THE
PANZER
KILLERS

THE PANZER KILLERS

The Untold Story of a Fighting General
and His Spearhead Tank Division's
Charge into the Third Reich

DANIEL P. BOLGER

CALIBER

CALIBER

An imprint of Penguin Random House LLC
penguinrandomhouse.com

Maps © 2021 by Chris Erichsen
Insert photographs © US Army Signal Corps

LIBRARY OF CONGRESS CATALOGING-IN-PUBLICATION DATA
Names: Bolger, Daniel P., 1957– author.
Title: The Panzer killers: the untold story of a fighting general and his
Spearhead Tank Division's charge into the Third Reich / Daniel P. Bolger.
Other titles: Untold story of a fighting general and his Spearhead Tank Division's charge
into the Third Reich
Description: First edition. | New York: Dutton Caliber [2020] | Includes index.
Identifiers: LCCN 2020006719 | ISBN 9780593183717 (hardcover) | ISBN 9780593183731 (ebook)
Subjects: LCSH: Rose, Maurice, 1899-1945. | United States. Army. Armored Division, 3rd—
History. | Generals—United States—Biography. | World War, 1939-1945—Tank warfare. |
World War, 1939-1945—Campaigns—Western Front. |
World War, 1939-1945—Regimental histories—United States.
Classification: LCC D769.305 3d .B65 2020 | DDC 940.54/1273—dc23
LC record available at https://lccn.loc.gov/2020006719

Printed in the United States of America
1   3   5   7   9   10   8   6   4   2

For Colonel Marc Axelberg,
First Sergeant Danny Laakmann,
and Lieutenant Colonel Scott Rutter

"He said unto his host 'Fight this day for your brethren.'"

1 Maccabees 5:32

Contents

THE
PANZER
KILLERS

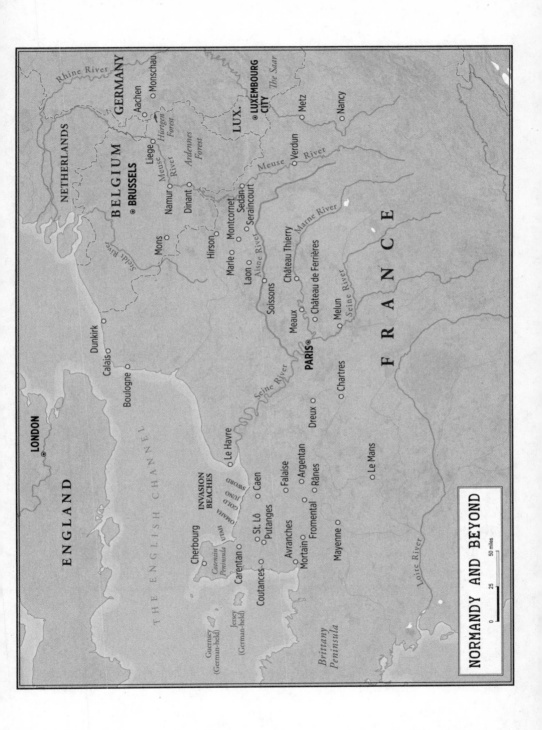

NORMANDY AND BEYOND

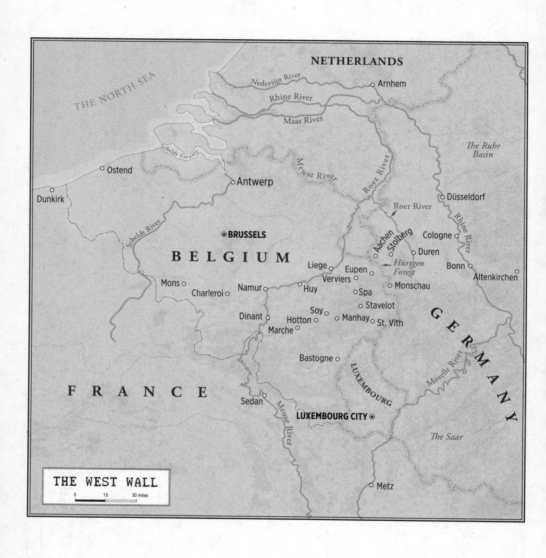

THE NORTH SEA

NETHERLANDS

Nederrijn River

Rhine River

Arnhem

Maas River

Scheldt Estuary

Ostend

Antwerp

Meuse River

Roer River

The Ruhr Basin

Dunkirk

Scheldt River

Roer River

Düsseldorf

⊛BRUSSELS

Aachen Stolberg Cologne

Duren

Rhine River

BELGIUM

Liege Eupen

Hürtgen Forest

Bonn

Altenkirchen

Mons

Charleroi Namur

Huy

Verviers

Monschau

Spa

Dinant

Soy Stavelot

Hotton Manhay St. Vith

Marche

GERMANY

Bastogne

LUXEMBOURG

Moselle River

FRANCE

Sedan

Meuse River

LUXEMBOURG CITY ⊛

The Saar

Metz

THE WEST WALL

0   15   30 miles

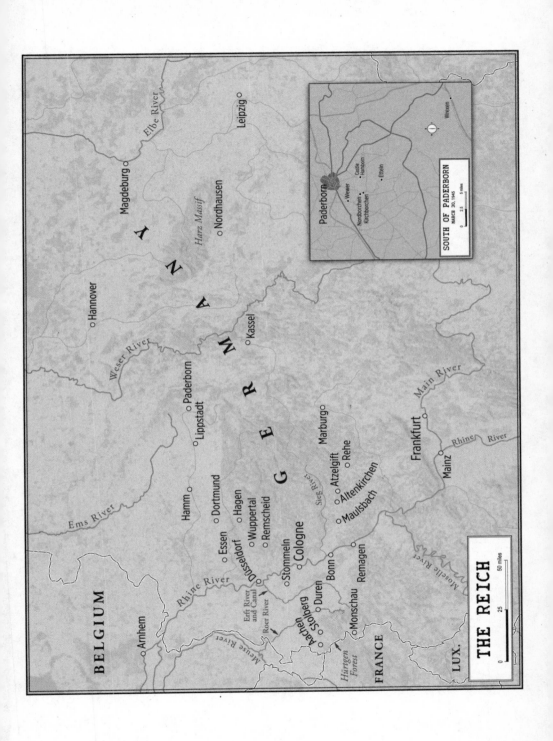

BELGIUM

Arnhem

Ems River

Meuse River

Hamm

Essen

Dortmund

Hagen

Dusseldorf

Wuppertal

Remscheid

Rhine River

Erft River and Canal

Roer River

Stommeln

Cologne

Aachen

Stolberg

Duren

Monschau

Hürtgen Forest

FRANCE

Bonn

Remagen

LUX.

Moselle River

Hannover

Weser River

Paderborn

Lippstadt

G E R M A N Y

Harz Massif

Nordhausen

Magdeburg

Leipzig

Elbe River

Kassel

Marburgo

Atzelgift

Rehe

Altenkirchen

Maulsbach

Sieg River

Frankfurt

Mainz

Rhine River

Main River

THE REICH

0   25   50 miles

SOUTH OF PADERBORN
MARCH 30, 1945

Paderborn

Wewer

Nordborchen

Kirchborchen

Castle Hamborn

Etteln

Wrexen

0   2.5   5 miles

Author's Note

They're almost all gone now. I remember them well. When I was growing up, many of the neighborhood adults fought in World War II. The man across the street served as a Marine on Iwo Jima. A girl's father two doors down flew as a gunner on bombers launching out of England and he brought home a wife from that green island. Her lilting accent provided endless fascination. (My own dad was one of the younger ones; he'd fought in Korea as an infantry sergeant.) When it came my time to join the U.S. Army, my first division commander had been a draftee in World War II. In years to come, I met plenty of former privates, corporals, tech sergeants, staff sergeants, petty officers, chiefs, and junior officers. As for Second World War generals, well, I'd seen *Patton*, watched *The World at War*, and read all the books. But I'd never met a general.

That changed when I went to The Citadel, a state military college in Charleston, South Carolina. In 1977 or 1978—can't recall the exact date, but it was during my senior year—I received an opportunity to meet a former Citadel president, four-star General Mark W. Clark, West Point Class of April 1917, veteran of World War I, World War II, and Korea, and best known for his command of the Fifth Army in the brutal Italian Campaign of 1943–1945. Prime Minister Winston L. S. Churchill called Clark "the American Eagle." Even in his dotage, you could tell this man had been a general commanding hundreds of thousands of soldiers. He radiated authority.

Three cadets went to see Clark. A faculty officer, a Marine veteran of Vietnam, gave us ground rules. The general will talk. You'll listen. If you get to ask a question, be careful. Do not mention Salerno, the Rapido River, Cassino, or Anzio. And above all, don't ask the general about his Jewish mother. His Jewish mother? I'd never read about that. Still, I'd been a cadet long enough to know how to keep my mouth shut. That I could do.

When ushered in to meet Clark, we all stood at attention until the great man motioned us to sit. His wood-paneled study featured walls covered with plaques, maps, photographs, and mounted weapons: swords, bayonets, pistols, and rifles. Clark started speaking—low rumbling, all bass, no treble. He talked in measured phrases.

Clark explained the difficult nature of Italian combat and the constant need to work with British allies. He liked the French mountain troops and thought a lot of the Canadians. The Poles fought bravely. Letting the Red Army take over their homeland—tragic, mused the general. As he described key maneuvers and former comrades his eyes lit up. He'd been there and done that, as we say today.

A cadet asked about Clark's work with General George C. Marshall, the U.S. Army chief of staff. In the summer of 1941, before Pearl Harbor, Marshall summoned Clark. "One day," Clark offered, "the chief said, 'Clark, I need the names of a hundred officers fit to command divisions.'" Clark drew up that list, and he proudly remembered all the fine men he'd recommended: Eisenhower, Bradley, Patton, his classmates Collins and Ridgway, and all the rest. Before the country even joined the war, Clark knew who would command its forces in battle. He was one of them.

A second cadet—not me—spoke up. He ventured a bit outside the lines. Was there anyone you did not name that turned out to be a good commander?

Clark paused. He steepled his long fingers. Then he answered.

"Maurice Rose."

I'd never heard of him. But then again, what did I know? Clark continued.

"He was outstanding," Clark said. "Top armored division commander. Very brave. The Germans killed him right near the end of the war."

Clark then moved on to other matters. I never did ask him anything. Don't miss a chance to say nothing, I guess. Spurred by Clark's comment, I determined to learn about this Maurice Rose. I found out some things back in 1977–1978. Then real life and my own military service got in the way. In the four decades-plus that followed, I also commanded an armored division in combat. Lately, though, I've been learning a lot more about Maurice Rose. There's a reason General Clark said his name.

Carentan D+7

He who has not fought the Germans does not know war.

British Army saying[1]

It was the hinge of the whole beachhead, and the Germans knew it. They had a nose for such things, a kind of predatory sense that led them right to weak spots and gaps and cracks. Well, the little Normandy town of Carentan amounted to all of those. Hit it and drive to the sea. That would split off the American landing forces at Utah Beach from those at Omaha Beach. And it just might unravel the entire Allied assault on Adolf Hitler's vaunted Atlantic Wall.

The Americans had landed 219,290 troops and 26,434 vehicles in the first week ashore. To their east, the British, Canadians, and a few Free French combined to field similar numbers. Off the American beaches steamed dozens of warships, including the great gray battleships USS *Arkansas*, USS *Texas*, and USS *Nevada*. Overhead flew hundreds of bombers and fighters.[2] And yet somehow, as usual in every war—including the greatest of all—the locus of maximum crisis at Carentan came down to a few hundred dirty, tired young Americans with hand weapons.

The Germans knew that as well. Maybe not the average privates.

As in the Allied armies, the junior rankers had a lot to learn. Many of the German rank and file were nervous teenagers and glum middle-agers who'd never fired a rifle except on a range. But leading them were enough cagey veterans, quick-thinking officers, and hard-eyed sergeants who'd mastered their bitter trade on the Russian front.[3] That battlewise cadre knew the deal. And the deal was to blow away the thin line of Americans, smash through at Carentan, and reach the English Channel.

Leading the way, as usual, would be the German tanks, the deadly panzers, a term well known to both sides and drawn from the official designation *panzerkampfwagen* (armored battle vehicle). The Germans named their latest panzers for the great hunting cats—panthers and tigers—but all of them, the new and the old, the big (49–77 tons) and the midsized (25–30 tons), existed to crush and kill.[4] Panzer cannons punched smoking holes through bunkers, buildings, and opposing tanks. Panzer machine guns tore apart trees, sandbags, thin-skinned trucks, and men unlucky enough to face that lethal stream of hot bullets. Worst of all, panzers bulled right ahead through mud, asphalt, rock, barbed wire, foxholes—with or without men in them—churning away with steel treads. Bullets and shell bursts might well kill you. A tank could smear you into the dirt. What remained wouldn't look human.

Panzers didn't just slay men. The driving German tanks stunned them, unmanned them, and turned their guts to water. Early in the war, troops facing panzers broke and ran in Poland, France, and Russia. In the 1940 campaign, the men of one unfortunate French artillery regiment abandoned their loaded cannons and took off screaming at the mere rumor of approaching panzers.[5] German armor attacks could do that to you.

Back stateside, U.S. Army training noncoms taught you from the book. And the book told American riflemen to hold their ground.[6] Other weapons will stop those metal beasts. Don't panic. Don't break. Don't run.

It sounded great in blank-fire drills on the far side of the Atlantic. But on the dusty ground west of Carentan, who really believed it? Until June 13, 1944, in the U.S. sector, men fought men. But those in their holes at dawn could hear the engines snorting and the heavy metal clanking in the far trees. As Lieutenant Preston Jackson bluntly put it: "An infantry soldier just can't beat a tank."[7]

The Germans knew that, too.

———

"Over the course of the war, 2nd Battalion, 506th PIR [Parachute Infantry Regiment] participated in many battles, but without a doubt the toughest fight of the war was the German counterattack on June 13, 1944." So wrote then Lieutenant Richard D. "Dick" Winters of the 101st Airborne Division's Company E ("Easy" in phonetic radio terms of the time), 2nd of the 506th, the tough paratroopers made famous in their twilight years by historian Stephen E. Ambrose, film star Tom Hanks, and HBO Films as the *Band of Brothers*.[8] Winters led these Americans throughout the war. And in his view, the "tightest spot" of World War II happened that June day at Carentan. The desperate clash merited a full episode in the miniseries. But that came decades later.

Nobody was thinking about a Hollywood production as dawn grayed the Normandy sky on June 13, 1944. It was a week since D-Day, D+7 by official reckoning. Word came down the line. The Germans looked to be bound for Carentan, then the beach. Winters and his weary paratroopers had to stop them.

The depleted regiments of the 101st Airborne Division aligned just west of Carentan. The Americans formed an arc from the northwest to the southeast. To the north stood the 502nd, then an impassable swamp, then Winters's battered 506th and their neighbors of the 501st, another marsh, and finally the glider men of the 327th. All four regiments had been part of the bloody final attack to take Carentan on June 12, 1944. That key city had been designated as an

American D+1 (June 7, 1944) objective. The Germans evidently thought otherwise.[9]

With Carentan at last in hand, the good news was that the 101st Airborne Division had finally come together after their badly scattered night jump in the first hours of June 6. The bad news was that they'd been fighting hard for a week. Food had been scarce. Most men had slept an hour or two here and there, if that. It added to the frictions already endemic in war. As one post-battle report on Winters's 506th summarized: "It appears to have been the case that most of the participants were by that time so exhausted that they had only vague impressions of what happened." The observer went on: "There are many missing pieces—arguments about objectives, disagreements about orders and messages, even disputes as to where certain units were when the action began."[10] U.S. airborne troops were well trained, well disciplined, and well led, and that élan kept them going when lesser outfits would have long ago faltered. But there were limits. The 101st Airborne men teetered on that fine edge.

On paper there should have been more than 8,000 Americans there in the shallow foxholes outside Carentan. In reality, the entire 101st Airborne Division fielded about half that number. The division's D-Day night parachute assault had gone just about exactly wrong, with most planeloads ending up well off the designated drop zones. Men landed in flooded swamps and drowned. Others fell to surprised German defenders. Most of the 101st Airborne paratroopers formed up in makeshift teams, sometimes with 82nd Airborne strays mixed in, and did what they could, achieving a lot despite the scrambled start. By June 13, Winters's 2nd of the 506th amounted to 300 effectives, if that. His own company commander, like so many others, was gone, dead, or lost somewhere in the marshes and the back stretches of the Atlantic Wall.[11]

To stop panzers, the paratroopers needed help. Somewhere in Normandy—maybe upended in a watery grave—were the 101st Airborne's 57mm antitank guns, but nobody in the 506th saw any at

Carentan. Antitank mines would have been handy. Those also weren't on hand. For Winters and his men, their personal anti-panzer arsenal came down to the thirteen-pound 2.36-inch (60mm) M9 rocket launcher, which looked like a 4.5-foot-long pipe with a handle on the center bottom and a small sight on the center top. Supposedly the 3.33-pound shaped-charge rocket could zip out 150 yards and knock out a tank. G.I. wiseacres called it the "bazooka" after an ungainly trombone invented by popular radio comedian Bob Burns.[12] Burns played it for laughs. But hunting panzers with a bazooka was no joke. To ensure a hit, a soldier needed to close to fifty yards and aim at the side, back, top, or bottom of the panzer. Getting that near a moving German tank, typically surrounded by alert enemy infantrymen on foot, amounted to a very high-risk proposition.

Far more useful than the daredevil bazooka was the SCR-300, the backpack radio. Artillery forward observers used the similar SCR-619.[13] These radios allowed Winters and others to call for field artillery missions. Excellent American fire direction techniques allowed the massing of fires from multiple cannon batteries within range. Army radios also offered a channel to the powerful arsenals directed by U.S. Army Air Forces' forward air controllers and U.S. Navy shore fire-control parties. The airplanes dropped bombs, shot rockets, and strafed with heavy machine guns. Big battleship cannons could range up to ten miles inland.[14] The Germans in Normandy lacked both of these devastating capabilities.

The U.S. Army's field manuals told you to start banging away as soon as you spotted the opposition. Bring in the air, then the battleship guns, next the artillery and the mortars, and finally the machine guns and the rifles and (God help you) the bazookas, grenades, pistols, and bayonets.[15] This kind of gauntlet of fire made all the sense in the world. And when it worked, as it often did, it stopped the Germans—sometimes even their panzers—cold.

Well-schooled at great cost in North Africa, Sicily, and Italy, the Germans very much respected American firepower. Still, Winters and his fellow paratroopers owned none of it, minus a few small mortars. If you wanted the storm of bombs and shells, you had to ask via a "call for fire." It was not an order, but a request. Sometimes the answer was no. But when you got the OK, as you usually did, artillery in particular was quite responsive, mere minutes away. Fighter-bomber aircraft and U.S. Navy support took longer to arrange, maybe twenty minutes to a half hour. In theory, the big, long-range stuff showed up first, while the hostiles remained far way. In practice, unless you got lucky with aerial spotting, or a well-sited outpost, or just plain combat-savvy guesstimation, the Germans would be right on top of you before any of the heavy fires arrived.

German leaders knew this well. To get ahead of devastating American supporting fires, any German attack had to go fast—panzer speed. At Carentan on the morning of D+7, the Germans formed for battle in a thatch of trees about five football fields away to the southwest—a few farm fields away. Their panzers would cover the intervening distance in two minutes, with German infantry on the run at most a few minutes behind. Could the U.S. artillery get there quickly enough? Dick Winters and his paratroopers bet their lives on it.

The best way to stop a panzer would be a U.S. Army M4 Sherman tank. But the 101st Airborne Division had none of those. That morning, the Germans had way too many.

———

Right after dawn, both sides opened up with machine guns, rifles, and mortars. The Germans endeavored to kill enough Americans to crack the line. The U.S. paratroopers saw the enemy tanks—couldn't hear them anymore with all the explosions—and concentrated on killing the hostile infantry. German artillery began pummeling the American lines. A few minutes later, U.S. howitzers joined the fight, hammering at the foe's positions in the trees. As Winters wrote later, the Americans employed "everything we had," opposed by "I'm sure everything they had." He called it a "hail of firepower going in both directions."[16]

Thirty-seven German panzers rolled forward, trundling around the edges of open fields. American reports identified enemy tanks, but in fact they were StuG IV (*sturmgeschütz*: assault gun, model IV), turretless, low-slung tracked armored vehicles, each with a wicked long-barreled 75mm cannon and the usual 7.92mm machine guns, too.[17] The panzers fired at each halt. Most of their high-velocity 75mm shots went over the dug-in Americans. The machine gun rounds, though, began to do their vicious work among the 506th foxholes.

Nazi propaganda films and U.S. Army newsreels of the era liked to show fleets of tanks racing across open prairies, dozens of armored war wagons bouncing along at thirty miles an hour like some overwhelming charge of the heavy brigade. It looked great on the silver screen, very exciting. And it would never work in real war. Tank attacks over actual ground didn't look at all like that. That proved especially so in the patchwork Norman countryside of small pastures and crop fields bounded by dirt walls topped by greenery—the hedgerows, the infamous *bocage* that characterized most of the region that wasn't underwater or true beachfront.

As the Germans came forth, what did Winters and his paratroopers see? Captain Ralph Ingersoll, a well-known prewar journalist who witnessed U.S. and German tank operations in Tunisia, explained:

> They [the tanks] advanced hesitatingly, like diffident fat boys coming across the floor at a party to ask for the next dance, stopping at the slightest excuse, going back, then coming on again, and always apparently seeking the longest way round. When they do have to cross a plain they postpone the evil moment as long as possible by clinging to the lower slopes of the nearest ridge until some invisible force pushes them unhappily into the open. When they follow a road, they zigzag in a series of tangents to it, crossing

it occasionally and staying on it only when there is no other way through difficult country.[18]

If a panzer crew came out in the open, they risked death by too many means. So smart tankers used the ground just like a stalking rifleman would. While Ingersoll might have found it less impressive than some wild steel onrush, in the long run, it did the job. Panzers working the terrain tended to burst out of a low place and vegetation right onto defending rifle troops. Panzer men loved that. The defenders? Not so much.

The Germans knew war, and they used all their weapons with great skill. Panzers followed their own supporting artillery concentrations, "leaning in the barrage," as the old sweats liked to say. With hatches clapped shut, armored vehicles could shrug off almost anything but a lucky direct hit by an exploding shell. And by slam-dancing with the German-delivered shrapnel bursts, the panzers could follow them right into their foe's foxholes. The Americans would be ducking down from the last artillery explosions just as the roaring steel monsters arrived.[19]

But there was more. Following the panzers were dozens of lithe figures in mottled camouflage smocks, pairs hop-scotching from tree trunk to hummock to ditch, weaving steadily forward, using the steel bulk of the StuG IVs to shield their brief sprints. You hardly saw them, mostly hints of movement in the distance. You might get a brief glimpse of a helmet, or spot a blur of dappled cloth. Framing these fleeting targets in a rifle sight wasn't easy. They appeared and disappeared like ghosts.

The Germans' infantry machine guns fired to protect their comrades' moves. When the Americans could raise their heads and catch a look, they might have seen that those to the north had the usual German coal-scuttle helmets with cloth camouflage covers; they came from the 17th SS Panzergrenadier Division "Götz von Berlichingen" (a notorious sixteenth-century German mercenary knight), as did the rumbling StuG IV panzers. The SS troops, stoked up with nazi-fied Teutonic ardor, advanced with a "murderous zeal," as a fellow German noted. The men to the south wore cut-down, nearly rimless German airborne helmets; they came from the 6th Parachute Regiment, worthy foes indeed. A 101st Airborne assessment later mentioned that "a high percentage of the attacking force carried light machine guns and machine pistols."[20] These guys meant business.

Yet good as they might be, the Germans had not come fast enough. This particular morning, the American supporting fires got there in time. The Germans paid for it. After an initial surge, the foot troops and their StuG IV panzers were stuck out there, gone to ground in the sunken farm trails and at the base of the hedgerows about halfway to their goal, from 500 to 150 yards out. German participants described the punishment inflicted by American artillery and mortars and a "hail of bombs and rocket fire from the air support."[21]

The firefight went on for much of the morning. It went as most engagements do, by fits and starts. A volume of shooting would build up then die down—nobody had unlimited ammunition, after all. Clutches of artillery shells showed up at odd intervals. American fighter planes swept down to bomb and strafe with their machine guns. It all resembled two beefy wrestlers grappling for position. Neither gained advantage. And neither quit.

That granted, the Germans were also tired. Their 6th Airborne Regiment paratroopers had defended Carentan tenaciously for a week before being finally forced out the day before. They were as exhausted as the Americans. The 17th SS Division *Panzergrenadiers* also seemed punchy. They'd endured days of relentless Allied air attacks as they motored 236 tortuous miles from southwestern France to the Normandy front.[22]

One game German StuG IV kept going, with a few more strung out behind playing follow the leader down the edge of a hedgerow berm. In days to come, attacking Americans would find out all too much about the limiting effects of the Norman hedgerows. But southwest of Carentan on D+7, the crazy-quilt of barriers and thickets favored the U.S. defenders. The lead German panzer hugged a low earthen wall. If it kept going, it would crash right onto the positions of Winters's Company E.

Company E's 2nd Lieutenant Harry F. Welch had seen enough. He ordered Private John McGrath to go to it with the bazooka. "Lieutenant," McGrath replied, "you're gonna get me killed." But he grabbed a loaded bazooka. Welsh followed with extra rockets, just in case.

The German panzer sat at the halt, hatches closed. Inside, the enemy crew was probably trying to find their way using the little slit periscopes that fringed the leader's and driver's positions. That could be difficult in sunny open terrain. In the shadows and overhanging bushes near Carentan, it took extra effort to peer out and estimate. The Germans didn't dare open the lid. There had been too much U.S. hot metal flying around.

With their adversary hesitant, McGrath and Welsh crept along a hedgerow. Their quarry remained stationary on the other side, engine rumbling. Seventy yards. Sixty yards. Fifty yards—close enough. The private scrambled up the berm, reared up, looked down, sighted, and fired.

The round hit squarely on the enemy gun mantlet.

And bounced off.

Seeking its tormentor, the StuG IV pivoted blindly toward the source.

McGrath's lieutenant didn't hesitate. He loaded another rocket and tapped the bazooka man's helmet. McGrath waited on his side of the hedgerow.

The StuG IV began to climb over the dirt barrier. The treads churned out sticks and leaves and clods of mud as the thing slowly edged up. The bow crested, then the flat metal underside between the tracks.

Belly shot.

McGrath took it.

The rocket slammed into the weak bottom plate and the StuG IV slid back, smoking, finished.[23]

One down, thirty-six to go . . .

It was all too much for some of the American paratroopers. In ones and twos, the men in Company F of the 506th began legging it toward Carentan. In Winters's words, the paratroopers "broke and ran." Shaken by the continuing German mortar barrage, gunfire, and advancing panzers, Company D "also retreated," recalled Winters. The official 101st Airborne Division post-combat account dressed it up rather laconically: "The 501 was immediately pinned down by heavy small-arms fire but managed to hold its position. The 506 was again struck by a heavy enemy counter-attack and forced back to within 500 yards of the west edge of the city [Carentan]."[24]

Sergeant Donald G. Malarkey of Company E stayed in his hole despite his right hand having been mangled by German mortar fragments. There were at least nine other Company E wounded, some completely out of it. There was no going back, either, no trip to an aid station. No trip anywhere except a German prison camp (maybe) or the final destination, the place every soldier feared most. Malarkey remembered the dire situation: "The Germans were relentless. We were close to being overrun. Tired. Losing guys. And hope."[25]

To the north of Malarkey, Winters, and the dwindling ranks of Company E lay that stretch of marshland, no-go for tanks. To the south were the empty foxholes of Company D. Short on ammunition, down to sixty or so men left, Winters and his band of brothers lived out their regimental motto: *Currahee*, Cherokee for "stands alone."[26] Smoke and dust drifted in the air. One more solid German push might well end it. From all around, the paratroopers heard the unmistakable growl of dozens of heavy gasoline engines.

––––

The tanks came, all right. But they came from the east, painted olive drab with white stars. They came in force. And they came spitting fire.

Dick Winters exulted: "What a wonderful sight it was to see those tanks pouring it on the Germans with their heavy .50 caliber machine guns and then plowing straight into the hedgerows with all those fresh infantry marching alongside the tanks as though they were on a maneuver back in the states." He saw the American Shermans engage the German StuG IV panzers. Winters thought he saw one stricken German vehicle blow up, then another. The accompanying armored infantry advanced by rushes, tree to tree, ditch to ditch, pressing the fight. The Germans backed away. By sunset, the 2nd Armored Division and the 101st Airborne held a line two miles west of Carentan. The day had cost nearly two hundred paratroopers and fifty-three armored soldiers killed and wounded, but the enemy threat to Carentan was dead. So were some 500 Germans.[27]

In the days and years that followed, different accounts offered various times for the moment the 2nd Armored Division showed up. The official history goes with 10:30 a.m. The tank headquarters listed 10:30 a.m. as the arrival of lead elements but also noted that the tank-led U.S. counter-push began at 2:00 p.m., with a second attack at 5:30. Malarkey thought midafternoon. Winters figured 4:30 p.m.[28]

It mattered not. What counted was that it happened. Winters, Welch, Malarkey, McGrath, and the rest of the Band of Brothers didn't know it, but there was a reason the supporting fires had been so timely and the tank column arrived right where it needed to be. Way up the chain, Lieutenant General Omar N. Bradley commanding First Army had access to the decrypted German message traffic produced by the Ultra program at Bletchley Park, Great Britain. The Bletchley team intercepted and cracked the German order to the 17th SS Panzergrenadier Division and the 6th Parachute Regiment. In the early evening of June 12, 1944, Bradley phoned Major General Leonard T. "Gee" Gerow, commander of V Corps. Without any reference to Ultra—Gerow wasn't cleared, nor were those below him in the hierarchy—Bradley told Gerow to move a designated tank battalion and a specific armored infantry battalion (riflemen that used half-track trucks) to back up the 101st Airborne Division at Carentan. When Gerow bristled at the micromanagement—U.S. Army corps commanders usually get a mission rather than an exact troop list and a directed location—Bradley sent preemptory written guidance. He softened it a bit, as was Bradley's way, but left no doubts. "Sorry to have to bother you but consider this highly important," wrote Bradley.[29]

Bradley also told Gerow exactly who to put in charge. He was a commander who Bradley knew well from Tunisia and Sicily, a man who got things done. As expected, the general did the job at Carentan, too.

Men of the 101st Airborne saw that particular senior officer in action west of Carentan. He didn't ride a tank. He walked with a purpose, alone, upright, personally scouting the way for his G.I.s. He kept his .45 automatic pistol in his hip holster. The dirty paratroopers marveled at the tall soldier's knee-high polished brown cavalry boots and green metal helmet with a single silver star.[30] Who the hell was this guy? Georgie Patton? Was he here?

It wasn't Patton, although that's who hand-picked the general for a moment such as this. The brigadier's own armored troopers knew exactly who he was. They called him "the immaculate, ruthless killer of Germans."[31]

Enter Maurice Rose.

I

NORMANDY AND BEYOND

CHAPTER 1

Lightning Joe's Lament

There are more tired division commanders than there
are tired divisions.

General George S. Patton, Jr.[1]

Brigadier General Maurice Rose knew what he was doing in Normandy. Too many of his Allied peers did not. Though the human cost was high, the mighty D-Day landings came off pretty effectively, smashing through the hard crust of Adolf Hitler's Fortress Europe. What came next didn't go well at all.

The senior people should have seen the trouble coming. Overall Allied ground force commander in Normandy General Bernard Law "Monty" Montgomery made his reputation on carefully planned operations. His famous triumph at El Alamein, Egypt, in 1942 marked a turning point in the war against Germany. Weeks before the first landing craft touched sand, Monty charted his view of how the war would go in the three months after D-Day. The British general worked with his staff to create a map with successive phase lines marked for D-Day through D+90. He forecasted taking Carentan on D+1, Caen about D+3/4 (maybe even on D-Day), Cherbourg by D+8, St. Lô at D+9, Coutances on D+12, Falaise by D+17, Avranches and Mortain at D+20,

Argentan on D+25, and the French capital city of Paris by D+90.[2] The map was neat and flat and made of high-quality paper.

Actual ground in Normandy was another matter altogether. Seen from an airplane, the bocage country looked like a patchwork quilt with uneven pieces: triangles, squares, rectangles, strips, and other odd shapes, each delineating a field of a quarter to a third of an acre. Around every area stood a dirt wall up to four feet thick and up to fifteen feet high, topped off by thick shrubbery and stands of trees that added another three to fifteen feet of height. Most of these sturdy barriers had been in place since the era of William the Conqueror, Duke of Normandy circa 1066. The bocage proved sodden, cut up by narrow dirt roads, and only too resistant to Allied bulldozers and high explosives.[3] Plus, it was full of Germans.

Monty's neat timetable didn't allow for any of that. It went right out the window. By late July, Carentan and Cherbourg had been taken, both well behind schedule. The south part of Caen town remained in German hands, as did Falaise and Avranches. As for Paris? It might as well have been on the back side of the moon. The Allies were stuck in Normandy, chopping their way forward hedgerow by hedgerow. To go a mile and a half through typical Norman bocage, one of Maurice Rose's U.S. Army tank companies of seventeen M4 Shermans could expect to face thirty-four separate earthen ramparts. To breach them demanded a half ton of demolition charges per hedgerow, in total seventeen tons of high explosives.[4] And that only shifted the dirt.

Killing the Germans cost extra, a lot extra. By one estimate, along with all the tank rounds, rifle bullets, and aerial bombs, it took about 200 artillery rounds to eliminate a single German defender. At that rate, it would require seven million U.S. artillery shells to wipe out the 35,000 or so German combat troops facing the Americans in Normandy. Put another way, American gunners needed to fire their maximum rate for a hundred days—and hope the Germans didn't reinforce, counterattack, or shoot back. Even the well-supplied U.S.

Army struggled to meet such profligate requirements. The Germans, of course, did not cooperate in the least.[5] All of this pain, and more, came with the hedgerows of Normandy.

"I couldn't imagine the bocage until I saw it," said Lieutenant General Omar N. Bradley after the war. Not prone to swearing, a frustrated Bradley called the Norman terrain "the damndest [sic] country I've seen."[6] Somehow, in all of the concentration on getting ashore under fire—admittedly a huge challenge—Monty, Bradley, and the rest of the top leadership paid almost no attention to the ground behind the waterfront. Then Brigadier General James M. Gavin of the 82nd Airborne Division said it best: "Although there had been some talk in the U.K. before D-Day about the hedgerows, none of us had really appreciated how difficult they would turn out to be."[7]

Bradley surely didn't anticipate the problem. Figuring out the battlefield belonged to Bradley, who didn't come across as a military savant. Rather, he reminded you of the guy who lived next door. These days, if Americans remember him at all, it's thanks to the brilliant portrayal by Karl Malden in the 1970 movie *Patton*. In one of the film's many face-offs between everyman Bradley and the larger-than-life Patton, the two argue about a unit's position. Patton offers an airy dismissal, and Bradley retorts, "I can read a map."[8]

Well . . . maybe.

The American First Army commander liked to pride himself on his grasp of infantry tactics and spent endless hours studying military maps. His superior in Sicily—and subordinate in France—Lieutenant General George S. Patton, Jr., found this affectation annoying.[9] After seeing Bradley in command in Tunisia and Sicily, Patton recognized that his infantry counterpart might be a pleasant fellow and a decent sort, but the man could not translate the squiggles on a map to the actual ground. Bradley knew the weapons ranges and the doctrinal frontages but found it impossible to envision it all on real dirt. The old military joke that when the ground and the map disagree, go with the ground. Bradley invariably went with the map, and it's not clear he quite understood that, either. He just didn't get it.

Had Bradley spent enough time under fire, experience might have helped him bridge the gap, to fill in the hole in his talents. But after his 1915 graduation from the U.S. Military Academy at West Point, New York, the future First Army commander spent World War I guarding copper mines in Butte, Montana, then training new troops at Camp Dodge, Iowa, getting ready for a deployment order that never came. Between the world wars Bradley attended U.S. Army schools and taught at some, too, including the Infantry School at Fort Benning, Georgia, and his alma mater, West Point.[10] His calm, studious demeanor reminded many of a Missouri schoolteacher, which he might well have been had he not chosen to serve in uniform. In any event, it all added up to years of theoretical map studies and not much practical hands-on troop command, let alone messy field exercises. The grand masters like Carl von Clausewitz spoke of a general's coup d'oeil, the ability to size up crucial ground at a glance, envisioning combat moves in time and space.[11] Napoleon and Wellington could do it. So could Lee and Grant in their time. Patton, too, had that gift, as did Maurice Rose. Not Bradley.

Limited brushes with the enemy made little impact. Sent forward in World War II at the behest of his West Point classmate General Dwight D. "Ike" Eisenhower—another very savvy American senior leader who missed the Great War of 1914–1918—Bradley experienced some close calls from hostile air attacks and artillery in North Africa and Sicily, but didn't follow Patton's example of seeking frontline action.[12] Bradley thought that to be grandstanding, not generalship.

At the request of the genial Eisenhower, well-known (and widely read) combat correspondent Ernie Pyle wrote stories about Omar Bradley, the modest "G.I. General." Other than proving that even Ernie Pyle could be buffaloed by Ike the smiling four-star, the Pyle articles played well on the home front and seem to have made Bradley happy. Bradley's own soldiers ignored the press buildup and the low-key, self-effacing Bradley, too.[13] They never saw him up front. He was just a name somewhere back there. Way back there.

By nature, Bradley preferred to run his war from a command post with good wire and radio communications and lots of well-marked map sheets. He didn't even move off the heavy cruiser USS *Augusta* and onto land in Normandy until D+4, June 10, 1944. Patton had been on the beach early in both the Morocco and Sicily assaults, seeing, being seen, and generally raising hell with friend and foe alike.[14] That wasn't Omar Bradley's style.

Now as his First Army bogged down in the Normandy bocage, Bradley stared at his eight-foot-tall map board and looked at the aerial photographs and just couldn't figure it out. Naturally, Patton would have known what to do. Of course he would. Patton knew all about the bocage. The mercurial cavalry general read Edward A. Freeman's magisterial *The History of the Norman Conquest*, toured the area before World War I, and spoke fluent French.[15] The Patton method would be to go to the nearest hedgerow and pitch into things, getting subordinates energized to try stuff, to experiment, to solve the puzzle. He'd generate action, but there'd be a maintenance bill. In his wake, Patton left a lot of broken crockery. He talked too much to journalists, badmouthed the British, and in Sicily slapped two soldiers hospitalized with battle fatigue, all incidents that Bradley abhorred, as did Ike. So Patton, who'd led Seventh Army in Sicily, topped out at command of Third Army. He wasn't in Normandy yet. Bradley was.

Those G.I. general puff pieces meant nothing in the high summer of 1944. To deal with "the Gethsemane of the hedgerows,"[16] Omar Bradley chose a way that suited him. He found a general who could read the map, the ground, and the enemy.

———

Joseph Lawton Collins looked like a general: handsome, stalwart, with piercing dark eyes and a square jaw. He had coup d'oeil, all right, taking it all in rapidly, deciding quickly, and issuing clear orders. Collins demonstrated a knack for going right to the problem point and applying effective pressure. He wasn't afraid of getting shot at, but he saw his role as getting others to face fire and get results. Day and night, you'd find him restlessly prowling division, regimental, and battalion command posts, poking and prodding. Joe Collins was all about achieving outcomes and doing so with urgency. His nickname was "Lightning Joe."

He earned that one on Guadalcanal in command of the 25th Infantry Division, the "Tropic Lightning" Division. Few would call the bloody, protracted jungle slugfest on Guadalcanal any kind of blitzkrieg. But the Americans won and Collins and his soldiers did their part. When combat veteran Collins came to Europe to take command of VII Corps, he said his troops had bestowed the title on him.[17] Maybe so. He made sure the "Lightning Joe" moniker made it out to the press. Reporters like colorful generals. Collins wasn't anywhere near the Patton or MacArthur level of outsized personality. Still, by D-Day, Lightning Joe he was. Now he had to live up to it.

He did so. Collins was probably the best division commander in the U.S. Army in the Pacific theater of operations and then the best corps commander in the European theater of operations. After the war, he'd go on to wear four stars and become U.S. Army chief of staff, the pinnacle of any soldier's dreams.[18] Yes, he was ambitious and not shy about it. But like Babe Ruth pointing to the fence then smacking a home run, Collins backed it up time after time.

Collins was a man in a hurry. When the United States joined the Great War, Collins and his classmates graduated early from West Point in April 1917. He missed the shooting war but at age twenty-two commanded a battalion in the occupation of prostrate Germany in 1919. In World War II, Collins became the youngest division commander in the Pacific and the youngest American corps commander. Good enough for most—but not for Lightning Joe Collins. By June 1944, Collins's classmate Mark W. Clark already wore three stars and commanded Fifth Army in Italy; Clark's soldiers liberated Rome on the eve of the D-Day landings in Normandy. Another classmate, Matthew B. Ridgway, commanded the 82nd Airborne Division and was leading the way in the Norman hedgerows, rifle in hand. Ridgway was marked for corps command, too. Collins intended to get ahead of both Clark and Ridgway, and to do that, he needed to deliver success with VII Corps. Ridgway's deputy, Brigadier General Jim Gavin of West Point's Class of 1929, summed up Joe Collins as "runty, cocky, confident, almost to the point of being a bore."[19]

Aside from his sometimes obvious self-promotion—not unusual in general officers, although most favored Bradley's more understated style—Collins shared a trait with German Colonel General Eduard Dietl, the tough-as-nails commander way up north on the Finnish-Russian front. The line went that Dietl was the best officer in the German army. The problem apparently involved Dietl's belief that every other German officer should be that way, too.[20] Collins certainly subscribed to that idea, at least with regard to subordinates. Perfect was good enough.

Because the majority of Collins's subordinates did not measure up to their general's exacting standards, the VII Corps commander chose to just do it himself. Collins handled the thinking. He directed minor tactics, to include personally placing battalions on the ground.[21] Joe Collins just needed good executors who did exactly what they were told to do. His consistent micromanagement filled in the blanks. Collins didn't encourage initiative, although he appreciated it in the rare cases when it arose. As for those who couldn't keep up, Collins had a quick trigger. Stumblers got fired. As the VII Corps crossed Europe, Lightning Joe torched a lot of colonels and generals. If you kept your job under Collins, you knew how to carry out your orders regardless of terrain, weather, time, Germans, or casualties. In retrospect, it seems heartless. But heartless measures win wars, especially against an opponent as tenacious as the Nazi Germans.

The Germans in the bocage stymied Bradley and Montgomery and a host of other corps and division commanders. Not Lightning

Joe. He'd already dealt with awful terrain on Guadalcanal and New Georgia, not to mention unyielding adversaries, on the other side of the world. While Bradley fretted in front of his maps and Monty worried about the schedule, Collins went to work.

————

"Send a bullet, not a man."[22]

That solved it. It took about six weeks to figure out the details, but Lightning Joe grasped the top line right away. He'd learned it on Guadalcanal.[23] And he applied the method in the Norman countryside.

The decision to rely on volume of weapons, not numbers of people, was baked into the American cake from the outset of World War II. It's an old adage that generals refight their last war, and the American generals of World War II certainly did. George Patton relived his tank exploits from the Great War. Omar Bradley immersed himself in his maps and musings from the campaigns he fought on paper teaching at West Point and Fort Benning. Lightning Joe Collins saw Guadalcanal in the thickets of the bocage. Maurice Rose re-created his stirring armored drive on Palermo, Sicily. Middle-aged men like to revisit their glory days. Generals are no exception.

The greatest of them all, U.S. Army Chief of Staff General George Catlett Marshall, late of the Virginia Military Institute (VMI) and the 1917–18 American Expeditionary Force, intended to get the world war right this time. In the Great War, the Americans bummed and borrowed British and French arms, suffered a grim bloodletting in the Meuse-Argonne Forest, and then saw the war end in an unsatisfying armistice that let the likes of Adolf Hitler claim Germany hadn't really been defeated. In this round, Marshall determined to use American economic might, the country's greatest strength, to crush the enemy decisively, to go right at the heart of Germany—no harebrained diversions into the Eastern Mediterranean basin, no quixotic expeditions to the Mesopotamian desert, no monkeying around in Norway, no sideshows, no delays, no wasted months. "We had to go brutally fast in Europe. We could not indulge in a Seven Years' War," said Marshall.[24] He determined to win this one much sooner. Marshall chose every senior U.S. Army general: Ike, Patton, Bradley, Collins, and most of the division commanders, too. They saw things his way.

Marshall's vision shaped the U.S. war effort. By head count in 1944, the United States had plenty of men (and women, too) in uniform, some 12 million in all. But once you deducted the two-ocean U.S. Navy (3.4 million), the six division (and supporting aviation) U.S. Marine Corps (600,000), and the globe-spanning U.S. Army Air Forces (2.4 million), you ended up with a relatively small U.S. Army ground contingent of 89 divisions and supporting combat and service forces (5.8 million), with some 40 percent of that in stateside and rear-area tail, not frontline teeth. America's Soviet allies raised more than 400 divisions for the Red Army (11 million) and needed every one of them; throughout the war, the Russians squared off with more than two-thirds of Adolf Hitler's troops. The British Army (2.9 million), in action worldwide since 1939, relied on 40+ divisions. The German Army (8 million) fielded more than 300 divisions. Despite its large population, the United States didn't follow suit. The official history of the U.S. Army refers to the "90 division gamble," the belief that rather than recruit hundreds of divisions, American industrial power, seapower, and airpower could effectively substitute things for bodies.[25] Send a bullet, not a man.

The British reasoned that way, too, but they didn't possess U.S. economic muscle. To fill in their gaps, London's leadership relied on Imperial and Dominion organizations and American numbers. Even so, by the summer of 1944, Great Britain, its dominions, and its colonies were down to the bottom of the barrel. Monty's military lineup in Normandy represented almost all the British Empire had left.[26] For their struggle against the Germans, the British would definitely be sending bullets—and tanks and shells—not men. On the western side, any major casualty toll must be borne by the Americans.

Generals like Omar Bradley, George Patton, Maurice Rose, and

Joe Collins knew that, but didn't like it. For them, ripping through young G.I.s constituted the last resort, and only after every mechanical and explosive option had been tried. That accorded well with American moral traditions of individual rights and self-worth, and the 90 division force cap demanded it anyway. There weren't enough U.S. Army ground elements to burn. Ammunition and armaments must suffice.

To Lightning Joe, that meant working the artillery, the air, and the tanks. Although he, like Bradley, came from the infantry, Collins knew his branch lacked the tactical skill to close with the enemy. As Collins learned on Guadalcanal, G.I. rifle platoons tended to make contact, hit the dirt, and call in supporting fires. Cavalryman Patton thought "the poorer the infantry, the more artillery it needs; the American infantry needs all it can get."[27] And why not use that firepower? U.S. Army rifle troops knew the score. Send a bullet, not a man.

Young Americans ended up in the U.S. Army infantry by default. The U.S. Navy and the Army Air Forces insisted on getting the brightest enlistees, the ones displaying a technical bent. On the ground side, those with mathematical abilities joined the artillery and the engineers, while the mechanically inclined went to tank, tank destroyer, and ordnance (maintenance) outfits. The Marines, the Airborne, and the Rangers demanded first dibs on aggressive, physically fit young men. Those who'd make fine sergeants and lieutenants in standard rifle companies ended up in the ranks in these elite volunteer units. Dick Winters and his hard-fighting 101st Airborne Division Band of Brothers benefited. Average U.S. Army line infantry outfits did not. American rifle platoons tended to be populated by those left over after all these cullings. Many were undersized. A few proved less educated. True, some proved to be very able indeed. There were rarely enough of those natural soldiers. As for the remainder, the Germans supplied a very abrupt—and costly—education.

A young officer who survived the lethal gunfights in the bocage and ended his service as a four-star general remembered a typical forty-man platoon. "You would always end up with a good sergeant or a good officer and three or four men doing all the work," said then Major William E. DePuy of the hard-luck 90th Infantry Division. "Unfortunately," he concluded, "the rest contributed to the casualties."[28] Whatever George Marshall's aspirations to preserve G.I. lives, the German army refused to play along. They kept right on killing Americans.

The casualty problem compounded itself as the campaign continued. Because the U.S. Army sent forth only 89 divisions—not even the allowed 90—every American division committed to combat had to remain in action. German, Russian, and British leaders attempted to rotate their combat units off the line now and then to add new soldiers, refit, rest, and retrain. Not so the United States. G.I. veterans stayed at it "for the duration," as the saying went, meaning you came home when the war ended. The number of old hands dwindled after every firefight. When men fell wounded, they had to be replaced. Those replacements arrived as individuals from stateside training camps and waited in forward transit depots, "repple depples." When a unit reported losses, replacements were pushed forward by truck and then foot to join engaged rifle platoons. In theory, it resembled feeding machine gun bullets into an open bolt. In actuality, though, people are not neat, rigid, unfeeling bullets. Especially in the deadly bocage, American replacements faced a steep learning curve bridging the gap between training exercises and true war. Remaining veterans didn't trust the newcomers. Too many newly arrived individuals died unintegrated, unloved, and unknown. And those casualties required more replacements, "the invisible horde of people going here and there but never seemingly arriving."[29] It was impersonal, inhuman, and un-American. But that's the way it went.

With his infantry of questionable quality, faced with dense terrain held by resolute Germans, Lightning Joe Collins sought solutions. From the first day he went ashore at Utah Beach, Collins recognized

the scale of the problem. American infantry lacked the tactical acumen to advance by rushes, alternately firing and moving from cover
to cover to clear the hedgerows. American artillery shells had to be
targeted properly, not simply tossed en masse into the next tree line.
American air support needed defined friendly and enemy positions,
no easy matter in these all too similar geometric hotboxes, this chess
board from hell. As for the tanks, well, they had two choices. Drive
down the few obvious farm roads, all covered by German 88mm
(3.5-inch) antitank guns and the like—not good. Or, the tanks could
try to top the berms. But that almost guaranteed an antitank rocket
in the underbelly, just as the 101st Airborne had done to the German
panzers at Carentan. Naturally, maddeningly, the Germans in Normandy owned their own, more effective versions of the U.S. bazooka,
the tube-like, reloadable 88mm *panzerschreck* (tank fright) and the
one-shot *panzerfaust* (tank fist).[30] So showing a Sherman's bottom to
Germans was a bad idea, too.

At First Army headquarters, Bradley offered his two cents': "Can't
we run tanks up there and chew those ditches apart with a few shells
and a burst of machine gun fire?"[31] No, Brad, that wouldn't work. But
even as Bradley turned back to his maps and paperwork, he planted
a seed with Joe Collins. Cracking the hedgerows required unleashing
the tanks, and that had to be done with American firepower, not
waves of precious riflemen. Could Collins and his subordinates figure out how to do it?

Early attempts went by the book. Each American division commander looked at the field manual and issued attack orders as if on
maneuvers back in the Carolina pine woods. Officers drew neat lines
on the map, marking off doctrinal frontages: 1,000 yards per infantry
battalion, 500 yards per rifle company. Battalions advanced with two
companies forward and one in reserve, two up and one back, the approved school solution at Fort Benning, Bradley's old stomping
ground. Regiments put two battalions forward and one back. Divisions employed two regiments up and one back. The formula worked

every time on classroom map problems and stateside maneuvers. It went over fine in Morocco, Tunisia, and Sicily, despite occasional bloody noses.[32]

In Normandy, wide frontages and two-up, one-back failed miserably. A thousand-yard front concealed four or five hedgerow compartments. American rifle companies under German fire found themselves split into frantic, milling knots of desperate men, caught on narrow dirt roads and impaled on earthen barriers. Those who spilled into the grassy open centers of the bocage patches were pinned down, cut down, and pummeled by German mortars and artillery.[33] Better-trained U.S. infantry might have tried night attacks. Those didn't occur much.

What about sending bullets, not men? In the dense bocage, it didn't much matter how many shells the American howitzers fired or how many bombs the P-47 Thunderbolt fighters dropped. Too often, American supporting artillery and air hit G.I.s. After all, by U.S. Army practice, anything striking within 600 yards—which is to say almost every projectile used in every hedgerow cell fight in Normandy—earned the warning "danger close," meaning friendlies must expect a random number of overs and shorts, and allow for hot metal screaming out of each impact to a bursting radii up to a hundred yards wide for the bigger munitions.[34] Accurate target location prevented a lot of that. The challenge, however, involved finding the dug-in, camouflaged Germans.

Those guys rode it all out. German old-timers had seen worse in the Ukraine and coached the newcomers how to hide, shoot low, and get hits. When Americans tried to take a bocage box, German defenders fired back in volume and held tight. If somehow the U.S. troops gained the upper hand, surviving German soldiers invariably dropped back, sidestepped, or even advanced to another hedgerow. The ground itself was always in play, and the Germans seemed to own the only copy of the complete playbook. The Germans schooled one division after another: the 4th, the 9th, the 79th, the 82nd

Airborne, the 83rd, the 90th, then all the rest.[35] The blood-soaked cycle ran full-tilt. Lather, rinse, repeat.

German infantry defended each bocage patch by dominating the corners on their end. If American riflemen got over or through the first wall, German MG34 and MG42 machine guns—accurate, high rate of fire, the best in the war—opened up, firing at knee height, grazing the grass tops. The machine guns were squirreled into the base of the German-held corners, and you rarely saw the guys shooting them. If you made it into the open area, the Germans focused machine gun and rifle fire on the point of entry, the fatal funnel. Casualties stacked up. Progress stalled. That's what Collins and his VII Corps had to crack.

On June 9, 1944, Bradley ordered Collins to drive west twenty miles across the base of the Cotentin Peninsula and then swing north twenty miles to capture the port of Cherbourg.[36] The directive accorded with the usual Bradley thinking: big hand, flat map, and absolute disregard of the messy, dangerous details. Collins, though, knew what to do.

Getting across the Cotentin, then north to Cherbourg, meant fighting through hedgerows by the gross. But Lightning Joe was a quick study, "independent, vigorous, heady, capable and full of vinegar."[37] He'd already seen what Germans in the bocage did. Like the Japanese on Guadalcanal, the Germans were dedicated but immobile—not enough panzers and trucks. If the Americans could crunch through a series of hedgerows, they just might get through the enemy defenses and then be able to drive through the German rear echelon.

Ideally, Bradley would have given Collins the 2nd Armored Division, the tankers that bolstered the American paratroopers at Carentan. But Bradley's innate caution kept Brigadier General Maurice Rose and the rest of the armor force tied down near the junction between VII Corps and V Corps, just in case the Germans tried another counterthrust. So Collins had to use his own four divisions. The 9th Infantry Division and the 82nd Airborne Division were veteran, well-led outfits, and the 4th Infantry Division certainly showed mettle starting at Utah Beach. They all together did the business in nine days, reaching the far coast on June 18, 1944. Eight days later, with the beaten-up, half-strength 82nd Airborne finally on its way back to England to stage for future jumps and the new and well-disciplined 79th Infantry Division added to Collins's team, Cherbourg fell.[38] The port was a mess, but Joe Collins and VII Corps had shown some lightning for sure. By contrast, Bradley's other corps marked time and floundered in the bocage.

Collins sent bullets, not men. He insisted on very narrow frontages—one hedgerow corral at a time per rifle company—and swapped out lead battalions up to three times a day: one up, then the next, then the next. This kept the forward units fresh, let passed-up battalions treat casualties and resupply, and even allowed time to reconnoiter, plan, and rest, no small things in the heat and humidity of the Norman summer. Most importantly, swapping out U.S. lead elements maintained steady pressure on the Germans.[39] They never got a respite from the flaying administered by American firepower.

Since the Germans anchored their defenses with their superb machine guns emplaced in the back corners of each bocage enclosure, Collins demanded that his rifle platoons focus right there using all fires, starting with their own M1919 .30 caliber machine guns, M1918 Browning Automatic Rifles (the famous BARs), and trusty Garand M1 rifles. American infantrymen liked to engage known targets, as learned on training ranges back home, but in contested hedgerows G.I.s hardly ever saw live Germans. The U.S. troops learned to fire at dirt puffs, muzzle flashes, and the slightest glints of metal or hints of motion. If even those telltale clues proved furtive, the Americans simply banged away at the preferred German hangouts in the far corners.[40] These bocage cell tactics resembled those used by today's American infantry for close quarters room-clearing in enemy-held buildings. Dominating the corners drove the effort.

Bringing in effective artillery isolated each German bocage patch and added to the killing weight against those far corners. With the shells coming in "danger close," attacking American riflemen learned to shelter in the lee of the near dirt mounds and let the howitzers pound the far berm. Gunners set artillery fuses for delay to allow the shells to burrow deep before bursting, which did nicely in ripping open hostile bunkers. Then, to nail Germans huddled in open trenches and holes, the American artillerymen mixed in rounds with "quick" settings to blow instantly on impact with the dirt. To kill even more moving or exposed Germans, American artillerymen employed time fuses that popped above the ground, showering down jagged hot metal fragments. Forward observers accompanied every rifle platoon to call in and adjust these supporting fires. In addition to observers on the ground, the VII Corps put up L-4 Piper Cub spotter planes to direct field artillery. Collins emphasized taking the high ground, whether atop a near berm, on the crest of a low Norman hill, or looking out the window of a droning high-wing propeller plane.[41] Seeing the target took you a long way toward hitting the target.

American close air support also required an overhaul. Collins worked with the Army Air Forces pilots to get forward air controllers where they belonged—forward, with lead rifle elements, not hanging around the regimental command post six hedgerows back. With their bulky, high-powered ground-to-air radios mounted in jeeps and even tanks, the airmen learned to move right with the lead units. Major William E. DePuy of the 90th Infantry Division offered little praise for the airmen or anyone else in Normandy, but he remembered that bringing forward air controllers alongside the fighting infantry "worked pretty well. In fact, it worked very well."[42]

Tanks played a role, but Collins wasn't satisfied that they contributed all they could. In the VII Corps advance to Cherbourg American M4 Shermans stayed mostly on the narrow country roads. The Shermans relied on their 75mm (almost 3-inch) cannons and onboard machine guns to back up nearby rifle platoon efforts.[43] Shooting over the earthen mounds was OK, but not always effective.

To bore into the bunkered-in Germans, the tanks had to smash into the bocage boxes. That required bulldozers, but the exposed drivers couldn't survive the spasms of hostile gunfire. A dozer blade rigged for M4 Sherman tanks sometimes did the job, but these proved awkward to use, slowed the vehicle on open roads, and acted as a "shoot me" sign for eager German panzer crews. Knocking out American dozer tanks became an enemy priority because they were rare commodities, only four per U.S. tank battalion, not nearly enough. Frantic First Army requests for 278 more blades went up the chain of command. It would take weeks, maybe months, to ship the implements from factories across the ocean in the United States.[44] Dozer blades weren't the answer.

Lacking anything more reliable, American tankers turned to their friendly combat engineers with their numerous satchels of high explosives. When the demolitions worked well, the Sherman tanks popped through breached hedgerow walls. Plowing ahead out of a big black gout of dirt sometimes caught the Germans flat-footed. But the smarter opponents learned to key their panzer crews, 88mm gunners, and *panzerfaust* men on the site of such an explosion, a fatal funnel all the way. Even when the wall-busting worked, charging American M4 Sherman tankers often outran their accompanying infantry and ended up isolated in open fields, much to the delight of the Germans. To keep the riflemen and tanks together, and let each spot for the other, soldiers wired field phones to the rear of the Shermans.[45] It helped in teamwork. That granted, while the U.S. infantry, artillery, and air made significant gains, the tanks weren't quite there yet.

Even after the new tactics became widely known and adopted, the question remained: Could American commanders, especially generals, carry out such operations? Ever anxious for action and often well forward poking around, Major General Joe Collins applied what even he termed "severe pressure" on subordinate generals and colonels. Most figured it out at grave human cost. Few proved as adept or quick-witted as Collins himself. Although it galled him to do so, Lightning Joe grudgingly permitted each newly arrived division's leadership at least one ugly smashup in the first encounter with Germans in the bocage. For the 83rd Infantry Division, that opening round on July 4–5, 1944, resulted in more than 2,100 casualties, a regiment wiped out while the rest learned in the hardest possible ways how to prevail in the Norman hedgerows. Still, as Collins observed, the 83rd started "showing signs of settling down."[46] The 83rd proved a good organization thereafter.

Thus despite Collins's misgivings, perhaps influenced by the less exacting Bradley, each U.S. division commander in Normandy merited one free cock-up. Some didn't need it. Most did. After that first failure, though, look out. In VII Corps, repeated fumblings guaranteed the wrath of Lightning Joe. In his usual style, and with Bradley's full backing, Collins fired those who kept floundering. On June 13, 1944, after days of bloody confusion and multiple failures, Collins relieved the commander of the 90th Infantry Division, a particularly snake-bit organization. Bradley called the 90th Infantry Division "one of the worst-trained to arrive in the ETO [European theater of operations]," and noted its "deplorable condition." Two regimental commanders were also removed.[47] The VII Corps commander insisted on results. In the advance to Cherbourg, he got them. That was no small thing in the stalemated Norman summer of 1944.

Still, taking a trashed French port city almost two weeks behind schedule did not a victory make. Omar Bradley's other corps commanders lacked Collins's abilities, preferring to muddle through from their distant command posts. Their troops struggled in the bocage, barely grinding forward. As the Germans defending near Carentan observed, the Americans hadn't really gone anywhere except Cherbourg, a dead end on a backwater peninsula.[48] Paris remained far, far away, and the Germans continued to hang on like grim death itself. So far, Collins hadn't quite figured out how to spring the U.S. tanks. But that was clearly in the near future. If

Collins could find the right combined arms recipe, and the right leader, Lightning Joe might well get the Americans clear of the bocage altogether.

———

On the eastern end of the Normandy lodgment, Montgomery's British forces also sent bullets, not men. They, too, found a way to beat the bocage and the Germans, and the method showed promise. The British approach boiled down to a massive air and artillery bombardment and then a tank/infantry assault through the resulting moonscape, rolling over what remained of the German defenders. After D-Day, the British tried it three times in a series of attacks named for English horse racing tracks: Operation Epsom on June 26–28, Operation Charnwood on July 8–9, and Operation Goodwood on July 18–21. None of them worked. The Germans threw in their best, strongest panzer divisions to stop the British. For their part, the British pulled their punches. They couldn't risk the casualties.[49]

Nobody on the U.S. side liked casualties, either, and with the 90-division force limit, they couldn't endure more at the prevailing rate. At the pace the U.S. Army churned through riflemen in the bocage, infantry regiments expected to lose 100 percent of their assigned strength in ninety days. The training base back in America strained to send enough replacements.[50] Yet unlike the British, painful though it became, the United States kept up. In Normandy, however, Eisenhower, Montgomery, Bradley, and all the rest of the senior leaders agreed, as did the weary privates doing the fighting. It was past time to break out.

That meant rerunning the British Epsom/Charnwood/Goodwood scheme American-style. In a meeting at First Army headquarters on July 12, 1944, Bradley proposed a major offensive code-named Operation Cobra. He advocated initiating with a concentrated use of four-engine bombers dropping munitions directly on the German front lines near the key road junction of St. Lô. In the discussion that followed with Collins and the other three corps commanders, Bradley warmed to his subject. The First Army commander began to parcel out the fighting divisions, the nondivisional tank battalions, the tank destroyer detachments, and the various field artillery units, more or less distributing them equally across the four corps. At that, Major General Elwood R. "Pete" Quesada, commander of the U.S. Army Air Forces IX Tactical Air Command, spoke up. Why keep spreading out force increments like peanut butter on toast? To smash out of the bocage, make one corps "overwhelmingly strong," Quesada suggested. He looked right at Collins.[51] So the airman threw down the marker in front of the infantry generals. But he was right. Bradley knew it, too.

Collins got the nod and the forces for Operation Cobra. Lightning Joe himself framed the aerial beaten zone smack atop the best ground leading out of the damned bocage. Every B-17 and B-24 heavy bomber in the U.S. Eighth Air Force, as well as hundreds of two-engine medium bombers and plenty of single-engine fighter-bombers, too—2,246 aircraft altogether—prepared to pound the dug-in German Panzer Lehr ("school," troops from the training center) Division across a rectangle 7,000 yards (nearly four miles) long and 2,500 yards (a mile and a half) wide, oriented from northwest to southeast just on the enemy side of the rather straight Périers to St. Lô road. The American air crews readied to unload more than 4,000 tons of devastating high explosives, unquenchable white phosphorus, and blazing napalm on the unwitting German panzer men. Once the bombing stopped, 258 artillery pieces—twenty-one battalions in all—would open up, ready to expend 28,000 rounds a day for Operation Cobra. And all of that preceded the divisions' own assigned and reinforcing artillery (700+ tubes), tank cannons, and machine gun fires of the attacking divisions themselves.[52]

To rush through the blasted terrain, Lightning Joe received six of First Army's fifteen divisions, including the ones he wanted most.

Along with the reliable 1st, 4th, 9th, and 30th Infantry divisions, Collins's VII Corps also picked up both the 2nd and 3rd Armored divisions. Rather than the time-honored two up/one back formula, Collins created a power drive: three up, then three more, no reserve. Collins even joked about it, saying he'd never kept a reserve in any of his previous fights.[53]

Operation Cobra massed American combat strength in quantity and quality. West to east, the 9th Infantry, 4th Infantry, and 30th Infantry divisions would make the opening attack. Waiting right behind the 9th stood the 1st Infantry Division, "the Big Red One," the most combat-tested outfit in Normandy, veterans of North Africa, Sicily, and D-Day. The 3rd Armored Division expected to pass through the 4th Infantry Division. Finally, the 2nd Armored Division "Hell on Wheels"—Patton's old outfit—planned to move through the 30th Infantry Division. This division, too, had fought in North Africa and Sicily as well as Normandy. All three exploiting divisions aimed at Coutances to the west on the Atlantic coast.[54] Take Coutances and goodbye, bocage. Goodbye to tens of thousands of outflanked Germans, too.

That kind of rolling fight suited the two armored divisions, of course. Yet Collins's infantry, too, had wheels. By this time, all four of the VII Corps infantry divisions included familiar attached tank battalions, tank destroyer battalions, and extra artillery. The truck count allowed every American to go into action mounted. By German standards, each U.S. infantry division qualified as a highly mobile *panzergrenadier* formation.[55] They'd move out.

The two armored divisions functioned as the big hammers. When their tanks got loose, they'd open up the entire front. Behind the VII Corps advance, the newly landed divisions of Lieutenant General George Patton's Third Army stood by to exploit.

An additional innovation ensured success. In the 2nd Armored Division, Sergeant Curtis G. Culin tried welding scraps from German steel tetrahedron beach obstacles onto the bow of an M4 Sherman medium tank. Properly placed, anchored, and angled, the twin "rhinoceros" horns permitted a Sherman to dig into and burst through a hedgerow at any point using engine power, not demolitions. Leverage kept the tank's bow low, protecting the vulnerable bottom plate. Now the Germans couldn't concentrate on the fatal funnel of a demolitions breach, nor hold out to put a rocket in the bottom of a Sherman clambering over a mound. Moreover, with rhino steel cutters, U.S. tanks could punch through anywhere and in great numbers. German panzers in the bocage lacked rhino fittings. They remained roadbound.[56] The metal tusks offered a huge edge in mobility.

A demonstration for Lieutenant General Bradley on July 14 convinced the First Army commander to direct widespread adoption of the device. By the start of Operation Cobra eleven days later, nearly two-thirds of First Army's Sherman tanks featured Culin's cutters. In Brigadier General Maurice Rose's 2nd Armored Division, three of four Shermans bore the rhino horns. By Bradley's order, all First Army rhino tanks remained back from the front, awaiting their moment.[57] It wouldn't be long now.

Major General Joe Collins assembled everything he needed . . . almost. He fully trusted five of his six division commanders, and he knew well the regimental colonels and brigadiers like Maurice Rose. One senior officer, though, gave pause.

Major General Leroy H. Watson commanded the 3rd Armored Division, the organization with the starring role in Operation Cobra. The 3rd Armored endeavored to take the central axis through the German rear area to Coutances, a classic role for such a tank-heavy organization. Yet Lightning Joe Collins doubted the man commanding that effort.

Leroy Watson, a West Point classmate of both Bradley and Eisenhower, served on the Mexican border in the "Punitive Expedition" against Pancho Villa's bandits in 1916–1917 and then as an infantry officer in World War I, seeing some combat in France. He took over the 3rd Armored Division in August 1942, led the formation through stateside exercises, then brought his soldiers to England to prepare for the Normandy campaign.[58] Sedentary in nature, seemingly a decade older than his fifty years, he ran things from a tidy command post. A pleasant, open-minded gentleman, Watson threatened no one, including the Germans.

The 3rd Armored Division struggled in its first combat action in Normandy on June 29–30 at Villiers-Fossard, four and a half miles north of St. Lô. The armored force gained a mile, not bad in the bocage. But the attack cost 31 tanks, a dozen other vehicles, and 351 men. Most of the losses came in a disjointed massed tank charge across a disused airfield, one of the few wide-open spots in that stretch of hedgerow country. Watson compounded matters by complaining about his under-gunned M4 Sherman tanks.[59] While the gripe resonated, and indeed proved all too true, it didn't impress Joe Collins when he heard of it. A poor workman blames his tools. Strike one.

On July 7–10, Watson's division tried again near St. Lô in a mixed-up fight poorly coordinated with the 30th Infantry Division. While the two organizations combined to halt a counterattack by the Panzer Lehr Division, the fighting again levied a high toll: 52 tanks, a self-propelled howitzer, 52 other vehicles, and 455 soldiers. One of Watson's brigadiers was fired by the 30th Infantry Division commander, a preemptory act that any other division commander would never have permitted. Watson let it ride, as the officer running the 30th was his West Point classmate.[60] The entire imbroglio exposed Watson as weak in several senses. Strike two. And that amounted to one more than Lightning Joe ever allowed. Lucky for Watson, in his two troubled attacks he did not work for VII Corps.

Now he did. Indeed, he and his 3rd Armored Division occupied stage center for the biggest American ground attack since D-Day. All who knew Major General Leroy H. Watson thought him a nice guy. But as Joe Collins and irascible baseball manager Leo Durocher both knew, nice guys finish last.[61]

———

That other nice guy, Lieutenant General Omar N. Bradley, hoped to kick off as soon as July 18, but it took two more days to lock down shattered St. Lô and the start line roadway.[62] The delay allowed for extra training and important discussions with the air commanders. Then, with all set, the weather went foul.

In war, Mother Nature giveth and she taketh away. She squared up the Allies and biffed the Nazi Germans on June 6 with a sliver of so-so weather that allowed the huge cross-channel assault to proceed. But for too much of that French summer of 1944, Mother Nature backed Berlin. As the U.S. Army official history observed, "The amount of cloud, wind, and rain in June and July of 1944 was greater than that recorded at any time since 1900." Half of the allocated U.S. close air support missions never flew. The effects on health, morale, and movement of ground troops all dragged on the already sluggish Allied campaign.[63]

Finally, on July 24, the weather teams and the airman agreed: good enough. Bomb at 1:00 p.m. local. The planes started taking off in England. Then a thick gray cloud deck coalesced over St. Lô, and the forward air controllers waved off the air wings. Mission aborted.

That kind of on/off switch works in video games, but not in real life. The abort order came too late. Three of six U.S. fighter groups and most of one heavy bombardment division dropped anyway. Errant bombs whistled down, killing 25 and wounding 131 Americans, all in the 30th Infantry Division. Worse, despite Bradley's expressed requirement for the heavy bomber stream to parallel the St. Lô road on the hostile side, the large aircraft flew perpendicular to the American front lines; the pilots rightly hoped to stay clear of German flak batteries, but hadn't made that necessity plain to Bradley, Collins, and the rest of the ground generals. (The American fighter-bombers used the requested parallel routes.) Even though the American troops had backed off three-quarters of a mile, too many bombs landed on U.S. positions. The mistaken bombardment alerted the Germans that something was up. Worst of all, the air crews had no choice but to rerun the same pattern the next day. It was too late to make changes.[64]

Over on the other side of the road, among the entrenched soldiers of the Panzer Lehr Division, the day had gone well. They'd gutted out a major Allied air attack without heavy losses. Then, when U.S. front-line units tried to reestablish forward positions after the botched air strike, the German panzer troops handily smashed back the American probes, patrols, and limited attacks to grab certain hedgerow squares. This fighting added 350 more G.I. casualties to those already inflicted by the U.S. Army Air Forces. The Germans lost about the same number of troops.[65] In their arrogance, the German commanders thought they'd won another round.

At 11:00 a.m. on July 25, 1944, the air bombardment started again. This time, the effort went full out, saturation bombing for an hour and twenty-three minutes. In blast effects, the concussion equaled that of a four-kiloton atomic bomb, a horror as yet unknown in 1944. The earth shook. A vast dust and debris cloud rose. The sun dimmed. Relentless overpressure squeezed the air out of the chests of prone soldiers. It went on and on. Reporter Ernie Pyle, who'd seen a lot of war already, called it "the most sustained horrible thing I've ever gone through."[66]

Again, bombs fell short. The official U.S. Army history refers to the fatal foul-ups as a "relatively light bombardment." That would have been news to the 111 men killed and 490 wounded in the 9th, 4th, and 30th Infantry divisions, the outfits designated to launch the follow-up attack. Thirty officers and NCOs, almost the entire command post crew of the 9th Infantry Division's 3rd Battalion, 47th Infantry Regiment, fell dead and wounded. Bombs shredded the tents, crushed the radios, and tore apart the soldiers of the fire direction center of the supporting 957th Field Artillery Battalion. All four lead rifle companies in the 4th Infantry Division's 8th Infantry Regiment suffered losses. The 30th Infantry Division reported 164 cases of outright combat exhaustion (today's post-traumatic stress disorder, PTSD) in heavily hit lead units. Some battalions took more casualties in the mistaken bombardment than they sustained on any other single day of combat in the war. As Omar Bradley said, "We believed our own casualties were devastating, perhaps so great that Cobra would have to be cancelled."[67]

Lightning Joe Collins, though, saw something many others did not. Despite justified rage and shock over the fatal bombing errors, Collins turned his speculations to the Germans. They'd taken the full weight of the pulverizing cascade of munitions, not just a deadly, painful temblor, but the entire searing horror show, Krakatoa upended and poured down for an apocalyptic eighty-three minutes. However bad it looked on the north side of the St. Lô road, the south side must be a whole lot worse.

Collins's instincts were right. Conditions in the Panzer Lehr sector defied description: craters gouged, trees flattened, panzers overturned, and men entombed. Communications wire had been cut to pieces and radios knocked out. Hundreds of torn corpses dotted the smoking, battered landscape. Filthy panzer men—deafened, drooling, babbling—wandered the desolate wasteland.[68]

Collins didn't flinch. He ordered in the lead infantry divisions. When generals objected that their stricken lead battalions couldn't possibly go, Collins didn't back down. War left no time for sentiment. Sub out and move out. To be blunt, the frontline regiments had endured worse losses back in those evil June days blundering through the bocage. As always, Collins's will prevailed. Off they went.

Amazingly, the surviving Germans fought back. To the west, the 9th Infantry Division advanced about two miles, crossing through the smoldering beaten zone. In the center, the 4th made similar progress. The 30th to the east made it just past a mile as night fell. By bocage standards, these gains registered at the high end. But somehow, the German remnants held out in a firm defensive line. There'd been no breakthrough.

And yet, Collins sensed something. That coup d'oeil thing, the innate understanding of ground and time and enemy that he had and so many did not, served him well again. The Germans hadn't counterattacked. They always did so. But not today. It was time to unleash the tanks.

The book told Lightning Joe not to do it. Before Cobra began, Collins told himself that "we shouldn't count too much on fast movement of armored divisions through this country; if we make a breakthrough it is OK, but until then . . ." The doctrine said hold the tanks. Now Collins said go.[69]

Of course, Collins being Collins, he diddled with the details. Getting Leroy Watson's 3rd Armored Division involved at crunch time—Collins didn't want any of that. Yet he most certainly wanted, and needed, to send the 3rd Armored's tanks into the fight, so he attached that division's Combat Command B (a regimental-sized task force of tanks, armored infantry, and self-propelled artillery) to strengthen the reliable 1st Infantry Division. Unsure of Watson and his 3rd Armored Division, Collins pointedly kept the rest of them well back behind the lines. Very sure of the 2nd Armored Division, Collins attached the 22nd Infantry Regiment, then waiting behind the jump-off line for the 4th Infantry Division. Collins knew that Brigadier General Maurice Rose had trained the 22nd riflemen to ride on Shermans, like the Russians did on the Eastern Front. As an experienced German NCO warned, "Americans use infantry too cautiously. If they used it the way Russians do, they would be in Paris now."[70] That German was about to see his fears come true.

Starting at 7:00 a.m. on July 26, 1944, the 1st Infantry Division and its attached tankers attacked west, bound for Coutances, ten miles away. They became balled up in the remnants of the German front

line just past the bombed-out region. The 2nd Armored Division followed at 9:45 a.m. after some difficulties passing through the cra-
tered ground in the 30th Infantry Division zone. Then the pace picked
up. Brigadier General Maurice Rose and his Combat Command A of
2nd Armored Division reached St. Gilles by midafternoon in what
Collins hailed as a "slashing drive."[71] That achievement signaled the
rupture of the main German defensive belt.

Rose wasn't done. As the sun went down, he pressed on to Canisy,
heading for Le Mesnil-Herman, well behind whatever was left of Panzer Lehr. Tired G.I.s begged him to halt for the night, to refit, rearm,
and reorganize. Rose refused. He told his soldiers that "the whole
American offensive depends on moving forward. I won't stop before
I've taken the objective no matter how dark it is, or how many men
we lose."[72] He kept going.

The next morning, July 27, Collins's 1st Infantry Division also
broke loose. Patton's Third Army, not formally activated until August
1, took charge of the U.S. divisions on the coast north of Coutances.
The corps over there hadn't been part of Operation Cobra. But they
were in it now, with Patton determined to break out, too. As the fiery
cavalry general exulted, "Things are really moving this morning and
so am I at long last."[73]

With the enemy in disarray, Collins bit the bullet and committed
Watson's 3rd Armored Division to advance to Coutances, the key objective of the entire operation. Collins almost wished he hadn't done
it. While the 1st Infantry Division and 2nd Armored Division continued to move out smartly, Watson's outfit dithered. They slowed to
pick a path through the bomb crater field, then spent much of July 27
battling German holdouts bypassed by the 1st Infantry Division. The
column stopped for the night to regroup. In the morning, the division advanced tentatively, halting well short of Coutances.[74]

When Joe Collins raced to the outskirts of Coutances on the afternoon of July 28 to find out why the 3rd Armored Division hadn't made

it there, he found an incredible traffic jam. George Patton and his senior people were on site, expediting the movement of their tanks, a scene re-created in the famous 1970 film *Patton*. Where was Watson? Collins finally tracked him down, sitting in his command post many miles away. In a cold fury, Collins ordered Watson forward. By the time Watson made it there, the sun had set. The 3rd Armored Division's lead task force stopped for the night. Tanks from Patton's Third Army took Coutances early on July 29, 1944.[75]

That night, Collins told Bradley he intended to dump Watson. It wasn't because Patton's tanks took Coutances first. That kind of stuff entertained journalists and provided grist for G.I. bragging rights, but the goal remained beating the Germans. Watson wasn't up to it. Collins thought an armored division needed a commander who would never quit, never stop, never let up.[76] He wanted Maurice Rose.

———

Cometh the hour, cometh the man. George S. Patton, Jr. himself picked Maurice Rose for greater things. Following the great 1941 maneuvers in Tennessee, Louisiana, and the Carolinas, and not long after Pearl Harbor, Patton elevated Rose from one of more than fifty lieutenant colonels in the 1st and 2nd Armored divisions to be the 2nd Armored Division chief of staff, the senior full colonel in the outfit, Patton's strong right arm. As former Third Army staff officer, noted military historian, and Patton biographer Martin Blumenson wrote, "Patton could have chosen any number of officers for this important position. It is significant that he selected Maurice Rose."[77]

Rose proved equal to Patton's confidence. When Patton moved up to corps command, Rose worked for Major General Ernest N. Harmon, a hard-charging, tough old cavalryman known to the G.I.s as "Old Gravel Voice." Rough in dress and language, Harmon spent his time out with the troops in the Patton mold, personifying the 2nd

Armored Division motto "Hell on Wheels." He expected Rose to handle the command post and keep the division organized during the
organization's early days at Fort Benning, Georgia, and then in North
Africa. Harmon sized up his tall, ramrod-straight chief of staff as "a
cool, able soldier, distant and removed in temperament." Omar Bradley called Rose "Harmon's brilliant young chief of staff." When Harmon went forward to Tunisia in 1943 to take command of the
troubled 1st Armored Division, he took only three men: his aide, his
operations officer, and Maurice Rose, who became the new 1st Armored Division chief of staff.[78]

No desk soldier, Rose earned two Silver Stars for valor while carrying out crucial tactical tasks at Harmon's direction. He led troops
under fire, created battle plans, supervised the staff, ran the division
command post, and even found time to negotiate a major German
component's surrender. That all impressed Patton, who agreed with
Ernie Harmon that Rose merited promotion to brigadier general.
Bradley saw it likewise. While Harmon stayed with the 1st Armored
Division for the upcoming campaign on the Italian peninsula, Rose
received his first star and the helm of Combat Command A, 2nd
Armored Division, destined for the Sicily invasion under Patton's
Seventh Army.[79]

This was an important appointment for a brigadier. In the
divisions that fought in the American Civil War and World War I,
brigadier generals did what their title implied: they commanded
brigades. American World War II divisions still included a pair
of brigadiers, but in the airborne and infantry formations, one served
as the assistant division commander (the deputy) and the other ran
the artillery. The two-star major general commanded the division.[80]
The duo of junior generals helped.

An American armored division organized differently. There, the
two brigadiers really commanded, often in detached independent
roles. An armored division comprised three "combat commands": A,
B, and R (Reserve). Each amounted to its own little division, a mix of

tanks, armored infantry, and self-propelled armored artillery, as well as engineers, signalers, medics, and other supporting arms. Task organization depended on the mission. Battalions and companies could be added or deducted as need be. Brigadier generals led Combat Commands A and B and a senior colonel headed R. (World war or not, the U.S. Congress scrupulously audited exactly how many generals the Army could promote; then and now, two one-stars per division remained the limit.) Orders listed these organizations as "CCA," "CCB," and "CCR" respectively. This flexible system matched the German *kampfgruppe* (battle group) method.[81] Today combat commands are known as brigade combat teams and form the standard structure for all U.S. Army divisions. They're commanded by colonels now.

Back in 1943, though, the best brigadiers took charge of combat commands. Maurice Rose and his CCA distinguished themselves in Sicily, leading Patton's attack to secure Palermo. Rose earned his third Silver Star.[82] At Carentan a week after D-Day, CCA's just-in-time advance backstopped the 101st Airborne Division. And then Rose and CCA made the first substantial penetration of German lines in Operation Cobra. Rose was ready to command his own division. All the wise heads agreed.

Patton, Bradley, Collins—they all knew him. Or did they? Old Gravel Voice Harmon, as gregarious as they come, never put a hole in Rose's armor. Harmon said of Rose that "no one could know him well."[83] The senior people thought of Rose as his World War II service record, a fine one, no doubt. And that's about all they really could say about the man.

In the small world of the interwar U.S. Army officer corps, your reputation preceded you. Patton and his wealthy wife flashed a lot of money during the Depression, and he made outrageous remarks in public, though he clearly understood his craft. Bradley liked to hunt birds and play bridge, and he epitomized the solid team player; he'd never upstage a superior. Collins came from a big Catholic Irish

American family in New Orleans and clearly intended to go places in the U.S. Army. Eisenhower proved a shrewd hand at poker and seemed to spend a lot of time in the throne rooms of demanding generals like Fox Connor, John J. Pershing, and the imperious Douglas A. MacArthur. Very few called frosty George C. Marshall by his first name, and he supposedly had a black book with the names of those who'd be generals in the next war.[84] If that little record existed at all—a big if—Maurice Rose's name most likely wasn't in it.

He had not gone to West Point. Indeed, he'd never attended college, and may not have completed high school. As America recruited soldiers for the Great War in 1917, Rose scored highly on a test to identify potential officers. A graduate of the First Officer Training Camp—today we'd know it as Officer Candidate School—at Fort Riley, Kansas, in August 1917, Rose served as an infantry officer in World War I. Wounded by German shellfire near St. Mihiel, Lieutenant Rose returned to his battalion of the 89th Division for the Meuse-Argonne offensive that ended the American part of the war.[85]

After the war Rose mustered out, sold meat for a year in Utah, then regained his infantry commission on July 1, 1920. For wartime performance, he made captain the next day; he remained at that rank for sixteen years, pretty typical for the shrunken U.S. Army of that era. Rose's infantry service alternated troop duty with school time until 1930, when he transferred to the cavalry, an unusual move. He stayed with cavalry squadrons until his promotion to major in 1936, when he attended the prestigious Command and General Staff School at Fort Leavenworth, Kansas. He didn't make any particular impression there, as evidenced by his next posting, a pedestrian stint as a National Guard advisor. Rose did well enough to gain admission to the Army Industrial College in 1939–1940, a senior service school equivalent but clearly of lesser caliber than the venerable U.S. Army War College, incubator of future generals. Rose graduated from the one known for bean-counters and second-stringers.[86] He remained in the background, there but not there.

Joe Collins went to the same Fort Benning infantry course as Rose in 1925. Collins, who networked with one and all, didn't appear to remember Rose. Neither did then Major Omar N. Bradley, one of the Benning instructors. Captain Rose missed George Marshall's Fort Benning tenure—and the future U.S. Army chief's alleged book of prospects—by a year. Rose had been married twice, but nobody recalled his first wife, Venice, and his second spouse, Virginia, was mainly recognized as the daughter of Major James Lew Barringer of the Veterinary Corps, not exactly a man on the make.[87] To those in the know, Rose appeared to be an average—possibly above average—time-server, careful in his dress, taciturn in his speech, another non–West Pointer filling out the room, a spear carrier, not a star. The war changed that.

Yet Maurice Rose never really changed. He remained who he'd been all along. Bradley, Collins, Harmon, Patton, and all the rest found out much later that the new 3rd Armored Division commander hailed from a family once known as Rauss, a Polish Jewish name "fixed" like so many others in that time. Maurice Rose's mother was Katherine Brown, recast from Bronowitz. Maurice's father, Samuel, owned a dress shop in Denver, Colorado. In 1925, following in his father's footsteps, seventy-year-old Samuel Rose became a rabbi. In the home, the Roses often spoke Yiddish, the traditional Jewish language drawn from German and Hebrew leavened with Slavic borrowings.[88] This constituted Maurice Rose's upbringing.

Among his fellow soldiers, Maurice Rose didn't mention his background. He listed his religion as Protestant, married second wife, Virginia, in an Episcopalian ceremony, and did not attend Jewish services nor, except on rare occasions, Christian ones. Still, when his son Maurice Roderick Rose was born in 1941, father Maurice arranged a circumcision with a rabbi outside Fort Knox, Kentucky.[89]

Maybe the approaching deployment to war reminded Maurice Rose of his roots.

We don't know because he never discussed the matter. Yet there he stood, a rabbi's son and a rabbi's grandson turned American general, pitted against the hard-core soldiery of the most virulent anti-Semitic movement in history. Maurice Rose said nothing of how this affected him. He let his actions speak.

CHAPTER 2

Slaughter Pen

It's a madhouse . . . You can't imagine what it's like . . . All
you can do is laugh out loud. Don't they read our
dispatches? Haven't they been oriented? They must be
living on the moon.

Field Marshal Günther A. F. von Kluge[1]

Immediate counterattack—every German soldier knew the drill.
Whether a hedgerow box, a key hilltop, a beachhead, a bridge over
a vital river line, or a rupture of the entire Norman front, German
Army doctrine offered one answer.[2] Hit back. Don't let the adversary
rest. Catch them off-balance. Go hard and fast, with as much force as
possible, right at the advancing opposing elements. Of course, as always, German panzers would lead the way.

By long practice, the first major German riposte should have been
the duty of the mobile division on the spot, Panzer Lehr. But that
once-formidable formation lacked any capacity to counterattack.
Even before Operation Cobra, nickel and dime bocage scraps and
daily American air strikes ground down Panzer Lehr to less than half
strength, maybe 40 tanks and 3,000 frontline troops.[3] Then came the

cataclysm of July 25, 1944: Ragnarok, the end of days. The exhausted, pitiful remnants of Panzer Lehr weren't up to anything resembling a counterstroke.

While more than 100,000 Americans and columns of hundreds of olive drab tanks and trucks poured through the yawning gap west of St. Lô, the German high command scrambled to form some kind of viable panzer group to stem the ever-increasing American tide. Yet here the Germans tripped up, courtesy of British General Bernard Law Montgomery's often criticized master plan. On the eastern end of the Normandy lodgment, the British and Canadians still remained stuck in the southern third of the smashed-up city of Caen, once hopefully listed as a D-Day objective. Despite failed attack after failed attack by Monty's men, their sacrifices were not in vain. The ceaseless British pressure attracted most of the German panzer forces, and those divisions remained stuck in place and bleeding out in front of the British Second Army around Caen. Even in the teeth of the un-folding crisis in western Normandy, it took days—too many days, nearly two precious weeks—to pry loose panzer regiments to go after the rampaging Americans. By the time the Germans assembled their counterattack contingent, Patton's Third Army's tanks roamed into the Brittany peninsula. Other Third Army units pushed east into north central France, heading toward Le Mans, an important Ger-man supply hub 140 miles southeast of St. Lô.[4] On the German high command's situation map, the traces of the attacking American divi-sions spread out like the streamers of a Roman candle.

Characteristically, German Führer Adolf Hitler blamed his gener-als. He fulminated against their failure to inspire their troops to hold every Norman hedgerow to the very last bullet and soldier. He excori-ated the field commanders for the delay in mounting the counterat-tack to repair the gaping hole. The former lance corporal of the 16th Bavarian Reserve Regiment in the Great War enjoyed berating the vaunted professionals of the German general staff. What did they know of real war? Rather than concentrate on throwing back what Hitler labeled the "Jewish-Bolshevik" threat in the east and "Jewish-plutocrat" invaders in the west—in his deranged rants, the führer consistently espied the Jewish hand moving against the Thousand Year Reich on all fronts—some of Germany's senior military officers seem to have been involved instead in the unsuccessful July 20, 1944, attempt to assassinate Nazi Germany's supreme leader. In fact, the circle of plotters turned out to be small, actively involving only a few generals. The führer, as was his mistrustful way, suspected them all. In Hitler's cynical estimation, his damnable generals couldn't even pull off a proper coup d'etat, let alone win the war. Along with fighting the Americans, the British, and the Russians, Hitler's top commanders also had to fear the midnight knock on the door from the dreaded Gestapo.[5] In the fever dreams of Radio Berlin, the führer's military genius promised a glorious panzer victory in France, smashing the Allies and driving them into the sea.

On planet Earth, most notably in the headquarters of OB West (*Oberbefehlshaber West,* the top command in France), Field Marshal Günther A. F. von Kluge hoped for much less. Launching an effective panzer counterattack might stanch the flow of American troops from the bocage, which could permit disengagement and flight by the majority of the slow-moving German infantry. Nazi blitzkrieg hype aside, nine-tenths of the German army still marched on foot and dragged their cannons behind horses. Von Kluge needed to compel about a two-week delay, enough to let his walking troops get away. Then they could re-form, dig in, and entrench along a stop line anchored on a significant barrier like the Seine River. The Allies might get to Paris but no farther. To buy this vital time, von Kluge designated the objective for his panzers as the coast at Avranches.[6] Cut off Patton's Third Army. Slow the American onslaught.

With the front broken and Patton's Third Army running wild, both sides intuited it must come to a heavy metal showdown,

American tanks vs. German panzers. Maurice Rose wanted to kill Germans. Adolf Hitler gave him the chance to do so.

———

As Hitler's panzer troops motor-marched into action on the morning of August 7, 1944, Brigadier General Maurice Rose assumed command of the 3rd Armored Division. The general showed up a week after Major General Joe Collins asked for him. As Collins well knew, and fully approved, Rose had been too busy fighting to get there sooner.

Indeed, Rose had spent the last few days still heading Combat Command A of the 2nd Armored Division, battling desperate German die-hards south of St. Lô. Those clashes cost 560 G.I.s killed and wounded and 37 Sherman tanks knocked out. These ugly firefights gained no headlines, yet mattered a great deal. In engaging the Germans, containing them, and killing them, Rose's final efforts with his former unit, joined with similar fighting by all of Collins's VII Corps and the rest of First Army, ensured Patton's Third Army to the west kept rolling. As then Lieutenant General Omar Bradley described the fight, "We kept punching ahead, mile by mile, shoving the Germans back, so we could crowd more divisions through the breakout."[7] First Army served as the stout shield. Third Army became the flashing rapier, which certainly suited Patton.

Maurice Rose's views on this evolving strategic picture remain unknown. What is known is that the general arrived at his new organization's command post, then set up at Chérénce le Héron, a Norman hamlet ten miles back from any gunfire.[8] He walked into the operations tent alone and unheralded—not the way things normally went. Most generals appear in a cloud of protocol and fuss. They tend to accumulate a retinue of favorite staff officers, aides, drivers, bodyguards, gofers, and flunkies that follow their general's star like the dust in a comet's tail. Not so Rose. Apparently, he didn't consult the general officer handbook. Rose brought no one from his former outfit.[9] He eschewed an entourage. He'd work with the team the U.S. Army gave him.

That team turned out to be far fewer than Rose expected. Collins fired Leroy Watson as commander of the 3rd Armored Division on July 29, 1944, but that unfortunate soul remained in limbo, still in command as a lame duck while Rose continued to tangle with his share of Germans. Determined to neuter Watson, Collins reached down and stripped out the division's combat power. By VII Corps order, Collins assigned almost every bit of it to the two combat commands. Effective July 30, CCA went to the 1st Infantry Division and CCB was attached to the 4th Infantry Division. Even the CCR headquarters was used to reinforce CCB. Poor Watson retained control of a portion of the Division Trains, a single armored infantry battalion (just enough to secure the current position), his command post, his aide, his driver, and his orderly. [10] That was all Maurice Rose inherited on August 7.

With German panzers on the move, Rose couldn't discern why he'd been sent to take over a division that didn't really exist. At VII Corps headquarters, Rose confronted Joe Collins. No shouter like Georgie Patton or Gravel Voice Harmon, and well aware of Collins's penchant for removing "troublemakers"—however ill-defined—Rose nevertheless lodged his objection, "for which I respected him," wrote Lightning Joe later. Collins justified the dishing out of the 3rd Armored Division's combat battalions by observing that he intended to give Rose "time to get acquainted with the personnel and operating procedures of the division, which I felt needed correction." Well, that kind of stately procedure made sense back home at Fort Knox, Kentucky. But in Normandy with hundreds of panzers bearing down? It sounded odd. Even so, Collins described the splitting of the division as a "temporary expedient," supposedly required by the large German panzer attack just getting underway.[11]

That the rationalization justified Collins's usual solution—micromanagement and simply doing it himself—went unsaid. Rose realized that he was on probation. Collins wanted to see what his new armor commander did next. Would Rose retire to his tent sulking and bitter, like Achilles before Troy? Or would Rose go forward to meet and sustain his committed combat commands, get up near the fight, and posture for the next phase against the Germans, playing chess, not checkers?[12] Stated more directly, was Rose another weakling? Or more hopefully, was he a good enough commander, a trustworthy executor of Collins's orders? Or might Rose really be who Patton thought he might be, a general able to be trusted to use his own initiative? Collins put few in that category, aside from himself. But this Rose guy? To be determined . . .

In a perfect world, Maurice Rose would have spent the summer campaign in France working for George Patton, the most experienced and aggressive armor officer in the U.S. Army. Even as Collins sized up Maurice Rose, to see if he really measured up to his new position, Patton's 4th and 6th Armored divisions roared across France, doing tank things, cavalry things—war-winning things. By contrast, with German panzers pushing hard, Rose found himself in early August 1944 delivering fuel and evacuating casualties in the messy scrum south and east of St. Lô, serving the senior echelon of First Army, a bunch that the ever-blunt Ernie Harmon dismissed as "slow, cautious, and without much zip."[13]

———

Rose immediately moved his command post closer to the fighting, choosing a site a mile and a half south of Chatillon-sur-Colmont, not far from the south side of the German advance. From there, a short drive took one right to either CCA or CCB. Code-named "Omaha," the division headquarters featured two parts: Omaha Rear, the Division Trains HQ, which handled logistics and stayed back several miles, and the main command post (daily battle tracking, intelligence, fires, and planning), known as Omaha Forward. G.I. wags soon began referring to Omaha Way Forward. By tradition, and in most outfits, the division staffers believed that "action was not supposed to be the concern of headquarters personnel." At Chatillon-sur-Colmont, the command post troops found out that in Rose's view, "there were no non-combatants in the 3rd Armored Division."[14] Rose endeavored to be up front. That habit commenced during his first twenty-four hours with the division.

Rose focused on the mission Collins gave him: sustaining his farmed-out combat commands. For the new division commander, that meant going out routinely to be with those under fire. Personally, Rose ranged forward in an open-top, four-wheel-drive Willys jeep, which in the armored force went by the name "peep," presumably because it allowed its occupants, often reconnaissance troops, to scout ahead and "peep" around the corner. Rose rode in the front right seat, with driver Technician 4th Grade Glenn H. Shaunce to his left and aide-de-camp Captain Robert M. Bellinger (inherited from the departed Major General Leroy H. Watson) in back, perched precariously next to the large rectangular SCR-506 radio, a device capable of transmitting and receiving out to seven miles. Although his peep carried that big radio, Rose also brought along an M20 armored car, a six-wheeled vehicle configured with additional radios; along with its two-man crew, the M20 carried two signal men, a battle-tracking sergeant, and the G-3 (operations) officer, Lieutenant Colonel Wesley A. Sweat. To direct fire support, Rose's division artillery commander, Colonel Frederic J. Brown, Jr., one of the few senior West Pointers in the 3rd Armored, also followed the general. Brown rode in a second peep with driver and his own bulky artillery radio. Two motorcycle-mounted military police soldiers served as messengers and security men. Three vehicles, two motorcycles, and thirteen soldiers, including the general, comprised Rose's extremely lean command group.[15]

Most of Rose's peers considered such a command group too light. The official U.S. Army table of organization and equipment offered an armored division commander an array of M5 Stuart light tanks, M3 half-tracks, M8 Greyhound (cousin of the M20) armored cars, and more peeps, to include an extra security platoon of armored infantry. The approved array totaled sixty-two G.I.s and fourteen vehicles. That was pretty big, a company's worth of troops. Major General Ernie Harmon, who commanded the 2nd Armored Division in Morocco, the 1st Armored Division in Tunisia and Italy, and then the 2nd Armored Division again in northwest Europe, used to emulate Maurice Rose and rely on his agile little peep to get around. German employment of stay-behind ambush tactics, snipers, and ample reliance on mortar and artillery fires changed Harmon's mind. "I dropped the custom, acquired in North Africa and Italy, of traveling by jeep [peep]" Harmon stated.[16] Old Gravel Voice, not averse to the front lines, judged an armored car element of about platoon strength to be a reasonable compromise. Rose chose to live dangerously.

With Rose out on his own, checking in by radio, the Omaha Forward team kept track of ongoing operations and kept VII Corps informed. University of Texas alumnus and field artillery officer Colonel John A. "Long John" Smith, at six foot six, one of few men in the division taller than Brigadier General Rose, ran the headquarters as chief of staff. Because of the propensity of the Omaha Forward to tangle with Germans, staff officers and NCOs referred being part of "Combat Command Smith."[17] They weren't joking, either.

The division's three fighting headquarters were CCA, CCB, and CCR with subordinate units attached and detached based on the assigned mission. All sixteen U.S. Army armored divisions used this same flexible command structure. Fourteen of these divisions organized with nine combat battalions: three tank, three armored infantry (mounted in half-tracks), and three armored field artillery (self-propelled M7 tracked howitzers), each given or taken as required by the combat commands. Study of previous battles showed that a 1:1 ratio of tank to infantry battalions worked best. German panzer generals solved this equation early, but the Soviets, British, and Americans soon enough agreed.[18] The U.S. Army reorganized its armored divisions accordingly.

But not all of them. The remaining two American armored divisions—the 2nd and Rose's 3rd, already in the European theater waiting for D-Day when the new organization went into effect—kept the older lineup of twelve battalions: six tank, three armored infantry, and three armored field artillery. Compared to the other fourteen such American armored divisions, the 2nd and 3rd included more soldiers (14,620 vs. 10,937) and more tanks (232 vs. 186 M4 Sherman medium tanks and 158 vs. 77 M5 Stuart light tanks).[19] Too many tanks, especially light ones, and not enough riflemen, the analysts decreed.

Each of these so-called heavy armored divisions also retained colonel-led regimental headquarters: two armored and one armored infantry. The smart guys back in the United States looked at practice to date in the war and found these regimental colonels and their staffs to be redundant, especially when you trimmed out three "excess" battalions of armor. All you needed were an equal number of tank and infantry battalions working directly for combat commands. So spoke the staff experts back home. Long-time tanker Major General Ernie Harmon growled that these constituted "painful alterations," and then Lieutenant General George Patton wondered why not add more infantry rather than subtract experienced full colonels and a lot of valuable tanks?[20] The veteran tank generals were ignored. Rose, like the rest, saw the logic, but couldn't help but notice that when things really got serious—Operation Cobra, for example—the higher-ups immediately called for both heavy armored divisions.

In the 3rd Armored Division, like the others, the combat commands did the daily hooking and jabbing with the foe. As a former combat command brigadier himself, Rose took a long, hard look at the leaders he found in place. Brigadier General Doyle O. Hickey, a pipe-smoking Arkansas lawyer, decided he liked the U.S. Army after serving as an artillery officer in World War I. Hickey's calm demeanor belied his demonstrated willingness to go into harm's way. He commanded CCA, built around the 32nd Armored Regiment and usually backed by the 67th Armored Field Artillery Battalion.[21]

Longtime cavalryman Colonel (later Brigadier General) Truman E. Boudinot commanded CCB. He attended the University of California at Berkeley before joining the U.S. Army during World War I. He also met Maurice Rose when they both attended the Command and Staff School at Fort Leavenworth in 1936–1937. Boudinot had another thing in common with Rose. Like his new division commander, Boudinot gained his command when his predecessor faltered in the bocage. The 33rd Armored Regiment formed the foundation of CCB, typically supported by the 391st Armored Field Artillery Battalion.[22]

Big, bluff Colonel William Wallace "Jug" Cornog, Jr. attended North Georgia Military College in 1918–1920. He commanded the 36th Armored Infantry Regiment. He also commanded CCR, sometimes referred to somewhat generically as "Division Reserve." Cornog usually gave up an infantry battalion to CCA and CCB respectively; in return, they sent him a tank battalion. When Rose took over on August 7, 1944, Cornog was forward as a task force commander with Boudinot's CCB. Normally, though, CCR provided the 3rd Armored Division's swing element, ready to reinforce CCA, CCB, or carry out a third task. Most often, the 54th Armored Field Artillery Battalion backed up CCR, but by long practice, artillery outfits were not kept in reserve, but sent forward to fire. Thus the 54th Artillery often ended up reinforcing CCA or CCB.[23]

The Division Trains made sure the division kept rolling. In coordination with the collocated Division Rear Command Post (Omaha Rear), the trains delivered fuel, ammunition, food, and spare parts. The trains also sent forward detachments to the combat units. The 3rd Ordnance (Maintenance) Battalion, Supply Battalion, 45th Armored Medical Battalion, and the rear echelon of attached outfits worked together to sustain those up front. Colonel Carl J. Rohsenberger, a long-serving cavalry officer, commanded. He took over on

August 2, 1944, just before Brigadier General Rose arrived in the division. Rohsenberger's elevation to command came because German gunfire killed his predecessor, Colonel James B. Taylor.[24] Taylor's death in a supposedly safe posting underscored that in a hard-fighting armored division duking it out with the Germans, there was not much "rear" to be found. And that was before Maurice Rose took over and imposed his vision of leaders being well forward.

————

What of the great German panzer attack?

The panzers showed up late, piecemeal, and disorganized, but show up they did, commencing their effort at 2:45 a.m. on August 7 with some 300 tanks and assault guns. Denuding the Caen front opposite the British, the Germans used the hours of darkness on August 6–7 to move into position. From north to south, the first echelon consisted of the 116th Panzer Division "Windhund" (Greyhound) going against the American 9th Infantry Division, the 2nd Panzer Division concentrating on part of the U.S. 30th Infantry Division, and the 2nd SS Panzer Division "Das Reich" (The Reich), beefed up by understrength battalions of the 17th SS Panzergrenadier Division—roughly handled since Carentan almost two months prior—keying on the southern battalions of the 30th Infantry Division. The Germans expected to penetrate in the center or south, overrunning the American 30th. Then, with a hole torn through the G.I. positions near Mortain, the 1st SS Panzer Division "Liebstandarte Adolf Hitler" (Adolf Hitler Lifeguard), aided by the battered Panzer Lehr reconnaissance battalion, would push ahead twenty-three road miles, take Avranches, and upend the entire American breakout.[25] So went the German plan, a good one . . . if it worked.

The two-week wait since Cobra kicked off made the imminent German effort only too obvious. Some British Ultra intelligence officers believed they'd delivered adequate warning. Omar Bradley begged to differ: "In this instance Ultra was of little or no value," offering only a few hours' alert. Still, Bradley already guessed something was up. After all, he'd already met the Germans in Tunisia and Sicily and well understood their preference for lashing back. Patton, also well aware of the usual German tactics, saw trouble brewing. He slowed up his Third Army, keeping the 35th Infantry Division available for action south of Mortain.[26] During the first few days of August, rampaging U.S. and British air squadrons tormented the rumbling German mobile columns, preventing proper assembly, provisioning, and prebattle reconnaissance. Even so, shrouded by the short summer night, when Allied air didn't fly, the veteran German panzer officers pulled off their attack. The Germans had a knack for finding a way.

The American 30th Infantry Division took the German main effort right in the teeth. Boudinot's CCB backstopped the 30th in their fight with the German 2nd Panzer Division and a battalion or so of the 116th Panzer Division. Most of the latter outfit bungled their attack; their commander supposedly did it on purpose to honor his alleged ties to the July 20, 1944, conspirators, thus validating every Gestapo suspicion fed to the already paranoid Hitler.[27] Such German-on-German general officer contretemps meant nothing in the hedgerows north and west of Mortain. There Boudinot's Sherman crews and riflemen fought it out with the dim, angular shapes and fleeting ghosts that loomed out of the graying dawn.

This time, the bocage worked very much in favor of the defending G.I.s. Their rhino tanks broke berms and caught German vehicles confined to narrow farm roads. Shermans faced down panzers time after time. G.I. rifle squads ambushed advancing Germans. Tracers sparked along each contested hedgerow wall. Artillery bursts flogged any vehicle or clutch of men seen in the open. It went on and on. In the words of a contemporary 3rd Armored Division account, "The Command [CCB] was shelled, bombed, and attacked by enemy infantry and tanks for five consecutive days." In these firefights, CCB lost 63 killed, more than 150 wounded, and dozens of tanks. In return,

Boudinot's troops wrecked most of 2nd Panzer Division's tanks. The Americans stopped the Germans cold a dozen miles short of Avranches.[28]

To the south, the 2nd SS Panzer Division stalled as the sun rose on August 7. Although they'd bypassed most of the overmatched 30th Infantry Division, two Waffen SS panzer columns could not force their way past one steady American outfit, the North Carolina National Guardsmen of the 2nd Battalion, 120th Infantry Regiment. Although hard-pressed, these 30th Infantry Division G.I.s held on to Hill 317 (its height in meters, over 1,000 feet), a dominant knob. As a result, U.S. forward observers and forward air controllers enjoyed clear visibility. They brought down great volumes of artillery shellfire and aerial bombs. Royal Air Force Typhoons flew 294 sorties and claimed 40 panzers destroyed. Often the fliers exaggerated. Not this time. The defending American soldiers suffered more than 300 killed and wounded, one of every two men on the hill.[29] But they held on, a bone in the throat of the 2nd SS Panzer Division.

Hickey's CCA ended up attached to the 2nd Armored Division, blocking German threats to the southwest. Here the fighting never approached the scale of the vicious engagements around Mortain. Nevertheless, Brigadier General Hickey's CCA did their part, suffering two killed, dozens of wounded, and a score of wrecked light and medium tanks.[30] The Germans didn't come close to getting through.

Throughout these hot, busy August days of renewed bocage combat, the 3rd Armored Division headquarters sent up fuel, ammunition, and replacement soldiers. The Division Trains doctors and medics assisted in treating the wounded. Graves registration teams brought out the dead.

New commander Maurice Rose took his peep here and there under fire. He spent most of his time in and around Hickey's nearby CCA outfits. The CCB action near Mortain was too far north. Even for an aggressive general like Rose, there were way too many angry Germans between the 3rd Armored Division command post and

Boudinot's CCB troops. That noted, Rose garnered some useful impressions of his new division.

The 3rd Armored Division soldiers knew how to fight. That became evident. Rose saw his tank crews, riflemen, and cannoneers at work and liked what he saw.[31] He found Hickey and CCA capable, the Division Trains well run, and the division staff at Omaha Forward on their game. Beyond that, Rose couldn't say. Not yet.

While Rose hadn't made it to CCB, one of the results of that command's operations demanded the new division general's immediate attention. At the height of the Mortain fighting, about 4:00 p.m. on August 9, 1944, a well-placed German artillery round killed four officers, including Colonel William J. Cornog, Jr., commander of the 36th Armored Infantry Regiment, and Lieutenant Colonel Vincent E. Cockefair, commander of the 36th's 2nd Battalion. This placed junior Lieutenant Colonel Jack R. Hutcheson, the 36th's executive officer (second in charge) in temporary, simultaneous command of both the 2nd Battalion and the 36th Armored Infantry Regiment. Naturally, Hutcheson focused on his battalion's critical mission of blunting the ongoing German counterattack. Regimental duties took a back seat.[32] Cornog's death meant that there'd be no real CCR until a more permanent solution became available. Solid infantry colonels were in short supply. Given all going on across Normandy, finding a quality backfill might take weeks. The 3rd Armored Division would have to make do.

Being on hand, but not fully in charge, chafed at Rose. These were his men and his losses. But this wasn't his fight. Evidently, though, the Germans wanted more. Maurice Rose and the 3rd Armored Division would soon give them all they could take.

———

Never reinforce failure. It's battlefield common sense, often echoed in military academies and war colleges. In that regard, once the major German counterattack foundered at Mortain by the morning of

August 8, 1944, the panzers should have backed off and gone to Plan B. But with Adolf Hitler, there was no Plan B. There's a reason that the German Army suffered millions of casualties in the 1914–1918 war yet never saw cause to promote Hitler past lance corporal. Even granting him that rank may have been generous.

Now the former lance corporal unleashed his all too predictable thunder: "I command the attack be prosecuted daringly and recklessly to the sea." German theater commander Field Marshal Günther von Kluge, nicknamed "Clever Hans" for his long-standing ability to offer happy talk to Hitler while cursing the führer in private, felt the hot breath of the Gestapo on his neck. Von Kluge felt he had no choice but to follow Hitler's delusional dictate and keep trying to chop through the strong American defenses. American artillery and Allied air flensed the German panzer battalions to the tune of hundreds of vehicles smashed and burned and thousands of men killed. [33] The entire debacle made you think of trying to pull your right arm out of a roaring wood-chipper by sticking in your left arm, too.

The continued German push created a large salient in central Normandy. Clinging to a stretch of Norman bocage some forty miles east to west and twenty miles north to south, the Germans struggled to contain the British Second Army and Canadian First Army in the north and the American First Army in the west and southwest, even as Patton's Third Army ran loose to the south. The towns of Falaise and Argentan marked the north and south limits of the fifteen-and-a-half-mile-wide escape path, the only way out for the surrounded enemy. What if Patton swung north and closed the trap of what both sides were beginning to label the "Falaise Pocket"? Up and down the Allied chain, they all saw the same thing: Eisenhower, Montgomery, and Bradley. Bradley exulted on August 9, 1944: "This is an opportunity that comes to a commander not once in a century. We're about to destroy an entire hostile army. If the other fellow will only press his attack here at Mortain for another forty-eight hours, he'll give us time to close at Argentan and there completely destroy him." He continued, "He'll have nothing left with which to oppose us. We'll go all the way from here to the German border."[34]

Bagging an entire German field army—two in fact, the Seventh and the Fifth Panzer, some 100,000 strong—might well resolve the Western Front, maybe the entire war, in a single stroke. To Germany's east, the Soviet Red Army had timed their massive 1944 summer offensive to match up with the D-Day landings. In Belorussia (today's Belarus), Soviet tank divisions encircled and destroyed much of the German Army Group Center.[35] If Bradley and his peers could do likewise in the west, the scale of these defeats might well bring down Hitler's Reich.

First, though, the Allies must complete this bold double envelopment. That required tough, veteran troops, and by now in Normandy, the Americans and British certainly had those in abundance, backed by superb, powerful airpower. Just as importantly, such a decisive maneuver demanded instinctive, gutsy generals up and down the line. Rose was ready; Collins and Patton, too. So far, so good.

Above the fighting level, though, caution was the dominant trait. Eisenhower commanded the European theater as a chairman of the board. He left the details in Normandy to his land commander, Montgomery. Monty excelled in well-prepared, set-piece battles like the opening D-Day assault. A roiling tank scrum around this untidy Falaise Pocket? Not so much. Plus, he had to be careful with his forces. Monty couldn't afford to squander Britain's last field army, the Second, let alone the limited numbers of the First Canadian Army and the Polish 1st Armoured Division. When those outfits bled out, there wouldn't be any more.[36]

By comparison, Bradley, hardly a lion, looked to be the boldest of the senior Allied commanders. And he enjoyed the authority to act. On August 1, 1944, Bradley stepped up to command the Twelfth Army Group in charge of Patton's Third Army as well as Bradley's former organization, First Army.[37] Bradley realized that driving hard to bag a mass of Germans offered a fine mission for Patton. Holding the nose and south side of the Falaise Pocket and squeezing the trapped Germans suited First Army, now under a new commander.

Lieutenant General Courtney H. Hodges was easy to overlook. Quiet, slight, and introverted, he lacked anything like the dynamic command presence urged on those aspiring to high command. Born in Georgia, Hodges started as Patton's West Point classmate. Both cadets failed first-year mathematics; Patton repeated his plebe year and graduated in 1909. Hodges quit and joined the U.S. Army as a private, gaining a commission from the ranks, also in 1909. In the Meuse-Argonne Forest in World War I, Hodges earned the Distinguished Service Cross as an infantry battalion commander. Another Fort Benning instructor like Bradley, Hodges taught Maurice Rose among others. Hodges didn't remember Rose. But then Lieutenant Colonel George C. Marshall clearly recalled Hodges and thought well of him as an unflappable, steady character. Now, after serving as Bradley's deputy from D-Day onward, Hodges took over First Army.[38]

Bradley described his fellow former Fort Benning instructor as "a military technician whose faultless techniques and tactical knowledge made him one of the most skilled craftsmen of my entire command." Those who knew Hodges in World War II might well have wondered precisely to whom Bradley referred. The Hodges who commanded First Army in 1944–1945 proved obtuse, inert, and eminently forgettable, the Man Who Wasn't There. Hodges rarely stirred from his distant command post. His orders often seemed inscrutable. He shared one of Bradley's more limiting faults, a galling inability to translate a military map to the actual ground, and added a few of his own, including lack of warmth, unwillingness to tolerate dissenting views, and a prickly devotion to minor aspects of general officer privileges. Hodges gained his name in the Great War and adhered to that conflict's stereotype of a château general—distant, unapproachable, and irrelevant to the effective conduct of day-to-day operations.

Patton summed it all up with his usual candor: "Courtney is really a moron."[39]

His postwar praise aside, Bradley apparently recognized Hodges's tendencies. From day one to the end of the war, Hodges's First Army always included Major General Joe Collins and VII Corps. In a better version of the campaign, Collins should have taken over First Army in August 1944 and Hodges should have returned to the United States to run some obscure training depot. But that didn't happen—more Bradley prudence, not to mention deference to the express wishes of U.S. Army Chief of Staff General George C. Marshall. Bradley did as he did with sorting out the bocage, taking Cherbourg, and mounting Cobra: leave it to Collins. For all his ambition, Joe Collins served Hodges with boundless loyalty. In return, Hodges let Collins run his own war and a good part of First Army's, too. When Collins's VII Corps led the way First Army shone, and when Hodges stirred to do whatever it was he did, First Army bumbled. It's noteworthy that Joe Collins insisted on keeping Maurice Rose and 3rd Armored Division with VII Corps throughout the war.[40] As Collins paced First Army, so Rose would come to pace VII Corps.

With the crisis at Mortain over and a vast sack of Germans immobilized west of Falaise and Argentan, Joe Collins reunited Maurice Rose with the combat battalions of the 3rd Armored Division.[41] Collins had need of them. It was time to kill panzers.

————

The Germans termed it a *kesselschlacht*, usually translated as "cauldron battle," the surrounding and destruction of an opposing army. As Omar Bradley rightly observed, no doubt conjuring up some half-forgotten West Point lecture on Hannibal or Napoleon, such events hardly ever came together in war. In the early days of their 1941 blitzkrieg, the Germans pulled off a few huge encirclements in Russia. The Soviets repaid the pain at Stalingrad in 1942–1943. In this war, the

British and Americans hadn't really created a classic *kesselschlacht*.[42] Now they would.

At Monty or Bradley altitude, success amounted to a matter of placing forces and fires in space and time, getting the lines right on the big map. With Omar Bradley involved, that was no sure thing. At the Maurice Rose level and below, this one would live up (or down) to the literal translation of *kesselschlacht*, a "kettle slaughter," tightening the screws while victims in a tight space clawed to get out. The Germans never just stood there and took it. They fought back.

Rose expected as much. Much as he disliked continuous hedgerow and village combat, that's where the Germans bogged down. So that's where the 3rd Armored Division must go. Bocage battles required combined arms: tanks, infantry, and artillery. This wouldn't be a Pattonesque dash across France. That might come later. But first, the Germans had to be crushed where they were.

The division assembled twenty miles south of the bocage belt and west of the French town of Mayenne on August 12, 1944. Rose issued Field Order No. 6, a few typed pages with an attached map overlay, a sketch of graphics to be traced onto a map sheet. Based on long practice, Rose wasn't prescriptive. He gave missions (task and purpose), assigned resources, and let his subordinates have at it. As Rose had written years before, "Being given a mission and allowed to work out the details is really a perfect 'set-up' which we too seldom encounter."[43] It offered a drastic contrast with some of Joe Collins's habits. But that inveterate micromanager had already discovered that he need not overcoach Maurice Rose.

Field Order No. 6 described a classic cavalry mission: advance to contact. U.S. Army field manuals, then and now, prefer the phrase "movement to contact," but that first word suggested some kind of glorified motor march. This one would be an attack all the way, finding the Germans and killing them. Knocking out the panzers took priority. Rose expected his G.I.s would do plenty of fighting to pry into the southern flank of the German pocket. Given what the intelligence staffers could predict about enemy dispositions, Rose picked the French crossroads town of Rânes, forty miles north of Mayenne by road, as a march objective, figuring the Americans would encounter Germans there in strength.[44] That fulfilled Rose's purpose. Get at them.

The new division commander realized that although the 3rd Armored Division demonstrated mettle in the defensive struggle around Mortain, when on the offensive, and certainly in Operation Cobra, the division developed a reputation for prodding and poking tentatively against any German opposition, no matter how minor. To put it crudely, in trying to winkle out every last German, 3rd Armored Division outfits sometimes found themselves treed by chihuahuas. While that made some sense in the dense hedgerow country, particularly in the confusing early engagements, it also played right into German hands, leaving the division's G.I.s and tanks crawling under hostile fire. That had to change.

On contact, Rose demanded violent action. Commanders meeting dug-in Germans had to plaster the foe with fire and immediately size them up. If faced with panzers, the Americans must hunt and destroy these dangerous opponents using tanks, tank destroyers, artillery, and, if need be, infantry with bazookas. If confronted by German infantry, a bunch often dug-in and hence somewhat immobile, the enemy must be "quickly overrun or bypassed, contained, and left to be dealt with by the closely following infantry."[45] A platoon of thirty German riflemen, maybe even a company of a hundred, could and should be smashed by U.S. firepower. Larger elements had to be engaged, then turned over to follow-on American infantry. Keep pressing forward, past the initial crust of hostile defenders. Get deep. Tear up the German rear area. If done at speed, it might well eviscerate the German supply lines, starve the panzers of fuel, and disrupt the enemy command network, paralyzing the enemy. Operation Cobra showed the way to do it.

Rose's scheme of maneuver built around this idea of going deep, getting to Rânes quickly to rock back the Germans on day one. That would stir them up, no doubt. The division's 83rd Armored Reconnaissance Battalion would lead, checking routes and reporting hostile positions. Given the by now well-understood challenge of the hedgerows, the division prepared to attack in column, CCA followed by CCB. Rose had already seen Brigadier General Doyle Hickey in action and trusted him; not so CCB. So Hickey's CCA would go first, with CCB ready to take over as need be. With no real CCR, Rose knew he'd have to assume a personal role in overseeing the use of the relatively small Division Reserve, although Collins at VII Corps told Rose that once the attack got going, the 60th Infantry Regiment of the 9th Infantry Division would be attached to help out. Rose planned to push his Omaha Forward command post right up there, just south of Rânes, although the exact location and nature of German resistance might dictate otherwise. Either way, Rose himself intended to be near the lead elements of CCA.[46]

The attack kicked off at 6:00 a.m. on August 13; the order specified 5:30 a.m., but the 83rd Recon reported that it "jumped off at 0600" (6:00 a.m.)—a half hour late. In past operations, the division dished out the four reconnaissance companies to the combat commands. On August 9, Rose had warned the recon battalion commander that those days were over. Rose planned to use the recon outfit directly under division control with the task of finding the foe, providing details of German positions and strength, and thus allowing the trailing combat commands to choose to attack or bypass as necessary. The 83rd's lieutenant colonel found it challenging to operate as a battalion. It was the first time he'd done so in Normandy.[47]

Two of the battalion's four companies scouted ahead, finding a clear road to the edge of the bocage at Pré-en-Pail by 11:30 a.m. At that point, about halfway to Rânes, the reconnaissance troopers sent Company B on ahead the remaining seventeen miles to Rânes. The rest of the battalion halted "for the night," a rather short work day.

The 83rd took no losses and found no Germans.[48] No runs, no hits, no errors—game on.

Just because the 83rd Recon didn't see Germans didn't mean they weren't there. They were. Short on ammunition, lacking a lot of fuel, the Germans let the 83rd Recon's parade of M8 Greyhound armored cars, M5 Stuart light tanks, M3 half-tracks, and nimble peeps pass by. German officers and NCOs knew what U.S. Army scouts looked like. They didn't want an appetizer. The Germans awaited the main course.

It wasn't long in arriving. Behind the scouts came CCA, advancing in two columns abreast. To the west, Lieutenant Colonel Walter B. "Rich" Richardson's battalion-sized task force (TF) of tanks and half-track infantry (a tank battalion with 36 Shermans and one rifle company, about 900 soldiers in all) protected their larger neighbor on the major road to Rânes, Lieutenant Colonel Leander L. Doan's regimental-sized TF of tanks and infantry (two battalions with 72 Shermans plus a reduced battalion of two rifle companies, about 1,800 soldiers altogether). On this opening day, Doan aimed to get through to Rânes or the German main body, whichever he found first. The opening twenty-three miles turned out to be pretty much a road march right out of the newsreels. Jubilant French women kissed soldiers, local citizens passed out bottles of wine and cognac, and some happy villagers literally threw flowers.[49] Had the Germans quit the war?

They had not.

About 11:30 a.m., on their route west of Pré-en-Pail, TF Richardson smacked into a hornet's nest at Couptrain, a spot the 83rd Recon reported clear. Contrary to the scouts' report, the Americans found a battalion-sized element, probably all that was left, of the German 728th Infantry Regiment.[50] The entrenched Germans used some 88mm antitank guns and their usual surfeit of machine guns to stall TF Richardson. In the past, this would have ended TF Richardson's day. But with Rose's urgency in mind, Richardson's men found a way to contain their foe. The armored column slipped away. The clash cost five Americans killed and a dozen wounded. TF Richardson kept going until midnight but didn't make it to Rânes. They stopped short, faced by an unknown number of truculent Germans at Joué-du-Bois ("The Play Woods"), about five miles south and west of Rânes.[51]

While TF Richardson tangled at Couptrain, CCA's TF Doan took advantage of their work and kept pressing north. They overran several German roadblocks and reached Rânes just after nightfall. There seemed to be a lot of Germans there. Men reported clanking sounds and engine noises. But in the darkness, who knew? Tanks needed fuel and there were American wounded to evacuate. TF Doan spent the night refitting. They prepared to go after the Germans in the morning.

Heartened by CCA's progress, Rose committed Colonel Truman Boudinot's CCB in their wake. Lieutenant Colonel William B. Lovelady's battalion-strength task force headed to Couptrain to finish off the Germans there. Boudinot directed the regimental-scale task force under Colonel Dorrence S. Roysdon to strengthen the attack. The two task forces couldn't do the job. Their battalion of half-track infantry wasn't enough to crack the German nut, despite a lot of artillery and air strikes. Dusk found both sides trading shots. This one wasn't over.[52]

As the day ended, the division headquarters soldiers at Omaha Way Forward found themselves in action at Pré-en-Pail. As the command post set up shop in the damaged hamlet, an excited French villager showed up. Through gestures and broken English, he pointed out a house with German troops in it. The voluble French citizen thought there might be six enemy in there, but something got lost in translation. In any event, the problem had to be addressed. Captain Ward D. Waits, Lieutenant Daniel O. Magnussen, and Sergeant Abe Moskowitz rounded up three willing private soldiers. Rifles ready, the six Americans carefully approached the house. The Germans replied with a wild hail of ill-aimed Mauser bullets. The G.I.s shot back, killing one German and wounding others. That did it. More than ninety Germans came trooping out, weapons dropped, hands up.[53] It reminded one and all at Omaha Forward that they were in the fight, too. Maurice Rose wanted it that way.

What did the general know of the fighting on August 13, 1944, the first day of his first division attack? In today's American military, satellite trackers and superb radio sets allow clear voice, text, and imagery across many miles. A present-day division commander can track individual tanks and rifle squads and talk to any unit with a radio. In theory, and sometimes in practice, the U.S. president in the White House could speak directly to a tank sergeant in combat. We know where our people are and how to contact them almost 24/7.[54] The system breaks down now and then, and our adversaries don't play nice. But it's pretty reliable.

Not so in 1944. The rudimentary pieces were there for Maurice Rose. But he dealt with a lot of holes in the picture. The 3rd Armored Division owned big truck-mounted radio, even teletype devices, with ranges up to a hundred miles. Those bulky animals worked swell when fixed in place with thirsty generators humming and tall antennas carefully arranged. That capability permitted good connections with VII Corps.[55] But inside the division? In place, you could run telephone wires, as in World War I. To deliver critical, detailed reports or certain specific orders, messengers used racing peeps or speedy motorcycles. On the move, though, commanders relied on short-range radio transmitters and receivers in rolling vehicles and on the sweaty backs of soldiers.

Radio reports told you only so much. With the division spread across thirty miles of French countryside and the usual frontline radio range seven miles at best, reports filtered back by relay, one station repeating what they heard from the other guys, passing it along. The G.I. signalers tried hard to be accurate, and commanders did the same, but in a clattering tank or under fire from a German 88mm cannon, messages passed through fragmentary, garbled, or not at all.[56] It was like playing the old party game of telephone, and by the time division got the word, it might not be quite right.

This was one reason Maurice Rose went to the scene of the action. He had to witness key firefights at crucial locations, and, when necessary, intervene to make things happen. The tested formula applied: a commander must see and be seen. The great ones—Erwin Rommel and George Patton, to name two—understood this to their bones. As Civil War Major General William Tecumseh Sherman said in a time of telegraphs: "Some men think that modern armies may be so regulated that a general can sit in his office and play on his several columns as on the keys of a piano; this is a fearful mistake. The directing mind must be at the very head of the army—must be seen there, and the effect of his mind and personal energy must be felt by every officer and man present with it, to secure the best results."[57]

Brigadier General Rose spent August 13, 1944, as Sherman recommended. He and his trusty peep puttered here and there, working to get a feel for the battle. Rose stopped to talk to G.I.s of all ranks. If they were busy—and especially if engaged in combat—Rose soaked it in and didn't meddle. On the road to Pré-en-Pail and the other route to Couptrain, Rose saw, heard, and smelled things: wrecked tanks and wounded men, chattering American .50 caliber machine guns and rasping German MG42s alternating in smoldering hedgerows, French houses burning, and the pervasive sharp tang of cordite and gasoline.

On the chipped pavement behind CCB's TF Lovelady near Couptrain, Rose saw something else: a few dozen prisoners, an indicator that maybe not all the Nazi supermen were feeling all that super. As one tank battalion officer remembered: "Apparently realizing they were fighting a lost cause, they would fire a few rounds or empty their clips, then give up as the great cordon of steel closed in upon them."[58]

It was the same thing as Captain Waits's skirmish at Omaha Forward. Plenty of Germans seemed full of fight at Couptrain, at Joué-du-Bois, and north of Rânes. Evidently the division had sussed out the perimeter of the German defenses straining to defend the Falaise Pocket. But how much oomph did these Germans have left?

The official view at both Collins's VII Corps and Hodges's First Army referred to "light resistance" on August 13. Rose wasn't so sure. His drive-around and past combat experience told him that the Germans were present in force. They might well be low on gas, short on ammunition, and stuck in a very bad situation. Some Germans appeared to be giving up. But not all. Somebody kept fighting back. Where were the SS men? What about the panzers? Rose figured they'd show up in the morning.[59]

They did.

––––

The heavy hitters appeared early on the morning of August 14, preempting CCA's TF Doan's attempt to renew the attack to the north. In the heat of action, some G.I. tank crews, probably rookies, claimed to see 63-ton German Tigers and 49-ton Panthers coming out of the mist, their long cannons spitting instant death. No Tigers stalked that dawn. But Panthers came, a dozen or so from the northwest, and another ten or more from the northeast, each panzer thrust trailed by a score of half-seen figures in camouflage smocks. German mortar and howitzer shells burst atop TF Doan's vehicles squatting behind hedgerow berms. The G-2 intelligence wizards later pegged these attackers as hailing from the 1st SS Panzer Division—they'd been at Mortain—and the 9th SS Panzer Division "Hohenstaufen" (named for a medieval German royal dynasty), although most records of the Falaise Pocket indicate the 9th SS operated on the British-Canadian front.[60] Could be—but this morning, whoever they were, they intended to force TF Doan out of Rânes. The G.I.s in TF Doan thought otherwise. That deadly brawl went on all day. If the Germans hoped to stop the 3rd Armored Division at Rânes, it worked.

The fight at Couptrain wrapped up in the morning, freeing CCB to press north to Joué-du-Bois. There, TF Richardson had its hands full dealing with more dug-in German infantry, more 88mm antitank emplacements, and a handful of well-hidden panzer assault guns, too. The 3rd Armored Division commander wanted to get CCB to Rânes to clean up that knot; instead it bogged down in another ugly fracas at nearby La Motte-Fouquet. The Germans at Joué-du-Bois certainly wanted to keep that bloody contest going. The stalemate forced Rose to use the armored infantry and tanks from the Division Reserve, then raise the stakes by sending in the newly attached 60th Infantry Regiment. With nobody but himself to take charge of the Division Reserve and the 60th, Rose spent his daylight hours endeavoring to sort out that furball. By day's end, at least TF Richardson wriggled its way out and made its way to Rânes to link up with TF Doan and consolidate CCA. From west to east, the division had CCB stuck at La Motte-Fouquet, the Division Reserve and 60th Infantry Regiment fully engaged on Joué-du-Bois, and CCA pinned in Rânes, right where the Germans wanted them. The lost day cost the division nine more soldiers killed, and convinced Rose he had to shake things up. [61]

On August 15, Rose jumped Omaha Forward to Rânes to direct ongoing operations and jump-start a stronger attack to the north. While the 3rd Armored Division marked time around Rânes, bedraggled Germans flowed east out of the unsealed Falaise Pocket. At the higher echelon, most attention focused on Patton's Third Army restrained (and mightily frustrated) at Argentan and the Canadians, including the 1st Polish Armored Division, trying to slog their way to Falaise and points south. Rose's men, however, also had to keep turning their own set of screws. That meant an organized drive north, headed through Fromental to Putanges. [62]

Combat around Rânes on August 15 took a toll, twenty-one killed and more than a hundred wounded, the worst day since Rose took command. Still, in the ferocious scrum in the bocage near Rânes, the G.I.s knocked out sixteen panzers. The Americans captured more than 1,800 soldiers, dejected, shuffling men, tired, hungry, and out of it.[63] Five miles to Fromental, and five more to Putanges and the British and all the Germans in front of Rose's division would be either prisoners or dead. One good hard punch—it could work.

In staging for the renewed advance, along with replacement junior soldiers for the tank and infantry outfits, a new commander arrived for CCR and the 36th Armored Infantry Regiment. Colonel Louis P. Leone took over on August 15, which freed General Rose from personally dealing with CCR/Division Reserve matters.[64] The division commander could spend the next day out and about, ensuring the major drive on Fromental came off OK.

Once the German counterattack spent itself, the task forces prepared to go back on the offensive. Refueling, rearming, and repairing kept G.I.s busy well into the night. In and around Rânes, Rose observed a number of abandoned Panthers—good—and too many derelict Shermans with no mechanics working on them—not good at all. Overall, the American tanks proved easy to maintain and fix, with nine of ten usually rolling. The bigger, better-armed and better-armored German Panthers spent a third of the time broken down. Even a damaged Sherman could often be fixed, or as a minimum stripped for useful parts. The hardworking mechanics of the division's 3rd Ordnance Battalion rarely seemed to sleep, eat, or do anything but turn wrenches. Where were they at Rânes? The division's move had left the maintenance teams behind. The ordnance battalion commander had to get that fixed, along with the broken-down Shermans.[65]

Both CCA and CCB attacked at 6:20 a.m. on August 16. Rose picked the time on purpose. In an era of wind-up wristwatches, missions tended to start on the hour or the half hour. Rose shuffled the deck a bit. It paid off.

The combat commands caught the tired Germans dozing after sunup. The two combat commands moved abreast, with strong air cover overhead. Fighting in a single broad column, rotating lead outfits at each road junction, Hickey's CCA took the main road to Fromental. Boudinot's CCB used the farm trails to the west. The Germans scrapped for each hedgerow and village.

At 3:00 p.m., a clutch of German panzers engaged lead elements of CCA. Cool under pressure, Doyle Hickey backed off his lead Shermans a thousand yards and called in P-47 Thunderbolt fighter-bombers, alternating air strikes with artillery bursts. After ninety minutes of back and forth, the surviving Germans scuttled away. By 10:00 p.m., CCA tanks halted on the eastern outskirts of Fromental.[66]

To the west, Truman Boudinot's CCB kept pace. TF Lovelady took the lead and "started fighting almost at once." German panzers hit two M4 Shermans, killed four Americans, and wounded a dozen more. TF Lovelady went right back at the Germans, taking out seven Mark IV Panzers (a fair match for a Sherman) and two assault guns. The G.I.s took "a large number of prisoners." At 11:30 p.m. CCB, too, stopped to refuel, rearm, and repair a mile and a quarter southwest of Fromental.[67]

Rose spent most of his day out in the peep, as usual. He spent time with both armored columns, and what he saw seemed to be working. It helped that most of the fighting occurred well within the radio range of the SCR sets on the tanks, trucks, and soldiers. Coordinating maneuver and fires went pretty well. The day, however, cost fifteen more American dead and another hundred wounded.[68] The Germans sure hadn't given up yet.

In the afternoon, Rose was summoned back to his division command post at Rânes. Lieutenant General Hodges of First Army arrived by three-quarter-ton Dodge WC57 command car, a sort of souped-up, more roomy version of a jeep. A contingent of security soldiers and staff officers completed the company-strength caravan.

Hodges offered nothing useful—he rarely did. But to his credit he came forward to see for himself. His staff escorts did, too. Some stared at buildings "still burning." Others soberly regarded roads leading in and out of town "lined with burnt-out and destroyed tanks and vehicles, some of which were ours."[69] What effect it had on Hodges was difficult to tell. The First Army general didn't say.

Rose, though, knew exactly what the achievements of August 16 foretold. According to the Germans' established rhythm of fighting, they'd counterattack hard in the morning. Rose assessed that the Germans had at least one more outburst in them. The word went out. Get ready.

August 17 turned out to be the toughest day of the offensive. The 35 Americans killed set a new and unwelcome high mark. CCA fought east of Fromental, CCB engaged west of Fromental, and CCR waited back near Rânes, ready to reinforce either. Rose, his commanders, and his hard-fighting troopers had their hands full.

The general removed one worry from the division's overfull plate. On Rose's order, Colonel Leone sent Lieutenant Colonel Samuel Hogan's tank-infantry task force five miles east of Fromental to join the 83rd Recon in securing a critical intersection near Ecouche. The First Army/Third Army boundary ran just to the east, and on the far side were the bumptious battalions of the 2nd Free French Armored Division. Burning to kill Germans and then liberate Paris, the French tankers "seemed to have no idea of march discipline or coordination." They shot their artillery across boundaries, a big no-no in the American military due to the danger of friendly-fire casualties. The French also "borrowed" roads as they saw fit, lines on the map be damned. Zealous West Pointer (Class of 1938) Sam Hogan proudly flew a Texas state flag from his command tank, and he turned out to be the right man to parley with the equally fervent French.[70] That problem went away.

For CCA, the battle in Fromental proved bitter. TF Doan's 1st

Battalion, 32nd Armored's experience offers a telling summary of the entire difficult episode. Having already lost the battalion commander at Rânes, four more officers succeeded for brief stretches. Captain Nicholas D. Carpenter commanded for an hour before the Germans captured and killed him; the pitiless SS did that all too often. Captain Foster F. Flegeal led the battalion for almost a day until badly hurt by fragments from an errant 500-pound bomb delivered by a U.S. P-38 Lightning. Major Frank S. Crawford commanded from his tank for three hours; a German panzer nailed Crawford's tank and wounded the major. Lieutenant Colonel Leander Doan sent up his own 32nd Armored Regiment executive officer, Lieutenant Colonel John K. Boles, Jr., to run the outfit. Boles saw things through until the Germans finally gave up. The battalion suffered nine killed and more than two dozen wounded. They hung on to eastern Fromental—and finished off a lot of Germans.[71]

In CCB's TF Lovelady close action was the theme of the day. The G.I.s. overran an extensive German ammunition dump spread out across several acres of hedgerow cells. It looked like the Germans had helped themselves just before the American arrived; the enemy shot back hard and fast all day. Shermans met panzers head-on at point-blank range, as little as 25 yards in some bocage lanes. Lucky for the Americans, these weren't thick-armored Panthers. TF Lovelady took out three Mark III Panzers, an assault gun, and a towed antitank cannon, as well as tens of hostile troops. Not long after the last German panzer creaked to a stop, sixty-odd Germans raised their hands and surrendered. In return, the Germans killed two Americans, wounded more, and smashed five American tanks. Hour after hour, American aircraft went hard after the enemy. TF Lovelady's unit log summarized the tough day: "Weather clear and sunny, morale good, men tired."[72]

As he bumped from firefight to firefight in his peep, Rose heard that the U.S. 1st Infantry Division to the west had linked up with the

British. His army air forces controllers reported "good hunting" to the north. The 3rd Armored Division artillery forward observers on high ground near Fromental looking north estimated that some 1,200 German vehicles could be seen. Some were moving; others not. The air and artillery pounded away.[73] The radio (and his senses) told Maurice Rose that it was almost over.

The next morning, TF Lovelady moved out early for Putanges, banging into some panzers. The Germans were nearly out of fuel and ammunition but gave it a try. Shermans accounted for six Panzer IVs, two assault guns, and a few hapless German infantrymen. The rest gave up. At 12:37 p.m., Sergeant Don Ekdahl, a tank commander in TF Lovelady, radioed: "Made contact with British armor on road to Putanges." Getting to the British 11th Armoured Division cost five American lives.[74] A G.I./Tommy handshake completed the 3rd Armored Division's mission in the Falaise Pocket.

The five-and-a-half-day fifty-mile drive resulted in ninety-two dead Americans and more than three hundred wounded. The division lost more than a hundred tanks and other vehicles.[75] Rose's men fought all the way. There had been mistakes, some made by Rose himself, most notably getting too entangled in handling the Division Reserve on August 14. Joe Collins at VII Corps bailed things out by attaching the 60th Infantry Regiment. New Colonel Leone and CCR deserved some attention. So did the commanders of the 83rd Recon and the 3rd Ordnance Battalion.

Much, though, had gone right. Doyle Hickey of CCA remained utterly reliable, and Rose's former Command and General Staff School classmate Truman Boudinot of CCB matched him. Several task force commanders—Doan, Richardson, Lovelady, and Hogan—displayed initiative and tactical skill. Long John Smith and Omaha Forward kept track of the battle and allowed Maurice Rose to get around. Notably, a big dog didn't bark. Avid gadabout Major General Joe Collins hadn't interfered at all.[76] That boded very well for whatever came next.

Well above the heads of Brigadier General Rose and his weary G.I.s, all was not well. Eisenhower blamed Montgomery for not pressing the Canadians harder to close the gap at Falaise. Montgomery pointed the finger at Canadian Lieutenant General Henry D. G. "Harry" Crerar. Bradley complained of Montgomery's unwillingness to change the agreed Canadian/American army boundary. Patton thought Bradley too cautious; indeed, on August 13, 1944, the old cavalryman wanted to ignore the map line and "drive the British back into the sea for another Dunkirk." Bradley, of course, indulged his innate caution and halted Patton. "I much preferred a firm shoulder at Argentan to a broken neck at Falaise."[77] Bradley got his wish.

So the Falaise/Argentan hole stayed open for a week. Instead of bagging both the German Seventh and Fifth Panzer armies, the Allies let about 40,000 of 100,000 enemy troops escape. Among the Germans who broke free were the remnants of six panzer divisions totaling 62 tanks, 26 artillery pieces, and around 2,000 men. Not much. Yet every one of those six—1st SS Panzer, 2nd Panzer, 2nd SS Panzer, 9th SS Panzer, 116th Panzer, and Panzer Lehr—brought out enough veteran cadre to reform and fight again. Together, the British, Canadians, Poles, Free French, and Americans captured about 50,000 Germans. Another 10,000 enemy troops never left the Falaise Pocket. Patton's Third Army performed a hasty survey of the material destruction and counted 220 tanks, 160 assault guns, 700 towed artillery pieces, 130 half-tracks, and 5,000 trucks, not to mention 2,000 wagons and their unfortunate teams of horses.[78] It wasn't complete destruction, but pretty close.

The sights and smells of the devastation appalled even the toughest soldiers. General Dwight D. Eisenhower recorded what he encountered after the shooting stopped:

The battlefield at Falaise was unquestionably one of the greatest "killing fields" of any of the war areas. Forty-eight hours after the closing of the gap I was conducted through it on foot, to encounter scenes that could be described only by Dante. It was literally possible to walk for hundreds of yards at a time, stepping on nothing but dead and decaying flesh.[79]

Thus ended the great battle for Normandy.

CHAPTER 3

War on the Michelin Map

L'audace, l'audace, toujours l'audace!

General George S. Patton, Jr.[1]

"On to Paris!"

So the French soldiers of the 2nd Free French Armored Division encouraged Lieutenant Colonel Sam Hogan, he of the Lone Star ensign—what he called the flag of "free Americans."[2] Well, the French tankers were all for freedom. Indeed, they very much desired to bring a big dose of it to those in their capital city. Who could blame them? Hogan and most of the 3rd Armored Division G.I.s assumed they'd be joining the liberation march of the Free French troops. According to the script, first you kill the Germans. Then you free the oppressed. Then . . . wine, women, and song. The nineteen- and twenty-year-olds who made up the vast majority of the 3rd Armored Division agreed with their French neighbors. On to Paris!

The American-equipped 2nd Free French Armored Division belonged to George Patton's Third Army during the pincers attack to close the Falaise Pocket. The French led the push north from Argentan to link up with the Canadians. As soon as the clashes in and around Argentan died out, French Major General Philippe François

Marie Leclerc made his intentions clear. His armored columns began refueling for the run to Paris. Patton, anxious to chase the retreating Germans, gladly washed his hands of the freewheeling Leclerc, who considered orders as suggestions, especially when such directives contradicted the guidance of self-appointed Free French leader Brigadier General Charles de Gaulle. (The haughty de Gaulle managed the trifecta of exasperation; British Prime Minister Winston L. S. Churchill, American President Franklin D. Roosevelt, and Soviet General Secretary Iosif V. Stalin all hated him.) Stuck by alliance politics with employing the heady Leclerc and his incorrigible French tankers, Bradley passed them to First Army's Courtney Hodges, who never complained to higher-ups about much of anything. Ignoring Hodges, the French immediately made for Paris, about 122 miles due east.

The lure of Paris, the shiniest of shiny objects, surely transfixed Leclerc's Free French Sherman crews and Maurice Rose's citizen-soldiers, too. The famous City of Light's metropolitan area teemed with five and a half million souls. When freed, these mouths would consume 4,000 tons of Allied supplies daily.[3] The logistics accountants didn't want to go there. Yet the innate decency of the Americans left no doubt: to bypass Paris would be both inhumane and inhuman. It wasn't going to happen.

In the cold light of military logic, Paris served as a distraction from the real Allied priority: pursuing and destroying the fleeing German army. Field Marshal Günther von Kluge of OB West committed suicide after the horrendous Falaise defeat, probably cheating the Gestapo. Hard case Field Marshal O. M. Walter Model took over. A keen Nazi reputed as the fireman of the Russian front, ever ready to solve a crisis, Model sure had one on his hands in France. With any hope of holding the Seine River long gone, the new OB West commander aspired to reform some kind of German defensive line at the border of the Reich. With that in mind, Model recognized the military value of Paris, at least in German eyes. The urban center of

France did what the German Mortain counterattack could not. Dealing with Paris might delay the Allies just enough, about a week in all, to let the remaining German battle groups break away and stream east, mile by mile, hour by hour, on threadbare tires, rusting panzer treads, creaking wagon wheels, loose horseshoes, and worn-out hobnail boots. The heartless Berlin inner circle certainly didn't care about Paris or its citizens. Indeed, on August 19, 1944, with the Falaise Pocket disaster compounded by a Paris-wide French Resistance uprising, Führer Adolf Hitler told his garrison commander to destroy the city. Each day that followed, Hitler badgered his general for confirmation that the French capital had been set aflame. The Nazi leader's daily query became the title of a famous 1965 book and then a 1966 movie, *Is Paris Burning?*[4]

It wasn't.

While the failure of the local German general to torch Paris and slaughter thousands brought on the usual Hitler tantrum, in truth, the surrender of Paris on August 25 gifted the Allies with exactly what they did not want. Rather than chase the withdrawing Germans, Hodges's First Army had to divert the 4th Infantry Division to back up Leclerc's 2nd Free French Armored Division. The U.S. Army's 28th Infantry Division got sucked in, too. Those G.I.s found themselves marching past the Arc de Triomphe in a street parade on August 29 while Eisenhower, Bradley, and Hodges looked on. De Gaulle beamed. The Americans fumed.[5]

General Bernard Law Montgomery did not join the reviewing party in Paris. He still commanded the ground campaign, and his master schematic showed the Allies in Paris by D+90, so in that sense all was well. "The present operations are absolutely as planned," he recorded happily.[6] With Monty, as long as he ran the show, and everyone did exactly as he said, events always unfolded in accord with his grand design. Even when that didn't happen, Monty tended to claim that it had.

Punctilious, peppy, demanding, hectoring, quick to take offense and slow to praise, a human terrier brimming with "I told you so," Monty proved eminently easy to dislike. Even affable Ike Eisenhower found Montgomery a hard pill to swallow. The normally tolerant Bradley detested him. Hodges . . . well, he was Hodges, which meant he never really said. Patton did, of course, dismissing Montgomery as a "tired little fart."[7]

Little he was. Tired he was not. His personal energy level seemed to have a single setting—intense. In truth, he was a thorough military professional, schooled (and shot through the lung) in the most unforgiving of classrooms, the trenches of the Great War. Montgomery beat the German Afrika Korps at El Alamein in 1942 and never let anyone forget it. By 1944, his country's limited manpower hobbled his options and forced him to rely on the same Americans who found him insufferable. Unlike Omar Bradley, Bernard Law Montgomery could indeed read a map and relate it to the ground. And he absolutely understood the German enemy. He warned one and all that the goal now was not holding ceremonies in Paris, a glittering but empty prestige objective that could only "detract from our main business," to wit: pursuing the Germans.[8]

Montgomery offered his prescription. "Great vistas are opening up ahead, and we want generals now who will put their heads down and go like hell."[9] Monty himself wasn't that kind of senior officer. But he recognized those who were: George Patton, Lightning Joe Collins, and Maurice Rose. Their time had come.

———

Not Paris but the backside of the running Germans—that was the target of Brigadier General Maurice Rose and the 3rd Armored Division. Even as the Free French and other American divisions broke for Paris, Rose issued orders to drive to the Seine River. Rose's division had the same hundred-plus miles to cross, and more, whatever it took to catch up with the Germans and finish them off, the classic cavalry mission of pursuit. In the words of the U.S. Army's *Field*

Manual 100-5 Operations: "Pursuit of a defeated enemy is pushed to the utmost limit of endurance of troops, animals, and vehicles."[10] That was what armored divisions were for.

As Lieutenant General George Patton stated, "if 'the greatest study of mankind is man,' surely the greatest study of war is the road net."[11] France owned a good one. Maurice Rose intended to use it.

To get going, the 3rd Armored Division needed to check out those French roads. The same U.S. Army bureaucracy that found itself unpleasantly surprised to find G.I.s dealing with the medieval-era Norman bocage also somehow forgot to push out sufficient quantities of map sheets showing the French route structure. Maybe the officers running the map warehouses in England thought the Normandy stalemate would persist forever. The breakout caught the map-issuers flat-footed. As the 3rd Armored Division began its pursuit across France, Captain A. Eaton Roberts of TF Lovelady observed: "One of our greatest bugbears was procuring maps. Before the proper ones could reach us, we were already half across another [map]." The troops made do, bumming "ordinary road maps of the give-away type" from French villagers and filling stations. From Maurice Rose to individual tank sergeants, the American soldiers learned, like millions of tourists before and since, to rely on *La Carte Michelin au 1/100,000.*[12]

The other solution was as old as war—sending out scouts to check the routes. That meant the 83rd Armored Reconnaissance Battalion. The troopers were brave and skilled, but the commander's work to date raised questions. The battalion didn't find the enemy all that well in the Falaise Pocket operation. The individual companies did fine work when attached to the combat commands. Rose could have let Brigadier General Doyle Hickey of CCA and Colonel Truman Boudinot of CCB reconnoiter for themselves. But Rose saw this as a divisional responsibility, which is to say his own responsibility. So Rose gave the mission to the recon battalion. He expected the outfit to produce. At 6:00 p.m. on August 21, 1944, twelve hours ahead of the lead tanks of the combat commands, the recon soldiers moved out for the proposed division assembly area located seventy-nine miles to the east between Dreux and Chartres. Reports filtered back—routes good to go, no contact.[13]

At 6:00 a.m. the next morning, CCA moved out, followed by CCB at 10:00 a.m. and CCR at 2:57 p.m. Omaha Forward trailed CCA. Rose and his trusty peep went with the lead task force of CCA. Major Haynes W. Dugan of Division G-2 captured the prevailing sentiment: "We were out of the hedgerow country and into fertile open country, among wheat fields with the sun shining." Captain Roberts in CCB noted that "our vehicles could not halt without being pounced upon by well-meaning friends, young and old, who, after four long years greeted their first liberators with tears, hugs, and warm kisses," as well as fresh eggs, fruit, and wine by the case. Roberts and the G.I.s of TF Lovelady asked directions of the townspeople. Local French Resistance leaders also supplied intelligence tidbits about the fleeing Germans.[14] The opposition was long gone.

It took well into the next day (August 23) to bring all of the division into the area between Dreux and Chartres. The roadways south of Paris were a mess, full of other U.S. Army traffic. With the division's single military police platoon utterly overwhelmed, Rose and the other senior leaders stayed busy directing traffic. In addition, Rose put out an order: no more wine and cognac. The celebrations were slowing the march column, and drinking and driving is definitely not a good idea in an M4 Sherman tank. The junior officers and sergeants tried to enforce the unpopular stricture, but found the best way to do so was to keep moving.[15] That accomplished Maurice Rose's intent rather nicely.

After refueling, fixing up the vehicles, and a few hours of rest—it helped to be young—the 3rd Armored Division soldiers resumed their march at 1:00 a.m. on August 25, heading for the Seine River near Melun, twelve miles southeast of Paris. Combat Command B led the order of march, followed by CCA, then CCR. The 83rd Recon scouts had left hours earlier and found an existing Third Army bridge. Traveling as usual with the lead task force, Rose alerted Lieutenant Colonel Lawrence G. Foster's 23rd Armored Engineer Battalion to prepare to lay down a second bridge to accelerate the division's passage. It took all night, but by dawn on August 26, a 23rd Engineer treadway bridge of 540 feet paralleled the existing structure.[16]

The crossing of the Seine was actually somewhat undramatic, more an exercise in traffic control than an opposed combat operation. (Later river-crossings would prove more eventful.) Even so, Rose knew well that at rivers, you never stop on the near side. Get across immediately with whatever you can—walking infantry, peeps, two-and-a-half-ton trucks—then build force. By all means, push tanks to the far side. CCB's Task Force Lovelady went over by 4:00 p.m. on August 25, with TF Roysdon right behind at 6:15 p.m. French Resistance informants told the Americans that German rear guards waited in ambush not far ahead.[17] By pressing the march—147 miles in three days—Rose's men had nearly caught up to their quarry.

Rose's regular movements alongside the lead task forces conveyed his sense of urgency. The division commander wasn't a rah-rah type. Standing by the side of the road as tanks and trucks rolled past, Rose's tall, rigid stature inspired respect, maybe a little fear, but no real affection. As one young officer said, nobody in the 3rd Armored Division would think of waving and hollering, "Hi, Maurice!" Rose listened more than he spoke, but when the general did say something, he could be pointed in his comments, especially when talking to an officer or NCO. Rose kept his messages direct, leaving no doubts. Throughout the flower-tossing and kisses and the long, long drive, Rose offered his soldiers, especially sergeants and captains, one message: stay ready. The Germans are just ahead of us.[18]

That thought might have been in the back of the minds of the exhausted G.I.s of CCB. Although dead-tired after the lengthy motor march and the stop-and-start crossing of the Seine, Captain John A. Haldeman's troopers reached their assigned assembly area at 2:30 a.m. Less disciplined men would have cashed it in and racked out. Not Haldeman's soldiers. They deployed their vehicles for defense, just in case. Like old-time cavalry troopers caring for horses before selves, the CCB soldiers then gassed up and checked ammunition—plenty there, as there'd been no contact yet—and posted sentinels. Only then did most of them drift off to fitful sleep.

The Germans redefined "rude awakening." At first light, enemy panzer fire began tearing through the position. Stricken American vehicles rocked back. One caught on fire. Three G.I.s fell, with one dead. Casualties eventually mounted to four killed and twenty wounded, serious losses indeed for a single company, no matter how well led. The enemy kept shooting but did not close. Haldeman's soldiers fought back, using their machine guns to discourage hostile infantry. Timely use of American artillery and the arrival of five M4 Sherman tanks ran off the German interlopers, later thought to be part of the 9th Panzer Division. Whoever they were, the engagement took all morning, and the action delayed the jump-off of CCB until 2:00 p.m.[19]

At the same time, CCA also attacked, bringing both combat commands on line, with CCA to the north and CCB to the south. The advance aimed to reach the Marne River and grab bridges there, maybe catching ahold of some Germans, too. Task Force Lovelady knocked out an offending quartet of Mark IV Panzers and four German trucks, too, plus some German infantry. Nobody stopped to count the dead enemy foot troops scattered here and there. The 3rd Armored Division reported the contacts as "sporadic," and Division G-2 analysts assessed these as the rear guard elements mentioned earlier by the French Resistance.[20]

Rose, of course, moved back and forth, sticking with the lead task forces. Behind CCA and CCB, CCR began rolling across the Seine River, using the new 23rd Engineers' bridge as well as the original one. It took until 7:00 p.m. on August 26 to complete CCR's crossing.[21]

With Rose well ahead and involved in the fighting, it fell to more junior division officers to monitor the steady movements across the Seine River bridges. Major Haynes W. Dugan of Division G-2 sat near a parked M-3 half-track. Using the vehicle's onboard radio, Dugan and his team called in each unit as it came up from the river. The major whittled a stick to pass the time.

About midmorning, Dugan saw a single three-quarter-ton WC57 command car. It must be someone big. It was.

Tricked out with a red rectangular plate with three white stars and bearing a tall, impressive, stern-faced passenger sporting two ivory-handled pistols, Dugan knew it could only be one man. The command car drew up even with Dugan, who'd scrambled to his feet, tossed away his whittling stick, and rendered a proper salute. Lieutenant General George S. Patton, Jr., returned it.

"Everything under control, major?"

Dugan replied in the affirmative.

"Give Maurice Rose my regards."

And off he went. Third Army's operations had spread out to the south. That's where Patton headed.

Dugan sent word to Omaha Forward, which duly informed Brigadier Maurice Rose.[22] It's not been reported what Rose thought about his former commander's greeting. Probably nothing much. Maurice Rose had a war to fight. Those German stay-behind elements suggested bigger game ahead. To the Marne—that's where Rose expected to catch them.

———

The 83rd Armored Reconnaissance Battalion did not find the Germans who surprised Combat Command B at dawn on August 26. Indeed, in that day's 2:00 p.m. attack, Rose reverted to the Leroy Watson practice and assigned the 83rd Recon's Company A to CCA and

Company D to CCB. It was time to make a change. Without rancor—but without pity, either—on August 27, Rose placed Major John R. Tucker, Jr., in acting command.[23] Maybe he'd do better than his predecessor.

Boudinot's Combat Command B launched at 7:00 a.m., bound for Meaux on the Marne River. To their south, Hickey's Combat Command A continued the attack at 8:05 a.m., also going toward the Marne. Combat Command Reserve under Colonel Louis P. Leone followed in zone, ready to go north or south as necessary. Maurice Rose told both Boudinot and Hickey to press hard, seeking the main body of Germans that had to be out there. The Division G-2 people estimated that the combat commands would bump into both the 9th Panzer Division and the 48th Infantry Division.[24]

Task Force Lovelady, as often happened, found the Germans first. As one of Lieutenant Colonel Bill Lovelady's subordinates recalled, "By starting our daily drives a little earlier, stopping a little later, and going a little faster, we were apparently straining the enemy's ability to coordinate his units and maintain his own lines of communication." Lovelady's tankers and half-track infantry stunned the German crews of two assault guns and two armored cars, capturing the lot intact. American Sherman crews also knocked out several German trucks and dispersed their infantry. The task force reached the Marne River not far from Meaux by 3:00 p.m. The Americans snagged a bridge, too.[25]

The bridge could bear individual soldiers as well as peeps and half-tracks, but maybe not 33-ton Sherman tanks. It needed wooden planking to be sure. The local people saw the problem and enthusiastically volunteered to help. Industrious French villagers fetched lumber, and tools . . . They began reinforcing the bridge. Even when a German Luftwaffe Messerschmitt Bf-109 fighter plane showed up and made a low pass—very unusual at this point of the war—the French volunteers barely glanced up.[26] The local civilians finished the job. The American tanks rolled.

The one-sided nature of the day's fighting, buttressed by encouraging news from the French Resistance, convinced Lovelady to press his task force into Meaux. That was not without risk, as Meaux was a substantial urban area with some 40,000 residents. A street fight would overtax TF Lovelady's single company of less than 200 infantrymen. But the French told Lovelady and his men that the Germans had left. The TF Lovelady log summarized things pretty neatly: "Arrived outside Meaux at 1700 [5:00 p.m.], decided to take town, moved in and secured it at 2000 [8:00 p.m.]." Combat Command A also made it across the Marne just to the south.[27] Rose could be well satisfied with the day's work. There'd be more tomorrow.

Maurice Rose had been in command only twenty days. Most of his soldiers probably could not recognize his voice. But many, especially Sherman crews and rifle squads, could pick out his tall figure. They all felt his impact, even when his peep wasn't purring through their formation, or he wasn't on foot in a village during a firefight. He'd seen them. They'd seen him. And he wasn't back in a tent sticking pins in a map.

That granted, young soldiers rarely think about generals. Sergeants, lieutenants, and captains dominated the lives of tankers, riflemen, artillerymen, engineers, and all the rest of the youths who made up the 3rd Armored Division. But generals like Rose? They come and go, even if this guy hung around up front more than most. When the troops did not see Maurice Rose—and most of the time, they did not, as even he couldn't be everywhere at once—the rankers forgot about him. If they considered Rose at all, they figured he must be somewhere pleasant, somewhere safe, wining and dining in high style.

Usually, they would be wrong. But on the evening of August 27, 1944, they were right. Omaha Forward set up shop in the pleasant apple orchard on the grounds of the Château de Ferrières, one of three dozen French estates affiliated with the famous House of Rothschild. The 1859 edifice looked more imposing than it was. German troops, looters, and squatters had worked the place over. Even so, it took your breath away to be in and around such a mansion. Junior staff officers and NCOs gawked. Yet they guessed rightly they'd be on their way in the morning, leaving behind tread marks and tire ruts.[28] Given Rose's background—utterly unknown to his fellow 3rd Armored Division soldiers—you have to wonder what the son of a rabbi thought about spending the night in the home of one of the most prominent Jewish families in history. Considering how hard Rose had pushed himself, a few hours of unbroken sleep probably seemed more precious than any Rothschild luxuries.

Maurice Rose didn't hang around to enjoy such things. Like his forward task forces, he headed out early, bound for the Aisne River and the old Great War landmark of Soissons, well known to a former doughboy like Rose. The Germans seemed to be just out of reach, but even that skilled foe couldn't outrun Rose's tanks forever. Maybe the Aisne—that had to be it.

Under Major Tucker, the 83rd Recon led the division forward, keying on finding ways across the Aisne River as well as any Germans defending that line. Spurred by Rose's strong direction, the scouts sought to get to the far side.[29] Good cavalry units fight for intelligence. The 83rd troopers understood that axiom. Now their battalion leadership was figuring it out, too.

The Aisne River would be a tough nut. It looped through the north part of Soissons. To get over the waterway, the 3rd Armored Division angled north. The division attacked with CCB to the west focused on Soissons proper and CCA pushing to take bridges at Pont-Arcy, about eight miles to the east.[30] One or the other—maybe both—should pay off. Perhaps this time the 83rd Recon would find a clean route and get the word back. Nobody counted on that. Both Doyle Hickey and Truman Boudinot assumed they'd have to sort out the river crossings on their own.

Task Force Lovelady led CCB and made contact on the approaches to Soissons. "Hunting was excellent," as noted in the task force log. In a series of firefights, American tanks, infantry, and artillery wrecked nine panzers (three Panthers, four Mark IVs, and a pair of assault guns), eight half-tracks, three armored cars, seven towed antitank cannons, and an "uncounted" number of trucks and dismounted German troops. The Americans suffered two riflemen killed and eleven tankers and infantry wounded. Two U.S. M5 Stuart light tanks were badly damaged but recoverable. TF Lovelady made it to Soissons by 8:00 p.m., but the main highway bridge had been blown. The TF Lovelady night position chosen outside the city began to attract German time-fused artillery fire—air bursts, not good. Occasional small-arms and flat-trajectory shots also zipped through the defensive coil of vehicles. It made for a very restless evening. TF Lovelady owned Soissons, but hadn't found a crossing yet.[31] The morrow promised to be eventful.

The larger contingent of CCB, regimental-strength Task Force Roysdon, also advanced into the eastern side of Soissons before halting on the edge of the Seine River. Lead tank crews reported a railroad bridge stretching across the Aisne River. Random German artillery shells exploded on the near side of the structure. Hostile machine guns ripped now and then. To take this thing would require a fight. And who knew if the bridge was rigged to blow up? Or if its supports had been damaged by the German shellfire?

The decision fell to the task force commander, Colonel Dorrence S. Roysdon, one of the originals who helped establish the 3rd Armored Division back at Camp Polk, Louisiana, in 1941–1942, which by this point counted for absolutely zilch. Roysdon was the "other guy" in Colonel Truman Boudinot's Combat Command B. Roysdon's junior counterpart, Lieutenant Colonel Bill Lovelady, consistently found and fought the Germans first. A "ramblin' wreck from Georgia Tech," the short, pugnacious Lovelady seemed like a compressed heavy-duty steel spring, ever ready to pop open and do damage. He got results. As for Roysdon, he and his bunch often seemed to be one terrain feature behind, doing their part, but not quite in on the kill. Something was off.

Roysdon did not lack for personal courage—far from it. In the July 1944 bocage fighting before Operation Cobra, Roysdon carried a Thompson submachine gun as he led an infantry attack on foot. That heroic episode levied a high price. Roysdon's young driver died in the firefight. Men saw the colonel break down in tears. As one lieutenant said, "This display of emotion was considered not as a sign of weakness but as a sign of courageous humanity."[32] Such scenes remind us that death in war affects colonels as well as privates. It clearly stuck with Roysdon. Thereafter, the colonel took pains—perhaps excessively so—in committing his troops in the face of German fire. While an understandable reaction to such a heart-wrenching experience, regimental task force commanders in combat can't afford sentiment. In a life-and-death encounter with a determined enemy, pausing even a minute or two can spell the difference between winning and losing.

Roysdon had always talked a lot. He'd long given his junior leaders a standard pep talk:

> Now the longer you stop, the more casualties you're going to have. Keep moving and you won't give 'em a chance to get you zeroed in. We have a job to do, and we're going to do it, whatever the cost. We must throw caution to the winds and be completely reckless. When you have casualties and lose vehicles keep right on going. If a company commander becomes a casualty, the second in command takes over immediately. As soon as you stop, in addition to wasting time, you're going to have more people killed and hurt. So whatever happens, absorb your losses and keep moving![33]

Tough words from a tough colonel—Roysdon said all the right things. In the weeks after that awful July 1944 clash, you had the impression he might be talking to himself. In the hedgerows he'd shown that mysterious coup d'oeil, the faint inner light, the ability to pull the trigger not just for himself but for 1,800 men at once. He'd had it. And now he appeared to have lost it.

War as practiced by Maurice Rose granted no credit for yesterday's triumphs. It was always "what have you done for me lately?" Now in the late afternoon of August 28, 1944, in front of the Soissons railroad bridge, Roysdon hesitated. Huddling with his battalion commanders in sight of the bridge, the colonel suggested that they look for another place to go over. This looked like a German trap, a little too inviting, and clearly well covered by enemy weaponry.

Right on time, up rolled Brigadier General Maurice Rose. His peep stopped. The general dismounted and walked the few steps to Roysdon's circle of officers.

"What's going on?" Rose asked. "Why have you halted?"

Roysdon tried to explain. Rose, not a shouter but not one to mince words, cut him off.

"Has anyone checked the bridge?"

"No," replied one of the subordinates.

"Then I'll do it myself," Rose said, as if announcing he was going to the corner store to pick up a newspaper. The general turned and headed for the bridge, moving by dashes from building corner to building corner to shield himself from hostile gunfire.

"General, sir!" an officer shouted. "The bridge is mined," another hollered. Indeed, soldiers of the 23rd Engineers had just removed several mines from the approach ramp.

If Rose heard the warnings, he didn't acknowledge them. Instead, he darted ahead, running crouched low, zigzagging onto the railroad tracks. The railway bridge stood fully exposed. Rose had no cover as he worked his way across, a forty-four-year-old reliving his Great

War lieutenant days. Now and then, Rose stopped to check for demolitions or mines. He assessed the strength of the bridge with his own weight and a practiced eye.

The Germans noticed the solitary man out on the structure. Bullets snapped in the air, flying by Rose with the zip-zip that tells you they're close. Mortar or artillery projectiles raised geysers in the Aisne River. Luckily for Rose that afternoon, German aim was off.

His personal survey complete, Rose worked his way back to Dorrence Roysdon's little gathering of leaders. The general told them to get going. They did.[34]

While the 3rd Armored Division commander carried out his one-man patrol, an order arrived from VII Corps directing the 3rd Armored Division to dispatch a tank/infantry task force to secure the World War I American Expeditionary Force battlefield of Château-Thierry, nearly twenty-six miles south of the ongoing fighting around Soissons. Apparently, Joe Collins of VII Corps thought this an appropriate tribute to the doughboys of 1918. Who knew? Collins never fought there or anywhere else in World War I. Maurice Rose did, but risking lives and wasting precious time on a stroll down memory lane meant nothing to Rose. He was consumed with catching and killing Germans at the Aisne River. Still, an order was an order. Combat Command Reserve sent Lieutenant Colonel Rosewell H. King's task force to handle the unwelcome mission.[35] Rose and the rest of the division remained firmly focused on the Germans and the Aisne.

With TF Lovelady enduring periodic harassing shots outside Soissons and TF Roysdon crossing the Aisne under German fire, Combat Command A also found a fight short of Pont-Arcy. Reinforced by TF Hogan from Combat Command Reserve, CCA shouldered aside the Germans and took an intact bridge over the Aisne. The 83rd Recon scouts did their part and paid the price, losing two killed and several wounded. But this time, they'd found river crossings . . . and the Germans.[36]

Those Germans didn't expect the 3rd Armored Division to show up so quickly and in such strength. Soissons served as a rail transit point for the German army, and the Americans now held that key junction. The Germans routinely moved by night to avoid the Allied air forces. As evening fell, German trains appeared on the tracks near Soissons. Railcars weren't standard tank targets. But they'd do.

The first rail engagement came at dusk. To the east, in the village of Braine near Pont-Arcy, soldiers of Combat Command A's attached battery of the 486th Antiaircraft Artillery Battalion—"Anti-Everything" they said—sighted a forty-two-car train. Private First Class John W. DeGrasse punched a 37mm (1.5-inch) round through the steam engine's boiler, which expired in a belch of white vapor visible even in the fading light. The German cars gradually slowed until they stood still. Then, German soldiers began to pile out of the nine passenger cars. Some shot from the windows. A few bold enemy troops ran to a flatcar bearing a panzer. The Germans intended to get that thing's big cannon going.

The American antiaircraft crews began bouncing 37mm rounds off the turret of the panzer—spectacular fireworks, but no damage. Far more effectively, the battery's half-track-mounted quadruple M45 .50 caliber machine guns opened up. The G.I.s called these "meat choppers." When you pressed the trigger pedal, these deadly implements hosed out 2,300 inch-and-a-half-long hot slugs a minute. Nobody could endure that. The meat choppers, also called "Kraut mowers," tore apart the light passenger wagons, chipped apart the twenty-one flatcars, sparked off the metal road wheels, and scattered the gutsy German panzer crew who'd gotten out and tried to board their vehicle. The brutal effects of the quad-50s ended it.[37]

The "Anti-Everything" gunners took seventy as prisoners. The G-2 analysts determined that this was what was left of a panzer battalion. Along with dead Germans, morning light revealed a scene described by Brigadier General Rose in his account: "The countryside was littered with all types of equipment, cosmetics, clothing, and wine bottles, abandoned by the loot-laden German soldiers in their panic." Although some jubilant Americans thought they'd torn up an SS outfit—the hated slayers of G.I. prisoners—this trainload appeared to be a regular German Army unit. The confusion arose because German panzer crews wore black coveralls with silver skull and crossbones insignia, a marking dating back to the Prussian cavalry of Frederick the Great. It was asking a lot to think nineteen-year-old American draftees could tell these groups apart in the heat of combat. More than once, unlucky German tankmen received the lethal consequences of American loathing for the Waffen SS.[38] How much of that happened at Braine, if any, isn't in the records.

Tankers of CCA's 32nd Armored Regiment and cannoneers of the 54th Armored Field Artillery Battalion caught a second train. Again, a well-aimed opening shot disabled the locomotive. This train had four big tanks on board, no-fooling Tigers, the dreaded Mark VI panzers with their long 88mm cannons. But these Tigers died tied to flatcars. American Sherman crews whacked the Tigers with broadside shots, the best way to engage these heavily armored brutes. Then the tankers and M7 105mm howitzer soldiers methodically machine-gunned the Germans trying to get to their trussed-up panzers. To end the night, near Soissons, Task Force Lovelady shot up a passing freight train, too.[39]

Colonel Long John Smith and his men of Omaha Forward also found themselves embroiled with fleeing Germans. Early in the day, as they prepared to move toward Soissons, a company's worth of German Luftwaffe flak troops drove right into the division command post perimeter. The staff officers, NCOs, and soldiers of Omaha Way Forward reacted strongly. In what one participant recalled as a quick but violent "pitched battle," the headquarters soldiers killed ten Germans and captured seventy. The G.I.s also took four cargo trucks, two smaller trucks, a motorcycle, two 88mm cannons, and three 20mm (three-quarter-inch) pieces. German return fire killed one American and wounded three.[40] Being part of Maurice Rose's staff was not for the fainthearted.

That night on the road northeast of Lévignen, another German column blundered into Omaha Forward as the headquarters moved by truck. In the darkness, both sides traded bullets on and off for four hours. The command post troops took the surrender of eighteen more German troops. Then it rained. Overhead, Luftwaffe aircraft droned in circles, dropping yellow flares. "Nobody got much sleep," the staff chronicler noted.[41]

Morning on August 29 brought a tough round of positional fighting as the 3rd Armored Division pushed battalions across the Aisne River at the railway bridge and CCA's Pont-Arcy site. Outside Soissons, Combat Command B troops located a huge ammunition dump estimated at 4,000 truckloads; the engineers blew it up.[42] That got attention.

Another development that day boded well for the division's future. It took Olympian efforts 24/7 to maintain the organization's 390 light and medium tanks and 3,810 other vehicles. The metal contraptions demanded their due regardless of German activity, weather, or road distances covered. Crews themselves did the basic work, fueling, greasing, tightening, and swapping out treads, tires, and the like. Serious breakdowns drew in trained ordnance teams. Fixing up battle damage—and there was no shortage of that—came extra. Getting the skilled mechanics, recovery vehicles, special tools, replacement engines, and spare parts forward demanded strong leadership. Maurice Rose liked what he inherited, but the long drive across northern France, marked by a trail of a few too many broken-down tanks and disabled trucks, suggested that more might be done. So when one of Patton's corps commanders requested the immediate services of Lieutenant Colonel Joseph L. Cowhey, commander of the 3rd Ordnance (Maintenance) Battalion, Rose OK'd the move without protest. Cowhey was good enough, although known to have quite a temper. He'd likely be some help at the corps level. Cowhey's departure gave Rose the opportunity to go with an impressive officer from the division staff, Lieutenant Colonel Rager J. McCarthy, to command the hardworking soldiers of the 3rd Ordnance Battalion.[43] Rose knew right away he was the right choice.

It took most of the day to squirt the long columns of tanks and trucks through two very narrow conduits. Rose spent much of the day at the bridges, sorting out traffic. The general pushed Colonel Leone's CCR through, too, sending that command into the center so he could spread out the bridgehead. From west to east, CCB, CCR, then CCA formed the array on the far bank of the Aisne. Skirmishing along the high ground cost twelve Americans killed.[44]

As the sun went down on August 29, CCB restarted the division attack to the north. As usual, TF Lovelady took the lead for CCB, departing at 7:30 p.m. When the U.S. armored column moved out, French Resistance partisans on the fringes of Soissons shot wildly, convinced that they saw in "every shrub a German tank, every shadow an enemy soldier," as one American officer remembered. The task force aimed for Laon, a city about ten miles northeast of Soissons.[45]

After a brief refueling stop at 4:30 a.m. on August 30, TF Lovelady pushed on. The task force took Laon by 7:00 p.m., concluding a very long twenty-four hours of hard combat. En route, G.I. tank crews, armored infantry, and artillerymen knocked out an 88mm cannon, two half-tracks, three armored cars, five trucks, two German jeep-equivalents, and a number of hostile rifle troops. Task Force Lovelady captured another forty Germans. Enemy soldiers fought back as bitterly as ever, killing ten Americans and wounding more than thirty. The opposition also knocked out two Sherman tanks.[46] Led by TF Lovelady, CCB aligned the division to keep pressing to the northeast. In their zones of attack, CCR and CCB followed suit. The division had encountered some doughty Germans, all right. But not enough. Not yet. Those guys sure were slippery.

By sunup on August 31, 1944, Rose's 3rd Armored Division ranged far out ahead of the rest of the U.S. First Army, some sixty miles ahead of most other units. Radio communications proved intermittent. Even Lightning Joe Collins couldn't keep up; he'd resorted to flying in and out by Piper Cub. Behind Rose's tankers, the VII Corps commander hustled forward the 9th Infantry Division and 1st Infantry Division. The follow-on infantry outfits closed on the Aisne River line as Rose launched for the next objective: Sedan, forty-five miles up the road in the Ardennes Forest.[47] The Germans beat the French badly there in 1870 and 1914, then did it again in 1940. Maurice Rose hoped to even up.

The attack kicked off on August 31. The revitalized 83rd Recon led out at first light, headed toward Sedan; the scouts reported various German outposts, and even took a few prisoners. The division's three combat commands moved abreast, although the planned 9:30 a.m. time of attack went awry. Combat Command B to the northeast went on two routes with TF Lovelady and TF Roysdon, although due to handover of the Soissons bridgehead to the follow-on infantry regiments, CCB did not launch until 12:24 p.m. Combat Command R in the center used a single column, moving at 10:00 a.m., late for no discernible or explicable reason—a mark against the new colonel there. Brigadier General Doyle Hickey's Combat Command A relied, as usual, on TF Doan and TF Richardson and got off promptly at 9:30 a.m. As the lead companies found enemy roadblocks, Colonel Louis P. Leone of CCR assessed opposition as "moderate," although the more experienced Turman Boudinot and Doyle Hickey both dismissed hostile reaction as "light." It was shaping up to be yet another day of sparring with feisty German rear-guard teams.[48]

Rose moved with CCR. Not long after noon, Lieutenant Colonel Sam Hogan's able tankers, half-track riflemen, and engineers met a German element near the crossroads of Seraincourt. Hogan knew his craft. He brought in supporting artillery as his Shermans and armored infantry squads closed on the foe.[49] Hogan's veteran sergeants and junior officers relied on tactics used over and over during this long march across France. Rather than swing around this firefight and keep going, the rest of Combat Command Reserve marked time in a long, long column.

Unlike CCR's Colonel Leone, the division commander didn't categorize this brand of skirmishing as moderate opposition. In World War I, Tunisia, Sicily, and Normandy, Maurice Rose learned the hard way the differences between hearing fire (common, no problem), receiving fire (getting interesting), and taking effective fire (get down, seek cover). A good battlefield commander figured it out quickly and chose an option: handle it with what you have, hold 'em and call for backup (reinforcing tanks, artillery, or air), or break off and reattack another way.[50] It was that coup d'oeil deal again. Take it in at a glance, then act. Just sitting there getting beat up, especially by the ever-alert Germans, ensured high losses for no gains.

In Seraincourt, the CCR colonel looked to be laboring to sort it all out. You could almost hear the gears spinning, like watching a person trying to do long division in his head. Rose had seen this movie before. Combat command is an art. Experience helped. But some basic talent in speedily calculating space, time, and weapons effects played into it. Book knowledge of U.S. Army doctrine only took you so far. After that, you either had it or you didn't. The on-scene commander must make the smart call, field manual bromides aside. As Rose himself later wrote of this engagement, "doctrine has not become dogma." "At other times," Rose continued, "there is little or no choice afforded the commander, who must accomplish his mission with the forces he has regardless of the type of operation involved."[51] The general was referring to himself. But he held his subordinate commanders to the same high expectation. Like Major General Joe Collins at VII Corps, Rose had only a fractional degree of patience for on-the-job training for subordinate commanders. Produce or move on.

At 1:15 p.m., the radio in Rose's peep crackled. The voice on the line told Rose this wasn't some mundane update. It was Colonel John Smith himself. The message was brief and spoken in double-talk, in case Germans listened. (They often did.) Rose listened, then spoke. Halt all columns. Coil in place. Stand by for new orders.[52]

———

"You could hear the brakes squeal when we radio'd the order to halt," said a staffer at Omaha Forward. Armored troopers pride themselves on the flexibility inherent in their mobility and radio communications, allowing them to change directions at motor speed. Now more than 14,000 American soldiers waited on "the word." Even as they did so, the five leading task forces remained engaged with German defenders.[53] The enemy didn't know what was about to happen. They'd find out.

Even with Long John Smith's spare verbiage, Rose immediately grasped the gist of it. The intelligence people up top had found the German main body, the entity that had thus far eluded Maurice Rose's division. Now the 3rd Armored Division, and indeed the entire VII Corps—the 1st and 9th Infantry divisions and all the corps artillery—would pivot nearly ninety degrees from slightly northeast to almost straight north to cut off and engage these retreating hostiles. Rose sized it up. Attack toward Mons, Belgium, to destroy what remained of the German Seventh Army.[54] Finish the work of the Falaise Pocket. Perfect. If done right, it just might kick open the door into the Reich itself. And that road led right to the end of the war.

Rose never heard of the cryptic doings at Bletchley Park, England. Eisenhower, Montgomery, Bradley, and Hodges dealt with all of that. Tight security restricted Ultra information to their level. Some previous events in Rose's experience traced directly to Ultra codecracking, such as the Carentan reinforcing effort on June 13, 1944, and the last-minute warning of the German counterattack at Mortain on August 7. The swing north to Mons had such origins. Allied air reconnaissance confirmed the German movements. Bradley and Hodges told Collins, who wasn't privy to Ultra. Lightning Joe jumped on the news.[55] Thus Rose and the 3rd Armored Division prepared to make a drastic change of direction.

At Fort Benning's Infantry School or Fort Leavenworth's Command and General Staff School, student officers like Maurice Rose learned how to form an estimate of the situation and draw up an operation order. It involved a lot of staffer scurrying, detailed discussions, and formal briefings. The method took many hours. That wouldn't work on this Mons mission. Catching these Germans meant moving immediately.

Right there on the side of the road at Seraincourt, Rose consulted with his peep-mounted artillery commander Colonel Frederic J. Brown and Division G-3 Lieutenant Colonel Wesley A. Sweat, right nearby in the M20 armored car. An officer from Omaha Forward, five miles away at Montcornet, arrived by truck with a copy of the VII Corps order. It wasn't much.

Rose sketched out a scheme on his map. He kept it simple. To move the sixty-four miles to Mons, the division had to start by realigning to head north. After breaking contact with the Germans already engaged to the east—no easy task—making about ten to fifteen miles would work for the rest of day one. After that, Rose intended to go as fast as roads, weather, and the foe permitted. Combat Command B, already on the inside track for such a turn, would send TF Lovelady toward Marle and TF Roysdon toward Vervins. Combat Command A focused on Hirson, with TF Richardson to the west aiming to pass through Rozoy-sur-Serre and the larger TF Doan on the east to push directly to Hirson. Combat Command Reserve would follow CCA, but be ready to go west to reinforce CCB if an opportunity developed. The 83rd Recon, already out to the northeast facing Sedan, was too far away to recall in time. Until the division reached

Mons, or found a lot of Germans the hard way, the 83rd had to make do with screening the eastern flank of CCA.[56]

His hasty scheme complete, Rose told his combat commanders—Hickey, Boudinot, and Leone—and his column commanders—Doan, Richardson, Lovelady, Roysdon, Hogan, and Tucker from the 83rd—to meet at Seraincourt at 2:30 p.m. Rose didn't want to waste time messing around with written directions or a trip by all back to Omaha Forward. The division commander knew that Wesley Sweat, like the good G-3 he was, would capture the notes and create a proper document, the eventual Field Order No. 12. The meeting didn't take long.[57] Helmeted heads nodded. Then they were off.

The rest of August 31 proceeded about as Maurice Rose figured. By midnight, CCB held with TF Lovelady at Marle and the other, larger task force a few miles short of Vervins. Combat Command A's two task forces only made it to Rozoy-sur-Serre, not Hirson. As for CCR, they stopped at a German roadblock a few miles south of Rozoy-sur-Serre, which "was not reduced prior to dark," as Rose wrote later. Breaking loose from the Germans exacted a price: eight Americans killed and more than twenty wounded.[58]

The day claimed one more. Following the commanders' meeting, CCB moved out. Rose's orders had been clear. Go north. Push hard. At a railroad underpass just north of Montcornet, TF Roysdon's lead tanks took what their colonel judged to be effective direct fire. Combat Command B commander Colonel Boudinot thought otherwise. "There's nothing in front of you but a thin line," he told Roysdon. Boudinot wasn't on the spot. Roysdon was. But Roysdon hesitated one time too many. Boudinot directed 33rd Armored Regiment executive officer Lieutenant Colonel Littleton A. Roberts to take over as acting commander.[59] Roysdon was finished.

The colonel reported to Omaha Forward, a few miles away, and waited on Rose, who was out and about until well into the night. When the general got there, he proved curt. Roysdon departed for duty in Eisenhower's headquarters. As Major Dugan put it, "Some of us, considering his [Roysdon's] prior action at Haut Vents in hedge-row country, found this severe."[60] Maurice Rose didn't ask for Du-gan's opinion.

————

The attack continued at 7:00 a.m. on September 1, 1944. All three combat commands pushed north, with CCB in the west, CCA in the east, and CCR trailing CCA. After moving all night, the 83rd Recon attached companies to CCA and CCB—acting commander Major John Tucker did plenty to pull that off, although Rose looked forward to getting a full-time battalion commander to get the most out of the scouts, to make them truly the eyes and ears of this entire mobile division, "the cav of the cav." Throughout the day, Rose in his peep spent time with each lead outfit, then circled back to check up on CCR. Up at First Army headquarters, the staff officers recorded resistance as "light."[61]

It felt a little more substantial on the ground. Combat Command B smashed through several German positions. Task Force Lovelady reported knocking out two Panther tanks, two armored cars, four trucks, and fifteen German jeeps. Lovelady's soldiers took 40 prisoners; their neighbors in TF Doan grabbed 160 more. Together, the two task forces ended their day at La Capelle, about twenty miles short of the Belgian border and forty miles shy of Mons. The fighting cost the G.I.s one dead and a few wounded. Task Force Lovelady's captain Roberts wrote:

> These were mad days. There were no two of them alike. Each was filled with new thrills, new adventures. These were Panther hunting days, and it was unusual if we didn't knock out two or more of these massive German tanks, along with smaller Mark IVs, armored cars, trucks, command cars, self-propelled guns and dual-purpose 88's.

Almost daily we would capture forty or more prisoners, and now we were beginning to contact many horse-drawn vehicles of enemy cavalry.[62]

Combat Command A worked through a more frustrating experience. A blown bridge resulted in a deluge of enemy shellfire on the stalled tanks and half-tracks. The Germans employed the dreaded *nebelwerfer* (fog thrower) multiple rocket launcher. The U.S soldiers called it the "screaming meemie" due to the distinctive sound as the curtain of projectiles rained down. Brigadier General Doyle Hickey's engineers managed to patch up the bridge enough to allow passage, and CCA bulled through the killing ground, suffering two Americans killed and five wounded. Combat Command A also scooped up German soldiers, some 400 in total. By midnight, Hickey's Combat Command reached Avesnes, about five miles north of La Capelle. Hickey estimated that he'd be in Mons late the next day.[63]

Combat Command Reserve struggled. Whereas CCA dealt quickly with a river crossing under fire, CCR did not. It took all day to sort out a blown bridge well to the rear of CCA. As a result, CCR only made it to Hirson at the cost of one American dead and several wounded. At that point, the combat command sat six miles southeast of Omaha Forward at La Capelle.[64]

Rose had seen enough. As recorded in the dry text of the Combat Command Reserve/36th Armored Infantry Regiment war diary, "Lt. Col. [Jack] Hutcheson asmd [assumed] command vice Col. [Louis] Leone relieved." Regimental executive officer Hutcheson had stepped in when Colonel Cornog died back on August 9. He'd done well. Still, bumping up the lieutenant colonel was a quick fix. It would do for the Mons operation, but this organization needed a solid colonel. The 36th Armored Infantry Regiment suffered the highest number of killed and wounded in the division.[65] Every attack, each defense, and all river-crossings demanded riflemen out on the ground. To date,

Rose had been operating with two reliable combat commands out of the three the division needed. That had to change.

September 2, 1944, brought the division to Mons. Combat Command B, led by Task Force Roberts, entered Belgium at 2:45 p.m. Combat Command A, with Rose right there, crossed at 4:10 p.m. Hutcheson's Combat Command Reserve, up on the line east of CCA, also pushed into Belgium. In the hamlets, civilians cheered and offered kisses, flowers, drink, and food, including the acclaimed Belgian waffles. Resistance leaders of the Belgian White Army offered the latest rumors on the Germans: close, very close. Rose told his men to ignore the welcome festivities. Get to Mons. Get set.[66] The Germans were coming.

As the sun sank in the west, the division's combat commands hurried on to Mons. When they arrived, Combat Command B put out roadblocks on routes coming from the west. Combat Command A did likewise to the south. Combat Command R pulled up to guard roads to the southeast. Beyond CCA, the 83rd Recon emplaced early-warning outposts in an arc across the road net to the south. While heading toward Mons, Company B scouts captured a German colonel bearing some useful maps showing proposed troop movements. It looked like most of the opposing forces, including part of the LVIII Panzer Corps, planned to make their way through Mons from the west and south. From what the colonel said, the Germans didn't realize the 3rd Armored Division had gotten to Mons first.[67]

On Rose's orders, Task Force Hogan detached from CCR and went to beef up CCA along the southern route. While Sam Hogan's M4 Sherman tanks found good ambush spots farther south along the highway, M5 Stuart light tanks and half-track infantry joined Omaha Forward, which had perched right next to the key approach, albeit in a choice locale. This particular evening, Colonel Smith sited the command post five miles south of Mons on a lovely country estate, the Château de Warelles—not quite the Rothschild digs, but nice indeed.[68] Neither Rose nor his staff had time to appreciate the place.

About 6:00 p.m. or so, Major General Joe Collins arrived via his M20 armored car, trailed by a mounted security force. The VII Corps commander hadn't seen Rose face-to-face since August 26, way back near the Seine River. At Omaha Forward, Collins hopped out of his vehicle and greeted Rose. Collins told the armor general that the U.S. 1st Infantry Division was meeting "a confused mass of retreating Germans" to the southwest and the 9th Infantry Division reporting similar contacts to the southeast. Tipped off by his 83rd Recon troopers, air reconnaissance updates, the Belgian Resistance, and Omaha Forward's good G-2 estimates, Rose warned Collins that the bulk of the Germans were en route. They'd be here soon.[69]

Collins elected to drive into Mons to gauge the vibes. They were all bad. As his caravan negotiated the empty streets, Collins didn't see many civilians, "always a danger signal." Like they used to say in Western movies, all was quiet. Too quiet. Lightning Joe sped back to Rose's command post south of town. He directed Rose to hold tight— a restatement of the obvious—then Collins got the hell out, motoring east toward the 9th Infantry Division.

With other divisions, Joe Collins would have stayed right there to buck them up. The VII Corps commander never shied from a fight, and by nature he couldn't usually keep his hands off the controls. But Collins trusted the 3rd Armored Division, which he believed "Rose had transformed into a great fighting machine."[70] Rose was exactly where he needed to be, doing exactly what he needed to do.

———

"You Americans don't want to fight," said the captive German officer. "You just want to slaughter us." He sure got that right.

For thirty-six violent hours, commencing at sunset on September 2, 1944, the 3rd Armored Division fought what American soldiers later labeled the Battle of Mons, an American-German sequel to the famous British-German clash of 1914. The third paragraph of a U.S. Army field order has long been titled "execution."[71] That's what happened beginning around dusk on September 2 in and around Mons, Belgium.

Action sparked at each node around the ring of U.S. roadblocks. Combat Command B's Captain Roberts of Task Force Lovelady offered a trenchant summary:

> Nearly every element of the division took an active fighting part in this fracas. The supply trains had to fight their way to the elements they supported. Task Force Lovelady had a real field day by knocking out more than a hundred horse-drawn vehicles, capturing more than two hundred and fifty prisoners together with much equipment. Germans were trying to escape in all directions, behind us, around us, through us. For them it was a bitter massacre, for us a brilliant victory.[72]

Combat Command A also did its share and then some. Task Force Doan and Task Force Richardson tank crews and riflemen took more than 3,500 prisoners, including three befuddled German generals. Brigadier General Doyle Hickey's men reported that "at this stage the enemy appeared generally disorganized with little or no knowledge of the position of our troops."[73]

At 3:20 a.m. on September 3, Combat Command R repulsed a panzer attack on one of its positions. The G.I.s knocked out two of three German panzers; the enemy abandoned the third. The Americans also killed eight Germans. The engagement cost one American killed and two wounded. Hundreds of hostile troops surrendered to CCR as the day went on. Lieutenant Colonel Jack Hutcheson and his soldiers did well—no issue there. But to stiffen CCR for the next few weeks, Rose sent in cavalry officer Colonel Carl J. Rohsenberger, commander of the Division Trains. He'd hold the fort at CCR while the division waited for a permanent replacement.[74]

In the gloom of night, unlikely opportunities arose. The 991st

Armored Field Artillery Battalion, a corps outfit backing up the 3rd Armored Division, normally delivered 95-pound 155mm (6-inch) artillery projectiles at targets 14.5 miles away. The gunners serving the "Long Toms" rarely saw the results of their shots. Near Mons, faced with the sudden, close-up appearance of groups of misoriented enemy troops and vehicles, the huge guns played blunderbuss. Crews leveled their cannons and fired flat-trajectory shots right into nearby panzers, half-tracks, and trucks. The artillerymen called this "direct lay." They laid out tens of Germans. Vehicle bodies, even steel panzer hulls, peeled open like smacked melons. Frantic enemy return firing killed four American artillerymen and wounded three. The G.I. gunners killed a great many more.[75]

Omaha Forward, a.k.a. "Combat Command Smith," saw action, too. Fighting alongside Sam Hogan's tanks and riflemen, the headquarters troops engaged a succession of German elements. Maurice Rose insisted on fielding a frontline command post. He certainly got his wish this time.

In the darkest stretch of the wild night of September 2–3, an Omaha Forward security team out on the main road identified an inbound German half-track. Alerted by a wire-line field phone, 143rd Signal Company privates Leonard Ethridge and Stanley Presgrave waited in their foxhole a bit farther north, their M2HB .50 caliber machine gun well-sighted on the highway. Ethridge snuggled in close, cradling the long belt of big .50 caliber rounds, ready to feed them steadily into the weapon. When the half-track appeared, Presgrave pressed the Y-shaped butterfly trigger on the butt-plate:

> He swung the heavy .50 caliber machine gun and hit the roaring half-track dead center with a long burst. For a moment, the vehicle continued on its mad course and then suddenly, it blew up in a flare of yellow flame and angry sparks. Out of the burning wreck came a number of [panzer] grenadiers, still shooting and throwing hand

grenades. American small arms, adding a background to
the steady clatter of the big machine gun, mowed them
down systematically. Within a few moments there was no
sound on the dark road excepting the snap and crackle of
the burning enemy half-track.[76]

In this and several other similar clashes, division headquarters soldiers captured 600 Germans. The division's military police platoon
inherited so many captives that the Americans herded them into a
sugar factory in the city of Mons. The MP guards, backed up by a rifle
platoon from the U.S. 1st Infantry Division, also intercepted a passing German column and picked up some 300 more prisoners.[77]

When the sun rose on September 3, unkempt rows of wrecked,
twisted, fire-blackened German vehicles stretched in front of each
American roadblock. Dead horses lay prostrate on the roadsides.
Some errant groups of enemy trucks, as well as bands of walking
Germans, kept at it during the day. Task Force Lovelady recorded
destruction of more than one hundred towed artillery pieces, trucks,
and panzers, as well as 300 more German quitters picked up. Other
task forces—Doan, Richardson, Lovelady, and Hogan—reported similar one-sided engagements.[78]

As these firefights flared and subsided, U.S. airmen joined in the
fray. In support of the American ground troops in and around Mons,
IX Tactical Air Command flew more than a thousand sorties. The
fighter-bombers claimed destruction of fifty panzers, 6,521 trucks,
452 horse-drawn wagons, and 485 "persons."[79] You had to hand it to
the pilots. They kept good ledgers. And they certainly savaged the
Germans.

So did the 3rd Armored Division. Rose's G.I.s captured 8,000 prisoners, added to more than 13,000 taken by the 1st Infantry Division,
plus a few thousand more nabbed by the 9th Infantry Division and
other corps units. In all, VII Corps rolled up more than 25,000 Germans. These included units from the LVIII Panzer Corps, II SS Panzer

Corps, and the LXXIV Corps (infantry). Along with prisoners taken from those elements, Rose's Division G-2 interrogators discovered members of the 6th Parachute Division, 17th Luftwaffe Field Division, 48th Infantry Division, 245th Infantry Division, and 272nd Infantry Division among their prisoners.[80] They'd slipped the noose in the Falaise Pocket. But not this time.

Perhaps 3,500 Germans died at the hands of VII Corps. The battlefield accountants didn't allocate these by division, which was just as well. The vicious series of engagements on September 2–4, 1944, cost the 3rd Armored Division forty-three killed and more than 130 wounded.[81] For those G.I.s who fought there, one grim glance, one pungent whiff, and they realized all too well what horrors had been inflicted on the opposition along the road net surrounding Mons.

When the American 1st Infantry Division officially took responsibility for Mons on September 4, 1944, the 3rd Armored Division was already moving out toward Namur.[82] Rose's G.I.s turned their backs on Mons, yesterday's news. The real business waited to the east. There lay the maw of the dragon.

II

THE WEST WALL

CHAPTER 4

Dragon's Teeth

The General said tonight that given ten days of good
weather he thought the war might well be over as far as
organized resistance was concerned.

    Major William C. Sylvan and Captain Francis G. Smith, Jr.[1]

The long columns of olive drab American tanks, half-tracks, and
trucks trundled east, ever east. "Moved at 1330 [1:30 p.m.] with
objective of Namur," recorded the operations officer of TF Lovelady.
The daily summary for September 4, 1944, continued: "Met very little
resistance and suffered no casualties. Still moving along highway at
2400 [midnight]. Bright moonlight, cold, morale good, men tired."[2]

The first tinge of autumn, the endless motor-march, and the G.I.s
were indeed tired, damned tired. The sergeants and officers definitely felt it; they'd been going on a few hours of sleep a day, if that.
The vehicles were sputtering, overdue for overhauls, spark plugs
fouled, treads loosening up, tires balding, burning oil—the works.
Two-thirds of the division's 232 M4 Sherman tanks had broken down
at least once and limped along with field fixes.[3] The 3rd Armored
Division had been fighting and moving steadily since July 26, covering nearly 300 miles in forty days. One hundred and ten miles more

would bring them to the German border and the fortified West Wall at the historic city of Aachen, gateway to the Reich. If the Americans could get there before the Germans . . .

Just that possibility very much worried German *General der Infanterie* (three-star equivalent) Günther Blumentritt, chief of staff at OB West. In his view, "The best course for the Allies would have been to concentrate a very strong striking force to break through past Aachen to the Ruhr area," the German industrial center. Blumentritt opined that "such a break-through, coupled with air domination, would have torn to pieces the weak German front and ended the war."[4] Push hard and finish.

Maurice Rose saw it, too. So did Collins, Hodges (even him), and Bradley. Rose never heard of Blumentritt, a name of interest in the bowels of Twelfth Army Group G-2, if there. But the 3rd Armored Division commander surely felt the hot breath of the horses pulling time's winged chariot. Kinder-hearted generals—and there were many—would have let up, rested the guys, given them and their overtaxed vehicles a break for a day or two, then gone back to the chase. Not Rose. As a subordinate observed, "He was firm and prompt of decision, brooking no interference by man, events, or conditions in order to destroy the enemy."[5] Rose's private fire burned white-hot. Only he knew why. But burn it did. As his men longed to let up, Rose applied the spurs, and when need be, the whip.

———

Field Order No. 13—an inauspicious number, that—charted the course: Mons, Charleroi, Namur, Huy, Liege, Verviers, Eupen, and then Aachen, Germany. A fine Belgian motorway paralleled the Meuse River as far as Liege, and the broader Meuse valley arrowed straight into Nazi Germany. The succession of towns along the Meuse called to mind the popular tune "A String of Pearls," a favorite selection of G.I.s lucky enough to hear Major Glenn Miller and his U.S. Army Air Forces band. With apologies to Major Miller, though, this Belgian string of pearls looked to host German die-hards bent on delaying the 3rd Armored Division's eastward thrust. To handle these anticipated obstructions, Maurice Rose sought bridges spanning the Meuse. These would allow the division to send columns of tanks and half-track infantry back and forth on either side of the waterway. Then the Americans could use a one-two punch, CCA north or CCB south, to prize the Germans out of their defensive posts.[6]

Combat Command B led out south of the Meuse River on September 4, 1944. Rose's peep accompanied the front column. That day, for the first time, Maurice Rose wore the two silver stars of a major general. His promotion finally came through, bumping him up almost a month into his division command. By U.S. Army tradition, promotions merit a ceremony and toasts. Rose had no time for such niceties. He pinned on his second star and moved out.[7]

In hopes of finding a bridge over the Meuse, Rose told Truman Boudinot to go right through Charleroi to Namur. Combat Command B did so, driving all night, sometimes getting the speedometer up to thirty-five miles per hour. The Americans pulled up in south Namur at 5:30 a.m. on September 5. But German engineers got there first. The main bridge was down.

After a brief fracas that cost three G.I.s wounded, TF Lovelady eliminated two German armored cars and a few game enemy riflemen, too. With the location cleared, brave American armored infantrymen hopped out of their half-tracks. Moving forward by sprints and stops, bent low to avoid German bullets, the G.I.s climbed, jumped, and dodged across the Meuse River, working their way over the slippery chunks of the dumped bridge. Two understrength platoons of American riflemen from Company E, 36th Armored Infantry Regiment eventually scrambled up the far bank. Task Force Lovelady didn't have a bridge. But they held a site.[8] That was something.

With the wrecked bridge approaches (relatively) secured, the American 23rd Engineers went to work despite occasional hostile harassing fire. Laying out 510 feet of treadway metal and supporting floats would not go quickly. The 23rd Engineer officers estimated that it might take until the morning of September 6 to complete the pontoon bridge. Somehow, defying the calculations, the engineers did the job by 7:00 p.m. Tanks and riflemen went over and took control of the far side.[9]

OK—but not fast enough for Maurice Rose.

At Rose's urging, the rest of CCB also spent the daylight hours of September 5 searching for a useable bridge. In the larger task force of Combat Command B, Colonel John "Jack" Welborn had taken command of the 33rd Armored Regiment. He was a keeper. A young West Pointer (Class of 1932), Welborn, like Rose, started in the infantry, then transferred to the cavalry, and finally to the armored force. Welborn fought in North Africa and Sicily with the 2nd Armored Division and landed at Utah Beach on D-Day in command of the 4th Infantry Division's attached 70th Tank Battalion.[10] This officer wouldn't require any prodding.

Determined to find another way across the Meuse, Welborn and his soldiers joined the bridge quest. It took well into the afternoon, but a patrol along the riverbank finally located a minor span. It wasn't great, but it might work as a one-way crossing. Combined with the 23rd Engineer pontoon project, the small connector sufficed to give Rose the flexibility he needed to move north and south of the Meuse.[11]

While CCB and the engineers grappled with Germans in south Namur, Brigadier General Doyle Hickey's Combat Command A passed through the north side of Charleroi. He'd allowed forty-five minutes to get through Charleroi, but the cheering crowds held up the Americans for almost three hours with the by-now customary bottles of wines, kisses, food, and flowers. It took well into the night to unscrew the impromptu street carnival. At 6:30 a.m. on September 5, Hickey's men finally pressed on and secured north Namur. Once again, joyful Belgians generated more trouble than any Germans. At a certain point, liberating got to be same-old, same-old.[12]

Behind Hickey's CCA, Rohsenberger's Combat Commander Reserve followed. They halted just west of Charleroi late on September 4. Rohsenberger's men also encountered crowds of celebrating Belgians. When CCR pushed on to Namur at 2:00 p.m. on September 5, the Americans met more local revelers. It took until well after dark for CCR's task forces to reach their designated night positions. During the night, Rohsenberger's soldiers picked up confused, dispirited German prisoners "in large numbers," as noted in the CCR war diary. It remained to be seen how Rose would use CCR as the advance continued. For now, they had orders to follow and support CCA.[13]

At Namur, most of September 5 went by as the engineers built their Meuse River bridge and TF Welborn metered vehicles one by one across their small span, too. The combat commands encountered scattered opposition. All to the good, but Rose was already looking ahead. He ordered Major John Tucker's 83rd Armored Reconnaissance Battalion to assemble for their next mission. At daylight on September 6—or as soon as the treadway bridge was up—the 83rd planned to move both north and south of the Meuse toward Liege. The battalion would be hunting more bridges, and Germans, en route. As the scouts waited for the 23rd Engineers to complete their pontoon crossing, a German bicycle platoon blundered into the 83rd's position. The recon men opened fire. The surviving bicyclists gave up immediately.[14]

During the day, Major General Joe Collins drove into Namur. His armored car and security vehicles waded into the crowds near the 23rd Engineers' bridging site. Even when a German 88mm antitank round whizzed overhead, the happy citizens of Namur continued to crowd the plaza near the river. Freedom and alcohol made for a lot of extra courage among the townspeople. Collins saw that the Germans were still actively shooting back on both sides of the Meuse.[15]

For the VII Corps commander, this wasn't a social call. He had an oral order to give. Collins sought out newly promoted Major General Maurice Rose at Omaha Forward. Tipped off on the radio by Chief of

Staff Long John Smith, Rose had showed up at his command post a few minutes before Collins. Omaha Forward occupied the lawns of another impressive mansion. This particular great house overlooked the Meuse River. German bullets and shells kept things lively—Omaha Way Forward, as usual.

Collins joined Rose just inside the open portico facing the Meuse. The dainty French door hung ajar as the men met. Gunfire cracked, and now and then the thud of something bigger crunched. It amounted to hearing fire, not taking fire—at least not a lot. Collins was not amused.

"Maurice, where is your front line?"

Rose pointed just across the river. That set off Collins. Everybody said the corps commander had a temper. This afternoon, Lightning Joe didn't hold back. Maurice Rose received both barrels.

Nearby staff officers and NCOs continued with their command post duties. But they strained to hear the details. They couldn't make out much. Except for the harsh tone, all from one party—that sure came through. "There ensued a chewing out of one general officer by another never before heard and was most embarrassing to the hearer," remembered Major Haynes Dugan of division G-2. Dugan thought he heard Collins wrap up with "If you ever do this again, I will relieve you." Rose, of course, didn't say much except "Yes, General" and "No, General."[16]

After venting, Collins got down to business. Farther south on the Meuse at Dinant, the 9th Infantry Division had run into a significant defending German force, maybe two infantry battalions with some panzers, too, the whole lot backed by artillery. It constituted the first well-organized German opposition since the end of the Falaise Pocket battle. Collins ordered Rose to send a battalion-sized tank/infantry task force to help the stymied 9th Infantry Division. [17]

These periodic diversions of combat power rankled Rose, but they were a Collins trademark, constantly diddling with a battalion here, a battalion there, like the earlier venture to the old World War I battlefield of Château-Thierry. Normally, Rose objected. Shipping a valuable tank/infantry task force backward to screw around at Dinant—that wasn't going to do anything to crack the West Wall. But given Collins's initial outburst, the division commander assented.[18]

The corps commander then offered his impressions of the Belgian crowds in Namur. Rose had already seen plenty of that for himself, but again, the 3rd Armored Division commander kept his mouth shut. Rose never said much. This looked to be an especially good opportunity to stay quiet. Collins concluded by shaking Rose's hand, congratulating his subordinate on his promotion to major general.[19]

The two men weren't friends. Neither knew the other well, aside from their relationship as fellow soldiers. They might both wear two stars, but each understood fully who was in charge. Still, the proprieties must be observed.

———

At daybreak on September 6, 1944, the 83rd Recon didn't get off smoothly at all. It was a dull gray rainy day, not a good one for moving on slick roads or through muddy fields. Company D to the north of the Meuse ran immediately into antitank and mortar fire. The thin-skinned M8 Greyhound armored cars, ill-armed M5 Stuart light tanks, and four-wheel-drive peeps had to back off. Companies A and B couldn't get south of the river. They didn't get to the two bridges in time, and the combat commands took priority. The recon teams wouldn't be getting to Liege anytime soon. Frustrated, Rose told them to advance to Huy, about halfway to Liege, to try to find bridges there. The scouts pulled that off, pinpointing a pair of intact crossings and notifying the combat commands.[20] Well, that counted for something. For Rose, the 83rd remained a work in progress.

The 83rd's problems mirrored similar frictions in the combat commands. To the south, soaked by the rain, CCB finally attacked at 11:40 a.m. German outposts popped up at every other road junction.

Task Force Lovelady, for example, reported engaging an antitank gun, a half-track, three trucks, and a bus full of German troops. At one point, a single Luftwaffe fighter plane dove down and strafed the moving task force column. Three G.I. riflemen in a half-track were wounded. The series of enemy contacts slowed up the task force. They only got as far as Huy.

This time, though, they grabbed a standing bridge, one of the two found earlier and reported by the 83rd Recon. On the road near the span, the task force's lead Sherman crew put a main gun round into a racing German vehicle which erupted into "a fountain of fire." That was probably the demolition stock.[21] In any event, TF Lovelady owned a sound Meuse River bridge.

The larger CCB task force, built around the 33rd Armored Regiment, also ran into several enemy roadblocks. Task Force Welborn fought well. The rain, though, imposed a penalty. Without the helpful spot reports provided by friendly pilots—funny how the outnumbered Luftwaffe flew despite the foul weather—the lead American Shermans moved tentatively. No crew wanted to eat a blazing 88mm bolt in the bow. Even after a long day trying various sloppy farm roads, TF Welborn couldn't pick a way much past Huy.[22]

They did, however, follow the scouts of the 83rd Recon to a small roadway span across the Meuse. This crossing might bear 33-ton M4 Sherman tanks as long as the Americans sent them over one by one. As Jack Welborn's accompanying engineers squinted through the rain and prepared to make a proper assessment of the structure, Major General Maurice Rose's peep appeared from the middle of the stopped row of American tanks and half-tracks. Rose ignored Welborn's little gathering. At the general's insistence, his driver, Tech-4 Glenn Shaunce, gunned the peep's motor and the quarter-ton truck bounced onto the shallow up-ramp. Without the slightest pause, the general's peep rolled right across the bridge. Nothing blew up. That worked for Welborn. The colonel waved across the first tank.[23]

Combat Command B did more than take bridges on September 6.

As directed by Major General Collins, CCB sent a task force south under command of Lieutenant Colonel Rosewell King, who'd been patched up after being wounded near Soissons on August 29. Task Force King started out at 9:40 a.m., the first task force to cross the Meuse. Maurice Rose clearly understood the priority of this mission. The task force neared Dinant by midday and went into action. Backing up the embattled 9th Infantry Division, King's tankers and armored infantrymen engaged German SS troops, killing an unknown number. At one point, Major General Collins watched armored infantrymen, backed by Shermans, storm houses held by the unyielding Waffen SS soldiers. Task Force King secured key high ground at the cost of one American killed and several wounded. The next morning, the 9th Infantry Division grabbed the Meuse River crossing at Dinant.[24]

To backfill TF King, Rose sent Sam Hogan's task force from CCR to Combat Command B. TF Hogan also banged into an enemy roadblock. The task force linked up with CCB and refueled by 10:00 p.m. on September 6.[25] Thanks to the 83rd Recon, TF Lovelady, and TF Welborn—with an assist from Maurice Rose—Truman Boudinot's CCB owned two Meuse River bridges at Huy to use in the morning.

North of the river, Combat Command A had to wait until almost 3:00 p.m. to get going. American troops shivered as sheets of rain pelted the stalled columns. Once the tanks and half-tracks rolled, they found problems. At alternating tree stands, German rear guards used well-concealed antitank guns and *panzerfaust* rocket launchers to delay the advance. Each knot of hostiles required a firefight and used up valuable daylight. After the gray day faded to black, CCA stopped north of the Meuse near Huy.[26]

The slow going on September 6 didn't sit well with Maurice Rose. Wet weather dumped on both sides, and Liege had the general's full attention. The Belgian industrial center had rings of forts dating back to medieval times. If a lot of Germans settled into those hardened positions, it would be extremely painful to dig them out. The

3rd Armored Division probably couldn't do it without bringing in two or more American infantry divisions.[27] And that kind of ugly set-to would end any chance of getting to Aachen.

Rose couldn't risk a street-by-street donnybrook in Liege. According to the G-2 estimates and pilot reports, the Germans expected more of the same, one American combat command advancing north of the river and one to the south. The enemy disposed accordingly, with obvious positions visible on the western edge of Liege. Rose saw his chance. The Germans looked for U.S. attack right down the highway handrailing the Meuse. Well, give it to them. Mount an obvious push with CCA, the matador's cloak, to distract the enemy. Keep the Germans busy. Then swing around with CCB, take the dominant heights in eastern Liege, and slam the back door shut—another Mons.[28]

The 83rd Recon got away cleanly before dawn on September 7, 1944, a very fine start to the day. The scouts reached western Liege by 3:00 p.m. and reported Germans present, including panzers. At least two bridges were gone, wrecked completely. The Meuse River turned almost due north at Liege. So to continue on toward Aachen, Germany, those crossings needed eventual attention.[29] But killing Germans came first.

Major General Rose followed the scouts' reporting by radio. The recon soldiers told him enough. The Germans faced west. Betting on the value of speed and maneuver, the general unleashed both CCA and CCB at 1:00 p.m. Doyle Hickey's Combat Command A went right at Liege north of the Meuse. This clearly attracted a lot of German attention.

At the same time, Truman Boudinot's Combat Command B swung well south of the river. Lieutenant Colonel Bill Lovelady had checked out a route that used pretty decent farm trails. Maurice Rose, naturally, moved with TF Lovelady, relishing the increasing evidence that the Germans were looking the other way. It wasn't raining on September 7. Even on the dirt country paths, Combat Command B moved out.[30]

TF Lovelady, the bigger TF Welborn, and Maurice Rose in his peep arrived on the high ground in the southern neighborhoods of Liege by 7:19 p.m., just as the last light faded. The Germans missed the entire envelopment. Now they'd pay. Boudinot set out five strong tank/infantry roadblocks, as at Mons. Boudinot and Rose both expected substantial German traffic overnight.

Boudinot was not disappointed, thanks to Combat Command A. Approaching the western districts of Liege north of the Meuse, Hickey's soldiers ran into four batteries of German flak guns: at least six 88mm pieces, several 40mm (about 1.5 inches) pom-poms, and a few nests of 20mm light cannons, some vehicle-mounted, some not, but all dug in, about two dozen in all. German 88mm cannons could shoot down planes or hit tanks. These gun crews trained their tubes for the latter. The German flak commander evidently hoped Hickey's tanks and half-tracks would impale themselves on these lethal weapons. Instead, Hickey turned to his accompanying gunners, the 67th and 54th Armored Field Artillery battalions. They coordinated a time on target, bringing down thirty-six 105mm (4-inch) shells at the same instant, then repeating the fatal deluge multiple times. The hammering went on for more than ten minutes. As the final explosions echoed, a pall of dust rose over the open-topped German positions and vehicles. When the dirty shroud subsided, nothing moved. Cannons pointed up at crazy angles. No men in gray German uniforms could be seen. They were finished. Hickey's tanks and half-tracks surged past the wrecked batteries and onward into Liege. Behind them, Rohsenberger's CCR followed. Except for TF Hogan over with CCB, CCR hadn't been needed yet.[31]

As Maurice Rose hoped, the night of September 7–8 turned into another Mons event. "Chaos reigned for the Germans," wrote TF Lovelady's Captain Roberts, "and the very madness of it all was somewhat confusing to us." Hundreds of Germans in vehicles and on foot bumbled into well-chosen American roadblocks.

In one night encounter, *Generalleutnant* (two-star equivalent) Konrad Heinrich of the German 89th Infantry Division and his staff car driver tooled up to a U.S. position. The TF Lovelady riflemen riddled what G.I.s described as a "sporty convertible cabriolet," killing the general. As the evening wore on, the G.I.s rolled up 150 captive enemy soldiers, too. In the wee hours of the next morning, TF Hogan's infantrymen captured *Generalmaior* (one-star) Bock von Wolfingen along with 600 other prisoners. TF Welborn added 700 more. Combat Command B's road watch teams knocked out an assault gun panzer, two trucks, twelve sedans, thirteen wagons, and eight towed 20mm antiaircraft cannons.[32]

North and west of Liege, Combat Command A didn't have as much action, but they added to the bag of prisoners. Most of the Germans were flowing east, toward home. Seven Mark IV Panzers motored into the gunsights of CCR Shermans; the enemy lost all seven, their crews, and some accompanying infantrymen.[33] It was the one potentially dangerous opposing combat unit that appeared during the German bug-out from Liege. Combat Command Reserve erased it quickly.

The 3rd Armored Division spent most of September 8 cleaning up the enemy resistance in and around Liege. The 23rd Engineer Battalion built another treadway bridge over the Meuse, this time blessedly unmolested by German fire. The two days had been costly for Rose's division, with sixteen Americans dead and nearly a hundred wounded. The 1,500 or so enemy soldiers taken captive represented a decent haul, but not much compared to the numbers taken at Mons. Maybe there weren't many Germans still willing to duke it out. Or possibly, the rest had slipped away. But not all. Hundreds of German remains lay all around Liege, an unwelcome burden for the otherwise ecstatic Belgians. The 3rd Armored Division declared the city secure at 6:10 p.m.[34]

Maurice Rose didn't stop to enjoy it. He never did. Beating the Germans to the West Wall—the idea consumed Rose. And how that man could concentrate his energies. As Liege's people cheered and milled about, and G.I.s oiled their M1 rifles and tinkered with ailing Sherman tanks, Rose looked east. He ordered the 83rd Recon to prepare to head out at 5:00 a.m. on September 9, 1944, and the combat commands to follow, destination Verviers, halfway to Aachen. The German frontier was forty miles ahead.[35]

––––––

The 83rd Recon wriggled a few patrols all the way to the east side of Verviers by 3:00 p.m. on September 9, 1944. Their reports proved sobering. The Meuse was no longer an issue, but with each mile traversed, the ground rose steadily on either side of the main highway. Thickets of trees grew closer to the roads. The secondary farm trails narrowed to one Sherman in width. And there were German panzers hidden in the woods south of the major route.[36]

Moving on country lanes north of the main highway, Hickey's Combat Command A faced what they called "light resistance," a few hit-and-run scrapes. Navigating the tricky back roads took a long time. Hickey's soldiers didn't reach the high ground northwest of Verviers until 9:00 p.m. There the task forces coiled for the night, setting all-round defenses like an Old West wagon train. The infantry placed a ring of two-man listening posts at least a hundred yards out. Then came a hard circle of tanks and half-tracks with men ready on the machine guns. Infantry foxholes secured the combat vehicles. Finally, in the center went the aid station, the ambulances, the command post, and the supply trucks. It was a procedure run nightly.[37]

Combat Command B, with Rose accompanying, had a much tougher day. The Germans didn't have much remaining in Belgium. But what they had left showed up on the way to Verviers. A brand-new German outfit, the 105th Panzer Brigade, offered the first serious opposition in weeks.[38]

The 105th Panzer Brigade represented yet another Adolf Hitler brainstorm. Unhappy with his veteran panzer generals, the irascible führer refused to replenish their battered mobile divisions. Instead, the erstwhile lance corporal demanded creation of new formations, each a sort of German combat command: one panzer battalion and one *panzergrenadier* battalion. The 105th built up around officers and NCOs drawn from survivors of the 18th Panzergrenadier Division, an organization smashed by the Russians in their summer 1944 offensive. The 105th's battlewise leaders inherited rookie soldiers imbued with Nazi fervor but not a lot of training. The brigade's thirty-three Panthers and eleven Mark IV assault guns arrived factory-fresh, so new they hadn't even benefitted from the manufacturer's usual break-in checks.[39] The just-issued panzers and their hopped-up but ill-prepared crews would get their shakedown courtesy of the 3rd Armored Division.

With TF King returned from their Dinant sojourn, Boudinot's Combat Command B sent TF Hogan back to Liege to wait with Combat Command Reserve. At 11:00 a.m., CCB rolled east at full strength. General Rose accompanied. Based on the 83rd Recon updates, all anticipated trouble.[40]

They found it.

At 3:49 p.m., Task Force Lovelady started taking high-velocity 75mm shots. Panthers. It had to be. The German panzer men knocked out three Shermans in quick succession; three Americans died and twelve were wounded, all three crews gone in seconds. Lovelady's other tank crews backed off the roadway, seeking cover. A minefield protected the Germans. This knot would take some work to unravel.

To suppress these German panzer men, the 391st Armored Field Artillery Battalion went into action. Their M7 self-propelled 105mm howitzers could stop and start shooting in minutes. Over the next few hours, the artillerymen banged out hundreds of rounds, pummeling the Germans and pinning the hostile panzers in place.[41] All the G.I.s knew the drill. Send a bullet, not a man.

Major General Rose was on hand, as usual, right at the edge of TF Lovelady's firefight. Lieutenant Colonel George G. Garton of the 391st and a few of his staff officers stood near Rose, watching the back-and-forth. At 5:45 p.m., an accurate batch of German mortar projectiles impacted almost on top of the officers. Red-hot, jagged metal shards whirled out, killing Captain Ballard P. Durham and cutting up Garton and three others. By some miracle, the deadly fragments all whizzed right by Rose. The general helped get the wounded to the medics for treatment. Then Rose walked right back to his prior spot.[42] The firefight wasn't over yet.

Fortunately, not long after Durham's death, U.S. P-47 Thunderbolt fighters appeared overhead. Directed by a savvy forward air controller, the American fighter pilots knocked out three Panthers. They would have gotten more but the airmen ran out of munitions. Before they departed, the fliers reported the location of several other German panzers. Guided by these welcome spottings, TF Lovelady's experienced Sherman crews went Panther stalking. To kill one, it helped a lot to know where a Panther sat. A Sherman's 75mm cannon couldn't punch through the foe's sloped frontal armor. To nail a Panther, you had to hit it from the side or back. Lovelady's tankers did just that, taking out four enemy armored vehicles. Even so, the long fight used up almost all remaining daylight. They weren't going to get into Verviers today.[43]

Task Force Welborn also ran into panzers. Overexcited G.I.s saw large dark shapes in the tree line and reported two Tigers. They were Panthers, but that fine distinction mattered little with armor-piercing slugs winging back and forth. The Germans hit a U.S. Sherman and an accompanying half-track, killing one G.I. and wounding ten. Again, American P-47 Thunderbolts intervened with effect. The fighter-bombers knocked out more than one panzer; the rest pulled out for parts unknown. Minefields, blown-down trees, and road craters, each guarded by a few plucky Germans, held up TF Welborn well into the night. They, too, halted short of Verviers.[44]

Cleaning out the rest of the 105th Panzer Brigade occupied most of September 10, 1944. Colonel Rohsenberger's CCR moved up southwest of Verviers to prepare for the next day's operation. Combat Command A knocked out more Panthers; the rest left, heading east. Combat Command B also had some fleeting contacts, breaching small minefields and shouldering aside more felled trees. Task Force Lovelady drove off some suspected panzers at dark and picked up ten prisoners, too.[45] Whatever remained of the 105th had lost interest in opposing the Americans, especially their fighter-bombers.

In a development that gratified many, TF Welborn's lead elements found an abandoned German Army warehouse on the south side of Verviers. The enemy's black bread and sausage didn't go over well. But the chocolate and cigars sure did. The treats went well with the friendly welcome in the streets of Verviers. Once again, the local citizens merrily rejoiced in their newfound freedom. Belgian Resistance men whispered warnings, though. There were Germans ahead—a lot of them.[46] That unhappy story never grew old.

At first light on September 11, the 83rd Armored Reconnaissance Battalion headed east toward Eupen, the last major Belgian town, the end of the line. A few miles out of Verviers, German stay-behind teams with burp guns and *panzerfäusten* struck at a scout M8 Greyhound armored car, killing two Americans and wounding four. Other hostile ambushers engaged nearby 83rd platoons. The U.S. recon men reported "stiff resistance." They couldn't get to Eupen. The scouts held up short. Both leading combat commands moved right through them.[47]

Nine other Americans died on the road to Eupen. With Rose along for the ride, Combat Command A moved out at 8:00 a.m. Again, they used the north side of the main highway. German harassing fire killed four American soldiers and wounded a dozen more. Hickey's men reached the north side of Eupen by midafternoon. Following CCA, Combat Command Reserve spent the remaining daylight hours on the road. By midnight, they'd halted to the west of Eupen.[48]

Also launching at 8:00 a.m. on September 11, Combat Command B advanced to the southern side of Eupen. On the way, Task Force Lovelady clashed with German riflemen, two antitank gun crews, and a single Mark IV Panzer. The Americans prevailed in the firefights but lost a Sherman and two more U.S. soldiers killed plus several wounded. The task force led the rest of CCB into Eupen around 3:00 p.m.

No well-wishers turned out. The streets were largely deserted. A few houses and businesses displayed Belgian flags. Many more buildings showed white bedsheets. "There were no flowers, no tidbits, no hugs or kisses," recalled an officer in TF Lovelady. Wary Americans noticed the many signs written in German.[49]

Every G.I. in the 3rd Armored Division knew what came next.

———

It all boiled down to the next few days. Both the Americans and the Germans felt it, the former running on empty, the latter bloodied and reeling. Could Major General Maurice Rose and his G.I.s break through the West Wall?

The spirit was willing but the flesh—and steel—were weak. Gasoline was getting harder and harder to come by. Artillery shells didn't arrive in volume anymore. Beat-up vehicles creaked and moaned. Riflemen stumbled ahead in a daze. For the deepest personal reason a man could have, Maurice Rose possessed all the willpower in the world to finish the great drive with the killer blow. And yet . . . and yet.

Captain A. Eaton Roberts, surgeon of Lieutenant Colonel William B. Lovelady's hard-fighting 2nd Battalion, 33rd Armored Regiment, recognized the problem. They had come so far, done so much, and now at the moment of truth, at the fearsome gates of Mordor, the wheels were literally coming off. Roberts saw it and wished he did not.

Signs of high endurance were beginning to line the faces of tankers and infantrymen alike. There had been practically no physical rest and certainly no mental rest since the very day of our commitment, early in July. Our vehicles were beginning to feel it, too. They lugged and chugged and tossed and turned like old men with bad stomachs.[50]

Bernard Law Montgomery saw it, too. He'd warned of this moment over and over, at length. Before D-Day, the American generals and most of the British, too, were fixated on getting ashore. Prior to June 6, 1944, only Monty looked past the beachhead, playing chess instead of checkers, seeing the endgame on the horizon. Patton glimpsed it, too, but he was not high enough in the chain to make a difference.[51] So it fell to Monty to make the case.

"The quickest way to win this war," Montgomery argued, "is for the great mass of the Allied armies to advance northwards, clear the coast as far as Antwerp [Belgium], establish a powerful air force in Belgium, and advance into the Ruhr." The Ruhr contained the core of German military production. Take that, and Hitler's war machine would cease to run. Monty sent his proposal directly to Eisenhower on August 22, 1944.[52] But the British commander had been saying it for months. Of course, Monty had someone in mind to take charge of this war-winning thrust: himself. Modesty wasn't one of his virtues.

Monty referred to his scheme as the "single, full-blooded thrust." In the field marshal's reckoning, by September 1 he'd employ his own Twenty-First Army Group (fifteen divisions), Bradley's Twelfth Army Group (twenty-one divisions), and the First Allied Airborne Army (five divisions, two British and three American), a mass of forty-one divisions, although Monty graciously rounded down to forty without ever mentioning that any others that may be needed had to be American. The British didn't have any extra divisions left.[53]

Where would this pile driver hit? They'd go at the Ruhr "via Aachen and Cologne," exactly the route ahead of Joe Collins and VII

Corps, led by Maurice Rose's 3rd Armored Division. Montgomery intended to punch through the West Wall there, with a supporting attack to the north going past Antwerp then through the southern Netherlands and into the north part of the Ruhr basin; the West Wall was incomplete on that part of the German frontier.

For what it was worth, the top-ranking Germans dreaded the very offensive Montgomery advocated. It amounted to their 1914 Schlieffen Plan, but in reverse—same good routes, same potentially decisive outcome.[54] Of course, the Schlieffen Plan failed when the German foot soldiers couldn't out-march determined French, British, and Belgian defenders. There was a lesson there, and gasoline engines didn't guarantee a better result in 1944. At any rate, the German generals' opinions only emerged after the war ended. In August and September 1944, nobody on the Allied side ran their plans by Berlin.

Had the concept been presented by anyone but Monty, the Americans might have listened. But by the late summer of 1944, the Yanks had lost their patience with Bernard Law Montgomery. It grew easy for American generals to poke fun at the sometimes pompous bantam Englishman who, as of September 1, 1944, became Field Marshal Montgomery by grace of His Majesty King George VI. Monty forever prattled on and on about "knocking Jerry for six" or "tidying up the battlefield" like some Hollywood caricature of a supercilious Brit. He left no doubt that he considered Eisenhower a hopeless amateur lacking in frontline experience, Bradley a colorless plodder mired in routine, and Patton some sort of occasionally useful madman. Monty didn't consider Hodges at all. (Who did?) Until September 1, 1944, the date of his elevation to five-star equivalent, Montgomery ran the ground war in northwest Europe.[55] Like him or not, American senior commanders Bradley, Hodges, and Patton had to obey him.

Now that changed. With his Supreme Headquarters Allied Expeditionary Force (SHAEF) established in France, Ike Eisenhower took over the ground war effective September 1, adding land force commander to his role as overall Allied theater commander. It drove Monty to distraction. The British field marshal clearly realized what must be done, and why. But Ike and his American generals just didn't get it.

On September 11, as Maurice Rose and his men stood at Eupen, Belgium, the Allied front from the North Sea to Switzerland belonged to six armies: Monty's Canadian First Army and British Second Army, Bradley's U.S. First Army and U.S. Third Army, and the new Sixth Army Group's U.S. Seventh Army and French First Army, both having landed near Marseilles on August 15, 1944. Up and down that long line, there were two good ways into Germany. Montgomery correctly named the best, the axis leading to the Ruhr factory towns. The second-best traced through Metz and into Germany's other production nexus, the Saar basin. Though hampered by worse terrain, the Saar avenue offered an option to jab north toward the Ruhr. George Patton's Third Army happened to be aligned on the Metz-Saar approach.[56]

Therein lie the problem. Monty's thinking would be the right answer in a staff college war game. Indeed, the Ruhr thrust would garner high marks, with a B- for those who selected the Metz-Saar alternative. But in a real war, with real people, other considerations mattered. Among his frustrated American peers, Anglophile Eisenhower already had a reputation as being way too accommodating to Montgomery. Putting all Allied eggs, including Bradley's divisions, into the obnoxious Monty's basket? Ike just couldn't do that to his West Point classmate Omar Bradley, nor to his fellow U.S. generals, especially Patton, who would have bridled at such a decision.[57] The reaction of the long-suffering American public can only be imagined, and by the way, 1944 was a presidential election year. So the supreme commander wanted options, a way to make all happy. Why not go with both drives, Monty in the north and Patton in the south? (The Sixth Army Group didn't figure much; by disposition and composition, especially their shaky French units, they were confined to a supporting effort.) In an ideal setup, fireball Patton would be pointed at Aachen rather than the lackluster Hodges. Ike, though, was a realist and a shrewd poker player. He'd play the cards he'd been dealt.

So that would be it—a broad front, Monty's Twenty-First Army Group to the north and Bradley's strong horse Patton to the south, sort of a continental version of Maurice Rose's recent tactics along the Meuse River.[58] Surely the richest countries on earth could afford both pushes. The two attacks might well befuddle the Germans, stretch them thin, and if one didn't succeed, maybe the other would. Perhaps they both would. All it took from the Eisenhower level was adequate provisioning.

That's where Ike's even-handed plan came a cropper. By September 11, 1944, Allied logistics neared implosion. While the American-led Sixth Army Group drew sustenance from Marseilles, Montgomery's and Bradley's forces received most of their supplies through the Normandy beaches. The ports that should have supplied the two northern army groups—the core of Monty's "full-blooded thrust"—remained closed. German die-hards holed up in Brest, Lorient, St. Nazaire, Boulogne, Calais, and Dunkirk. The Allies gained the harbors at Cherbourg, Le Havre, and Ostend, but all three barely functioned due to considerable sabotage by their final batch of German defenders. The British handily took Antwerp, home to a superb set of quays and docks. Unfortunately, though, the Canadian First Army found itself enmeshed in a lengthy campaign to clear entrenched German regiments guarding the fifty-mile Scheldt estuary, the water connector to Antwerp. Without control of the Scheldt, Antwerp's fine facilities sat idle. On top of these serious port issues, the French railroad system had been bombed to smithereens prior to D-Day, a great way to foul up German troop movements, but also a major headache once the Allies broke loose from Normandy and motored east to the German border.[59] The farther the Allies moved east, the greater the strain.

One hundred and thirty-two American quartermaster truck companies with 5,958 vehicles, including some stripped from late-arriving U.S. Army combat divisions, rolled east day and night in the famous Red Ball Express. They delivered an average of 7,000 tons a day, supplemented by about 500 tons of daily aerial resupply, weather permitting. That all sounded great, except Bradley's fighting forces needed 13,650 tons every twenty-four hours. Being closer to the coast, Monty's British and Canadian armies, along with the single Polish division, suffered only spot shortages.[60]

Still, running on half-rations assured problems, and with each passing day, things got worse. Units slowed, guns didn't fire, and vehicles broke down. Division after division ran out of gasoline by early September. Supplies, or the lack thereof, began to reduce Eisenhower's choices far more than any spat with Montgomery. Predictably, the British field marshal wagged his finger and indulged in smug lecturing. With only half the necessary sustainment, only one thrust would do—his. Monty's remonstrances grew so strident and so personal, that at one point during a September 10 conference, the normally even-tempered Eisenhower growled, "Steady, Monty, you can't speak to me like that. I'm your boss."[61]

Yet in the interests of sound strategy, logistical limits, Allied solidarity, or perhaps just an unwillingness to keep arguing, Ike split the loaf again. Monty received SHAEF's only uncommitted force, the First Allied Airborne Army, for a strike across the Dutch extension of the northern Rhine River; this would become the Arnhem operation, the ill-fated "bridge too far" drop. Hodges's First Army, still under Bradley's command, gained supply priority to cooperate with Montgomery's major airborne-armor push—so much for the touted Aachen axis, now reduced to an ancillary effort. To mollify the slow-boiling Bradley, Ike continued to offer logistical support for Patton's Third Army advance toward the Saar.[62] Everybody got something. Nobody got enough. Except the Germans. They gained a handful of critical days; not many, but sufficient to man the West Wall. Decisions, to include compromises, have consequences.

———

The West Wall loomed like an ominous, continent-spanning open jaw. Nazi publicity photos long highlighted the barricade's most recognizable feature, the West Wall's murderous welcome mat: five rows of close-set, man-sized triangular steel-reinforced cement prongs able to rip the underside off any Allied tank, and thereby leave would-be attackers stalled and helpless, easy meat for well-aimed German gunfire. Both sides called these stark impediments dragon's teeth. According to ancient Greek legend, Cadmus sowed a plowed field with dragon's teeth, and each razor-pointed seed spawned a fierce warrior.[63] In September 1944, desperate German commanders, short on troops, trusted that their dragon's teeth might do as much.

Names matter. The Americans referred to the dragon's teeth and the covering bunker complexes as the Siegfried Line even though to Germans, it was always the West Wall. The actual Siegfried Line dated back to World War I. Doughboys of the Great War like Maurice Rose and Courtney Hodges remembered that fortified belt as the Hindenburg Line.[64] They misnamed and underestimated that one, too.

If you can't even get the name right, it doesn't bode well. Most of the American G-2 experts thought little of the German border defenses, supposedly outmoded, ill-prepared, and sparsely defended. The First Army G-2, Colonel Benjamin A. "Monk" Dickson, told Lieutenant General Courtney Hodges to figure on meeting a hodge-podge of "Police, L of C [lines of communications, logistics elements], Signal and other service units, hastily gathered and thrown in to man the West Wall." Dickson rated these troops as "probably miserable" in quality. He assessed the enemy's options as "minimal resistance," "retreat," or "collapse and surrender." So there. Gratified by Monk Dickson's optimism—never a good trait in an intelligence chief—Hodges referred on September 11, 1944, to "the Siegfried Line—or what there is of it."[65]

Flush with such happy talk, Hodges ordered his First Army's three subordinate corps to close on the West Wall. By design, and his own strong influence on Hodges, Major General Joe Collins's VII Corps had long set his course for the prime real estate of Aachen and the

Stolberg corridor, teeing up a straight shot to Cologne and the Rhine River only fifty-four miles to the east. Hodges hoped for another jolt courtesy of Lightning Joe.[66]

For his part, Collins didn't try anything tricky. The VII Corps would bum-rush the West Wall with three formations abreast. From north to south, the 1st Infantry Division keyed on Aachen city, Maurice's Rose's 3rd Armored Division received what passed for the best tank ground in front of Stolberg, and the 9th Infantry Division drew the short straw, an assignment to crunch through the dense Hürtgen Forest, a place that soon became infamous. Collins ordered his generals to "push on to the east with the hope that we might crack the West Wall before it could be fully manned."[67] Hope is not a recommended method of war. Yet given how well things had gone for the past seven weeks, who could blame Lightning Joe for indulging in some wishful thinking?

Maurice Rose saw it differently. He was ever a cold-eyed realist, especially with regard to the Germans. Those people never quit easily. Now they defended their home ground, the "sacred soil of the Fatherland" so often invoked by Hitler and his fellow Nazis. Rose did not dismiss the West Wall as some slipshod joke. These same Germans built high-quality MG42 machine guns, mighty Panther tanks, and rugged Focke-Wulf 190 fighter planes, as well as the formidable Atlantic Wall beach defenses and the impressive *autobahn* (automobile trail), the world's first modern highway system. If the Nazi regime constructed protective border fortifications between 1936 and 1938, one should expect quality work, whatever the actual structures entailed. But as Rose's key subordinates recalled, "The intelligence picture was quite vague up to this time."[68] Rose knew what he didn't know. It was high time to fill in the blanks.

On September 12, 1944, with the division grouped near dreary Eupen, Belgium, Rose did something he hadn't done since he took command. He stopped insisting on constant forward movement and ordered his lead task forces to take a good, hard look at the fortifications ahead. In military terms, the pursuit was complete. To Rose, this West Wall effort shaped up to be a deliberate attack, a prepared penetration of the German border defenses.[69] Such an operation demands a solid picture of the enemy's layout. As the British liked to say, time spent on reconnaissance is seldom wasted.

The 83rd Armored Reconnaissance Battalion gave it a try after dawn on September 12. They got almost nowhere. Endeavoring to go overland in their unarmored peeps and lightly protected half-tracks and armored cars, the scouts found the closely wooded terrain leading to the German frontier to be so muddy as to be "impassable." When the recon teams tried roads, they found all varieties of intentionally blown holes in the pavement, nests of interlocked downed trees, and clusters of man-made iron and concrete obstacles. Many of the roadblocks sported active German protectors. The scouts couldn't get by. Well, Rose hadn't counted on much from the 83rd. This difficult ground didn't suit their wheeled vehicles.[70] More than any equipment upgrade, the outfit desperately needed a true cavalryman in command, a man with a nose for the bad guys.

Rose had just such a man: Lieutenant Colonel Bill Lovelady, commander of the 2nd Battalion, 33rd Armored Regiment. This sawed-off dynamo showed a knack for finding a way into the foe's vitals. When Rose directed both CCA and CCB to send forward patrols at 8:00 a.m. on September 12, the division commander knew damn well who would get the nod in Combat Command B. Lovelady did not disappoint. Under a leaden sky, the task force commander threaded around mud bogs and abandoned roadblocks. The lead American vehicle crossed the international boundary at 2:51 p.m. Within minutes, the G.I.s rolled into the village of Roetgen, Germany. As the olive drab tanks clanked down the main street, locals waved white towels and sheets—no stomach to tangle with rumbling Shermans. When he received the radio report, Colonel Boudinot exclaimed, "Tell Lovelady he's famous! Congratulate him and tell him to keep on going!"[71]

Lovelady needed no urging. By 4:02 p.m., the forward tank pla-toon broke out of a dark stand of trees. Just a few yards into the open grass pasture, the first Sherman lurched, the tank commander hold-ing up his right fist. All halt. A few hundred yards ahead the dirt trail ended abruptly. Stretching from left to right, as far as the Americans could see, ran a cordon both medieval and sinister, gray as the scud-ding clouds above. Five densely packed rows of concrete pyramids, most chest-high, the storied dragon's teeth spiked up in grim serried ranks, exactly as the intelligence analysts had warned. Well, here they waited, a formidable obstacle indeed. No tank or truck could drive through the dragon's teeth. A few bursts of machine gun bullets from the east announced that somewhere out there, the Germans saw TF Lovelady. That would do for today. Having already lost two G.I.s killed and ten wounded while destroying two German trucks and taking twenty prisoners, Bill Lovelady backed his vehicles into the wood line.[72]

North of TF Lovelady's probe, Colonel Leander L. Doan led his tanks and infantry forward. In a few sharp roadside fights en route, TF Doan lost three tanks and seven G.I.s killed, plus more than twenty wounded. Battling through, TF Doan halted a few hundred yards south of the last set of trees fronting the dragon's teeth. They reached that spot by 4:38 p.m. on that sad, dim afternoon. Leander Doan, West Point Class of 1927, was a tall, rangy Texan whom wise guys nick-named "Tubby," which he was not. He was, instead, a man who pre-ferred to see things for himself, much like Maurice Rose. Doan kept his vehicles hidden back in the shadowy timber, but he and some staffers carefully worked forward tree to tree. They stopped at the edge of the opening. A broad mat of grass beckoned. Two football fields ahead, athwart any possible advance, squatted the forbidding, silent rows of dragon's teeth. As Doan and his colleagues took a gan-der, a few German civilians and a Romanian man walked up to the Americans. The Romanian stated he'd once served in the German military—when or where, he did not say—and told Doan there were no German forces guarding the frontier. Doan listened, but wisely decided to send out his own men that night to take a closer look.[73]

Three infantry foot patrols sallied forth. The one farthest south came back after a trip 600 yards past the dragon's teeth. They didn't see any hostiles. The next, just about aligned on where Doan made his own visual inspection in the late afternoon, turned around after seeing a "large group of Germans," number and exact activities undefined, on the American side of the concrete barricade. The northern patrol made it to the dragon's teeth and walked around them. The American soldiers found stakes for barbed wire but no such tangle-foot present. The patrol leader believed that the cement tetrahedrons might be cracked with demolitions. As he wasn't an engineer, that represented an educated guess at best. Doan thought the patrol results "incomplete and unsatisfactory."[74] Or, in other words, typical—men like Doan lived in the world of half-truths and suggestive indicators, hints as to what might be. Good commanders connected the dots. Doan's task force would have to work it out under fire in the morning.

What did Rose make of the day's work? The Armored Force School at Fort Knox would advise against using an armored division to crack a fortified line. That duty should go to infantry outfits, with tanks plunging through to exploit the gaps blown, like in Operation Cobra back in Normandy. Well, the 1st Infantry Division near Aachen and the 9th Infantry Division before the Hürtgen Forest had their own challenges. Rose might get an infantry battalion from one or both of these neighbors if Joe Collins felt generous. By and large, though, 3rd Armored Division would have to skin this cat themselves.[75]

So Maurice Rose thought about it. He'd personally gone far enough forward to see the dragon's teeth. Behind that obstacle belt would be German machine gunners in concrete bunkers, 88mm antitank gun cannon crews hidden in camouflaged firing emplacements, and panzers tucked in behind earthen firing ramps. The Germans wanted the Americans to come right at them, head-to-head, shoulder-to-shoulder. Instead, Rose borrowed a tactic from

Georgie Patton. Based on Lovelady's and Doan's reports, Rose decided to "grab 'em by the nose and kick 'em in the ass." Doyle Hickey's CCA would go straight into the Germans, holding the enemy's nose, punching hard. And Boudinot's CCB, with Lovelady sniffing out a seam in his own inimitable way, would burrow from south to north to unhinge the German defensive belt, ass-kicking to follow.[76]

Nobody in the 3rd Armored Division had trained to bust fortified lines. But the veteran officers and NCOs certainly remembered hedgerow tactics. Rose would cash in on that experience. After all, Rose and the other old-timers understood that the West Wall wasn't the Great Wall of China, but instead the usual diabolical German pinball machine, created to bump a confused attacker between mutually supporting pillboxes and bunkers dotted every few hundred yards to ensure crisscrossing fields of fire. You could spend many days—and way too many lives—ensnared in such a fatal labyrinth. The dragon's teeth were simply an extra good deal, stuck there to keep the tanks on the wrong side of the fighting, out of range of the key German machine gun bunkers yet exposed to high-velocity German panzer shots. Aerial photos indicated there was a second such band of dragon's teeth and concrete bunkers five miles east of the first set. The entire West Wall defensive zone extended six miles in depth.[77]

If Hodges and Collins and Monk Dickson had it right, the outmatched Germans would battle back a bit then fold up, like in Operation Cobra or what just happened west of Liege. You'd feel them starting to give way, West Wall or not. Rose would know in a day or two. So be it. The general set the time of attack for 9:00 a.m. on September 13, 1944.[78]

———

Rain drizzled on the olive drab tank hulls west of the dragon's teeth. Rose stood right there at the rim of the forest as Tubby Doan's armored infantry moved forward on foot. The riflemen slipped through the concrete obstacles and fanned out. Engineers trailed behind, dragging satchels of demolitions. Sherman tanks banged at the firing slits of a covering pillbox. No response. Nothing.[79] The rain dripped off helmet edges. Maybe that Romanian guy was right.

He wasn't.

About 12:30 p.m., as the American riflemen wound their way through a draw to go toward the next visible gun emplacement, two German machine guns rasped, the fast yammering of the deadly MG34s. Caught in the open, squads of surprised G.I.s dropped prone, squirming for folds of cover in the broad field. Most were trapped out there. Some sprinted back to the dragon's teeth, where the riflemen tried to hunker down behind the triangular objects. American tank guns punched back at the same pillbox they'd hit ninety minutes earlier. Evidently the Germans inside still wanted to play.[80]

One brave G.I. medic raced forward, sprinting while crouched low to the ground. He went to aid two wounded Americans out near the enemy enclosure. In the lee of the concrete mushroom, the medic reached the pair of stricken infantrymen. The corpsman spoke German and hollered for the Germans inside to surrender. The reply was decidedly negative. With that, the medic dragged his casualties to cover in a nearby dimple of dirt. But those U.S. infantrymen, as well as the ones still stranded in the open expanse or huddled back at the dragon's teeth, were stuck. The constant rain meant no air support today. Of course, American artillery could help, but the only known target—the pillbox—was way too close to the prostrate friendly riflemen.

Doan had to get his tanks through the cement spikes. For two hours, defended by their infantry colleagues and protected by Sherman tank gunnery, soldiers of the 23rd Engineers worked under fire, setting and blasting charges to break apart the dragon's teeth. The rain made the wires slick and the fuses touchy. Even when the explosives went off, the pesky robust pyramids shed a few brittle chips and shrugged off the rest of the blasts. Meanwhile, German machine gun fire, punctuated with occasional mortar bombs, tormented the engineers and ensured the American riflemen did not advance. Two hours crawled by.[81]

About 3:00 p.m., an infantry lieutenant came up on Tubby Doan's radio net. The man was a replacement, so Doan didn't know his name. But the young officer clearly had his head in the game. He sent welcome news. Three hundred yards south of the luckless engineer attempts, the lieutenant and his platoon found a way over the dragon's teeth. It appeared local farmers piled up dirt between the teeth so they could bring tractors and wagons to and from their fields. The earth bridge was in some low ground, handily out of sight of that dangerous German bunker. The passage looked tricky, muddy, and probably mined, too.[82] It had to do.

With Rose's urging, Tubby Doan sent 1st Lieutenant John H. Hoffman, commander of Company E, to take charge. Hoffman led up four tanks to test the mud mound. Hoffman's first M4 Sherman pushed a flail. The implement looked like a pavement roller attachment with chains on it. As the thing rotated, the ground pressure and flapping chains would detonate land mines. That was the idea, at least.

This wet afternoon, the flail didn't find any mines. But the driver found the going too slippery, and the 33-ton tank slid slowly to the side, blocking the path. Brave tankers dismounted and hooked a tow cable to their Sherman; Hoffman got out and linked the other end to his own tank. Then the lieutenant's vehicle engine howled. Mud clots flew.

Nothing. The flail tank stayed mired. A German mortar shell burst a football field away. Somebody had seen the American tank effort going on.

Hoffman waved up a third tank. That one connected up a cable and the two mobile Shermans pulled together. Up popped the flail tank. OK, enough. Hoffman ordered his M4 tanks to move out.[83] Go, go, go.

Doan immediately told the rest of the battalion to follow. Within ten minutes, twenty U.S. Shermans roared through the gap. In Doan's words, "the tanks began to cruise the pillbox area." In quick succession, Tubby Doan and his tankers knocked out six enemy bunkers. The Americans found several 88mm cannons unmanned; their panicked Luftwaffe crews had taken to their heels.[84]

As his Sherman crossed the sloppy dirt pass-through, Doan found out he had a major problem with his infantry, which he very much needed to keep going. Doan's 1st Battalion, 36th Armored Infantry Regiment teammates had been savaged, reporting more than sixty men dead and wounded. The real number might be much higher. The battalion commander, Captain Louis F. Plummer, was out of it, badly hurt. A lieutenant took charge over whatever able-bodied men could be assembled. From way back at Combat Command Reserve headquarters in Eupen, Lieutenant Colonel William R. Orr hurried forward to take charge. But with night coming on, it would probably be morning before the armored infantry reorganized. Right there to see the problem, Maurice Rose sent word to VII Corps: to keep going, we need a battalion from the nearby 1st Infantry Division. Luckily, Major General Joe Collins had anticipated the problem. The 1st Battalion, 26th Infantry Regiment would arrive after nightfall.[85] Problem averted.

The Germans, however, had other ideas. A few minutes after the American tanks began to shoot up the first line of pillboxes, the Germans unleashed what Doan called "a murderous artillery fire." Worse, as the tanks pushed east to get clear of the shell bursts, they thumped right into a second row of bunkers with panzers and 88mm cannons interspersed. Several brave German *panzergrenadiers* from the 9th Panzer Division—those guys again—even ambushed four separate Sherman tanks using *panzerfaust* rocket launchers. These Germans weren't going anywhere. Without their infantry partners to go after the German *panzerfaust* teams, Doan's tanks suffered horribly. Ten Shermans went up in flames, to include the battalion commander and a company commander. Tough Lieutenant Hoffman went off the radio net—he was wounded, his tank immobilized.[86] The great triumph turned to wormwood in a few tragic minutes.

By midnight, the Americans had only eight tanks still working east of the dragon's teeth. Although the 1st Infantry Division's battalion marched in to do their part, the 1st Battalion, 36th Infantry Regiment was in bad shape. So were CCA's two tank outfits; Lieutenant Colonel Rich Richardson's task force had gone into the maelstrom, too. At Maurice Rose's order, Lieutenant Colonel Sam Hogan's tanks and infantry were on their way up from Eupen, but they'd only allow CCA to hold on—maybe—to the narrow crack they'd clawed through the first band of the West Wall.

The long, brutal day had levied quite a toll on Combat Command A, with dozens killed and hundreds wounded. Disrupted communications meant nobody, from Rose down to the squad sergeants, could be sure of the actual numbers. Two battalion commanders down, numerous company commanders gone, three battalions shredded, men missing, horrific wounds—and Maurice Rose witnessed every bit of it from all too close up.[87] The Germans stood strong. It sure didn't feel like a breakthrough.

———

While Major General Maurice Rose watched Colonel Tubby Doan's slugfest to the north, Combat Command B attacked in the south. Painful as CCA's West Wall purgatory became, in the cold calculus of combat, the sacrifice might have accomplished its purpose by grabbing German attention. Rose's plan envisioned hitting hard with CCA and thereby freeing up CCB to pry a hole into the German depths. A lot rode on this prong of the division's push.

Thanks to Lieutenant Colonel Bill Lovelady's reconnaissance in force on September 12, Colonel Truman Boudinot's Combat Command B marked two likely lanes of passage through the dragon's teeth. Accordingly, Boudinot committed Lieutenant Colonel Rosewell King's task force to the north and Task Force Lovelady to the south in a side by side advance.[88] One or both would get through.

The old sweats, of course, guessed it would be Lovelady. It usually was.

Whereas CCA tried an infantry attack to lead the way, CCB's two task forces went with the old formula: send a bullet, not a man. As engineers slipped forward to yank cable, cement blocks, and steel girders out of the single-vehicle gap trails discovered in the dragon's teeth—presumably put there to permit German counterattacks, like sally ports in a feudal castle—CCB's field artillery battalions opened up. They smothered identified cement bunkers with shell after shell. The six howitzer crews of Battery A, 391st Armored Field Artillery Battalion, reported shooting 581 105mm projectiles. Their impacts barely scarred the thick domes of the pillboxes, a tribute to German engineering and the sadistic overseers of Organisation Todt, the Reich slave labor directorate. But those inside the sturdy bastions evidently suffered drastically from the relentless shake, rattle, and roll. Sped by the artillery suppressive fires, both TF King and TF Lovelady scooted right through the five rows of dragon's teeth. By day's end, the task forces were locked in head-to-head engagements with the denizens of the next set of pillboxes, the back end of the first fortified belt.[89] So far, so good.

Then it wasn't. When the first barrier of cement teeth were overrun, German engineers focused on the obvious American routes. Before the lead Shermans rounded the bend, the Germans detonated buried charges, blowing holes in the none-too-good roadways. Both TF King and TF Lovelady found their paths blocked. As their American riflemen and engineers worked to secure and clear the holes, German mortars dropped round after round. The foot soldiers suffered losses, first in ones and twos, then by fives. The Germans understood just how to use their obstacles like flytraps to draw in the G.I. ground troops, then hammer them. Task Force King lost two tanks and a lot of riflemen as night fell. With the rain and the loss of leaders, King couldn't tabulate the casualties.[90] King's men needed help.

In front of TF Lovelady, as their riflemen struggled, a pair of Panthers of the 9th Panzer Division appeared. The big panzers drilled holes through four U.S. Shermans and a half-track, killing multiple American infantrymen and tankers and wounding even more. That did it for the day. With his attached 36th Infantry Regiment rifle company woefully shy on healthy officers and sergeants, Lovelady pleaded for more riflemen. King seconded the request; his infantry, too, had been torn up. Apprised of the situation by radio, Maurice Rose committed his last armored infantry battalion, CCR's 3rd Battalion, 36th Infantry Regiment. They wouldn't get to CCB until midnight. Colonel Boudinot sent them to buttress TF King. The 83rd Recon Battalion, Rose's final uncommitted element, fell in behind TF Lovelady to provide more combat power.[91] The scouts with their peeps and armored cars and light tanks were completely wrong for the job. But they were all the 3rd Armored Division had left.

Come another gray, rainy morning on September 14, 1944, both task forces advanced, fighting all the way. Another costly day ensued. Rosewell King himself was hit, his second wound in two and a half weeks. This time, he wouldn't be coming back. The changeover to Major Herbert M. Mills slowed the task force. They fell in behind TF Lovelady.[92] It all came down to that bunch. Again.

Somehow, by tenacious efforts, TF Lovelady threaded through German roadblocks and past bunkers. After blowing away a German antitank gun crew using Sherman gunfire, infantry maneuver, and artillery bursts, Lovelady approached the second belt of dragon's teeth by sunset on September 14.[93] One more good push . . .

They got there, short of ammunition, shy on tanks, not many infantry, out of everything but guts. By the end of September 15, 1944—drizzling, misty, no air for the third day running—Lovelady's exhausted G.I.s stood at the far end of the second band of the West Wall. They'd bulled through, barely. Ferocious German counterattacks stopped them cold. Lovelady's final thrust cost the Americans seven tanks, a tank destroyer, and an ambulance, and even worse, five men killed and thirty-three wounded. That sad outcome added to the entire division's list of 953 soldiers killed and wounded, plus 79 M4 Shermans burned out, with more travail to come as TF Lovelady and the other forward task forces dug in and held on to their dearly-won, needle-thin corridors through the West Wall.[94] In front of Bill Lovelady and his G.I.s the high road led to Cologne and the Rhine River. Never Never Land. They'd almost made it. Almost.

Almost.

CHAPTER 5

The Dark Wood of Error

It was Passchendaele with tree bursts . . .

Ernest Hemingway, *Across the River and Into the Trees*[1]

For the Allies, September 1944 became the month of "almost." Maurice Rose's near-run puncture of the West Wall joined all the rest. War is a contest of time and distance. A few days or a few miles can make all the difference. Up and down the Western Front, the Allies got very, very close. But not close enough.

To the north, Montgomery's massive airborne-armor operation took a bridge over the Dutch Rhine River but the brave British "paras" couldn't hold the prize against alert Waffen SS panzer outfits. British tankers, American airborne troops, and Polish paratroopers fought fiercely to get through, but it was not to be. The defeat left Monty in possession of a finger of liberated Netherlands turf pointing toward the Dutch Rhine at the price of 17,000 dead and wounded British and American soldiers. Monty tsk-tsk'd it away as "90% successful." Even he didn't believe his bunkum this time.[2]

To the south, George Patton's great attack to seize the Saar basin sliced into the French/German borderlands, reaching the fortress ring around Metz. That's as far as the Third Army went. As Patton wrote to his wife, Beatrice, "For the last three days we have had as bitter and protracted fighting as I have ever encountered. The Huns [Germans] are desperate and are attacking in half a dozen places." Metz did not fall. Instead, Patton's troops bogged down in the network of forts amid "nasty country where it rains every day and the whole wealth of the people consists in assorted manure piles." Inconclusive engagements exacted 16,618 American casualties.[3] The famous Third Army had faltered.

In First Army, VII Corps did the dirty work in that supposedly best axis of advance into Germany around Aachen. There, the triumph of hope over experience dashed the former and added all too much to the latter. Aachen remained in German hands. Outside Charlemagne's one-time capital, the 1st Infantry Division had yet to breach the second line of the West Wall. Maurice Rose and his beat-up 3rd Armored Division held a toehold just past the German fortified belts. To Rose's south, the 9th Infantry Division in the dank, haunted Hürtgen Forest hadn't even gotten through band one of the West Wall. This first month, ensnared in the West Wall, resulted in nearly 16,000 casualties for First Army. Too many came from VII Corps.[4] Among the chipped cement jungle of the West Wall in the lee of that glum September, it seemed like World War II ended and World War I broke out.

––––––

"By this time," wrote a veteran rifle company commander, "the 3d Armored Division was like an athlete who breaks the tape but falls spent and exhausted."[5] The analogy is compelling as far as the division's depleted condition, but not quite right in terms of achievements. Yes, the division pierced the West Wall. Yet the race wasn't over. It certainly hadn't been won.

Reluctantly, in accord with orders from VII Corps, the 3rd Armored Division went over to the defense on September 25, 1944. The worn-down task forces of Combat Command A and Combat

Command B outposted an arc running through the industrial town of Stolberg, the head of its namesake corridor that stretched thirty-three miles to Cologne. No American tankers or riflemen would be going that way anytime soon. In the duty log of Task Force Lovelady, the daily notations for late September 1944 repeated the same four words: "situation still the same." The monotonous weather remained "rainy with fog." German artillery and mortar fire added to the misery. Both sides backed off, fought out for now. [6]

Late September's lowering skies and steady drizzle coincided with the Jewish High Holy Days. The Jewish G.I.s in the 3rd Armored Division marked the occasion, more or less, as duty permitted. Maurice Rose acknowledged nothing to his men. He never did. What he carried in his heart can only be guessed. Not far to the east of the Americans defending Stolberg, Nazi SS detachments carried out unspeakable acts at scores of forlorn concentration camps, like the West Wall the awful handiwork of Organisation Todt. Nobody in the 3rd Armored Division, not even Maurice Rose, the rabbi's son wearing two stars, realized the full import of these sordid matters. But from Major General Rose to the rawest replacement private, American soldiers certainly recognized the abject brutality of their Nazi foes, especially the prisoner-slaughtering Waffen SS. All heard dark hints of the tragic plight of Jews in German hands—nothing confirmed, but surely believable given what more than a few Germans did on the field of battle, let alone the bloody crimes promised in Adolf Hitler's public ravings. With the Allied forces stalled at the German frontier, hideous tortures and killings inside the Reich not only continued, they accelerated.[7] That, too, was the consequence of almost breaking through. Such thoughts could cross one's mind on the eve of Yom Kippur.

Killing Germans, breaking through, winning the war—that's what could be done, what must be done. But to take up the fight again, the 3rd Armored Division needed to regroup, rearm, and replenish. The First Army rumor mill suggested that Lieutenant

General Courtney Hodges intended to renew the offensive on October 1, 1944.[8] So for Rose's division, every day counted.

Sorting out the leadership came first. Rose hadn't even been in command two months, but the attrition among key officers had been horrendous. Some might point to the commanders dismissed by Rose from the 3rd Ordnance (Maintenance) Battalion, the 83rd Recon Battalion, the 33rd Armored Regiment, and the 36th Infantry Regiment. Those removals, while harsh, paled in comparison to the scything administered by the enemy: one regimental commander out of three and fifteen battalion commanders among the nine tank/infantry task forces. The 1st Battalion of the 32nd Armored Regiment suffered the death or wounding of five commanders; two others filled in briefly. The 2nd Battalion of the 32nd, the 1st Battalion of the 33rd, and the 1st Battalion of the 36th Armored Infantry Regiment each went through three commanding officers, a total of nine, with seven killed or wounded. The 2nd Battalion of the 36th sustained one commander killed and another wounded, as well as a short period under the authority of an interim filler. The 3rd Battalion of the 36th had one commander wounded and another placeholder who passed through. Two determined officers, lieutenant colonels Elwyn W. Blanchard and Rosewell H. King, returned from battlefield wounds only to get hit again and evacuated again. Two more, Captain (later Major) Thomas G. Tousey, Jr. and Major R. T. Dunn, also came back to command after being wounded; they'd made it, so far. These many change-outs occurred while the division battled to compress the Falaise Pocket, pursued broken German formations across France, confronted the enemy at Mons, attacked across Belgium, and assaulted the West Wall. Casualties among company commanders, platoon leaders, and key noncommissioned officers followed suit.[9] Yet the division fought on, next man up. Just enough good men hung in there. The amazing thing about Lieutenant Colonel Bill Lovelady wasn't simply his combat acumen, but his success in evading German bullets. The man was rolling sevens on every turn of the dice. Sooner or later, you'd turn up snake eyes.

That certainly applied to Major General Maurice Rose, too. To an extent, the killings and woundings of the battalion and company leadership reflected the example set by Maurice Rose. Because the general went forward, so did the rest. They could do no less. Brigadier General Doyle O. Hickey of CCA and Brigadier General (as of September 24, 1944) Truman E. Boudinot did as Rose did.[10] Like Bill Lovelady, somehow the 3rd Armored Division's three generals failed to run into all the German metal flying around. But the more G.I. leaders moved up under fire, the more the odds tilted in favor of the adversary.

Good fortune might have graced the 3rd Armored trio, but American generals in northwest Europe in 1944 enjoyed no special dispensation from death. Four had already died. Brigadier General Don F. Pratt of the 101st Airborne Division was killed in a glider crash on June 6, 1944. Brigadier General Teddy Roosevelt, Jr. (son of the 26th president) of the 4th Infantry Division succumbed to a heart attack on July 12, 1944. Lieutenant General Lesley J. McNair, an observer from stateside, died in the July 25 short bombings related to Operation Cobra. Brigadier General James E. Wharton of the 28th Infantry Division fell to German rifle fire on August 12, 1944.[11]

Did the last one get Rose's attention? Was that why Joe Collins chided him in Namur? It doesn't appear Rose took it that way. On September 21, 1944, the division commander planted Omaha Forward on the grounds of the Hans Friedrich Prym House right at the southeast edge of embattled Stolberg. German bullets, mortar bombs, artillery shells, and Luftwaffe night intruders arrived all too often. When he wasn't taking his chances at Omaha Forward, Rose continued to spend most of his time with the front line elements.[12] You couldn't go after the Germans on a map sheet. Rose did it his way. See and be seen. Sooner or later, though, the bad guys would see you first. It's best not to dwell on that. Rose didn't.

Two holes in the leadership demanded immediate solutions. Both had nagged at Rose for seven weeks. The temporary fixes hardly sufficed and distracted the major general from his primary duties. Some of the 3rd Armored Division's commander's tactical mistakes in the long advance traced directly to his efforts to work around this pair of command problems. It was past time for remedies.

The 83rd Armored Reconnaissance Battalion hadn't fulfilled its role as the "cav of the cav." Too often, the scouts couldn't chart the key routes, locate critical bridges, or pinpoint the opposing positions. Or if the recon men found these things, word didn't get back, or filtered back too late to matter. The 83rd had no shortage of courage and skill at the company and platoon levels. But the battalion needed a quality commander, a real cavalryman, a Jeb Stuart or a Phil Sheridan. In September 1944, one emerged. Lieutenant Colonel Prentice E. "Mike" Yeomans came from the 703rd Tank Destroyer Battalion. The motto of that community was "Seek, Strike, and Destroy." Yeomans epitomized the ethos: aggressive and smart, "leather-lunged and capable," according to subordinates.[13] From the day Mike Yeomans took charge, Rose never had to look for the 83rd again. They were ever out front, hunting Germans.

The 36th Armored Infantry Regiment also needed an upgrade. Not at the battalion, company, and platoon level—the resilient riflemen, their officers, and their sergeants led the way under fire in almost every clash. Because they participated in almost every attack, almost every defense, and the vast majority of the patrol actions, the half-track infantry suffered the highest losses in the division.[14] There were never enough armored infantrymen on hand. In the deadly maze of the West Wall, that deficiency hobbled the entire 3rd Armored Division. Tanks could take ground. But only rifle troops could hold it.

Thus the 36th Armored Infantry Regiment had to be sound from bottom to top. The bottom and middle worked, although at high cost. But the high end hadn't been right since Colonel William Cornog's death near Mortain on August 9. The various backfills did what they could, but it wasn't sufficient. In Belgium, experienced cavalry officer

Colonel Carl J. Rohsenberger stepped in from his usual role commanding the Division Trains, but that solution billed the division twice. Rohsenberger never fully gripped the infantry regiment, and the trains troops languished without their colonel's attention. So the armored infantry contingent and division logistics both limped, and did so right when the division required a full-court press at the West Wall.

Moreover, aside from inspiring, organizing, and directing the division's half-track rifle forces, the colonel of the 36th Armored Infantry Regiment also commanded Combat Command Reserve, the division's third mobile striking arm. That organization hadn't really done much besides act as a holding pen for uncommitted units. Combat Command Reserve's constituent battalions, notably TF Hogan, fought under CCA and CCB, and did so effectively. Yet CCR itself contributed little. A good brigadier would be the ideal way to go, but the U.S. Army only authorized two. To run the 36th and CCR, Maurice Rose asked for a man ready to get his star, the best colonel available.

He got him. Colonel Robert L. "Bobby" Howze, Jr., like Tubby Doan and Jack Welborn, graduated from West Point, Class of 1925. Bobby Howze hailed from a West Point cavalry family. His father had earned the Medal of Honor battling the Lakota in 1891, then became a famous general in World War I. Bobby's younger brother Hamilton served in the 1st Armored Division in Italy in 1943–1945 and, like his father, eventually wore stars. So did Bobby in years to come. He was the right commander for Combat Command Reserve. Rose remembered Bobby Howze from the 1930–1931 course at the Cavalry School at Fort Riley, Kansas.[15] Some might have gone with an infantryman. Not Rose. Credentials didn't matter. Rose sought results. With Howze, he'd get them.

————

Maurice Rose graded hard when it came to his subordinate commanders. How about the rank and file? What about them?

The division fought—that's for sure. Bravery and drive character-ized the effort. Time after time, at Rânes, Fromental, Soissons, Mons, Namur, Huy, Liege, and the West Wall, the division kept going when lesser outfits might have slowed or stopped. Good men with initiative—Hickey, Boudinot, Doan, Lovelady, Hogan—found a way. The sergeants made sure their tank crews shot true, their riflemen advanced under fire, their gunners pumped out shells on target, their engineers bridged and breached, their medics saved lives, and their mechanics kept 'em rolling. When a public affairs officer mentioned a headline from a Jack Thompson article in the *Chicago Tribune* that read "Tank Men from Chicago Help Beat Nazi Best, Third Division Feat Wins Name 'Spearhead,'" Rose jumped on it like a bridge across the Meuse.[16] Spearhead!

The division didn't really have a nickname. Some officers pro-posed "Bayou Blitz" because the division formed at Camp Polk, Loui-siana. OK, but not right. Under Major General Leroy H. Watson, about a million years ago, the division went by "Always Dependable," which nobody liked and nobody used. The 1st Armored Division was "Old Ironsides," the 2nd Armored the flashy "Hell on Wheels"—George Patton there—and the younger armored outfits also sported slick monikers. The 5th went by "Victory." The 6th called itself the "Super Sixth." The 7th favored "Lucky Seventh." As for the 8th, they chose "Thundering Herd," the 9th liked "Phantom," the 10th preferred "Tiger," the 11th went by "Thunderbolt," and the 12th decided on "Hellcats." Not to be out-catted, or jinxed by their number, the 13th selected "Black Cats," embracing the theme. The 14th Armored Divi-sion elected to go with "Liberator." The 16th used "Armadillo." The 20th invented the label "Armoraiders." The 4th Armored Division didn't have a nickname, although veterans of the 4th liked to say their number was "Name Enough." Clearly, the G.I.s of 1944 liked nicknames. For the 3rd Armored Division, "Spearhead" was a clear winner. It told every new replacement that he'd joined the division that cracked the West Wall.[17]

A lot of fresh faces heard about "Spearhead" when they arrived at the end of September 1944. The division lacked 1,341 soldiers (80 officers and 1,261 enlisted).[18] To a bean counter, the division remained at 90 percent strength. So no big deal, right?

Wrong. Aggregate numbers briefed well on the wall charts at Twelfth Army Group and First Army. But that missing 10 percent of the 3rd Armored Division represented a lot of combat power. Most casualties came from the infantry, then the tank crews. The recon battalion, engineers, and artillery suffered, too, but not usually in high numbers. With Maurice Rose's forward leadership style, service troops, signal sections, and command post teams also came under fire and lost people. But the infantrymen and tankers endured the worst. As Lieutenant General George Patton warned, when a division "has lost four thousand men, its offensive value is zero, because ninety-two percent of these four thousand men are riflemen." Thankfully, the 3rd Armored Division hadn't been ground down that far. But with 2,389 infantrymen and 4,848 tankers needed at full strength, the division's no-kidding maneuver combat power stood not at a healthy 90 percent but at about 82 percent overall, with the infantry down to an alarming 51 percent.[19] In an outfit that depended on the tank/infantry team to fight, that had to be addressed. Rebuilding was in order.

It wasn't as easy as plug and play. Most replacements came in with infantry training; few tankers showed up. The forecasters back stateside underestimated the tank crew loss rate. As one inspector noted, "The handling and delivery of armored replacements has been a colossal failure." So it was. The 3rd Armored Division couldn't wait for this to sort out. Among arriving replacement troops, men trained as infantry had to be taught how to be tankers. They were fed into experienced M4 Sherman and M5 Stuart crews and taught in very quick frontline familiarization sessions.[20] Of course, tanker replacements had about as much learning incentive as any humans alive—if they wanted to stay that way.

The U.S. Army replacement system has been rightly pilloried as impersonal and numbers-driven, but in the fall of 1944, those tendencies broke in favor of the 3rd Armored Division and the rest of the diminished U.S. divisions in northwest Europe. Shaking the bushes to find more manpower, especially riflemen and tankers, the powers that be in the Pentagon curtailed two selective educational efforts brimming with high-quality privates, smart and physically fit. With more than enough pilots in the pipeline already, the aviation cadet ranks gave up 24,000 flight candidates to the ground forces. The Army Specialized Training Program (ASTP), a curriculum that taught chosen men to be military engineers and scientists, forwarded 73,000 college students to frontline outfits. Among those who found themselves shifted from the ASTP to combat battalions were men like comedian and filmmaker Mel Brooks, Senator Bob Dole, diplomat Henry Kissinger, New York City Mayor Ed Koch, and author Kurt Vonnegut. The 3rd Armored Division didn't inherit any of the famous-people-to-be, but received its share of former flight cadets and ASTP G.I.s. Most went right into the 36th Armored Infantry Regiment and the six tank battalions.[21]

Some of those coming to the Spearhead Division in September were not rookies, but old friends returning from wounds, non-battle injuries, and illnesses. Even that good news story became tainted in bureaucratic folderol. Number crunchers at First Army, determined to address statistical deficits and priorities, proposed to dispatch returning G.I.s to whichever unit needed them most rather than sending them back to their former outfits. It's not wise for a rear-echelon clerk armed with a clipboard to try to enforce such an inane policy on combat veterans with M1 rifles in hand. Most returning soldiers went right back to their original units. The paperwork eventually caught up.[22]

In other armies or other times, the 3rd Armored Division would have been pulled to a rear area to refit and retrain. Some of that happened near Stolberg. Still, G.I.s had to defend their posts. Every day division soldiers patrolled and exchanged fire with the Germans. It was the roughest brand of on-the-job training. Veteran lieutenants became captains. Able privates earned sergeants' stripes. Hundreds of newcomers filled out the tank crews and rifle squads. And men kept dying and bleeding, with twenty-five more dead and another six dozen wounded from September 25 through 30, 1944, a supposedly quiet period.[23] Even so, the grim reaper always got his share.

Sergeants and soldiers in an armored division can go only as far as their equipment will allow. For weeks now, the tanks, half-tracks, self-propelled howitzers, trucks, and peeps had all been "rode hard and put up wet," to use the old cavalry adage.[24] That wasn't healthy for horses or vehicles.

According to the U.S. Army technical manuals, drivers and ordnance teams should have performed all kinds of checks and services on their iron steeds. To do such things by the book required several hours a day for a complicated armored vehicle like an M4 Sherman tank or an M7 self-propelled howitzer or an M3 half-track. That degree of attention happened back at Fort Knox, Kentucky, but not much overseas. In day-to-day bouts of combat split by sixty-mile motor marches, squirting some grease, topping off the oil, and pouring in gasoline had to do.[25] Then you dealt with maintenance problems as they cropped up. With each passing day, more did.

The M4 Sherman tanks exemplified the newly christened Spearhead Division. By the last days of September 1944, the fleet seemed shaky indeed. Only about a hundred Shermans of 232 assigned had made the entire run from Normandy to the West Wall. With newly issued tanks added in, the division reported 153 Shermans operational on September 18, putting the force at two-thirds strength.[26]

Even that amount was deceptive. Eighty-five Shermans could only move in the lowest three forward gears out of five. Thirty crawled along strictly in the lowest gear. As well as transmission troubles, problems dogged the engines, the starters, the on-board radios, the automatic turret traverse mechanism—when working, a huge advantage over the hand-cranked German models—the suspension system, and the treads.[27] If any one of those items failed at an inopportune time in combat, well ... that's where all those missing tanks went.

The September hiatus came none too soon for overworked M4 Sherman mechanics and tankers. Long-deferred maintenance deficiencies received attention. Tanks received overdue servicing. The basic soundness of the Sherman tank allowed recovery from a lot of lapses.

In addition to fixing up the older tanks, some fortunate crews drew new ones. To bring battalions back up to full strength, the Spearhead Division received M4A3 Sherman variants featuring a new Ford V-8 engine (500 horsepower) instead of the standard 9-cylinder Wright radial engine (400 horsepower). The 20 percent extra gusto sure helped in the autumn mud.[28]

Sixty-five of the new M4A3 tanks also included a more powerful, longer-barreled 76mm main gun. It had been tested in Italy on tank destroyers and seemed better than the Sherman's usual 75mm gun. The veterans weren't convinced. The 76mm armor-piercing rounds still couldn't reliably punch through the front end of a Panther or a Tiger. But now and then, within a hundred yards, the gun did the job.[29] It reminded you of the bazooka, a fine weapon if you sought the Medal of Honor.

———

The German panzers still waited out there. While Maurice Rose's Spearheaders reorganized, so did their enemies. Somehow, with the Allies driving hard, the Germans stopped them at the West Wall, then rebuilt the gray-clad ranks. German generals deemed the recovery the "Miracle of the West." Adolf Hitler took full credit, of course.[30]

Hitler's Nazi Party officials rallied all of Germany to the cause. Mixing patriotic exhortations with the urgings of Luger pistols, German authorities rounded up teenagers and old men for *volksgrenadier* (people's soldiers) divisions structured around a backbone of veteran officers and NCOs. These units bore familiar numbers and titles and looked fine as pins stuck in the führer's maps. In reality, training fell well below traditional German army standards; Nazi rah-rah had to make up the shortfall. In the pillboxes of the West Wall, backed by a few panzer outfits, they'd do. Such draconian drag- nets raised German army strength to seven and a half million soldiers, admittedly a broad use of that title for the latest levies.[31] Still, a sixteen-year-old with a *panzerfaust* (and the guts, or naiveté, to use it) could blow open a Sherman as well as any hardened Ger- man paratrooper. Quantity still counted for something.

Shoved back to the Reich frontier, German forces benefited from much shorter supply lines. Although lashed by Allied heavy bombers, German factories in the autumn of 1944 cranked out 5,505 panzers (including 644 Panthers and 112 Tigers), 9,000 artillery pieces, 100,000 machine guns, 750,000 rifles, and 1.25 million tons of ammunition, more than enough for a two-front war (three counting Italy). German soldiers did not lack for arms.[32]

There were unanticipated threats, too. Tinkering in the glow of what British Prime Minister Winston L. S. Churchill called "the lights of perverted science," ingenious German designers delivered Hitler's long-promised "wonder weapons": Me-262 jet fighters, V-1 pulse-jet cruise missiles, and long-range V-2 rockets. Senior Allied military commanders correctly assessed these devices as intriguing stunts, too little, too late. Those on the receiving end begged to differ. Waves of V-1s and V-2s rained down on London, Paris, and Antwerp and other randomly chosen spots, killing thousands of civilians. Ger- man engineers and SS guards compelled slave laborers to produce the two types of "vengeance weapons" in an underground lair at Nor- dhausen, some 250 miles northeast of Stolberg. Night after night, soldiers of the 3rd Armored Division looked up as the so-called buzz bombs sputtered overhead, bound for points west. One Spearhead officer even watched two V-2 rockets shoot up from some remote site on the eastern horizon.[33] The G.I.s didn't quite understand what they were seeing. But they knew it wasn't good.

Doing something about the V-weapons wasn't really 3rd Armored Division's problem. Doing something to break past the German border zone was. Getting well on manpower and armaments recast the Spearhead. What to do with it? That was the question.

Up at SHAEF, Ike Eisenhower offered the answer: the broad front. Monty and Patton hadn't delivered, probably because Ike did not pick one, and so the campaign fell between two stools. Eisenhower didn't wallow in recriminations. That wasn't his way. He looked ahead. The Allies were where they were, stuck along the Reich boundary in dodgy terrain. Any idea of a quick win blew away with the brown autumn leaves. The trends, the overall math, still strongly favored the Allies. The Russians would do their part in the east. So the strategy appeared only too obvious: keep up the pressure. Go with the broad front. Everybody give it a shove. Try to get to the Rhine River before spring 1945.[34] It had all the originality of the Battle of the Somme circa 1916. Hopefully it wouldn't end up with the same butcher's bill.

The broad front turned things over to the army group commanders. In the north, Montgomery's Twenty-First Army Group followed their field marshal's proclivities and tidied up the battlefield. The Canadians, with British help and one U.S. division, doggedly cleared German hold-outs from along the Scheldt estuary. Other British forces, with two American divisions assigned, fought to advance slowly through the Dutch-German border country. In the far south, the American-French Sixth Army Group waded into the forested Vosges Mountains of Alsace, pressing bunker by bunker the wrong way through the east-facing 1940 French Maginot Line.[35] Eisenhower didn't expect much from either end of the Allied front.

Ike hoped for better work from his West Point classmate. This led General Omar N. Bradley to consult his wall of maps. The usual bafflement followed.

Bradley's Twelfth Army Group fronted on three potential avenues to the Rhine: Aachen/Stolberg-Cologne, Monschau-Bonn, and

Metz-Saar-Frankfurt. The arithmetic wasn't too daunting: two armies, three corridors. Third Army matched up with the Saar, and you never had to prod Patton.[36] Bad weather and tough Germans would slow Third Army, but he'd find a way. He always did.

First Army had a choice: Aachen or Monschau? Bradley didn't leave this to Courtney Hodges. He steered him to choose the Aachen lane, and even brought up a new headquarters, the Ninth Army, to handle the stretch north of Aachen up to Monty's area. As for that Monschau axis, it meant traversing the dense, rugged Ardennes Forest, known to the Germans as the Schnee Eifel (snow mountains). Stay out of there. It's not tank country. Bradley discounted the area and used it to rest battered divisions and acclimate new ones. Of course, the Germans launched an entire panzer army through the Ardennes in May 1940. They'd crossed it in August 1914, too.[37] But they wouldn't do that again, would they?

Hodges had a pretty clear task—force the Aachen-Stolberg corridor and press to the Rhine River at Cologne. The reasonable solution would be to turn things over to Major General Joe Collins's VII Corps and use the rest of First Army to make limited attacks to engage the rest of the Germans in and around the West Wall. Taking Aachen, a city of 165,000, wasn't crucial. You could work around it. Once you made it to the Rhine, Aachen might well drop in your lap like a ripe peach. The 3rd Armored Division already had gotten by Aachen, as had the 1st Infantry Division.

Even with the answer filled in on his test sheet, you never knew with Courtney Hodges. The former Fort Benning instructor also prided himself on his interest in map-board tactics. He rarely spent time with forward units. When he did, he stopped by corps headquarters, and now and then dropped in to see division command posts, usually on quiet days. He only graced Spearhead's Omaha Forward on five brief visits (November 1944, twice in February 1945, and twice in March 1945), plus the time he saw Rose in the streets of Rânes back in August 1944. Hodges, the Great War veteran, passed his days like one of that conflict's infamous "château generals," staring at his large map, drawing and redrawing unit boundaries.[38] He was looking for something and not quite seeing it.

Never quick to decide, or to decide at all, Hodges demanded reams of information, more and more, as if within that mass of papers and numbers a diamond of insight might gleam. A subordinate corps G-3 officer who'd served up and down the front in 1944 recalled that "when you did a situation report for Third Army you showed the positions of the regiments. When you did one for First Army, you had to show platoons."[39] He was probably exaggerating. But not by much.

Hodges said little. The man was a sphinx. And unlike Maurice Rose, also a general of few words, Hodges seldom stirred from his maps and sheaves of dispatches. With Rose, presence and actions spoke. With Hodges, you got almost nothing. When he did comment, the words made your skin crawl. At one corps headquarters, Hodges's aide took this note:

> General Hodges, who has felt since the beginning that too many of these battalions and regiments of ours have tried to flank and skirt and never meet the enemy straight on, was opposed to the maneuver outlined, believing it safer, sounder, and in the end, quicker, to keep smashing ahead, without any tricky, uncertain business of possibly exposing yourself to being cut off.[40]

There you go. Head down, hit the line, three yards and a cloud of dust. It worked, after a fashion—a very blood-begrimed fashion—at the Meuse-Argonne in 1918 for then Major Hodges. Now Lieutenant General Hodges issued the orders for an entire field army for an offensive to reach the Rhine. He wanted to go on October 1, 1944, but wretched weather postponed the start twenty-four hours.

It wouldn't be another Operation Cobra, a Collins product created when the more open-minded Bradley ran First Army. This time,

Hodges's First Army staff officers cooked up their own version. It was pretty thin gruel. Hodges chose not to concentrate; instead, each corps would attack, and each seemed to be the main effort, which meant no definite focus existed. First, XIX Corps and VII Corps would encircle and then seize Aachen. Then XIX Corps was to head toward Düsseldorf and VII Corps would drive to Cologne, both on the Rhine River. To the south, V Corps was to push east from Monschau through the Ardennes toward Bonn and the Rhine. In other words, given two possible routes to the Rhine, First Army selected both, and added the Düsseldorf angle, too. Evenly dispensing combat power, First Army allocated two infantry and an armored division to each corps, and then gave each corps eleven artillery battalions. To reduce Aachen, XIX Corps and VII Corps gained two more artillery battalions apiece. Even in that, both corps had priority of fires, and so neither really had the stick.[41]

As an afterthought, a separate order to VII Corps directed Collins to clear German troops out of the Hürtgen Forest, a place of endless G.I. woe.[42] All of these geographic objectives—Aachen, Düsseldorf, Cologne, the Hürtgen, Bonn, the Rhine—represented the worst possible examples of big hand, little map. For a general who wanted platoon positions posted and drew his own unit boundaries, Courtney Hodges simply didn't grasp the awful nature of the terrain before First Army. In classic Western Front 1917 style, the general issued his orders and retired to his chambers.

————

Joe Collins never wanted to take Aachen. In the initial run to the West Wall, Lightning Joe desired a quick rupture and a follow-on leap to the Rhine River. Messing around inside an enemy-held city made no sense. When overstrained Allied logistics, exhausted troops, foul weather, and the ever-determined Germans conspired to block a fast pass into Germany, Aachen again came up in late September 1944. At the urging of the 1st Infantry Division commander, whose

Airborne forces gliders circle and land in Normandy early on the evening of June 6, 1944. The major parachute and glider assaults occurred that same day in the predawn hours. The hedgerows of the bocage terrain are evident.

A G.I. inspects a knocked-out German *sturmgeschütz IV* assault gun in Normandy in June 1944. The 75mm high-velocity cannon could destroy an American Sherman tank or fire high-explosive rounds into American paratrooper positions. An onboard machine gun was deadly against U.S. ground troops. Panzers of this type led the German counterattack at Carentan on D+7.

An American soldier aims an M9 2.36-inch rocket launcher. Known as the bazooka, this antitank weapon fired a projectile that could penetrate German panzers, but only from a very close range and only if aimed at the side, rear, top, or bottom of a hostile armored vehicle. Shots at the frontal armor of a German Panther or Tiger would likely bounce off. German troops used a larger (3.5-inch) version called the *panzerschreck* (tank fright).

Major General J. Lawton "Lightning Joe" Collins commanded the VII Corps in 1944–1945 in Northwest Europe. Collins traveled in an M20 armored car with a mounted security platoon for protection. He spent a lot of time forward with fighting units. The 3rd Armored Division served under Collins for all but a few days of the war.

A U.S. Army M4 Sherman tank with "rhino" hedgerow cutters breaks a dirt wall in Normandy in July 1944. This is a training exercise, with supporting infantrymen riding on the tank, although these same methods were used during Operation Cobra in July 1944 and during the Falaise Pocket fighting that followed. These breaching devices enabled the Americans to smash through German bocage defenses.

A P-47 Thunderbolt fighter-bomber fires two rockets. Armed with rockets, bombs, and .50-caliber machine guns, these aircraft ravaged German forces in the Falaise Pocket in August 1944. To survive under the relentless Allied air attacks, German units were compelled to move by night and take advantage of bad weather.

Two wrecked Panthers sit abandoned in Normandy in the summer of 1944. Allied airpower, artillery, tanks, and infantry combined to devastate German panzer forces in the Falaise Pocket in August 1944. The 3rd Armored Division played a key role in this fighting.

This overhead view shows four scout vehicles, an M8 Greyhound and three Willys jeeps, known as "peeps" in the U.S. armored community. The 83rd Armored Reconnaissance Battalion relied on these vehicles during operations in 1944–1945.

Two M5 Stuart light tanks advance in Normandy in the summer of 1944. In the 3rd Armored Division, the 83rd Recon Battalion and all six tank battalions employed a company each of Stuarts for scouting, convoy escort, and attacks on hostile infantry. With a 37mm cannon and thin armor, the Stuart could not stand up to a German panzer.

American M3 half-tracks of the 36th Armored Infantry Regiment cross a pontoon bridge during the pursuit across France in August 1944. The 23rd Armored Engineer Battalion built this bridge and many others, often under fire. The 3rd Armored Division relied on half-track infantry and hard-working engineers in every combat operation.

Liberation! Enthusiastic crowds swarm a 3rd Armored Division Sherman tank with riflemen aboard. In both France and Belgium, boisterous locals greeted American soldiers with flowers, kisses, and wine. The gratitude was appreciated but often slowed the pace of the U.S. advance.

Major General Maurice Rose watches a half-track approaching the Belgian border on September 2, 1944. Rose routinely accompanied forward units. Many times, he and his peep constituted the foremost element of the 3rd Armored Division.

An M12 155mm "Long Tom" cannon fires on the enemy. The Long Toms of the 991st Armored Field Artillery Battalion provided heavy, long-range fire support for most 3rd Armored Division operations. Although officially not part of the division, the 991st considered themselves honorary Spearheaders. The 3rd Armored Division's three assigned artillery battalions (the 54th, 67th, and 391st) used the similar but smaller M7 105mm self-propelled howitzer.

Sherman tanks of the 3rd Armored Division move to battle near Mons, Belgium, on September 2, 1944. The division pivoted 90 degrees on short notice to go into action. The resulting meeting engagement in and around Mons on September 2–3, 1944, proved confusing and deadly, but the 3rd Armored Division took a total of 8,000 German prisoners drawn from multiple enemy units.

Lieutenant General Courtney H. Hodges studies the situation map at First Army headquarters on September 15, 1944. Based on his assessment of the situation, Hodges ordered a series of costly attacks into the German West Wall defenses in the First Army zone. The seizure of Aachen went fairly well. Multiple pushes into the Hürtgen Forest did not.

An American Sherman tank and accompanying infantrymen cross the dragon's teeth obstacles of the German West Wall in September 1944. The rapid American pursuit across France and Belgium ended in the German border fortifications. Although the 3rd Armored Division successfully penetrated the hostile lines, logistic shortages and strategic miscues resulted in a stalemate that lasted for the entire autumn of 1944.

This U.S. Army lieutenant carries a captured German *panzerfaust* (tank fist). These tank-killers could burn through an American Sherman, although like the G.I. bazooka, an enemy soldier had to get close to get a hit. Each *panzerfaust* could be fired once; the spent launch tube was then discarded.

Major General Maurice Rose drove around the battlefield in his ¼-ton Willys peep. The container near the general's right leg holds an M1A1 Thompson submachine gun. Captain Robert M. Bellinger, the general's aide, sits atop the big radio set in the back seat.

Two American Sherman tanks and a few infantrymen clear a street in Aachen, Germany, in October 1944. The riflemen stayed behind the tanks, using their armor as cover. Going out into the center of the road risked death.

Supreme Commander General Dwight D. Eisenhower visits Major General Maurice Rose at the 3rd Armored Division headquarters in Stolberg, Germany, on November 8, 1944. The two men barely knew each other. Note that Eisenhower carries a cigarette. He smoked three to four packs a day. Rose, as usual, wears his shined cavalry boots.

Lieutenant Colonel Clifford L. Miller, Major General Maurice Rose, and Colonel Leander L. "Tubby" Doan watch an ongoing attack near Stolberg, Germany, on November 25, 1944. Operations in and around the West Wall were slow-paced and costly. Poor weather limited American air support, and U.S. efforts gained little ground against tough German defenders.

A Sherman tank burns in the Hürtgen Forest. The dark, dense woods favored the German defenders. American tankers of the 3rd Armored Division found the area slow-going and dangerous.

A German Tiger II (also known as a Royal Tiger or a King Tiger) passes American prisoners in the early days of the Battle of the Bulge. The great German offensive caught the Americans by surprise. As a result, the 3rd Armored Division raced south to stop the German advance.

Major General J. Lawton "Lightning Joe" Collins (VII Corps), Field Marshal Bernard Law "Monty" Montgomery (commander of the Twenty-First Army Group), and Major General Matthew B. Ridgway (XVIII Airborne Corps) commanded the forces that stopped the Germans on the north side of the Bulge. The 3rd Armored Division worked for Ridgway in the crucial first few days, then back with their usual commander, Collins, thereafter. All three of these generals were very much "hands-on" commanders.

Major General Maurice Rose (standing) talks to Brigadier General Doyle O. Hickey (seated in the peep) during the Battle of the Bulge. Poor weather, icy roads, and long distances complicated American efforts to respond to the huge German attack. Hickey's Combat Command A spent days on a secondary mission to round up German paratroopers dropped in the First Army rear area.

A burned-out German Panther marks a crossroads west of Manhay, Belgium. The 3rd Armored Division fought a sequence of desperate battles to block Waffen SS forces attempting to press north through Manhay to take bridges on the Meuse River.

A pair of U.S. Sherman tanks advance up the snowy roads near Manhay, Belgium, in December 1944. The Shermans had special "duck feet" growers installed on their treads to allow better mobility on icy, snow-covered roads. The bad weather limited Allied air support, but it made movement hard for both sides.

An American T26E3 Pershing heavy tank advances in Germany in March 1945. The 3rd Armored Division received ten of these powerful tanks with 90mm guns. They could engage a German Panther or Tiger on even terms, something the standard M4 Shermans could not do.

This fire-damaged German Panther succumbed to Staff Sergeant Bob Earley's T26E3 Pershing tank crew on March 6, 1945, in the shadow of Cologne's medieval cathedral. Earley's 90mm rounds made short work of the panzer. The rapid-fire tank clash was filmed by a nearby G.I. motion-picture team.

Two G.I. riflemen take cover during the 3rd
Armored Division advance through Cologne
on March 6, 1945. Experienced riflemen made
smart use of the urban rubble. The twin spires
of the Cologne Cathedral are visible in the
distance.

Before the 3rd Armored Division could take it intact, the Germans destroyed Cologne's
Hohenzollern Bridge on March 6, 1945. As a result, the 3rd Armored Division had to cross
the Rhine River elsewhere. The delay held up the final advance to finish off the German
Army.

Major General Terry de la Mesa Allen cut a rakish figure as commander of the 104th Infantry Division. Long-time cavalryman Allen insisted he was Major General Maurice Rose's close friend. During the attack toward Paderborn in late March 1945, Allen attached an infantry regiment to reinforce Rose's 3rd Armored Division.

African American rifle platoons trained at Noyon, France, in February 1945, the first small break in the World War II U.S. Army's color line. Three of these platoons served in the 104th Infantry Division, to include the contested final advance on Paderborn.

Major General Maurice Rose presents an award to his driver, Technician 4th Grade Glenn H. Shaunce. Shaunce was wounded earlier in the campaign. He'd be wounded again driving Rose on March 30, 1944.

Sergeant Aurio Pierro was one of the 3rd Armored Division's brotherhood of experienced tank commanders (TCs). He was the only man in his original platoon to complete the entire 1944–1945 campaign. Pierro's platoon broke into the Nordhausen death camp on April 11, 1945. In this photo, Pierro stands atop a wrecked German panzer.

Soldiers of the 3rd Armored Division evacuate a liberated inmate of the Nordhausen death camp on April 11, 1945. Division soldiers had heard rumors of such facilities, but what they experienced at Nordhausen appalled even the most hardened combat veterans. The Germans forced the Nordhausen prisoners to build V-1 buzz bombs and V-2 rockets in underground factories.

American generals serve as honorary pallbearers at Major General Maurice Rose's funeral in Ittenbach, Germany, on April 2, 1945. At front left is General Omar N. Bradley, still wearing his former three-star rank of lieutenant general although he'd been promoted to four-star rank a few days earlier. Behind Bradley, in the dark uniform, is Lieutenant General George S. Patton, Jr. To the right front is Lieutenant General Courtney H. Hodges. Behind him is Major General J. Lawton Collins. Other generals follow, with an honor company from the 3rd Armored Division marching behind them.

Major General Maurice Rose's helmet was recovered from the battlefield near Castle Hamborn. For years it was exhibited at the Patton Museum at Fort Knox, Kentucky. Postwar investigation suggests that the two holes were punched through the helmet while it was in the air rather than on Rose's head.

men would bear the brunt of a block-by-block battle for Aachen, Collins once more spoke up. "Aachen," he argued, "had very little military significance to the Americans or Germans now that the XIX Corps, as well as our VII Corps, could bypass it on the way to the Rhine." Collins advised Courtney Hodges: isolate the urban center and move on. Collins remembered the terrible struggle for Cherbourg and had no desire to repeat it. For his own obscure reasons, however, Hodges thought otherwise. He wanted Aachen taken.[43]

The cathedral of Aachen, a city known to the French as Aix-la-Chapelle, hosted the tomb of Charlemagne, Karl der Grosse to the Germans. Hitler and his fellow Nazi ideologues claimed Charlemagne's kingdom as the First Reich. This gave Aachen iconic value, especially to Hitler. The führer insisted that Aachen be held to the last bullet and the last man.[44] Such was Hitler's default setting anyway.

Because First Army's orders specified a two-corps encirclement before taking the city, an already difficult task became even more complicated. After the Falaise Pocket misstep—and the much cleaner effort at Mons—one might think Hodges would just hand the entire situation to Joe Collins, give him the combat power, and let him sort it out. It worked splendidly at Mons.

Hodges, though, didn't only wish for Aachen. He also wanted his main man Joe Collins to drive to the Rhine and clear out part of the Hürtgen Forest as a sideline. But Collins couldn't pile up his guys on Aachen. His VII Corps had too much else to do. Having spread divisions and artillery battalions like cream cheese, a nice even schmear, it fell to First Army to coordinate the efforts of XIX Corps and VII Corps. As Hodges didn't do such things, Collins found himself nudging, pleading, and cajoling his fellow corps commander to cooperate.[45] It worked out in the most excruciating fashion.

In VII Corps, Collins let the 1st Infantry Division carry the ball for Aachen. South of Aachen, Collins told Maurice Rose and his 3rd Armored Division to defend the Stolberg corridor and be ready to send in a task force, or even an entire combat command, to reinforce the advance into Aachen. With Collins, Rose had to know that would be coming. Lightning Joe liked to shift battalions here and there. To the 3rd Armored Division's south, the 9th Infantry Division planned for another bite at the rotten apple of the Hürtgen Forest.[46] In the rush to get going, even the normally perceptive Joe Collins missed the flaws. Two-thirds of his corps, including his armored division, wasn't doing anything to take Aachen or get to the Rhine. And the 9th prepared to plunge for the second time into a timbered hellhole with zero strategic worth. As the saying goes, orders are orders. Somewhere the ghosts of Verdun and Gallipoli nodded.

After fourteen bloody days bashing pillboxes and crossing dragon's teeth in both belts of the West Wall, the 30th Infantry Division of XIX Corps and the 1st Infantry Division linked up at 4:15 p.m. on the dim fall afternoon of October 16, 1944. Right on schedule, orders came from Joe Collins at VII Corps to Maurice Rose at Spearhead Division: send a tank/infantry task force to bolster the 1st Infantry Division in Aachen. Collins directed the size of the column—a big one.[47]

Maurice Rose turned to Lieutenant Colonel Sam Hogan. The stalwart Texan moved with both his own 3rd Battalion, 33rd Armored Regiment and 2nd Battalion, 36th Armored Infantry Regiment, plus supporting engineers, an antiaircraft battery, and tank destroyers— a regimental-scale task force. Rose trusted Hogan. Sam Hogan linked up with the 1st Infantry Division commanding general at 9:00 a.m. on October 17. By 3:00 p.m. that day, TF Hogan began moving tanks and half-track infantry to the bombed-out factory quarter in northeast Aachen. Once the 1st Division's 26th Infantry Regiment secured a foothold in the streets, TF Hogan would be brought in to knock out enemy strongpoints. The G-2 people delivered a hair-raising list of the adversary's Aachen garrison: 1st SS Panzer Division, 2nd Panzer Division, 3rd Panzergrenadier Division, 116th Panzer Division, 245th Infantry Division, and, of course, the 506th Heavy Panzer Battalion with Tiger tanks, some 13,000 men and dozens of panzers. Some

American analysts suggested that up to 5,000 *volksturm* (people's assault—the militia) should be added to the total.[48] In TF Hogan, the old sweats shrugged. They couldn't all be in there. In any case, this wouldn't be like the dash through Soissons or Liege. City fighting—ugh.

It turned out that wasn't TF Hogan's role, not exactly. The Spearheaders ended up working on the west side of Aachen, catching German "squirters" trying to escape the relentless attack of the 26th Infantry Regiment. Overrunning West Wall bunkers on the outskirts of the city, Hogan's troopers took a key German position on the knob known as the Lousberg. Although they should have hung in there, disheartened adversaries on the hill didn't put up much opposition. Hogan's G.I.s captured 700 German soldiers. In four days of fighting, TF Hogan suffered twelve killed and forty wounded.[49]

Consistent with his usual habits, Joe Collins also moved in a battalion from the 28th Infantry Division, brought from the edge of the Hürtgen Forest. In the city center, heavy air bombardment and liberal use of artillery, 9,500 rounds a day, rubbled entire urban blocks. The infantrymen used a self-propelled 155mm Long Tom cannon as a door-knocker. Even the most fanatical Nazi Germans couldn't stand up to that. Aachen surrendered at 12:38 p.m. on October 21, 1944. Taking this prestige objective cost about 4,350 Americans killed and wounded. Precise figures are hard to come by, as it became unclear how much to attribute to Aachen proper and what to tag for related secondary missions in the West Wall. The 26th Infantry Regiment reported 75 killed, nine missing, and 414 wounded, about half of all who entered Aachen in the outfit's understrength pair of lead battalions. Along with hundreds killed, 11,637 surrounded Germans eventually raised their hands and quit.[50]

Hodges's contribution to the effort consisted of back-seat driving. The First Army commander only came up from his command post five times during the twenty days of the operation. He spent his hours hosting visitors, including King George VI and General George C.

Marshall. Other senior commanders in the middle of a major offensive, Monty for sure and Patton probably, might have tried harder to avoid or strongly limit this battlefield tourism. After all, the war took precedence, and both the king and George Marshall would have heartily agreed. Hodges never raised the matter.[51]

Courtney Hodges also stared at his wall map. The scribblings told him things, it appears. In a phone call to Major General Charles H. Corlett of XIX Corps, Hodges complained that 30th Infantry Division commander Major General Leland S. Hobbs was always "bragging or complaining." Hobbs and his 30th had been the heroes of Mortain back in August. That was then; this was now. Hobbs's 30th and its parent XIX Corps were winning, just not fast enough to please the First Army commander. Hodges said more: "I always thought you ought to relieve Leland. He hasn't moved an inch in four days." Corlett thought not. So Hodges fired Corlett, perhaps *pour encourager les autres*.[52] It was a hell of a way to run a field army.

Joe Collins and Maurice Rose took notice, as well they should have. Prior good deeds, even decent progress in difficult ongoing tasks, merited little. For Hodges, it was all about taking the named geographic objectives. With Aachen in hand, but the rest of the great offensive stillborn, Hodges reconsidered the marks on his wall. The Hürtgen Forest—not taken yet. It drew Hodges like a moth to a flame.

————

Maurice Rose didn't fight in Aachen. He checked on Colonel Bobby Howze, who backed Hogan with fuel and ammunition, brought out his dead and wounded, and kept Rose up to date on the doings in Aachen. As his Spearhead Division replenished their ranks and their tanks, the restless major general spent his time prowling the forward positions near Stolberg. There the Germans shelled and shot day and night. So did the Spearheaders. Barbed wire, night patrols, trench foot—it really was like somebody turned back the clock three decades. Aside from TF Hogan's casualties in Aachen, the rest of the division lost thirty-nine killed and more than 150 wounded while marking time on the Stolberg front.[53] Attrition is not a pretty way to make war.

Rose and his men got lucky with the Hürtgen Forest, a statement that not many in First Army could make in that damp, gloomy fall of 1944. Although a bit of the seventy-square-mile triangle of woods extended into the southeast part of the 3rd Armored Division's front, the Spearheaders sidestepped the worst. In their stead marched an unhappy succession of infantry divisions: the 9th, 28th, 1st, 8th, 4th, and 83rd, fed into the terrible dark maw of that evil patch one by one, like logs sliding into a whirring saw blade. From September to December, fighting in the woods resulted in some 23,000 American dead and wounded, plus 8,000 nonbattle losses, a number including hundreds, maybe thousands, of "psychiatric" (PTSD) casualties; the U.S. Army didn't like to discuss such matters.[54] The Hürtgen's lethal groves drove men mad.

The grim Hürtgen killing ground remained a divided responsibility between VII Corps and V Corps, mostly the latter. Had Bradley been able to read a map, or had Hodges not been Hodges, one or both of them would have realized that the forest could be passed to the north—Rose's division had already done it—or the south, in the Monschau avenue, the one Bradley judged as not good tank country. Collins probably intuited the attraction. The Hürtgen reminded Hodges of his younger days earning the Distinguished Service Cross in the Meuse-Argonne Forest.[55] In any event, First Army stayed at it.

The Germans in the Hürtgen anchored their stubborn defense on the West Wall fortifications. Both sides learned that their artillery shells, if fused for point of impact detonation, burst in the tall firs, showering down red-hot, jagged fragments. These tree bursts characterized combat in the Hürtgen. Moving erect risked evisceration. Open foxholes became open graves.[56]

Overhead explosions drove G.I.s to hit the dirt. In the Hürtgen, even the ground turned on you. Mines dotted the spongy forest floor.

Little *schu* (shoe) devices blew off feet. Hubcap-size Teller mines ripped apart tank treads. And "Bouncing Betty" mines, when stepped on, popped up to belt-buckle height and shredded men where they felt it most.[57] The most simple tasks—walking to eat chow, hopping off a tank to refuel, standing up to massage cramps—became dicey indeed.

From October 25 until November 10, 1944, the 3rd Armored Division backed up the enervated, shot-up 47th Infantry Regiment of the 9th Infantry Division. The unlucky 47th, a fine outfit with a great fighting record, had already gone twice before into the Hürtgen Forest. In these clashes, the 3,258-man regiment suffered a sadly numerically coincident 47 percent casualties, a horrendous rate all too typical for units committed to the dreaded locale. While attached to the 3rd Armored Division, the 47th defended in place, trying to integrate the hundreds of replacements trucked forward. Working with the men of the 47th Infantry Regiment, the Spearheaders lost twenty-two dead and almost eighty wounded.[58]

Out in the foxholes and in the turrets of the tanks, the scuttlebutt circulated: expect another push soon. This time, the 3rd Armored Division would be fully involved. Pessimists whispered that the Spearhead Division's good fortune was over. They'd be going through the Hürtgen, too.[59] Soldiers' moods matched the weather. Bleak.

Up at First Army, wheels turned. In a rather tone-deaf move, after Aachen fell, Hodges's staff relocated to Spa, Belgium's magnificent Hotel Britannique, former headquarters of the Second Reich's German High Command in World War I. Hodges blithely moved into the room where Field Marshal Paul von Hindenburg once slept.[60] You couldn't make this stuff up. One could only imagine what G.I.s squatting in freezing sleet at a Hürtgen roadblock might have thought. Hodges made it a point not to ask.

In their nice new digs, First Army staffers concocted a new plan. Eisenhower and Bradley still insisted on getting to the Rhine River. The October offensive grounded out after the seizure of Aachen and the continuing floundering in the Hürtgen Forest. So now the planners lowered their sights a bit. Getting to the Roer River might do. Secure that waterway, then bound forward to the Rhine.

The Roer? When did that otherwise unimportant river become important? The top staff officers at First Army finally read an October 2, 1944, report prepared by a very sharp major in the 9th Infantry Division warning about the peril posed if the Germans opened two Roer River dams. The Roer paralleled the West Wall and stood about seven miles ahead of the current American front, bisecting the way to the Rhine. If the Germans blew the dams and inundated the broad Roer valley, the prescient 9th Division major thought, "destructive waves" would result, a biblical event, and not a pleasant one. It might take weeks for the raging waters to subside. There'd be no First Army drive to the Rhine. Even worse, what if the hostiles popped the dams after the American lead columns passed the Roer?[61] The U.S. assault force would be stranded on the enemy side of a massive inundation.

This risk worried Hodges. In fact, in laying out the scheme for the upcoming offensive, Hodges directed that "troops will not, repeat, not advance beyond line of Roer (Rur) River except on Army order." The two Roer dams stood in towns on the northeast fringe of the Hürtgen Forest. First Army staff people seized on the threat of the dams. The two structures offered a great ex post facto rationalization for all the gory sacrifices in the Hürtgen and accorded nicely with Hodges's obstinate insistence on clearing the fatal forest.[62] See, offered the headquarters apologists—Hodges knew. Maybe all that time looking at the map paid off. Maybe.

The First Army plan was an improvement over the October version, admittedly a low bar. Collins's VII Corps (three infantry divisions and 3rd Armored Division, plus sixteen supporting artillery battalions) drew a sixteen-mile-wide zone of attack opening on the Stolberg corridor and part of the Hürtgen. Objective: Cologne on the Rhine. To their south, on a twenty-seven-mile front, V Corps (two infantry divisions, one armored division, and thirteen artillery battalions) had to take the two dams by going right through the Hürtgen Forest. The Monschau corridor in the Ardennes promised a fine way to get around the Hürtgen and take the pair of key water barriers. But Hodges followed Bradley's lead and left that avenue, and indeed the entire eighty-mile stretch of the wooded Ardennes, to the defending VIII Corps (three infantry divisions, one armored division). That was a rest area for chewed-up divisions and newly arrived organizations. The major action would all be in the north, with VII and V Corps. The U.S. Army Air Forces prepared another huge bombardment on the scale of Operation Cobra; that ought to blow the Germans out of what remained of the West Wall. Hodges set the date of attack for November 5, 1944.[63] First Army staff guys talked themselves into it all—another Cobra, the terrible Hürtgen Forest in the rearview mirror, the Roer dams under firm control, and Rhine River bridges there for the taking. Hodges, as usual, said little.

———

Hodges came by Omaha Forward on November 5, but it wasn't for the offensive. The mighty air show demanded good weather, and November in Stolberg dealt only in rain, chill, and banks of low gray clouds. It felt like dusk at noon. So the attack date moved to November 10, when the meteorologists thought there might be a break. Or not. Who really could say?

Hodges found Major General Maurice Rose waiting for him. The First Army commander, small, slight, and rumpled, sported his cigarette holder. Rose towered over the three-star. As usual, despite the drizzle and mud, Rose wore a spruce uniform and his knee-high polished riding boots. His bearing impressed Hodges's aides.[64] Had Hodges stopped by more often, he and his assistants would have expected as much from Rose. They knew him not.

Hodges came and went like a gust of autumn wind. Yet Rose's staff officers, even Colonel John Smith, the chief of staff, or the brace of lieutenant colonels, who saw Rose every day, really didn't understand their division commander any better than Hodges did. With the Spearhead command post at Stolberg since September 21, even allowing for Rose's many hours forward with the troops, the staff officers and NCOs had opportunities to learn more about Maurice Rose. They didn't figure out much.

Sergeant (later 2nd Lieutenant) George Bailey, a G-2 interrogator, watched Rose around Stolberg. To Bailey, "appearances were not deceiving." He described the general as "thin-lipped, sharp features, closely cropped hair, a ramrod of a man." Bailey thought Rose "the toughest looking officer I have ever seen." There was more: "There was not a man in division headquarters who did not fear Rose. I saw staff officers," he wrote, "full colonels, standing at attention before Rose, sweat pouring off their faces, visibly shaking in their tankers' boots."[65] Maurice Rose was all business.

As a result, when he sat down for a meal with his officers, which happened more at Stolberg than anywhere else in 1944–1945, Rose didn't participate in the usual bonhomie and small talk. The general did not discuss his family or anything else personal. Conversation was stilted, so much so that Long John Smith had to prod his officers to speak to the general. When one officer mentioned a *Time* magazine article about tank destroyer tactics that worked well in Italy, Rose asked pointedly, "Why didn't I know about that?"[66] The war mattered. Everything else came in a distant second.

The Omaha Forward enlisted men didn't break bread at the general's table. But they, too, noticed things. Rose got up early, drove off in his peep, and didn't come back until evening, if then. His aide, Captain Bob Bellinger, and his driver, Tech-4 Glenn Shaunce, had both been wounded while out and about with Rose. While the pair recovered and quickly returned to duty, it served as a reminder of what went on every day with Maurice Rose. Nobody's luck held up forever. But this guy Rose . . .

The G.I.s talked about one incident. It happened at Stolberg. Soldiers couldn't place the date. Some said late October; others thought

November. The semi-official chronicler of Omaha Forward pegged it as early December. It hardly mattered. One day was very much like the next—overcast, wet, chilly, dim, and subject to random German shelling. Now and then, the Germans did injury. This was one of those instances.

On that particular morning, just after the skies grayed a bit, soldiers busied themselves with their morning regimen on the grounds of the Prym estate. Some soldiers had lined up for chow. Drivers fussed over their half-tracks, trucks, and peeps. Rose stood near his vehicle, getting ready to head out. Same old, same old.

Then a clutch of German artillery rounds impacted. The hot blasts blossomed among the Americans. Division artillery fired back within minutes, silencing the enemy guns. But thirteen U.S. soldiers had been wounded, two quite badly. Some men lay there. Others stumbled in a daze. Medics ran to treat those who'd been hit.

Sergeant George Bailey described what followed:

> The wounded who could still walk lined up outside the division surgeon's office for treatment. Rose came up and talked with them all until the last man had been treated by the surgeon. Then he stepped up and said, "All right, doc, now you can take care of me." No one had noticed it but Rose had taken shrapnel in both shoulders.[67]

Rose did not permit the surgeon to submit him for a Purple Heart, although his lacerations qualified according to the regulation. Having been hit more seriously in the Great War, the general evidently didn't consider his minor cuts to be wounds. He literally shrugged and moved on. No big deal. Among the rankers, word went around. For his part, Maurice Rose never mentioned it.

Some of this was Rose's nature, reserved and laconic, "deeds not words" to borrow the motto of the 36th Armored Infantry Regiment.[68] But Rose's behavior also reflected his habits of command.

Most American generals, high and low, ran their war from command posts and led through their staff. Eisenhower and Bradley fit squarely into this bunch; Hodges, too, although he could be rather obtuse even to his senior staffers. Staff-centered commanders gathered information by briefings—often anything but brief—then worked out decisions in successive meetings, sometimes with dozens present, now and then in selected small groups. Collegially arranged decisions became plans and orders. The staff made it all happen and followed up, requiring reports and making inspections. Junior commanders were brought in and told what to do and, too often, how to go about it, too.

A minority of American generals, like George Patton and Joe Collins, knew where they wanted to go and how they wanted to get there. They worked with their commanders, not their staffs. Patton described, leaving subordinates to craft the methods. Collins prescribed, steering and guiding much of the way, even with men he trusted, like Rose. Both Patton and Collins believed in personal supervision, seeing and being seen.[69] The staff just policed up the details and handled the routine reporting. These guys didn't need much from their staffs. They knew more about their outfits, and the war, than anyone back in the command post. Rose epitomized this approach. It explained what Patton saw in him back stateside, and why Collins, a very tough judge, saw Rose as "my top division commander."[70]

The 3rd Armored Division plan for the November offensive was a typical Maurice Rose concept, simple but allowing options. Joe Collins originally planned to keep the Spearhead Division back until VII Corps closed up to the Roer River, then wait until V Corps secured the two Roer dams. Once those crucial facilities were in hand, Collins intended to slingshot Rose's tanks across the Roer to make for Cologne and the Rhine. To be ready to launch, Rose prepared his combat commands to follow the 1st Infantry Division in column: CCB, then CCA, and finally CCR. Once they pushed through the main

German defenses, the Spearheaders could fan out.[71] It shaped up to be a textbook armor mission, exploiting the gap.

Rose, though, knew well Collins's ways. Rose expected that he'd be told to detach task forces, perhaps entire combat commands, to beef up the U.S. infantry attacking in front of the 3rd Armored Division. This time, Collins didn't wait for the time of attack. With the weather delay from November 5 to November 10, Collins assigned an opening day mission to the 3rd Armored Division, a single combat command to open a key road near Hamich, a village in the northwest end of the Hürtgen Forest. It would goose the attack, maybe pry open a seam.[72] Collins was thinking Cobra, no doubt.

So the Hürtgen it would be—again, tree bursts and land mines—starting with Combat Command B. This time would be different, Collins said. A fast start, another Cobra-like breakthrough, depended on the concentrated power of the planned heavy bomber strikes. Orders went down the chain. Stand by for fireworks on November 10, 1944. Beside their olive drab Shermans, propped up in muddy foxholes, the G.I.s waited. And waited.

And waited.

———

November 16 turned out to be the day, "spotty sunlight" being as good as it got. With ears cocked to the radios, at 10:15 a.m. the great men gathered at First Army headquarters in Spa. As the waves of American and British four-engine bombers, 2,379 in all, roared above, sometimes visible through the intermittent clouds, the generals spoke of the Cobra breakout. Maybe Joe Collins would again unleash the lightning. Hodges's aide wrote, "General Bradley believes [the operation] will be the last big offensive necessary to bring Germany to her knees."[73]

The Germans chose not to play along. The much-ballyhooed aerial bombardment dumped 9.76 kilotons of high explosives, twice the tonnage expended for Cobra. Twin-engine medium bombers and

single-engine fighter-bombers joined the fray. The deluge of munitions turned a lot of soggy dirt, and did some damage. But fears of
short bombings, the scourge endured in Normandy, pushed the Allied bomb line more than two miles beyond the VII Corps jump-off
positions, and the designated attack box stretched nine miles. The
U.S. and British airmen claimed "enormous" effects. German regiments reported 1 percent to 3 percent losses.[74] The bombing didn't do
the job.

The American artillery preparation, however, wreaked havoc.
First Army guns for both VII Corps and V Corps pounded German
frontal bunkers and trenches with 51,600 rounds. This hurricane tore
up German wire lines, adding to disruptions caused by the Allied air
arm. As a result, attacking American regiments reported only seven
enemy artillery firing events during the afternoon of November 16.[75]

Into the beaten zone went Combat Command B. At 12:45 p.m. Bill
Lovelady's tanks punched right through in two hours, gobbling up
the hamlets south and west of Hamich. Seventy-eight Germans surrendered. Some were unwilling *volksgrenadiers*, bubbling over with
useful intelligence. But a few dour enemy sergeants said nothing.
Their eyes conveyed contempt and an air of "you just wait." Once the
1st Infantry Division took the ridge just to the east, Lovelady's Sherman crews and half-track troopers envisioned a quick thrust to the
Roer.[76]

Herb Mills's men had a much rougher time. They ran into a knife
fight, the entire Hürtgen horror show. The lead platoons found themselves mired in mud and mines, the usual grisly trifecta: Tellers cutting treads, *schu* mines amputating lower legs, and Bouncing Betty
types ripping abdomens. German mortar bombs smacked the tree-
tops, shotgunning down hot shrapnel on Sherman tank commanders standing exposed in open hatches, ripping through open-topped
tank destroyer turrets, and scattering dismounted infantrymen.
German 88mm cannons worked out. Hostiles with *panzerfäusten*
did, too. By dark, TF Mills had only advanced a few hundred yards,

with sixteen of their Sherman tanks knocked out and nine G.I.s killed, including two of three tank company commanders. As the regimental log noted, "Other personnel casualties were not determined."[77] Darkness and confusion swallowed all.

With TF Mills stymied and the 1st Infantry Division also battling a mile back, the Hamich ridge remained wholly German. Enemy observers began calling down artillery fires on Bill Lovelady's troops. When the lieutenant colonel climbed down from his tank to talk to some nearby soldiers, a German projectile struck the Sherman, killing one man and wounding another. German gunners banged away, killing an American officer and wounding twenty-one more G.I.s. Well-hidden enemy antitank guns picked off three U.S. tanks. Another four American Shermans struck mines; those could be repaired.[78] The shroud of night came over none too soon.

November 17 saw more of the same, with drenching rain to boot. Bill Lovelady's men held on, waiting for their neighbors to catch up. Task Force Mills wedged forward to come even with TF Lovelady, but the Germans kept the high ground. By 6:40 p.m., TF Mills was down to seven M5 Stuart light tanks and eight Shermans. Truman Boudinot's CCB was down to 50 percent in tank strength. On November 17, the two task forces lost a total of nineteen killed and more than a hundred wounded. Maurice Rose, who'd been forward for most of the day, told Colonel Bobby Howze of Combat Command Reserve to be ready to move on an hour's notice.[79] The pair of lead task forces were out on a limb.

At first light on November 18, a German shell exploded high in the timber above TF Mills. Scorching hot fragments killed Lieutenant Colonel Herbert Mills. Major Kenneth T. McGeorge took over, the fifth battalion command changeover in that task force since the first week of August. But the awful opening did not mar the rest of the day. With Boudinot and Rose on hand, American tank crews and infantrymen spent the day rousting out determined German observation teams from the lower slopes of the Hamich ridge.[80]

Rose, who seldom betrayed much emotion, was in a surly mood. He moved between TF McGeorge and TF Lovelady, insisting on continued attacking to finish off the Germans.[81] It was the only way to stop the opposing artillery. Poke out their eyes.

Lieutenant Colonel Bill Lovelady and his soldiers saw Rose at work. Lovelady recalled that "General Rose didn't mind coming up [to] the front line." At one point, with things at an impasse, the general told his G-3, Lieutenant Colonel Wesley A. Sweat, that it was time to can Lovelady. Sweat evidently didn't overreact. The storm passed. Lovelady kept his job.[82] But the fact that Rose even considered firing one of his premier commanders says much about the general's agitated state. Mr. Cool had his limits.

When two companies of bold German infantry commenced a counterattack against depleted TF McGeorge, the major replied American-style: send a bullet, not a man. At 5:45 p.m., McGeorge's artillery forward observers asked for an artillery concentration, massing the fire of multiple howitzer batteries. Gunners mixed point-detonating rounds—tree bursts—with delay fuzed projectiles that plunged all the way to the pine needle forest floor. The American artillery stayed at it for fifteen searing minutes.[83] That put paid to the German counterthrust.

Elements of the 1st Infantry Division linked up on November 19, 1944, and completed clearing the rest of the Hamich ridgeline over the next two days. To push forward a few miles since November 16, Combat Command B lost two-thirds of its 103 assigned tanks. The armored infantrymen again paid a high price, with the attached 2nd Battalion, 36th Armored infantry Regiment reduced to 50 percent strength, to include another battalion commander wounded and evacuated. The CCB casualties proved harrowing: 14 killed, 69 missing in action, and 70 wounded. Most of the missing were dead, but it took weeks to recover their remains.[84] Some were never found, gone in the mud and damp pine straw of the Hürtgen Forest.

Bradley gravely summed up: "Collins advanced a mere six miles in miserable weather and at a terrible cost." The Americans reached the Roer River line, but no farther. To their south, the Germans held tight to the valuable Roer dams. The enemy still dominated half of the Hürtgen Forest.[85] At this rate, the war might end in 1947. If then.

———

For the next three weeks, combat continued. Nobody said anything else about breaking out. Rather, Collins referred to these operations as "limited objective attacks," American-speak for what Monty called "tidying up the battlefield."[86] Like "mopping up," it was a term the G.I.s rightly disdained. Losing men to straighten the front and to get all divisions neatly arrayed on the Roer River didn't do much for morale. But the Spearheaders knew the refrain. Orders were orders.

True to form, on November 24, 1944, Joe Collins directed Rose to send a battalion-sized outfit to help the 1st Infantry Division take a key hummock near the Roer. Pitted against German machine gun nests and antitank gun positions, not to mention the usual mud, Lieutenant Colonel Rich Richardson's task force fought for three days, losing fourteen killed, six missing, and nearly a hundred wounded. They gave a key boost to the U.S. infantry as they secured the offending knot of high ground, mission accomplished.[87] It hardly seemed worth it.

Another VII Corps attack on December 10 found Rose leading with Colonel Howze's Combat Command Reserve. Bobby Howze's twin task forces grabbed three small German crossroads and ended up, at last, on the Roer River. This small gain resulted in forty-four Americans dead and 101 men wounded.[88] After another round of regrouping, the Rhine came next. The map told you so.

The Germans tenaciously protected each grimy bunker, every well-placed minefield, all the shattered villages. The foe shot his machine guns and 88s and used his mortars and his artillery tubes. You'd expect that. It's what Germans did. The enemy couldn't win the war. All but some overeager Hitler Youth and a coterie of Nazi true believers seemed to get it. Yet here in the shadow of the West Wall, on the front porch of the Thousand Year Reich, the Germans fought on.

For Maurice Rose and the experienced Spearhead regimental and battalion commanders, for the veteran captains and sergeants in the ranks, something felt "off." The Germans always scraped up their armored reserves and smashed back. Rose's G-2 people had lost track of the usual suspects: 1st SS Panzer Division, 2nd Panzer Division, 2nd SS Panzer Division, 9th Panzer Division, and 116th Panzer Division.[89] Those dangerous formations had been hanging around the Aachen/ Stolberg region well into October. Now in mid-December—zilch.

Where were the panzers?

CHAPTER 6

Panthers in the Snow

If you go into that death-trap of the Ardennes, you will
never come out.

Général de division Charles Lanrezac[1]

Be careful what you wish for. Despondent over the bloody impasse in and around the West Wall, Lieutenant General Omar
Bradley wanted the Germans to quit ducking and covering and defending every ramshackle pillbox to the last man. Come out and play.
Come out into a mobile scrum in more open terrain where American
firepower could tear them up.

At 5:30 a.m. on December 16, 1944, the Germans obliged.

"Well, Brad, you've been wishing for a counterattack," said Lieutenant General Walter Bedell Smith, Eisenhower's SHAEF chief of
staff. "Now it looks as though you've got it."

"A counterattack, yes," replied Bradley. "But I'll be damned if I
wanted one this big."[2] The Twelfth Army Group commander got it
anyway, courtesy of Adolf Hitler, no less. A winter offensive employing almost every viable mobile unit the Germans had left—no ratio-
nal top commander would undertake such a massive gamble. But a
megalomaniacal Austrian-born lance corporal? Why not?

The Germans struck hard against the First Army. Shielded from the Allied air armada by foul "Hitler weather," the foe slammed into the southernmost 99th Infantry Division of the ill-used V Corps— still ensnared in the Hürtgen Forest—and tore up the strung-out VIII Corps: the brand-new 106th Infantry Division and the Hürtgen-ravaged 28th and 4th. The four U.S. divisions thinly outposted an eighty-mile front, the same Ardennes region that Bradley told himself wasn't suitable for tanks. Poor Bradley. The map done him wrong again. Now three German field armies, a thousand panzers and a half million men, were on the move. The enemy envisioned going all the way to the just-opened port of Antwerp. Cut up the Americans, cut off the British, and possibly, at least in Hitler's febrile mind, force the Allies to the bargaining table.[3] Based on the thunderclap opening, Hitler's troops might pull it off.

What now, Brad?

A book man to his bones, and fortunately not prone to panic, Bradley thought back to what he'd learned at West Point, Benning, and Leavenworth. Contain the breakthrough. Hold the shoulders. Block the foe's leading panzer outfits at the major road junctions. Anchor on the high ground and rivers. And when the skies cleared—if that happy day ever came—tear 'em up.[4] To do these things, Bradley needed more forces.

Here the Allied broad front approach, the U.S. 90-division force cap, and the British manpower shortage left the cupboard rather bare. Eisenhower had very little to offer his classmate Bradley. The SHAEF reserve consisted of XVIII Airborne Corps with the 82nd Airborne and 101st Airborne divisions. Both divisions were refitting after the September "bridge too far" operation in Holland. Although composed of well-led, hand-picked, highly trained volunteers, the airborne outfits were small (authorized 8,596 soldiers vs. a standard U.S. Army infantry division's 14,253 men) and undergunned, with no tanks, no tank destroyers, and no standard field artillery.[5] They'd have to pick up reinforcing units en route and make do.

That was something at which the paratroopers and glider men excelled.

With the airborne troops en route, Bradley had to reconfigure his other chess pieces. Twenty-First Army Group to the north probably had nothing to provide; Monty had been borrowing U.S. divisions all through the fall of 1944. Sixth Army Group to the south had their own fish to fry and nothing to spare. So Bradley turned to his own three armies: the Ninth north of Aachen, the First with a gaping hole in its south end, and Patton's Third Army fighting in the Saar. Bradley tapped the Ninth for the 7th Armored Division to speed toward the German penetration; the Ninth later sent the 30th Infantry Division, the 84th Infantry Division, and the 2nd Armored Division as well. Patton's Third Army also received word to cough up the brand-new 10th Armored Division. Being Patton, and having already divined the German counteroffensive before it launched, the Third Army commander prepared to pivot his forces 90 degrees and attack into the south flank of the German forces. When the time came, Patton would be ready.[6]

What about Hodges? His forces had taken it right in the teeth. But two-thirds of his First Army lay north of the German push. A good general would immediately march to the sound of the guns, moving right to the point of crisis to see and be seen, to steady the line. Not Hodges. The First Army commander did what he did best. Nothing. The fateful 16th of December passed calmly at the Hotel Britannique in Spa. The maps looked OK, and the bulk of the reports weren't too alarming. The fact that a great many updates from the embattled VIII Corps were missing raised some eyebrows—that obviously wasn't a good sign. Even so, the First Army commander didn't stir from his headquarters. Indeed, Hodges kept his normal office schedule, to include hosting military visitors from SHAEF and going to bed on time. The general was nursing a head cold.[7]

When looking at transcripts of fragmented radio messages from American headquarters in the Ardennes, Hodges told staff officers that the German offensive thrusts "were only what the General called 'spoiling attacks'—to take the pressure off the important V Corps drive towards the Roer River dams." The general assessed the German advances as being "in large patrol strength and others in battalion strength." As a precaution, after calls from Joe Collins and the other corps commanders, Hodges consented to put the 1st Infantry Division, regrouping off-line, on six-hour alert for possible movement to the Ardennes. Hodges thought he might send a regiment off to backstop the hard-pressed 99th Infantry Division on the critical northern shoulder of the enemy offensive. The First Army commander was "neither optimistic nor pessimistic." He was just Hodges. In later years, some would point to all of this as evidence of Hodges's phlegm, resolution in the face of peril.[8] Could be. Inertia became him.

Along with notifying the 1st Infantry Division to prepare to truck south, Hodges also sent an order putting the 3rd Armored Division on six-hour notice to go, too. It appears that the directive to ready the 1st Infantry and 3rd Armored divisions represented the First Army commander's personal decision. Hodges picked the 1st Infantry Division because it was behind the front and available. He picked the 3rd Armored Division because of Maurice Rose.[9]

———

Four days earlier and a lifetime ago, before the German onslaught, Hodges invited Major General Maurice Rose to the VII Corps command post near an abandoned segment of the West Wall. Joe Collins was there, of course. With hardly any preliminaries, the reticent First Army commander genuinely surprised Rose with an impromptu presentation. As a junior officer read the citation, Hodges stepped directly in front of his taller subordinate and pinned on the Distinguished Service Cross, America's second-highest valor award. Only the Medal of Honor stands higher. The citation referred to Rose's "extraordinary heroism" and "intrepid actions, personal bravery and zealous devotion to duty" from September 6 through September 9, 1944, during the advance across Belgium. As Hodges's aide wrote afterward, Rose was "one of his [Hodges's] favorite generals."[10] That constituted a very exclusive set given Hodges's dour demeanor and disinterest in most of those he outranked.

The unexpected honor meant a great deal to Rose, as it would to any soldier. United States Army generals collect many medals, and in World War II that certainly held true. Most generals received the Distinguished Service Medal, prestigious no doubt, but presented for carrying out demanding responsibilities, not for valorous acts. Wiseacre G.I.s referred to it as the "generals' good conduct medal," the star-level version of a medal normally given to an enlisted soldier with a clean disciplinary record. Some World War II generals were awarded Silver Stars. Then Brigadier General Rose had one from Sicily to go with the two he'd received as a colonel in North Africa. He'd earned all three of them. Others seemed a bit gratuitous. Bradley, for example, received a Silver Star for "gallant actions" in 1945, although it's not clear exactly what he did.[11] Bravery comes in many forms.

The Distinguished Service Cross, though, came from a different category. That one resonated up and down the ranks. Hodges earned the award in 1918, and the First Army commander never approved a recommendation lightly. You could argue, as some Spearheaders did, that Rose deserved the medal more for the Rânes fight, or the contested Aisne River crossing, or Mons, or the bloodletting at the West Wall. No matter. Hodges signed what someone put on his desk, and did so without a second thought. With Maurice Rose, soldiers from general to private could vouch for his battlefield presence. They might not—indeed did not—know the man. But they knew where to find him.

Now with flotillas of German panzers crawling all over the floor of the Ardennes Forest, Rose got the call. It came late and garbled, transmitted from First Army through VII Corps. At 5:30 p.m. on December 18, 1944, Combat Command A moved out. They had orders to motor southwest and take up positions south of Eupen, Belgium. The Spearheaders hadn't been in that neck of the woods since September. If the intelligence analysts had it right, enemy panzers were headed that way to link up with a German parachute drop.

Combat Command A's Brigadier General Doyle O. Hickey asked a reasonable question. For whom did he work? The answers, and non-answers, spoke volumes.

First Army Headquarters initially claimed direct authority, but that didn't last long. With reports of German SS panzers only seven miles south of Spa—and those frantic messages weren't that far off—First Army command post troops began a hurried withdrawal to a secure location near Liege. Although later writings downplayed the degree of panic, the departure proved precipitate. Liaison officers from subordinate units who arrived at the deserted Hotel Britannique saw classified papers strewn about and marked maps on the wall. Telephones remained active. Even a fully trimmed Christmas tree had been left behind. Apparently, with his staff packing up and his forces in disarray, a dispirited, sick (and sick at heart) Hodges spent some time with his head on his desk. At least he got something useful done that day.[12]

None of that helped Hickey and CCA. Hickey checked with V Corps headquarters, an organization busy with German infantry and panzers trying to overwhelm the north goalpost of what G.I.s had begun to call "the Bulge." Weeks later, that became the name American soldiers used to refer to the bitter Ardennes combat. For CCA, there'd be no confrontation on the rim of the Bulge. Not yet. Their role involved hunting down German paratroopers dropped overnight on December 17–18. With that mission from V Corps, Hickey's troops went to work.[13]

The German airborne task force included officers and NCOs who'd fought at Carentan way back on June 13. There were other experienced men in the ranks, and some of the Luftwaffe Ju-52 transport pilots showed ability. Most of those doing the delivering and making the jump, however, were neophytes. Nazi Party fervor only took them so far. Buffeted by winds and dumped out by unsure pilots, 1,200 German jumpers scattered all over the north side of the Bulge. Some were put out as far to the east as Bonn on the Rhine River. After the botched assault, at least 125 enemy paratroopers gathered near Monschau and tried to cause some mayhem.[14] Their ambuscades unnerved American rear echelon troops and headquarters staffs, including those at Hodges's First Army. So Hickey's CCA got told to sort it out.

A few bands of enemy airborne men ended up in the forests near Eupen. There CCA infantrymen and tankers made short work of the Germans. The Americans spread out, seeking parachutes draped in the trees along the main road running south from Eupen. Combat Command A patrols gathered up mis-dropped enemy ammunition, mortar, and machine gun cannisters, limiting the German airborne men to their shoulder arms and a few hand grenades. After a few brief clashes, a good number of the Germans raised their hands. The more enterprising melted into the woods, presumably heading for home.[15]

With CCA already gone, the rest of 3rd Armored Division moved out on December 19. Beginning at 1:15 p.m., Combat Command B began heading to Spa to join XVIII Airborne Corps and stop the powerful German panzer force that flushed First Army headquarters. Courtney Hodges's staff got away OK, but just south of Spa near the village of Stavelot lay an open-air depot containing a million gallons of gasoline. While First Army service trucks scrambled to gather these valuable stores, it proved no quick process. If a Waffen SS panzer column grabbed the fuel, they'd have enough gasoline to cross the Meuse River, no problem. The Allied strategic bombers had gutted much of Nazi Germany's oil industry. But these Germans were more than willing to settle for gasoline from Oklahoma and Texas. Individual U.S. corps-echelon engineer battalions, displaced antiaircraft batteries, groups of truck drivers, and other orphan units blocked key routes snaking north toward the vital Stavelot gasoline yard. Sent by truck from north of Aachen, the American 30th Infantry Division filtered into the area company by company. Combat Command B rumbled south to join this critical fight.[16]

A few hours after CCB departed, Major General Rose received orders to take his remaining forces (Omaha Forward, Combat Command Reserve, the 83rd Recon, and the Division Trains) sixty miles south and west to Hotton, Belgium, south of CCA's para-hunting and west of CCB's evolving Stavelot fight. Rose, too, had orders to report to XVIII Airborne Corps.[17]

The motor march started as the gray day faded to inky blackness. Snow and sleet drifted down steadily all night, coating much of the roadway with a glaze of ice. The frozen moisture made it very tough to see, and the small vehicular telltale markers—in order to disguise the move from Luftwaffe aerial snoopers, headlights were not used—barely showed up a few feet away. The entire armored column of 1,200-plus vehicles extended dozens of miles. An officer described the situation:

> The movement was a pure nightmare. Despite the system of guides and sentries the MPs [Military Police] had worked out on short notice, there was still lots of confusion and a stop and start situation all night. The intervals were extremely erratic and often after prolonged stops the vehicles would get stretched out. When this happened, the vehicle in the rear would drive rapidly to catch up, but in the mist and darkness it often came upon another stopped vehicle and banged into the rear of it. If a two-and-half-ton GMC [General Motors Corporation] truck happened to hit a three-quarter-ton weapons carrier, it would simply knock it off the road. If a tank skidded into a jeep it would squash it flatter than a pancake. I made sure I didn't get in front of a tank that night.[18]

Right in front rode Maurice Rose in his open-topped peep. Darkness and rotten winter weather may have grounded Allied air squadrons. But the unmanned German V-1 buzz bombs kept at it. Several pulsed overhead as Rose and his long column moved south. Liege was a favorite target, and at least one hit near the new First Army headquarters, killing sixteen officers and NCOs and wrecking two trucks. The V-1s added another danger to a night already replete with them.[19]

As Rose's peep passed Liege, the general's aide Captain Bob Bellinger heard a buzz bomb's characteristic putt-putt engine cut out. Not good. Out of the inky wet sky came a whoosh of air then a brilliant blossom of fire and thunderous detonation less than a hundred yards away. The blast wave skidded the peep to a stop, tossing Bellinger out. The aide picked himself up—head ringing, but all parts attached and working. He got back in the quarter-ton truck. Rose mentioned a headache, but nothing else. Off they went toward Hotton. The division's tanks and trucks followed in fits and starts.[20]

Just before midnight, near Hotton, frigid road guards of the 82nd Airborne Division's 1st Battalion, 325th Glider Infantry Regiment met what they identified as the "armored 'point.'" It was Major General Rose leading the way. The glider men weren't that surprised. Their division commander, Major General James Maurice "Slim Jim" Gavin, was cut from the same cloth.[21]

Gavin's superior, Major General Matthew Bunker Ridgway, also led from the front. In Normandy in June 1944, both paratrooper generals stalked the hedgerows, rifles in hand. In Holland in the autumn, the pair did likewise. By then, Gavin commanded the 82nd Airborne Division and Ridgway commanded XVIII Airborne Corps. But in Holland the British ran the show; Ridgway was just stopping by to see his men. Gavin remembered Ridgway's sangfroid under German bombardment. Even for Gavin, it was too much: "You don't just stand there looking at tree bursts. I told him to go be a hero someplace else."[22]

Now someplace else was the Ardennes, and Ridgway's lightly armed airborne forces faced multiple panzer divisions. The paratroopers and glider men needed tank backup. Having been required to ship his 101st Airborne Division off to Bastogne and glory, Ridgway wanted Maurice Rose's 3rd Armored Division yesterday. The XVIII Airborne commander realized that "the 3rd Armored was far away and coming piecemeal." In typical Ridgway fashion, late on December 19, the paratrooper general went forward personally to find Maurice Rose.[23]

In a Belgian hamlet not far from Hotton, Ridgway walked through the dark streets. Blowing snow and freezing rain made the going tough, even on foot. The corps commander saw a collection of M8 armored cars and peeps parked at a corner. The helmeted G.I.s aboard huddled against the wind, hands on their weapons. Ridgway and his aide waved. No problem. A gloved soldier in an M8 turret waved back. As Ridgway passed the halted armored car, the general spied a yellow light shining through a slightly open door. He knocked, a wise idea when those inside and out have firearms. The door cracked wider.

In the small room, a few soldiers had a map spread on a wooden table. Flashlights lit up the crumpled sheet. The Americans were from the 83rd Recon. They didn't seem shocked at all to see a two-star general. They were used to Rose popping up all over. Their lieutenant showed Ridgway the 3rd Armored Division's route. Ridgway thanked the men and left.[24]

So the 3rd Armored Division was very close, and arriving just in time, too. There were a hell of a lot of panzers out there. Ridgway hadn't served with Maurice Rose. But he'd heard of him, and later thought Rose "one of the most gallant soldiers I have ever known."[25] It takes one to know one.

For the first time during Rose's command tenure, the Spearhead Division was working for someone other than Joe Collins at VII Corps. These paratrooper generals seemed crazy-brave; Rose could relate to that. Ridgway was Collins's West Point classmate and like Lightning Joe, the airborne commander missed combat in World War I. Ridgway had sure made up for that in Sicily, Italy, and now in northwest Europe. But he'd been a division commander then. Trying to hold the north side of the Bulge represented Ridgway's first corps-level operation. Frankly, he'd inherited a mess, with bits and parts of units intermixed with the Germans.[26]

That worked for Ridgway. An airborne assault starts by dumping men and gear out of the sky, often at midnight. In concept, the parachutists and glider teams land right on predetermined targets. In too many cases, drops degenerated into 52-pickup, with little groups of paratroopers improvising, adapting, and overcoming. So the situation in the Ardennes looked a lot like the night jump in Normandy: find American units and stick them together like Legos. Hold that line. That was what Ridgway did, and it's about all he could do. Later diagrams of the situation on December 20, 1944, depict a neat wall of American divisions, the 9th, 2nd, 99th, 1st, 30th, 82nd, and now 3rd Armored. The reality was much, much more jumbled.[27]

The XVIII Airborne Corps owned only two-thirds of the 3rd Armored Division, as Combat Command A remained glued to the road net south of Eupen chasing German para-ghosts. Given constant reporting about German jumpers, spies, saboteurs, and even hostiles in American uniforms—all of them grounded in some kind of truth—CCA was stuck. To block any German lunge toward the Stavelot fuel stocks or the Meuse River bridges to the north, Combat Command B passed directly to the command of the 30th Infantry Division, their higher headquarters from the Mortain battle back in August 1944. This left Maurice Rose with the 83rd Recon and Combat Command Reserve at Hotton, hanging out in the breeze.[28] There were more U.S. forces on the way. But for now, the only things west of them were more Meuse River crossings.

And soon enough, the Germans.

————

This would be a tank battle, a big one. The Spearheaders had clashed with enemy panzers many times: Mortain, Rânes/Fromental, Mons, the West Wall. But these encounters usually featured a handful of panzers and dozens of American tanks. Now on the forest roads near Stavelot and Hotton, the odds would be pretty nearly even. That got Rose and his G.I.s thinking.

More than half of the enemy panzers running around the Ardennes were Mark IVs or their turretless assault gun cousins. Those 28-tonners mounted a long 75mm cannon that outranged a Sherman's shorter 75mm, although not by a lot. At five hundred yards or so, it was a fair fight. The 3rd Armored Division's forty-eight Shermans with 76mm barrels could ventilate the front end of a Mark IV out to a thousand yards.[29] If only Mark IVs showed up, great. But there were other denizens lurking.

The opposing menagerie's apex predators were only too obvious, the dreaded Tigers and Panthers. Both overmatched 3rd Armored Division's tanks. Among the American tank crews, men spoke with respect of Tigers and Panthers, as well they might.

Although the Tiger was often reported, especially by nervous G.I. new arrivals, facts seldom caught up with allegations. Tigers came in two versions, the 63-ton Tiger I and the 77-ton Tiger II, also called the King Tiger or Royal Tiger. These massive, sluggish giants overstressed bridges, cracked pavements, and sometimes struggled in mud. But when they moved out, they struck with power. Both used 88mm cannons deadly to a Sherman at 2,000 yards. Tiger frontal armor could ward off Sherman projectiles, although if it caught an angle just right, the U.S. 76mm gun round might penetrate at about a hundred yards or so. Fortunately for the Allies, the Germans fielded few of these behemoths. Only 1,393 Tiger Is and 458 King Tigers were produced during the entire war, and most went to the Russian front. These monsters could be found in special heavy tank battalions. Only two Tiger battalions fought in the Ardennes. Combat Command B of the 3rd Armored Division met one of these outfits.[30]

Unlike Tigers, Panthers proved all too available in the Ardennes. Spearhead Division units ran into these big panzers in several clashes. The almost unstoppable Tiger might bring on night sweats. But the numerous Panthers offered a more likely threat. They moved in packs, hit hard, and died hard, too.

A Panther weighed just under 50 tons. Although clearly heavier than the 33-ton Sherman, a Panther rode on wide tracks that spread the weight better, a quality known as ground pressure (12.3 pounds per square inch, compared to 15.1 for a Sherman). Panthers employed a long 75mm gun that outperformed the Tiger's 88mm weapon inside a thousand yards. A Panther main gun round could rip through a Sherman from any aspect. If surviving American tanks returned fire, the Panther's heavy sloped frontal armor shrugged off both U.S. 75mm and 76mm shots, although those cannons could now and then get a lucky hit inside a hundred yards. American Sherman tank guns had a good chance of penetrating the sides or back even a thousand yards out.[31] Of course, that presumed the Americans maneuvered successfully to gain those advantageous positions. If you manned a Sherman hunting Panthers, these raw statistics certainly gave you pause.

Folk wisdom in the ranks of the 3rd Armored Division said a Panther enjoyed a five-to-one edge over a Sherman. Put another way, Americans expected to trade one platoon per Panther. German panzer men understood the terrible arithmetic. "One of our tanks is better than ten of yours," they snorted. "But you always have eleven!" [32] Such metrics might be OK for the ones marking the charts way up at First Army, Twelfth Army Group, or SHAEF. But those getting "traded" certainly didn't appreciate the exchange rate.

So how did Shermans beat Panthers?

Rather than simply swap like for like, at 5:1, 10:1, or even 1:1, Maurice Rose and his men learned to use all their panoply of armaments. As Rose expressed in a formal report that went to General Eisenhower, "We compensate for our inferior equipment by the efficient use of artillery, air support, and maneuver."[33] It was the familiar prescription. Send a bullet, not a man. Rose believed in it, taught it, and insisted on it. He was right there to make sure it worked.

But Rose also knew there were things that simple side by side number-crunching missed. Shermans stayed in action; they were fixable and robust, with nine out of ten running most days. Panther crews struggled to keep their elegant machines operational. The strong German panzers often fell off the line of march, burdened by inadequate transmissions and a lack of spare parts. German mechanics counted 29 percent of their Panthers in the shop as the Ardennes offensive began. Of forty-seven abandoned Panthers examined by American technical teams after the Battle of the Bulge, twenty had no battle damage. They'd simply stopped working.[34]

The Americans also stuck to the path blazed by innovators like Eli Whitney and Henry Ford: interchangeable parts and standardization. From 1939 to 1945, the Germans fielded four main battle tanks: the Mark III, the Mark IV, the Panther, and the Tiger (two versions), not to mention a bewildering variety of related and unrelated assault guns, obsolescent Mark I and Mark II models, borrowed foreign equipment, and experimental "wonder weapon" variants. None of these things was much like the other. The Americans, however, went with the Sherman and only the Sherman. In the 3rd Armored Division, the M7 self-propelled howitzer and the attached M10 and M36 tank destroyers all built on the basic M4 Sherman design, and thus shared engines, transmissions, parts, and tools. Even the 17-ton M5 Stuart light tank shared some common items.[35]

This standardization lent itself to fairly fast and uniform fleet upgrades. Stateside arsenals provided the M4A3 Sherman with the improved 76mm cannon and the higher horsepower Ford V-8 engine. Front-line mechanics developed the sharpened metal bow forks that uprooted the Norman hedgerows. With winter coming, divisional ordnance teams also installed mass-produced end connector extenders. Sort of the tank equivalent of snow tires, these modifications widened the Sherman's treads, reducing the ground pressure to 12.4 pounds per square inch, similar to that of the Panther. The troops called these track growers "duck feet."[36] They'd come in handy in the snowy Ardennes.

Besides having a more reliable tank, the Americans also had better tankers. Rose certainly thought so. "There is no question in my mind," he wrote, "but what [sic] our gunnery is far superior to that of the Germans." While a few wily panzer aces still manned the German turrets, by 1944 most of the enemy's crews consisted of men who'd driven only a few hours or fired but a few live rounds in slapdash training. The Spearheaders had no shortage of fuel or ammunition to teach new guys the ropes. Rose realized that experienced G.I. tankers learned to go for side and rear shots at less than 800 or more than 1,000 yards. Sometimes it came down to a face-off on a one-lane farm trail. That sort of thing got very sporty.[37]

See first, shoot first, hit first. So preached the old-hand tank sergeants. A postwar U.S. Army study of armor engagements in 1944–1945, including the Battle of the Bulge, confirmed the validity of this mantra. Tank vs. tank fights tended to exemplify the formula Thomas Hobbes ascribed to life expectancy in primordial times: nasty, brutish, and short. The side that got off the first round won, tending to knock out four opponents for each friendly loss. German hits came at an average of 946 yards out. Americans struck their targets at an average range of 893 yards, pretty much the same. The moving vehicle was at greater risk, as motion enabled detection. Stationary defenders hit first in 84 percent of these brief, violent clashes of armor.[38] Winning such quick smash-ups depended on smart, well-trained crews.

The Americans had them. A Sherman relied on the teamwork of five soldiers. Intercoms in their helmets let the men talk back and forth. Two G.I.s worked the hull: the driver, who kept the tank going in the right direction, and his assistant, who manned the radio and fired the .30 caliber bow machine gun. Three soldiers handled turret duties. The loader found the right main gun projectile—armor-piercing, high explosive, or white phosphorus incendiary/smoke—and placed it in the breech; he also fed ammunition to the machine guns. The gunner sighted on the target and fired both the main cannon and its coaxial .30 caliber machine gun. The tank commander (TC) stood high in the turret, usually with his hatch open. He ran the crew. The TC also fired the big .50 caliber heavy machine gun, a weapon that had no German counterpart. The .50 caliber could tear up dismounted troops, shred wooden and masonry walls, eviscerate trucks, and even hole thin armor plate, as on German half-tracks. In a pinch, you could man a Sherman with but a driver, gunner, and TC. Assistant driver and loader were apprentice positions. When the Spearheaders had to retrain infantry replacements as tank crewmen the newcomers normally started in those introductory roles.[39]

Sergeants formed the vast majority of 3rd Armored Division's TCs. Running a tank absolutely constituted NCO business—blue collar, hands-on, no-nonsense, life and death. The need for quick reflexes, upper body strength, athletic agility in cramped quarters, and endless endurance made tanking a young man's game. The 3rd Battalion, 32nd Armored Regiment's Staff Sergeant Lafayette G. "War Daddy" Pool, twenty-five years old in 1944, was considered an elder. Among the greatest of the many fine TCs in the division, Pool earned the Distinguished Service Cross, knocked out dozens of panzers— 258 by one count—and had two Shermans shot out from under him before he finally lost part of his right leg in West Wall fighting on September 15, 1944. War Daddy Pool's experiences provided plot elements for two Hollywood movies, *The Tanks Are Coming* (1951) and *Fury* (2014).[40] Not all Spearheader TCs measured up to Pool. But even aspiring to that level set a high bar.

You couldn't lead men like Pool by babbling on the radio from a heated tent. The sergeant TCs respected officers who fought from a tank. The NCOs expected their lieutenants and captains to lead by example. So, too, with armor battalion majors and lieutenant colonels like Bill Lovelady and Sam Hogan, who commanded from the turret. As Pool's experience warned, this was an exceedingly risky business. It explains the many Spearhead Division tank battalion commanders killed and wounded as the war ground on.[41]

Above battalion level, armor colonels and generals rarely led from a tank. They had to work with infantry, artillery, engineers, and service troops as well as tank crews. The U.S. Army's organizational charts offered such senior leaders the choice of an M5 Stuart light tank, an armored car, a half-track, or a peep, plus affiliated security teams.[42] Maurice Rose chose an utterly unarmored quarter-ton peep. The young tank sergeants knew the deal. They respected Rose's guts. He went where they went. In armored combat, Rose's way was like playing in an NFL football game wearing only a T-shirt. No matter your speed or savvy, sooner or later, you will get hit hard. But Rose and the TCs never talked about that, and it's not likely they thought about it, either. That wasn't healthy.

What was healthy was focusing on killing panzers. See first, shoot first, hit first. With Panthers, go for the flank and butt end. To do so, Rose's NCOs and junior officers preferred to find a good site, squirrel away, and then bushwhack advancing panzers. Of course, that tactic worked if you knew the panzers were coming. On December 20, 1944, they most certainly were.

———

"Initiate intensive reconnaissance in the Hotton-Grandmenil sector, to locate the enemy, and to secure a line running east from La Roche to crossroads 576853 [a military map location southeast of Manhay], and to tie in with the 82nd Airborne Division on the left [east] and the 84th Infantry Division on the right [west]."[43] Thus Matt Ridgway of XVIII Airborne Corps directed Maurice Rose to carry out a series of tasks that would be difficult under any conditions but verged on impossible given the 3rd Armored Division's strength, disposition, and probable opposition.

Hotton and Manhay—these towns mattered. Hang on to them

and the Germans couldn't blitz north to the Meuse crossings. The enemy still might head west, but that was a long, long way to the Meuse River, let alone Antwerp. The forest thinned out with each mile you drove west. And sooner or later, this cruddy Hitler weather would give way to blue skies full of P-47 Thunderbolts. Rose figured all of that out on the dark, wet ride from Stolberg. When he reached Hotton and assembled the division staff in a hotel borrowed to house Omaha Forward, Rose didn't ask for clever ideas. He gave orders.

With CCA and CCB busy elsewhere, Rose's truncated division would be hard pressed to defend Hotton and Manhay, thirteen miles apart. So be it. The book said it couldn't be done. But Maurice Rose chose to see opportunity. The Germans didn't know how much, or how little, of the 3rd Armored Division stood in front of them. Rose went at it like a cavalry officer. He attacked.[44]

Four task forces prepared for action on December 20, 1944. Each combined 83rd Recon scouts, tank companies, armored infantry, engineers, and self-propelled artillery. Rose picked the commanders. Lieutenant Colonel Sam Hogan of CCR went to the west, aiming to reach La Roche. Major John Tucker of the 83rd Recon took the center route toward Dochamps. Lieutenant Colonel Matthew W. Kane of CCR drove east toward Manhay. As backup, Lieutenant Colonel William Orr waited near Hotton; his battalion task force stood ready to go where needed. As for protecting Hotton town itself, Omaha Way Forward, a.k.a. "Combat Command Smith," drew the mission. Along with the headquarters soldiers and the 143rd Armored Signal Company, Company E of the 23rd Engineers helped prepare defenses.[45] Nobody else was left to do the job.

Sam Hogan recounted what he and his men had to go on. "The information of the enemy given to us was zero," he wrote. "This was only a little less than usual." This time, though, friendly information "was also zero, and this was quite a bit less than usual."[46] Hogan and his G.I.s anticipated meeting German units as well as displacing U.S. elements. All the Spearheaders expected panzers.

Task Force Hogan didn't find any. Instead, when they reached La Roche, they met the division trains of the 7th Armored Division. When a reconnaissance team pushed south, they found a German roadblock. The enemy piled thick timber on a blind curve with a steep hill on one side and a drop-off on the other. A hidden antitank gun set afire the first American M8 Greyhound scout car, wounding the crew. With night coming on, that would do it. Hogan pulled his men into a night defensive coil around La Roche. The trains troops from the 7th Armored Division shared rations and cigarettes, a good end to a long day.[47]

On the central advance, by midafternoon, Major John Tucker and his task force reached Dochamps without a problem. There they met a peep carrying Lieutenant Colonel Andrew A. Miller, Quartermaster Officer of the 7th Armored Division. He had 25,000 gallons of gasoline and 15,000 rations on the ground two miles south in the village of Samrée. German recon vehicles had been sighted. Could Tucker help? Well, he'd been sent to find the enemy. Task Force Tucker advanced toward Samrée in a single file on a narrow road bounded by tall trees.

Tucker's column ran smack into waiting Panthers. The Germans saw first, fired first, and hit first, taking out six Shermans in a few minutes. The Americans reversed out of there. They didn't know it yet, but Tucker's men had found the lead companies of the 116th Panzer "Windhund" (Greyhound) Division. For their part, the enemy gobbled up 25,000 gallons of precious gasoline. Tucker's task force scuttled north toward the crossroads of Amonines.[48] The opposing panzers had been well and truly found.

To the east TF Kane made it to Manhay and pushed patrols outside town by dusk. That critical crossroads at Baraque de Fraiture, the 576853 map reference, lay three miles out ahead. Kane met Americans in Manhay who told him a unit from the U.S. 106th Infantry Division occupied Baraque de Fraiture. Rather than risk a "blue on blue" firefight among friends, Kane elected to wait until morning.[49]

Maurice Rose did not. The general sifted through the results of the day's fighting. He'd only seen his tanks and half-tracks moving today, having just missed both Hogan's dustup south of La Roche and Tucker's unhappy meeting engagement at Samrée. Rose did the mental math, and thought through his lineup. Sam Hogan was good to go. He'd sort out whatever showed up. Matt Kane had more work to do but seemed to be on the right track. John Tucker in the middle found real trouble; he needed help. Although he didn't have much to commit, Rose peeled off Lieutenant Colonel Bill Orr's 1st Battalion, 36th Armored Infantry Regiment to strengthen the center task force; Orr would take over, too. As Rose's reserve, Colonel Bobby Howze's CCR consisted of a Sherman tank company, a half-track infantry company, and an engineer company.[50] It wasn't much to react to whatever the Germans tried next.

The enemy tried something all right. At 4:30 a.m., prior to first light on December 21, soldiers hidden in roadside outposts southeast of Hotton heard vehicle noises, throaty engines, steel clanking. A radio check to TF Hogan reported no action there. Had the Germans gotten around Sam Hogan's men?

They certainly had.

At 7:30 a.m., with the day as bright as it would get, German artillery and mortar rounds began falling in Hotton. German infantry appeared to be moving in the woodline southeast of town. Panzer sounds, metal on metal, motors racing, echoed through Hotton. Omaha Forward and 23rd Engineer troops raced to their foxholes, all hands on deck. A stranded U.S. Sherman and a Stuart, both in Hotton for minor repairs, joined the effort.

Two Panthers appeared right on the edge of Hotton. The Sherman shot first, but this time a Panther shot better. With that, Hotton's defenders resorted to the tool of desperation, the bazooka. Engineers have secondary roles to fight as infantry. At Hotton, they did. In close, Sergeant Vern Sergent and Private Hugh Lander whacked the first Panther, setting it ablaze.

The partner Panther responded by drilling a hole in the M5 Stuart light tank. That American vehicle represented no problem to the Panther. But engaging the Stuart left the Panther crew unaware of another bazooka team, Corporal Phillip Popp and Private First Class Carl Nelson. They scored a close-in hit on the side of the Panther's turret. Scratch the second panzer. In the distance, the German *panzergrenadiers* dropped to ground in the tree line. They had no idea they were fighting a scratch bunch of staff officers, engineers, clerks, and signalmen. To the east, at Maurice Rose's order, Colonel Bobby Howze committed a platoon of Shermans and a platoon of half-track infantry to bail out Hotton. They arrived at 11:25 a.m.[51] The 3rd Armored Division's Combat Command Reserve amounted to part of a tank company, part of a rifle company, and a company of the 23rd Engineers. Margins were getting razor-thin.

Both sides paused.

The Germans awaited reinforcements, more panzers, to be exact. But one of the Windhund Division's tank/infantry columns banged into TF Hogan. Colonel Bobby Howze ordered Sam Hogan to drive north to break up the hostile thrust on Hotton. But Hogan only got as far as Marcouray, seven miles southeast of Hotton. Germans stopped TF Hogan, then cut the roads both north and south, surrounding the Americans. But they couldn't budge the tough Texan and his 400 or so troopers.[52]

In the center, TF Orr also held up part of the 116th Panzer Division. Orr's soldiers attempted to advance south to retake Dochamps—an aggressive act that threw off the Germans, even though the push failed and Orr had to withdraw back to Amonines. German Panthers and infantry threatened to push out Orr's outnumbered task force. But Orr and his guys owned good high ground, and the German panzers needed to move up the roads one vehicle at a time. That favored the defenders.[53]

To the east, TF Kane made it to the much-mentioned Baraque de

Fraiture, map grid reference 576853, "X" marks the spot. The cross-roads turned out to be atop an open hill with three small houses, the second-highest ground in the entire Ardennes Forest. No wonder XVIII Airborne Corps wanted it held. Kane found that as he'd heard, several 106th Infantry Division units guarded the vital junction: three towed 105mm howitzers, three antiaircraft half-tracks, and perhaps two hundred Americans. By Battle of the Bulge standards on December 21, 1944, that constituted a major force. Kane couldn't stay. With Hotton in peril and TF Orr pressed hard, Rose told Kane to attack west toward Dochamps to cut off the German panzers menacing TF Orr. It did not work. But it confounded the Germans, and that counted for something.[54]

Rose spent December 21 shuttling back and forth between em-battled Hotton, TF Orr at Amonines, and TF Kane to the east. At 3:30 p.m., welcome news came that Combat Command A was on its way back. But CCA wouldn't arrive until the next morning. Doyle Hickey's combat command was returning with strings attached. Rose had to place them to the west, toward Marche, to make a firm link with the 84th Infantry Division as that new outfit showed up. Rose negotiated with Ridgway to spring loose Lieutenant Colonel Rich Richardson with a tank company and a half-track rifle company. Task Force Richardson had to go to Manhay. But that wouldn't be possible until December 22, if all broke just right.

In Manhay as he moved through en route to TF Kane, Rose ran into Major General Jim Gavin of the 82nd Airborne Division. Gavin wasn't happy. His division's western end hung loose, too loose even for a paratrooper. Why wasn't TF Kane holding Manhay? Why were they attacking west, toward Dochamps? Rose, literally down to a few uncommitted platoons, assured Gavin he'd juggle his tanks and in-fantry and get something to block the road at Baraque de Fraiture. Rose was thinking TF Richardson. But that battalion-size organiza-tion might be twenty-four hours away at best. Both generals wondered if the German panzers would get to Baraque de Fraiture and Manhay first. The 2nd SS Panzer Division "Das Reich"—brutal bastards, heavily armed, fresh—had dropped right off the American intelligence overlays.[55] What about them?

As the sunlight faded on December 21, thick dark low clouds promised snow on the morrow, a lot of it.

————

While Rose and his subordinate commanders shifted forces back and forth to frustrate German attacks, the high commanders gathered at the Twelfth Army Group's rear headquarters at Verdun on December 19. There, just-elevated General of the Army (five stars) Ike Eisenhower brought together the major actors, with Bradley and Patton prominent in the group. Monty, as he often did, pleaded ongoing business and, in true passive-aggressive style, sent his chief of staff. Nobody invited Hodges.[56] Nobody missed him, either.

The situation review described a huge penetration, sixty miles wide and already twenty-five miles deep. Bad stuff, but not all bad. The Ultra code breakers in England had missed most of the German buildup; inside the Reich, Hitler's generals used German telephones, not radios, and those phone wires hadn't been tapped. Now, with the enemy in motion and radios transmitting, Ultra again offered insight. The Germans had planned to be across the Meuse River by December 20, 1944. It didn't look like they'd get there.[57]

The two stanchions, up north (99th, 2nd, and 1st Infantry divisions) and down south (4th Infantry Division and part of 9th Armored Division), held up. The inexperienced 106th Infantry Division suffered horribly, with two regiments, 8,000-plus men, surrounded; they'd surrender by day's end. The Hürtgen-bloodied 28th Infantry Division fell back in relatively sound order. The XVIII Airborne Corps with the 82nd Airborne and 3rd Armored divisions would shore up the north. The 101st Airborne Division had the task of holding the road nexus of Bastogne at all costs even as enemy contingents closed off exits from the city.[58] The Germans drove deep. But the Meuse, not to mention Antwerp, lay far away.

In this meeting, Ike ratified two undertakings already in train. Every available force, to include brand-new divisions, sped to the front. The 75th Infantry Division, the 87th Infantry Division, and the 11th Armored Division (just arrived on December 17) all headed to the Bulge. Along with the divisions came separate artillery battalions, engineer outfits, tank destroyer units, antiaircraft batteries, and every other kind of combat power. Allied air groups stood ready to strike as soon as the weather broke. The meteorologists promised a "Russian high" in the wake of the predicted December 22 blizzard. Temperatures would plummet—agony for G.I.s in the Ardennes. But clear conditions augured success for the deadly Allied fighter-bombers.[59] Soon.

Eisenhower also approved George Patton's counterattack. Patton stunned the gathering by announcing he'd attack with a three-division corps on December 22. All present knew he'd do it, too, the old cavalryman riding to the rescue of the encircled 101st Airborne at Bastogne. As a subsequent newspaper headline blared: PATTON, OF COURSE.[60]

Ike's most important decision didn't come during the meeting. Eisenhower recognized that Omar Bradley located his Twelfth Army Group headquarters in Luxembourg City, south of the Bulge. Bradley hadn't seen Hodges face-to-face since the German offensive began. Communications to First Army near Liege were adequate for Bradley. But Ike didn't give much credence to electronic encouragement. Hodges deserved more. And he was definitely going to get it.

No doubt swallowing very hard, Eisenhower turned to Field Marshal Bernard Law Montgomery. Effective noon on December 20, 1944, Monty gained command of the American Ninth and First armies. Bradley retained Patton's Third, the star player, to be sure, but only one army for an entire American army group HQ to look after. Monty, of course, could barely contain his glee. Bradley felt betrayed by his West Point colleague.[61] Ike ignored these dramatics. Somebody needed to get a grip on Hodges. Nobody gripped like Monty.

The bird-like little British field marshal arrived at First Army headquarters promptly at 1:30 p.m. on December 20, 1944, "like Christ come to cleanse the temple." Monty found conditions not to his liking: "divisions [including the 3rd Armored] in bits and pieces all over the place," "a complete muddle," "no reserves anywhere," and, of course, "no grip." Monty judged Hodges out of his depth, having not gone forward to see his subordinates. Monty asked Eisenhower to sack Hodges. As an American general noted, Hodges was "too old and too frail." (He was two years younger than Patton and the same age as Montgomery.) In any event, Ike refused to let Montgomery get rid of Hodges.[62]

So Monty did what Bradley and Ike did. He worked around Hodges. To lead the counterattack from the north, Montgomery asked for Lightning Joe Collins. Monty would only get VII Corps headquarters; Collins's remaining divisions, less the 1st Infantry and 3rd Armored, stayed in place on the hard-won Roer River line. For his part, Collins gave his druthers. To lead Monty's counterpunch, Lightning Joe requested the U.S. Army's two heavy hitters, the 2nd Armored Division and, of course, Maurice Rose's 3rd Armored Division.[63] An impressive array—but first, the Germans must be stopped.

———

For Maurice Rose, counterattacking under Joe Collins was off in the distant future. Dealing with rampant Germans came first. Did it ever.

From west to east, Rose's division faced enemy pressure. Hotton held with its small pickup team, backed by artillery fires that kept the Germans at bay. A defiant *panzergrenadier* battalion held part of the road east to Soy, where Colonel Bobby Howze's Combat Command Reserve had found its meager ranks bolstered by the full-strength 1st Battalion, 517th Parachute Infantry Regiment, courtesy of XVII Airborne Corps. Howze and the paratroopers had the mission of clearing the Germans off the Soy-Hotton road—easier said than done. The heavy snowfall on December 22 made advancing on foot akin to slogging through knee-deep sand. It also kept the U.S. tanks road-bound. Howze's tankers and the airborne troops stayed at it all day and well into the night. Nothing worked, except the American medics.[64] They stayed plenty busy.

South of Hotton, Sam Hogan's task force defended Marcouray. Even though they were only five miles from Hotton, they couldn't move. Throughout that snowy day, Germans cut the road north and south and kept the perimeter under desultory small-arms fire. If the Germans wanted to take Hotton, they'd have to excise the hard knot of TF Hogan. Hogan had good radio communications, and so he made fine use of supporting artillery. Marcouray sat in the center of open fields. All-round defense worked well:

> We had a regular turkey-shoot knocking out several [German] trucks and jeeps. One of the knocked-out jeeps apparently had a map or something of value in it because the Germans kept trying to get something out of it. Every time they would approach it we would lay in a round of tank fire. Later, one of our artillery pieces was laid in with the jeep as a base point and an occasional round kept the jeep clear until dark. Even then, we lobbed one in now and then for luck. The combination of moon and light snow enabled us to shoot up several German patrols which probed at us during the night.[65]

Good stuff, and Hogan had a lot of ammunition, too. But Hogan's vehicles, especially his Shermans, averaged about a third of a tank of gas. Task Force Hogan needed to go but five miles to reach an American position. They had enough fuel. But they had too many Germans.

East of TF Hogan, Bill Orr's task force tried again to take Dochamps. The 116th Panzer Division had brought up infantry reinforcements from the 560th Volksgrenadier Division. Orr's men
floundered in the snow. It was TF Hogan's situation in reverse, and
again, the attacking side suffered. Orr pulled back to Amonines. He'd
sustained so many infantrymen wounded or badly frostbitten that
he dismounted tankers to hold key foxholes. Half-track drivers and
cooks, too, helped hold the line.[66]

East of TF Orr, Matt Kane's tankers and infantry also attempted
attacks on Dochamps. Two attached companies of the 509th Parachute Battalion joined the effort. Even though the airborne men tried
two night attacks, the Germans didn't budge.[67]

Maurice Rose spent the day working back and forth between the
two Dochamps efforts. At Rose's order, mindful of the 82nd Airborne's worries about Baraque de Fraiture, Rose told Kane to send
something to back up that stitched-together defensive team. All Matt
Kane spared, and even this hurt, amounted to two Shermans. They
joined the three howitzer crews, half-track antiaircraft platoon, and
Company F, 2nd Battalion, 325th Glider Infantry. In the morning,
Rose promised more.[68]

Although Rose and his beleaguered G.I.s didn't know it, their stub-
born, continuous resistance convinced the commander of the 116th
Panzer Division to give up on routes to the Meuse through Hotton or
Dochamps/Amonines. Days behind schedule and many miles from the
Meuse, the Germans thought they confronted a much larger opponent.
A few tanks here, a few tanks there, dug-in infantry, local counterat-
tacks at Dochamps, and continuous fatal dosages of American
artillery—an all-weather brand of firepower—made the foe hesitate.
The 560th Volksgrenadiers stayed in contact. But the 116th Panzer Di-
vision began to pull out. They'd try their luck to the far west.[69]

December 23, 1944, dawned biting cold but clear. This would be a
day of retribution for Allied pilots. The sunshine scattered the Germans into the woods, who knew well what P-47 Thunderbolts and

P-38 Lightnings did. The Germans between Hotton and Soy melted into the trees. But they didn't give up the road or their wooded high ground. Combat Command Reserve kept at it all day, backed by air strikes. Hotton, though, remained firmly in American hands.[70]

Sam Hogan's personal Lone Star flag still flew at Marcouray. His task force occupied the hole in the doughnut. Well-hidden German *volksgrenadiers* persisted in their choke hold. But now Hogan's wounded, more every few hours, needed key medical supplies. His vehicles were running on fumes. The entire thing started to smell like that famous 1836 Texas stand at the Alamo. That one hadn't ended well.

Maurice Rose let his cannoneers try firing bandages and blood plasma into Marcouray inside hollow 105 shells normally used for propaganda leaflets. What landed looked like cold pizza, a mess. An airdrop later in the day also failed. The Germans picked up the bundles and the U.S. Army Air Forces lost cargo planes.[71] The outlook for TF Hogan appeared bleak.

The 560th Volksgrenadier Division continued to press TF Orr at Amonines and TF Kane east of Dochamps. Wary of the roaming American aircraft, the Germans settled for attacking by fire, mortars mainly, plus an occasional antitank gun round. The Germans waited for darkness. The Americans waited for more troops.[72]

At last, Rose had some to give. Combat Command A returned to the fold, closing in an assembly area north of Manhay at 1:30 a.m. on December 23. While most of CCA moved west to Marche to gain a firm handshake with the incoming 84th Infantry Division, Lieutenant Colonel Rich Richardson's task force came under Spearhead Division control. Richardson came with more than expected, his usual cast, built around his own 3rd Battalion, 32nd Armored Regiment and Company I of the 36th Armored Infantry Regiment. Most of Richardson's tankers and infantry moved to backstop Manhay, equal to embattled Hotton as the other anchor of Rose's thin green line.[73] The Germans hadn't pushed there . . . yet.

About noon, Rose directed Richardson to send a Sherman tank platoon and a half-track rifle platoon south to Baraque de Fraiture. The infantry got hung up at a roadblock—ominously, Waffen SS there—but the five Sherman crews closed their hatches, shrugged off the German small-arms fire, and clanked onward. They got to the critical crossroads at about 1:00 p.m. American glider men there told of a failed SS attack that morning.[74] Evidently the 2nd SS Panzer Division had made its appearance. There'd surely be more.

There was.

About 4:00, as the sun set—and the American airplanes went away—German artillery and mortars commenced a twenty-minute concentrated bombardment. The bare hill at Baraque de Fraiture offered no cover other than the trio of farmsteads. The Germans methodically shredded those. American glider troops crouched in their foxholes. Tank crews rode it out with every lid shut. Hot fragments rattled on the Sherman hulls.

Right on cue, the way they taught you in any good infantry school, the SS *panzergrenadiers* came running from the south and west, hopscotching from dim hummock to barely seen dip, almost touching the last few shell bursts, coming on the American infantry holes just as the last German mortar bombs deonated. Mark IV Panzers appeared. Two Shermans flamed. So did two Panzers. The 106th Infantry Division howitzer crews knocked out two more Mark IVs. So far, so good—then the Panthers showed up.

The Panthers immediately blew away two more Shermans. A third American tank tried to use the foundation of the Belgian house as cover. The G.I. crew edged out and shot twice at a Panther, but the 75mm rounds hit the Panther's sloping front plate and zinged away, "like throwing peas at a plate glass window." The Panther nailed the Sherman, and then two more. Meanwhile, the SS *panzergrenadiers* pawed through the wreckage of the three buildings. The enemy overran the position. Only a few Americans made it out. The glider infantry company reported seventy-one men missing. The crews from 3rd

Armored Division never came back. The Germans had grabbed the vital crossroads at Baraque de Fraiture.[75] Next came Manhay. Then the Meuse.

———

The moment of crisis had arrived. Everything Maurice Rose had was in the fight. The 82nd Airborne had no more to loan to the Spearheaders. This battle had to be won with what the 3rd Armored Division owned—not much, maybe not enough. Rose knew it, too.

And it had to be the 2nd SS Panzer Division "Das Reich," notorious slayers imbued with Nazi propaganda. The Americans heard the stories, bad ones. The Waffen SS had already murdered eighty-six American prisoners at Malmedy, and Bill Lovelady's task force in Combat Command B reported slain Belgian civilians at the tiny village of Parfondruy. There a Waffen SS unit shot an old man in bed, drilled another elder in the street, killed a family, including a six-month-old baby, and murdered six more children. Lovelady's men took SS troops captive who freely admitted the slaughter. The enemy officers encouraged them to "fight in the old SS way."[76] No prisoners. And now an entire panzer division of these Nazi zealots drove on Manhay.

Rose didn't hesitate. He'd spent days in and around Manhay, thinking about how to defend the place. The village itself wasn't the key. No, the high ground to the northwest near the hamlet of Grandmenil formed a bow that also ran athwart the highway to the Meuse. Hold that ridge, from just past Grandmenil around to the north end of Manhay.[77] Hold it with tanks, infantry, engineers, and pounding artillery and the Germans weren't going anywhere, Waffen SS or not.

It's of interest that Field Marshal Montgomery also grasped the importance of these crucial heights. In his traditional efficient style, on December 20–23 Monty made daily whirlwind tours of his new American corps headquarters, seeing and being seen, and offering bon mots—"see him off with a bowl," "hit him for a boundary"— incomprehensible and vaguely condescending to non-cricketeer

Americans. Monty quickly sized up conditions and commenced his tidying thing, making straight the ways in the spirit of the approaching Yuletide. Effective December 23, 1944, Matt Ridgway's XVIII Airborne Corps stopped at Manhay, to be held by the battered 7th Armored Division and the rump of the 106th Infantry Division. Joe Collins's VII Corps inherited everything west of Manhay, starting with Maurice Rose's 3rd Armored Division at the vital Grandmenil heights and on west through Amonines to Soy, to Hotton, to Marche, and out to the Meuse crossings at Dinant. Behind the designated American line, rather clean on Monty's map board, British armored brigades moved into position at the crucial Meuse bridges: Dinant, Namur, Huy, and Liege, sticky wickets all.[78] Neat, clean, and gripped up; so ruled Monty.

But the mixed-up situation on the ground did not so swiftly unsnarl itself, especially with the 2nd SS Panzer Division pushing north toward Manhay. And Monty wouldn't run this fight near Manhay. Rose would.

Overnight on December 23–24, Rose's orders went out: Howze and CCR must clean up Soy-Hotton once and for all. Orr and Kane need to hold the center: Orr at Amonines, Kane at Grandmenil. Richardson had to tie tightly into TF Kane and defend the heights north and west of Manhay; he also must cooperate with the hodge-podge gathering there from the 82nd Airborne and 7th Armored divisions. And Hogan? One more day, one more airdrop, then pull the plug. Whatever that might really mean. Rose couldn't dwell on it. The weather people presented good news for Christmas Eve, another good flying day, with Christmas likely the same. The fighter-bombers would be active. Rose's artillery chief, Colonel Fred Brown, promised eighteen battalions in range and on call.[79] Air and artillery, big hammers— and the Spearheaders had need of them.

Rose insisted on one more action. Overnight on December 23–24, Rose told Richardson to get a force, as much as he could scrape up, down toward Baraque de Fraiture to make contact with the Waffen

SS. The Germans would probably wait until night before renewing their attack toward Manhay. Richardson sent Major Olin Brewster with a swept-together task force of seven tanks, four half-tracks of armored riflemen, Company A of the 509th Parachute Infantry Battalion, and Company C, 1st Battalion, 290th Infantry, 75th Infantry Division. That last unit had just shown up for duty. They had no prior combat experience, and now had to stand in the face of the 2nd SS Panzer Division. Brewster's makeshift battalion made it as far as a defile at Belle Haie. They felled trees and blocked the road, then dug in for a 360-degree fight right on the main enemy axis of advance. Brewster's orders came from Rich Richardson, who'd gotten the word from Maurice Rose: "hold at all costs."[80] With Baraque de Fraiture gone, by first light on December 24, TF Brewster formed the early warning outpost and a breakwater on the highway to Manhay.

Risking air attacks, the Germans spent the daylight hours on Christmas Eve slipping forces up toward Manhay to set up for a decisive night attack. As a result, Brewster's men battled small bands of SS *panzergrenadiers* all day. The rookies from the 75th Infantry Division got a faceful of Germans, a steep learning curve, all right. Brewster's tanks held their own. The Waffen SS weren't mounted in half-tracks, nor backed by panzers. Odd that—Brewster didn't realize it, but the Germans lacked gasoline. They'd siphoned and scrimped to fill up the lead vehicles in their Panther column. And that element didn't dare drive right up a defended defile road with Sherman tanks in ambush, artillery zeroed in, and quartets of P-47 Thunderbolt aircraft wheeling overhead hunting for prey.[81]

One of those Waffen SS panzer columns wriggled through the woods west of TF Brewster and moved north toward Grandmenil. Two Panther companies pushed north with SS *panzergrenadiers* riding the panzers to economize on scarce gasoline. Just after 8:00 a.m. at a hamlet called Freyneux, two miles southwest of Grandmenil, the Germans clanked into an open field. The dark Panthers contrasted nicely as they waddled through the sunlit snow.

Freyneux was defended by a team from TF Kane including five American M4 Shermans (one with the new, larger 76mm cannon), four M5 Stuarts, and forty-five 83rd Recon scouts. The Americans waited in carefully chosen concealed firing positions as the Germans blithely approached. German officers up in the turrets noticed nothing unusual. And then . . .

Sergeant Jim Vance opened fire with his tank's 76mm cannon, whacking a Panther on its vulnerable side. He then hit another Panther in its belly as the German vehicle crested a bump. Another American Sherman damaged a third Panther. The Germans backed into the trees. See first, shoot first, hit first—exactly like training at Fort Knox.

Vance and the other TCs then sprayed the withdrawing German Panthers with .50 caliber heavy machine gun fire. That unceremoniously unloaded the onboard *panzergrenadiers*. The four M5 Stuarts and dismounted recon men opened fire. The Stuart's puny 37mm main gun did nothing much to panzers. But against scurrying German ground troops, it more than filled the bill.

The German Panthers hit one Sherman and a Stuart, too. When four more Panthers attempted to cross the snowy meadow, TC Sergeant Reece Graham spotted them at 2,000 yards (more than a mile away), dark silhouettes on the white carpet, broadside to Graham's standard-issue 75mm gun. Sherman tankers loved Panther side shots. Graham engaged, quickly knocking out two of the distant Panthers; their stricken crews probably had no idea where the kill-shots originated. The surviving Waffen SS panzers backed away, retracing the dirt trail they'd used to get to Freyneux. Vectored in by alert forward air controllers with TF Kane, American fighter-bombers found them and set a Panther afire. Five Panthers gone, three damaged, numerous *panzergrenadiers* killed, wounded, or wandering in the trees. Clearly, this attack didn't work for the SS.[82] Kane's men saw to that.

Along the Hotton-Grandmenil road, greatly aided by U.S. airstrikes and fearsome artillery concentrations, Rose's task forces established a solid line for the first time since December 20. Combat Command A linked in with the 84th Infantry Division in Marche. Combat Command Reserve with another regiment of the 75th Infantry Division strongly held Hotton and Soy. Task Force Orr guarded Amonines. Task Force Kane just south and TF Richardson just north held the high ground west of Grandmenil. Matt Kane placed four attached tank destroyers inside the village itself.[83] When the 2nd SS Panzer Division main effort came, Rose's men dominated the good ground.

While the 2nd SS Panzer Division commanders reassessed their efforts to get around TF Kane and TF Brewster, Sam Hogan also met the Germans. One of his Sherman sergeants reported a German officer approaching alone on foot. The man carried a stick with a white flag. A lieutenant blindfolded the enemy leader and took him on a magical mystery tour—no need to let the German gain intelligence. After a reasonable length of time, the German came face-to-face with Hogan and his Lone Star flag. The U.S. escort removed the eye covering. In good English, the German officer told Hogan that three panzer divisions surrounded the American battalion. Surrender now, he said.

Hogan emphatically refused. A battlewise veteran by now, Hogan could see by his foe's uniform that this was no panzer man, but a regular infantry officer. Panzers or not, the Germans certainly outnumbered the Americans and held most of the cards. But as Hogan told his unwelcome guest, the Americans had orders to hold, and they would. The German was again blindfolded and escorted back to whence he came. A similar scene near Bastogne brought everlasting fame to the 101st Airborne Division.[84] But unlike the 101st, no Third Army divisions were driving to succor TF Hogan. Sam Hogan and his G.I.s stood alone. Maurice Rose had nothing to send them.

That afternoon, Army Air Forces C-47 Dakota transports again dropped supplies by parachute. The encircling Germans again enjoyed the American largesse, and shot down at least one airplane, too. Two airmen parachuted into TF Hogan's defensive position. Two more mouths to feed, thought Hogan, and with almost no gasoline left and ammunition shortages, too.[85] Defiant words aside, TF Hogan was nearly spent.

Christmas Eve night brought not peace, but pain. In Manhay, both the 7th Armored Division and the 82nd Airborne Division troops began the Montgomery-ordered realignment. By happenstance, a Waffen SS column of Panthers bearing *panzergrenadiers* stormed into town about 9:00 p.m., catching several American outfits by surprise just as the G.I.s loaded up to pull out. In a running gunfight, the Americans lost dozens of vehicles and sustained hundreds of casualties.[86]

The Germans grabbed the town as U.S. trucks, tanks, and foot troops scattered. For good measure, Waffen SS Panthers also chucked out the four TF Kane tank destroyers in the village of Grandmenil. All bad, all ugly—and all tactically irrelevant, as the Americans absolutely controlled the key terrain. Daylight would bring more rampaging P-47s. The Germans had taken Manhay. Merry Christmas. But Manhay didn't matter anymore.[87] The 2nd SS Panzer Division was out of fuel and out of options.

So were two of Maurice Rose's exposed task forces. With the 3rd Armored Division fought out after the slugfest along the Hotton-Manhay line, and unrelenting German pressure up and down that front, no viable force remained to rescue TF Hogan or TF Brewster. What would become of them?

Maurice Rose had been pondering TF Hogan's state for days. At midday on Christmas Day, Rose authorized Sam Hogan to destroy his vehicles and withdraw on foot under the cover of night. Lacking gasoline and engineer demolition charges, Hogan's men drained all the oil reservoirs and resorted to the preferred method of teenage vandals, pouring sugar into the gas tanks and then racing the engines until they seized up. Gunners collected breech blocks from howitzers and tank guns; these went down a well in Marcouray. Men with hammers and wrenches bashed radios to pieces, then for good measure cracked up gunsight optics. Battalion surgeon Captain Louis Spiegelmann volunteered to stay behind with the dozens of immobile G.I. wounded, some captured Germans, and the remains of the one American killed in the Marcouray perimeter. The walking wounded went out with Hogan.

At twilight, the Americans discarded their heavy, noisy metal helmets, rubbed ashes on their faces, and set out in disciplined platoons, no panic, all business. A recon team had found a gap in the German lines. "Hogan's 400" used it. The last man in the march turned out to be Sam Hogan himself, not due to any bold gesture—though he had guts aplenty—but because the task force commander wore fur-lined Royal Air Force flight boots, excellent for hours standing in a cold metal tank and thoroughly awful for tromping through deep snow. Even so, the Americans got cleanly away and reached American lines near Hotton on the bright morning of December 26.

When he met up with G.I. defenders, Hogan was packed into a peep and sent to Omaha Forward. Rose greeted him, congratulated him on his stalwart defense, and praised Hogan for getting most of his men out. When the general asked why Hogan walked in last, the Texan eschewed a chance to say something heroic, and instead offered, "My feet hurt."[88] American newspaper reporters and radio broadcasters told and retold the story of Hogan's 400. These soldiers epitomized American grit.

A different experience awaited Major Olin Brewster. His stitched-together battalion-strength task force at Belle Haie still held the place "at all costs," as ordered by Maurice Rose. But once Manhay fell to the Germans, that no longer made sense. The Waffen SS had gone from Belle Haie. But they'd be back. Brewster talked by radio to Rich Richardson, who OK'd a withdrawal in the wee hours of December 25. "Get out now if you can," Richardson said, "but don't use the road you went up on. Try east."[89] Bring out all vehicles and soldiers. Go toward the 82nd Airborne Division's area. Avoid Manhay.

Brewster tried the eastern road. It didn't go well. At about 3:00 a.m. on Christmas morning, the vehicle column slowly chugged down a tight one-lane farm track. Concealed German antitank guns nailed the lead tank and then the trail tank. German machine guns opened up from the south, not effective at first, but getting there. In a snap decision, fight or flight, Brewster opted for the latter. He ordered all his troops to dismount and head north through the dark woods. The Americans moved out with a purpose. It was not a bug-out, but an organized tactical effort, taking advantage of the darkness and German confusion, some of it caused by TF Brewster's previous stand at Belle Haie. The U.S. task force left behind a half-track, a peep, a two-and-a-half-ton truck, and five intact Sherman tanks. Men said they'd disabled the vehicles, and no doubt did what they could under German fire. But the need to break contact took priority.

By dawn, Brewster's soldiers met with friendly paratroopers. Like Hogan, the major was trucked to 3rd Armored Division headquarters. Brewster met a reception as cold as that Belgian winter morning. Maurice Rose sat silently behind an olive drab wooden field desk. His posture suggested judge, jury, and executioner. So did his tone.

"Brewster, what happened?"

Exhausted, unshaven, filthy, Brewster did his best to explain. He emphasized that he had Rich Richardson's approval to withdraw. Rose didn't buy it. He asked if TF Brewster still had fuel and ammunition. The major answered affirmatively.

"And you quit fighting?"

Brewster tried to reply. Rose cut him off.

"Brewster, you are under arrest for misbehavior before the enemy." Rose dismissed the shocked officer.[90]

Maurice Rose was as well-accoutered as ever that morning. But the general had gutted out a week on little more than an hour or two of sleep a day. He'd been going, and going, and going, roadblock to roadblock, Hotton to Manhay and all the nasty points in between, day and night. Rose had seen too many of his men dead, too much blood on the snow. Unlucky Brewster caught both barrels.

Once Brigadier General Doyle Hickey, Colonel Tubby Doan, and Lieutenant Colonel Rich Richardson intervened, and Rose got some sleep, the matter went down the memory hole. Olin Brewster went back to Task Force Richardson and served with distinction until wounded badly on January 8, 1945. Yet G.I.s talked to one another about what happened to Brewster. It wasn't fair, they said. And it wasn't like Rose. Apparently the crushing stresses of the Bulge got to him, too.

———

"The operation was a bluff," Rose explained afterward, "because on occasions the enemy had enough strength to overrun the division." In that decisive first week in the Ardennes, "the division succeeded in its mission because it attacked instead of passively defending." Rose referred to this period as the most critical five days of his entire military service.[91] Indeed it was.

The Spearheaders successfully fought off four German formations: 1st SS Panzer Division (Combat Command B's opponent from December 20–25), 2nd SS Panzer Division, 116th Panzer Division, and 560th Volksgrenadier Division. Except for the last one, those outfits constituted elite enemy troops, and the 560th proved themselves more than able, too. Maurice Rose's men had done as much as any American division to blunt the great German offensive of December 1944.

That achievement came at a high price. Rose's division lost 187 men killed and 1,386 wounded. German gunners took out 125 Sherman tanks—more than half the division's assigned fleet—38 light tanks, six self-propelled howitzers, and 158 half-tracks, armored cars, and trucks. No other single battle levied such a toll.[92]

The G-2 counters credited the 3rd Armored Division with killing 1,705 Germans and wounding 545. Despite the precise figures, those were estimates, of course, but within reason. The division took 2,510 prisoners by actual head count. Division troops claimed 118 panzers, 31 of them Panthers, by physical inspection of the wrecks.[93] Some of those probably represented double counts for Allied airpower or the 82nd Airborne and other units. More important than any roll-up, the Germans never crossed the Meuse River. The people of Antwerp never saw a single panzer.

The fighting in the Ardennes didn't end on the day after Christmas. Any German chance to win surely did. The new year of 1945 augured Allied victory in Europe. Somebody, a great many Spearheader somebodies, still had to pay for it.

III

THE REICH

CHAPTER 7

To the Rhine

Weary to the bone, frozen, cold-eyed now, cold-footed,
and cold-hearted to the core, he was sure only that up
ahead lay another river and beyond that another hill,
and that surely beyond that hill was still another river
to cross, on pontoons or by wading.

James Jones[1]

The Germans opened the Roer dams on February 9, 1945. After
all the tragedies of the Hürtgen Forest—the *schu* mines, the
tree bursts, the lost men churned into the pine needles, five months
wasted and 7,024 American lives sacrificed—things ended up right
where they started in September 1944. Even the huge Battle of the
Bulge altered nothing at the Roer. Rather than let approaching
Americans take the dams, the enemy acted as they might have at any
point along this long-term arc of woe.[2] The wide water wash the
Americans fought so hard to avoid now barred the way to the Rhine
River, exactly as Adolf Hitler desired.

First Army commander Lieutenant General Courtney H. Hodges
added this sad outcome to his many burdens. In the worst days of the
prior autumn's Hürtgen campaign, Hodges once stopped his vehicle,

got out, and stood on the muddy road shoulder in silent salute. The Great War veteran welled up in tears as a procession of grimy vehicles passed by. The deuce-and-a-half trucks bore exhausted 4th Infantry Division riflemen. "I wish everybody could see them," Hodges said.[3] All of that travail—and now, the deluge anyway.

German engineers did their usual meticulous work. Expert hands carefully sabotaged both the Erft and the Schwammenauel barriers, blowing open valves that allowed the contents of their reservoirs to spill steadily into the broad Roer River valley. Not a wall of water, but a burbling, unstoppable flow, the flooding guaranteed almost two weeks of delay.[4] In a bit of good news, the opposition could only flip this hole card once. When the ground dried, the Americans planned to advance to the Rhine.

They'd do so in the same old way, the patented Ike Eisenhower broad front advance to the Rhine. The Allies just barely came up shy back in September 1944, but the horrendous German losses in the Bulge—100,000 men gone and the panzer force gutted—combined with the renewed Soviet Red Army offensive in the east, changed the calculus. This time the full frontal push would work. All of Ike's senior generals thought so.[5]

With one exception, that is. Field Marshal Bernard Law Montgomery still insisted on a single thrust north of the Ruhr industrial center. He'd command. After all, hadn't he just done quality work in erasing the Bulge? Yes he had, by any measure. Even Lightning Joe Collins, no fan, thought, "Monty deserves much credit."[6]

But being Monty, he couldn't let it be. In a January 7, 1945, press conference egregious even by Monty standards, the wiry field marshal took full credit for the hard-won triumph. "The first thing I did was busy myself in getting the battle area tidy," he said, "getting it sorted out." After similar self-aggrandizing comments, Monty summarized: "The battle has been most interesting, I think possibly one of the most interesting and tricky battles I have ever handled." Given that only a few British units fought in or around the Bulge, and that

Monty only led the northern portion with an almost wholly American lineup, the public gloating caused an uproar in America and among senior U.S. generals in Europe. Monty had outworn his welcome. Incensed, Eisenhower offered a clear choice to the political and military authorities in Washington and London—him or me. Both capitals backed Ike. Monty apologized, kept his job, and saved further acrimony for his private thoughts and memoirs.[7] His Twenty-First Army Group would be part of a broad front advance.

With that distraction resolved, and the Bulge erased, the familiar fall 1944 command setup reemerged. In mid-January 1945, Omar Bradley's Twelfth Army Group resumed authority over Hodges's First Army, to include Joe Collins's VII Corps and Maurice Rose's 3rd Armored Division. By the first week of February, VII Corps headquarters and the Spearheaders returned from whence they came, the Stolberg corridor and the Roer River line, held in their absence by the 104th Infantry Division to the north and the 8th Infantry Division—another outfit scarred by the Hürtgen—to the south. All stood ready to go on the attack. Then the Germans blew the dams and the swollen Roer overtopped its banks. It reminded G.I.s of that most time-wasting of drills, stepping tall but going nowhere. Mark time, march.

———

Rose's Spearhead Division had already issued Field Order No. 26, ready to follow the two infantry divisions, then, once past the Roer, shoot through and lead the VII Corps drive on Cologne. It was supposed to kick off on February 10. Now the start date depended on the readings brought back every few hours by various engineer survey teams. The engineers guessed twelve days.

Nearly two weeks' delay helped immensely in the 3rd Armored Division. The flooded expanse kept the Germans well back, an unexpected blessing. During that stint the division recorded one soldier killed and a few wounded by German nuisance artillery rounds. Holding back their ammunition stockpiles to meet the expected

American attack to the Rhine River, German generals limited their howitzers to four rounds a day. American artillery responded in volume. "Ten shells for their one," a G.I. said. "That's the secret of it."[8] Send a bullet, not a man.

As for the men, the 3rd Armored Division brought in many replacements. As usual, most went to the 36th Armored Infantry Regiment and the tank outfits. For example, the 32nd Armored Regiment, home of CCA, including TF Richardson, brought in sixteen officers and 213 enlisted men, about 10 percent of the unit's strength. Some tank outfits suffered more. The Bulge, however, also inflicted significant losses on the 83rd Recon, the 23rd Engineers, the artillery battalions, the forward logistics elements, and Omaha (Way) Forward, too.[9] Two extra weeks of tank crew drills and basic infantry tactics ensured the rookies knew what to do once the Spearheaders headed for the Rhine.

The 3rd Armored Division tank fleet also benefited from two more weeks of preparation. Tanks with blown engines, over-torqued transmissions, damaged suspensions, or cracked armor could be fixed, and were. Hard driving over bad roads, through mud and snow, and across rough terrain caused a lot of this. American soldiers added to the strain on the Shermans. Ingenious G.I. crewmen and mechanics placed sandbags, extra road wheels, additional sets of track blocks, and even torch-cut steel plates to reinforce the Sherman's frontal armor slope. This extra weight took its toll on the innards of the Shermans. Engines howled going up inclines. Transmissions whined. Treads split. More tanks fell out on motor marches, an average of 17 percent vs. the usual 10 percent But the sergeant TCs wanted the extra field-expedient armor. They were willing to accept a speed dropoff and more breakdowns if their tanks could shrug off the next Panther shot.[10]

Repairing mechanically hobbled tanks happened regularly. Battle-damaged Shermans required an ordnance officer and NCOs to make tougher calls. Because the Americans held the battlefield at the end of the Ardennes campaign, T2 tank retrievers (Shermans modified as the tread-borne equivalent of tow trucks) clanked here and there to pull back wrecked American tanks. It beat doing so under fire, although they did that, too, often at grave risk.[11]

In the best case, a tank with a crippling hole in it went to the scrapyard and the crew received a brand-new model with a Ford V-8 500-horsepower engine. The ones with the 76mm long guns were not popular. The TC brotherhood preferred the old-school 75mm. They knew it well, and didn't quite trust the allegedly improved 76mm type. Rose backed his tank sergeants. So the division had only 44 Shermans with 76mm cannons by February 1945, down from 65 in September 1944.[12]

Yet even with prodigious American production, the maintainers had to refit every tank they could in theater. A bird in the hand, even a pretty torn-up one, beat waiting for the faraway stateside army to provide a new tank. Mechanics learned to clean up, fix up, and send up. Fresh white paint inside and olive green outside disguised a lot of unpleasant scarring. Sometimes paint did not suffice, thanks to a German habit.

Germans taught their soldiers—panzer crewmen, antitank gunners, and even Hitler Youth hauling *panzerfäusten*—to keep shooting at a tank until it caught on fire. American TCs taught G.I.s to bang away until the hostile panzer stopped moving and shooting. A bonfire was a nice confirmation. But the Germans emphasized going for flame. A topped-off M4A3 Sherman contained 172 gallons of 80-octane gasoline, not to mention 71 rounds of main gun ammunition. If that stuff ignited, a Sherman with the hatches open immediately sucked the heat skyward and the thing burned like a haystack. British tankers who used the Sherman nicknamed it "the Ronson" after a popular cigarette lighter that advertisers boasted "lights first time, every time." It didn't make for a nice tableau when mechanics looked inside at what remained. That gruesome smell lingered. Such tanks went immediately to the discard pile.[13]

Even if a smacked or burnt-out tank couldn't be restored, enterprising mechanics could always take parts off the beat-up hull and turret. The G.I.s called it cannibalization.[14] The term spoke for itself.

Along with the freshly issued M4 Sherman mediums and M5 Stuart lights came an unexpected surprise. Ten T26E3 Pershing heavy tanks showed up. Twenty had been sent to Europe as a test. Ten went to the 9th Armored Division, an outfit that saw a great deal of action in the Bulge. The other ten arrived in the Spearhead Division in mid-February. Word of the super tank even brought out Courtney Hodges from First Army headquarters to join with Joe Collins in Rose's forward division area. The three generals liked what they saw. So would Spearhead TC sergeants. The 46-ton Pershing mounted a 90mm gun and heavy armor and rolled on wide tracks. It could outgun a Panther or a Tiger.[15] Well, better late than never.

The 83rd Armored Reconnaissance Battalion also received sorely needed new vehicles. The M5 Stuart light tanks had long been relegated to ancillary roles. "The light tank is being used for working with infantry," stated one of Maurice Rose's former colleagues in the 2nd Armored Division. "We subject it to direct fire just as little as we can," the report continued, "for it is realized that the armor will not turn the German fire, or [sic] the 37mm gun damage the German tanks or SP [self-propelled] guns." For his part, Rose was characteristically direct: "There is no place in an armored division for a light tank whose principal weapon is a 37mm." To address these complaints from field commanders, the U.S. Army developed the M24 Chaffee, a sprightly 21-tonner powered by twin Cadillac V-8 engines. The M24 turned out to be as speedy as the Stuart but a bit better armored, though it still couldn't trade blows with a panzer. It could, however, kill one. The Chaffee used an improved version of the Sherman's 75mm main gun. The 83rd Recon swapped out its company of well-traveled M5 Stuarts for these agile new M24s. Unfortunately, the rest of the 3rd Armored Division had to keep using the obsolescent M5s.[16] There weren't yet enough new Chaffees to go around.

One other fighting arm badly needed two more weeks to get right. The division's three armored field artillery battalions—the 54th, 67th, and 391st—fired thousands of shells in support of division operations going all the way back to the summer of 1944. Technical experts back in America claimed that a 105mm tube enjoyed a service life of 7,500 rounds. They did their arithmetic based on the designated rate of fire of four projectiles a minute. But highly skilled howitzer crews pumped out ten a minute when necessary. It was often necessary. As a result, the 105mm barrels in the division had become pitted and corroded, with rifling grooves worn down to uneven dents. Smoothbore cannons might have been adequate in the face-to-face thousand-yard smash-ups of the American Civil War, but at seven miles' range, an M7 howitzer required predictable accuracy. Tired tubes meant wandering artillery rounds. When you sent a bullet, not a man, you had to be able to count on your shot hitting where you aimed. Off-target rounds missed Germans. Short rounds killed Americans. That had to be remedied. Every howitzer barrel in the 3rd Armored Division, fifty-four in all, had to be changed out.[17]

With a general like Maurice Rose in command, Spearheaders stayed busy training and refurbishing their gear while waiting for the Roer valley flooding to subside. Absent the daily threat and breakneck tempo of mobile combat, however, men found chances to talk. The old-timers, some of them in the ranks since Camp Polk in 1941, hoped that this last push might do it. The new guys wanted to be in on what looked to be the last offensive of the war. The great Rhine River acted as a physical barrier, no doubt. But it also formed a crucial psychological boundary, "Die Wacht am Rhein" and all of that. Breach it, and you entered the heart of Germany, the vitals of Hitler's Thousand Year Reich. Maybe, just maybe, crossing the Rhine could trigger a swift German collapse. Rookies were sure of it. Veterans had heard that stuff before at the Seine, at Mons, and at the West Wall. The old sweats scoffed in public. But privately, more than a few prayed that this really would be the final push. Men felt tired past tired. No two-week delay could take that away. And the Germans . . . well, hundreds and even thousands might surrender. But a lot fought on. Would those people ever quit?

That disturbing question conjured up the most horrific of rumors, the thoughts men shared inside darkened tank turrets or in foxholes at night. Have you heard about what those guys in the French First Army found down south, near Strasbourg? The Nazis had been running some kind of concentration camp, not simply to house slave laborers, which was terrible enough, but for industrialized mass execution of Jews, homosexuals, political resisters, and other so-called undesirables. Stories circulated about poison gas, ghoulish medical "experiments," and, in a sick display of Teutonic efficiency, very thorough records of the entire set of horrific proceedings. Some G.I.s had seen the *Life* and *Time* issues showing photos and reporters' descriptions of a similar camp at Majdanek in Poland. Even hardened Red Army officers, no slouches at slaughter themselves, couldn't quite take it in.[18] These Nazi Germans—what the hell do you do with an enemy like that?

Maurice Rose had an answer. Kill them. And when we kill enough, they'll quit. As the Roer waters gradually dissipated, the next round of killing loomed.

———

Lightning Joe didn't get that nickname for his patience. When the engineer river-checkers thought the Roer flooding had nearly run its course, Collins wanted to launch. First Army held the reins for a day or so, to coordinate with the Ninth Army to the north. Patton's Third Army had already started. Even Monty's Twenty-First Army Group was underway. Finally, on February 20, Hodges and his Ninth Army counterpart agreed. Go on February 23.[19]

At 2:15 a.m. on the appointed day, 936 American guns opened up, the largest preparatory program since the ill-fated VII Corps attack way back on November 16, 1944.[20] That was then. This was now.

The two infantry divisions went first to secure a bridgehead across the Roer at Duren. At 3:30 a.m., four regiments of American infantry cast off in flimsy assault boats, fifteen per rifle company, with the 104th Infantry Division to the north, the 8th Infantry Division to the south. Both division commanders scratched a smoke screen or illumination flares; better to simply get to the other side in darkness. The 104th Infantry Division's lead companies made it across quickly. The 8th Infantry Division's assault wave did not. Swirling river water drowned the small outboard motors, and only a few boats made it to the eastern river bank, and those thanks to herculean paddling by soaked riflemen. A few of the craft swamped; some capsized. It took well into the following night for the 8th to ferry enough G.I.s over to clear the far shore. [21]

Though the 104th enjoyed a more successful crossing, bridge construction proved very difficult. In the 8th's area, it was almost impossible. German artillerymen pounded away after daylight. The opposition made good use of all of those shells they'd been saving. At one point, the 8th Infantry Division reported 125 German rounds an hour. American engineers labored under cover of a dense smoke screen, so most of the enemy projectiles splashed in the water. But some hit, killing eight engineers and wounding 145. It took until midnight to get a single narrow bridge completed in the 8th's area, and no others were finished until February 25.[22]

Despite the slow rate of bridging, Major General Joe Collins of VII Corps noticed something important. The Germans mounted no counterattacks, no panzers, none of the usual. And the American riflemen scooped up prisoners right away. Even in the difficult 8th Infantry Division zone, twenty-three Germans surrendered as soon as the first few assault boats landed. German defenders didn't fight very hard for the small city of Duren, either.[23] Once the engineers installed the bridges, the 3rd Armored Division could pass over and really get going. There might not be much to stop the Spearheaders.

With four tank-worthy engineer spans built by dusk on February

25, Rose began to stage armored forces into the bridgehead under the cover of night. Combat Command B used the 104th's two northern crossings; Combat Command A went over the 8th's pair of southern bridges. They'd advance abreast toward Cologne, twenty-two miles to the east. Lieutenant Colonel Mike Yeomans's 83rd Recon parked between the two combat commands. The recon commander had the task to race ahead to grab an intact bridge or two over the next waterway, the Erft Canal, about halfway to Cologne.[24]

At 6:00 a.m., under a cold drizzle, five columns departed the Duren bridgehead, aiming at Cologne. From north to south, Rose's division deployed CCB's TF Welborn and TF Lovelady, TF Yeomans (structured around the 83rd Recon), and CCA's TF Kane and Doan. Combat Command Reserve followed CCB with TF Hogan and Richardson. To add much-needed rifle strength to the 3rd Armored Division, Joe Collins attached the 13th Infantry Regiment from the 8th Infantry Division. This paired a tank and infantry battalion in all six task forces, less that of Mike Yeomans. The Spearheaders trained with the 13th Infantry Regiment prior to the February 23 river crossing. Although the 13th came with their own trucks, they intended to travel on the decks of the Shermans, Soviet Red Army style.[25]

The terrain between the Roer and the Erft included a mix of farm fields, small villages, and some tree stands. Winter mud and the day's rain encouraged the Americans to rely on the autobahn, but Rose and his task force commanders knew better. The methodical Germans always protected the obvious routes. So Rose chose the way less traveled. He sent his task forces through the countryside north of the paved highway, trying farm trails. It might serve to outguess the overstretched, largely foot-mobile Germans. That could well flush any lurking panzers, too. For insurance against Panthers or even Tigers, Rose's task force commanders led each column with a T26E3 Pershing. Might as well check out these touted Tiger-killers; each went to an experienced sergeant TC and a picked veteran crew.[26] Rose counted on his sergeants, as usual.

The attack on February 26 went well in the north. Colonel Jack Welborn's task force started forty-five minutes late, held up by congestion in Duren. But once the tanks started rolling, they moved out. Although hindered here and there by the sloppy side roads, Welborn's men blew through "little enemy resistance," to include Hambach Forest, a mini-Hürtgen had the Germans defended it.[27] They did not.

Enemy proclamations made much of the Nazi *volksturm* militia in the villages near the Erft. Supposedly every able-bodied German, and some not so able, too, would turn out to repel the gum-chewing American gangsters. The few who assembled immediately raised their hands.[28] They did not want to play.

Neither did a family of three—mother, father, and daughter—that Spearhead G.I.s found in the hamlet of Berrendorf. The trio lay dead, side by side, cords around their necks. Somebody had cut them down from the barn rafter where they hanged themselves. Even their little dachshund had been killed. A German-speaking American soldier translated the neatly lettered note. "We cannot live in shame any longer."[29] What had these people seen? Worse, what had they done?

Most Spearheaders didn't have time to think about such things. That hour would come. But not on the wet afternoon of February 26. Getting to and across the Erft preoccupied the American tankers and riflemen. Stay on task.

Bill Lovelady sure did. He always did. His path brimmed with gluey wet mud, but TF Lovelady kept at it, crunching right through its stretch of the Hambach Forest. Unlike TF Welborn, Lovelady's men had some encounters, to include the stubborn crew of a German 88mm antitank gun. Two Shermans were knocked out, resulting in several G.I.s wounded. Lovelady's men destroyed that pesky German cannon and a panzer assault gun, too. The Americans took seven prisoners before halting for the night within a mile or so of the Erft Canal. Lovelady's intelligence officer thought the task force might have killed fifty Germans.[30] Nobody really could be sure. Still, the task force was almost at the waterway.

In the center, aggressive Mike Yeomans and his scouts made it halfway to the Erft before hitting a very hard knot of German infantry with antitank guns at a crossroads called Mannheim (not to be confused with the major city on the Rhine). The new M24 Chaffee light tanks couldn't pry the Germans loose.[31] The recon men weren't going to grab an Erft bridge screwing around at little Mannheim.

Yeomans talked with his neighbor, Lieutenant Colonel Matt Kane of CCA. The route south of him was the autobahn, and as Maurice Rose intuited, the Germans were all over that route. On that fine roadway, Task Force Doan had a major fight on his hands, and TF Kane had slipped past to the north after smashing through two dug-in 88mm guns. Tubby Doan's infantry platoons were clearing trenches in the manner of the Great War; the Americans had already lost seventeen men killed, numerous wounded, and four Sherman tanks. Doan's artillery had to fire smoke shells to allow the Americans to shake loose for another attempt to break through.[32] The autobahn battle wouldn't be over anytime soon.

Now Kane saw an opportunity. With Brigadier General Truman Boudinot's strong backing, Kane worked with Yeomans to take Mannheim. The 83rd Recon attacked from the west, and TF Kane struck from the south. This double-header broke the Germans. But it also dragged on well into the evening.

Maurice Rose spent the day forward, mostly in the center and south. There's a familiar military adage that advises a general to reinforce success. Combat Command B sat close to the Erft, but the German resistance to their front had gotten worse overnight. The 83rd Recon held Mannheim, halfway to the Erft. Task forces Kane and Doan had made it about as far as Yeomans's 83rd Recon. Rose wasn't worried about a neat, straight line—no Monty he. Rather, Rose wanted to keep pressing toward Cologne and the Rhine.[33] And that meant getting across the Erft.

Rose decided to commit Combat Command Reserve. The division commander directed Sam Hogan's tank/infantry column to pass through TF Welborn, and Rich Richardson's group to move through TF Lovelady. The general also spurred Mike Yeomans to get his scouts to the canal. The prize was a bridge. Rose promised a case of scotch to the first task force commander to cross over. The general didn't drink.[34] But those lieutenant colonels sure did, and so did a bunch of their officers and NCOs.

Yeomans's scouts headed for the water's edge first. Moving before sunrise, the lead peep hit a mine, killing a company commander and wounding three other soldiers. The 83rd didn't delay much. Medics treated the wounded and engineers proofed the road, then off went several recon teams. They found the ruins of a blown bridge. German machine gunners and mortarmen fired from across the canal.[35] No joy. And no scotch, either.

Hogan and Richardson waited for their cue. But first, Jack Welborn and Bill Lovelady and their soldiers had work to do. Task Force Welborn fought through Elsdorf, a small town just shy of the Erft Canal. In peacetime, the place could fairly be described as picturesque, a Rhineland jewel, replete with timbered, gabled homes out of Hansel and Gretel. But on February 27, Elsdorf was just another rat's nest to scour. Persistent German machine gun teams, *panzerfaust* men, and die-hard pairs and trios in stone-block cellars had to be cleared by tank main gun fire and U.S. riflemen with M1 Garands, BARs, and hand grenades. It took all day.[36]

Task Force Lovelady also battled on the east side of Elsdorf. The same determined hostile infantry refused to knuckle under. As Bill Lovelady's tanks and U.S. rifle troops worked their way into the battered houses, a gigantic shell impacted, killing an infantryman and two forward observers from the 391st Armored Field Artillery Battalion. Several Americans fell wounded. It was some kind of "Big Bertha" railroad gun, maybe a 380mm (15-inch) behemoth, firing from the east side of the Rhine River.[37]

The German panzers were not so effective. Two Mark IVs and a Panther attempted to intervene in the Elsdorf action. The German armored vehicles ran into a U.S. Pershing. The experienced American TC saw the enemy first. He and his crew shot first. And at a thousand yards range, they hit first, too. The 90mm projectiles lanced right through the Panther's sloped front plate and ripped open the other panzers, too. That disheartened at least twenty-five German infantrymen, who surrendered. As with TF Welborn, though, the combat used up all the daylight hours.[38]

To the south, Combat Command A closed up near the Erft, too. When the Germans counterattacked with infantry and panzers, the 67th Armored Field Artillery Battalion quashed the bid with heavy concentrations of shellfire. Again, progress had been made. But it took until night to run off the enemy. All of the clashes in CCB and CCA cost twenty-two Americans killed and more than a hundred wounded.[39]

A hard day indeed, and not much movement—and yet, Maurice Rose sensed wavering on the other side of the fighting. He ordered Colonel Bobby Howze of CCR to move up. At 4:30 p.m., TF Richardson passed through TF Lovelady. By 5:20, in twilight, TF Hogan rumbled past TF Welborn. Hogan had his Lone Star flag flying from his tank. Yet Rich Richardson, too, hailed from Texas.[40] Both commanders were determined to get across the Erft Canal before sunup.

Hogan's lead platoon found the residue of a dumped bridge. At 9:29 p.m., four platoons of the 36th Armored Infantry Regiment moved out, with tank cannons and machine guns providing covering fire. The American riflemen scrambled across the Erft Canal in the darkness. German mortar fire pinned the assault force to the far bank. But they were there.

Rich Richardson's lead tank crew also reported a bridge gone. But here, not even stumps or wreckage remained. Nevertheless, before midnight, dauntless riflemen from the attached 13th Infantry Regiment waded the icy canal. On the eastern side, the bone-cold Americans went prone as German mortars pummeled the area. Again, though, G.I.s found a way. The 23rd Engineers moved their bridge team in behind Richardson's toehold. By 9:45 a.m. on February 28, the first structure was completed. For the record, Rose sent the coveted container of scotch to Hogan. Sam Hogan properly split the prize with Rich Richardson. As it turned out, Hogan's tanks ended up crossing at Richardson's site.[41] Hogan might have gotten American foot troops over first. But the tanks went courtesy of TF Richardson. And in the Spearhead Division, tanks counted.

The next water barrier was the Rhine River.

———

Maurice Rose and Long John Smith pushed Omaha Forward into torn-up Elsdorf about the same time CCB chased out the last of the German defenders. As Rose's newly promoted aide Major Bob Bellinger commented, "It was very warm around there." He wasn't discussing the weather. The soldiers of Omaha Forward figured on that kind of reception. But as usual, Rose didn't hang around the command post. He motored his peep up to the bridging effort, as if his physical presence might will the metal treadway into being.[42] If nothing else, he shared the dangers with the laboring engineers, the covering tank crews, and the weary riflemen.

Getting a single span to the other bank amounted to step one. The 23rd Engineers didn't stop there. Rose wanted four crossings capable of bearing tanks, including the 46-ton Pershings. Throughout the gray chill daylight hours of February 28, under sporadic German fire and drifting clouds of friendly smoke, the engineers tried to erect bridges at Lovelady's crossing and Yeomans's location, too. During the day, Matt Kane's men found a fourth good spot. But suitable locations do not equal finished spans. For most of February 28, there was only one bridge, the metal span in TF Richardson's zone.

The enemy did what they could to slow the American passage over the Erft, dropping mortar and artillery rounds, killing eight G.I.s and wounding more than twenty in and around the crossing lanes. The 23rd Engineers suffered the worst of it. A poorly organized German counterattack against TF Richardson's bridgehead came too late. At 9:45 a.m. American Sherman tanks stormed over the just-finished first treadway, scattered the hostile infantry, and knocked out two supporting panzers, too. The division G-2 experts later identified the Germans as part of the 3rd Panzergrenadier Division.[43] Those once-vaunted opponents had clearly lost a step or two. With the Germans pushed back, for the rest of the day 3rd Armored Division vehicles passed one by one to the far side. With only a solitary bridge, it took a long, long time.

Rose stood at the busy treadway when Colonel Smith called on the radio. The division chief of staff said that Lightning Joe Collins had just showed up at Omaha Forward. Nothing new there—Collins often did so. The surprise involved his plus-one, Lieutenant General Hodges. Hodges hadn't been in the 3rd Armored Division zone during an attack since the clash at Rânes back in August 1944. Had it been only Collins, Rose might have stayed at the canal edge and the corps commander would have come there, too. But Hodges? He was as far up as he'd go. Rose had to make his way back to him.[44]

Rose hopped in his peep and bounced back to Omaha Forward in Elsdorf. As he neared the damaged town, the division commander saw batteries of heavy guns banging away. The 991st Armored Field Artillery Regiment 155mm Long Toms had already cranked shells into the outskirts of Cologne.[45] There'd be more of that. A lot more.

Hodges and Collins had been waiting about forty-five minutes by the time Rose arrived. The generals sat down with coffee. Collins enjoyed a warm relationship with Hodges. Although only nine years apart, Collins lived, looked, and acted much younger and Hodges often emulated Methuselah. Lightning Joe seemed to be the inscrutable First Army commander's fair-haired son, all right.[46] Rose also stood high in Hodges's eye, but their ties were all business, nothing personal. With Rose, it never was.

Having already gotten a tactical update from Colonel John Smith, Collins and Hodges didn't quiz Rose about the bridging operation.

Collins normally talked a lot, but in well-practiced deference to the reticent Hodges, Lightning Joe kept mum. Rose, as usual, also said little. After a few awkward moments, Hodges pronounced himself satisfied. When the First Army commander's aide crept into the room to whisper that it was almost dusk and thereby past time to depart, Hodges said, "I don't care what time I leave; for the first time in a month I heard a gun." Then he promptly left.[47] Of note, Hodges's First Army soldiers had been on the offensive for five days. Courtney Hodges sometimes gave the strong impression that he was visiting his own job. Not that it mattered on the Erft. Collins certainly gripped the picture, as Monty might say. And so did Rose.

So did the Germans.

With little else left to throw into the cauldron, the enemy turned to a force that hadn't been decisive for two years—the Luftwaffe. Random recon flights, V-1 buzz bombs, jet fighter-bombers, and occasional "bed check Charlie" overnight raiders had pestered and hurt the Spearhead Division on many prior nights. But the last night of February marked a surge by German pilots. At least seventy-five German planes made separate strikes. The bridges, finished or not, got attention, but so did American artillery batteries. Combat Command A's 67th Armored Field Artillery Battalion suffered several wounded. The attacks persisted into the predawn hours. An Omaha Forward sergeant wrote: "Then there'd be the erie [eerie], rising whistle of the bombs and, if they were close, the unbelievably loud crash." The 486th Anti-Aircraft Artillery Battalion gunners threw up a lot of flak and claimed five kills.[48] Maybe they got some of the intruders. Who knew? What the Spearhead soldiers did know was that most of the German bombs churned mud. American operations continued unabated along the Erft.

Working around Hodges's rare appearance, Collins realigned VII Corps for the push to take Cologne. Possibly, the Germans might oppose the Americans in house-to-house combat, but Collins thought not. A fast, powerful blow would bowl over the German defenders and run them out of Cologne, a city with a prewar population of 780,000 inhabitants, fourth largest in the Reich, and so potentially a formidable urban stronghold, a Nazi version of Stalingrad. By 1945, however, most Cologne civilians were long gone, either fled or dead. The city was a bomb-shattered ghost town. With the local German Army units chewed up and the city's remaining residents wholly war-weary, the U.S. seizure of Cologne seemed likely to go like Liege, not Aachen. That's what Collins intended. The VII Corps commander read ground well, and while most of the area west of Cologne stretched flat as a pancake, dotted with slag heaps, lignite coal pits, and villages, one terrain feature grabbed Collins's attention: the Vorgebirge ridgeline, a 500-foot-high hummock six miles west of the city that ran south from the town of Stommeln. That would be the pivot point. Collins intended Rose's 3rd Armored Division to seize that crucial road junction at Stommeln, then head right into north Cologne, keying on the massive triple-arch iron truss Hohen-zollern Bridge across the Rhine. The 104th Infantry Division would take south Cologne. The 99th Infantry Division covered the 3rd Ar-mored Division's north flank; the 8th Infantry Division (minus its 13th Infantry Regiment still with the Spearheaders) planned to do the same for the 104th's south side. The entire VII Corps scheme de-pended on the 3rd Armored Division. As Collins put it: "The task force commanders, Doan, Kane, Welborn, Lovelady, Hogan, and Richardson, were all great combat leaders, as were the combat com-manders, Hickey, Boudinot, Howze, and, of course, Maurice Rose."[49] Collins backed the right horses.

Rose set the start for very early on March 2. Day one involved se-curing a solid start line past the Erft Canal. Once the division held the launch pad, the armored task forces would blast off for Cologne and, if lucky, the famous Hohenzollern Bridge. Control of the canal line passed to the U.S. 4th Cavalry Group and the 395th Infantry Regiment of the 99th Infantry Division. Commencing at 3:00 a.m., Lieutenant Colonel Mike Yeomans's 83rd Recon pushed out a few

miles to secure villages on the west slope of the Vorgebirge. Colonel
Bobby Howze's Combat Command R then slipped through the 83rd
and took the key roads that headed to Stommeln. Combat Command
B followed behind Howze's CCR. To the south, Combat Command A
rolled through the 395th Infantry Regiment to grab more roads leading over the Vorgebirge. The day's fighting resulted in eighteen Americans killed and scores wounded. Rose was right there. He saw it all.[50]
This tough twenty-four hours set the stage.

Now, with the Germans rocked back some, Rose insisted on pick-
ing up the tempo and going faster than the walking foe, bereft of
most of its panzers, could hope to react. Captain A. Eaton Roberts of
TF Lovelady explained why: "Except for the too closely spaced towns,
the rolling plains of Cologne were more nearly suited to tank exploi-
tation than most of the terrain we had fought over. Here, the easy
maneuverability and speed of Shermans paid dividends over the
heavy, sluggish German monsters."[51]

Combat Command A went first on March 3. American rifle platoons
infiltrated German hamlets before dawn, catching exhausted German troops asleep at about 4:00 a.m. Colonel Tubby Doan's infantrymen didn't suffer a single casualty. They took 110 Germans prisoner
and captured two panzer assault guns and three laden ammunition
trucks. In the next town, Doan's men rousted 156 more German quitters, one the colonel of a *nebelwerfer* (rocket launcher) outfit. The Germans handed over their one remaining launcher, its half-track
towing vehicle, five trucks, three jeep-like vehicles, and a half-track
with an antiaircraft gun. It hadn't been much of a fight.

Task Force Kane had a rougher clash in their first hamlet. Aroused
just before daylight, German infantry called up a pair of panzer assault guns. The German panzers knocked out a Sherman and two
light tanks. Crafty American infantry with bazookas used the darkness and the house fronts to get very close to the preoccupied panzer
crews and punch fatal holes in both of their vehicles. With their

panzers out of it, eighty-six Germans raised their hands. They included a colonel, commander of the 767th Infantry Regiment. This beaten remnant was all he had left of his outfit.[52]

With the Germans worried about CCA's advance, Combat Command Reserve kicked off at 7:00 a.m. Task Force Hogan led in the north, clearing villages en route to Stommeln, the critical corner around the north knob of the Vorgebirge. Sam Hogan's soldiers knocked out a panzer and pushed away two others. By 8:35 p.m., Hogan's tank with its Texas flag entered northwest Stommeln. Fighting there continued.[53]

Lieutenant Colonel Rich Richardson's advance on Stommeln took a more direct route, always tricky with the Germans, who regularly blocked the best road to anywhere useful. They did it again on March 3. Almost as soon as TF Richardson moved east at 7:00 a.m., his first tank found an extensive minefield protected by dug-in enemy anti-tank guns. Both sides resorted to artillery. Things went back and forth all day. Major General Rose, on hand as usual, saw enough by midmorning. At 10:30 a.m., Rose ordered up TF Lovelady from CCB.[54] This committed Hogan, Richardson, and Lovelady, three battalions of tanks and three of infantry, to Stommeln. Rose wanted that road nexus very much in order to avoid trundling over the forested Vorgebirge and its defended slag piles.

Lieutenant Colonel Bill Lovelady's task force came in from the southwest, tying in with Richardson. The approach cost two tanks and some Americans wounded; Lovelady's men destroyed an assault gun panzer and two Mark IV types in return, and took 120 prisoners. Quartets of P-47 Thunderbolt fighter-bombers arrived just before sunset. The American pilots bombed and strafed the enemy in Stommeln, focusing on vehicles. As night fell, the Germans hanging on in Stommeln were very nearly encircled. The survivors fled overnight.[55]

With Stommeln well in hand, Rose sent forward Colonel Jack Welborn's task force, too. By 7:50 p.m., TF Welborn pressed past the

Vorgebirge's north end. The American tankers, infantrymen, and artillery gunners rounded up fifty enemy soldiers and knocked out three more panzers. Division G-2 analysts judged them to be from the 9th Panzer Division, a familiar opponent.[56] If so, they didn't have much left.

Maurice Rose rarely offered praise over the radio. That device served for reports and orders. Late on March 3, however, the general made an exception. He refused to use his own words—not his way. Rose didn't go in for the "Caesar's address to the legions" puffery. That suited guys like Georgie Patton. Rather, Rose chose to convey a message from Major General Collins: "My personal congratulations for a nearly perfect operation. Congratulations on spearheading VII Corps, the leading First Army troops, to the Rhine."[57] Cologne lay dead ahead.

———

That meant it must be Mike Yeomans's time. The 83rd Recon commander refitted on March 3. At 4:20 p.m., Rose sent the 83rd forward toward Stommeln. Get around that fracas, Rose told Yeomans. Then head for the Rhine River.

Yeomans's scouts pulled it off in exactly twelve hours. At 4:20 a.m. on the morning of March 4, a recon team reached the heights overlooking Germany's greatest waterway. The 83rd men were about five miles north of Cologne proper. The Americans got out of their scout cars and peeps and slowly crept through the underbrush until they could get a clear view of the Rhine. On the river itself, boats and ferries went back and forth. Roads along both the east and west banks teemed with marching men and German vehicles of all description. Come daylight, if the weather cleared, this would be a shooting gallery.[58]

To punctuate their success in reaching the Rhine, other companies of Yeomans's battalion rolled up the groggy members of a German artillery battery encountered en route to the big river. In the hour before the sun came up, 196 enemy troops surrendered, giving up four 105mm cannons as well.[59] Yeomans had blazed the trail. Now the other task forces would use it.

March 4 resembled March 2, jockeying for the best jump-off points, getting set. That did not mean a day of rest, even though it was a Sunday. War didn't allow for days off, especially not war in the Maurice Rose style. Instead, Combat Command B to the north and Combat Command A to the south prepared to attack into Cologne. That entailed more than refueling and rearming. It resulted in fighting, too.

Task Force Lovelady advanced to the Rhine to back up the 83rd Recon. Bill Lovelady and Mike Yeomans worked well together, as did their soldiers. Even with their new M24 Chaffee tanks, the 83rd lacked the firepower to clear enemy-held villages unless the recon troops found the Germans unprepared or willing to give up. Not all did.

As a result, TF Lovelady fought all day. When lead Shermans bypassed a deep ditch dug as a tank trap, an attached M36 Jackson tank destroyer took a fatal shot from an M4 Sherman. Lovelady's own lead tanks shot back, knocking out the errant Sherman. It turned out to be a "German Sherman." With their purloined panzer gone, 125 German soldiers surrendered. That offered no comfort to the four dead G.I. tank destroyer crewmen.[60]

Bill Lovelady's soldiers pushed on to the next town, right on the Rhine River. At twilight, American tanks and infantrymen began shooting down at river barges and boats. This energized a German counterattack led by two Tiger tanks, real ones, not nervous phantoms. The American tanks got one of the Tigers and chased off its partner. It's not clear if TF Lovelady's T26E3 Pershing administered the decisive shot; several TCs claimed credit. In any event, the 83rd Recon took over the position for the rest of the night. Task Force Lovelady had to move into its assigned post for the morrow's attack into Cologne.[61]

While the 83rd Recon reached the Rhine, with TF Lovelady doing likewise, Maurice Rose's Omaha Forward shifted to the vicinity of Stommeln. The half-tracks parked at the easternmost edge of the town, and the headquarters G.I.s set up shop in a relatively intact building. As usual, the soldiers of Omaha Forward found themselves ducking occasional gunfire and shell bursts. When Lightning Joe Collins stopped by on his rounds, he found a chunk of German artillery shrapnel sticking out of one of the command post's situation maps. Rose had just come in from another day with his men.

"Maurice," Collins said, "Do you *always* have to have your CP [command post] in the last house in town?" (Italics in original.)

"General," Rose replied, "there is only one way I know to lead this division, and that's at the head of it!"[62]

Collins let it go. By this time, Collins considered Rose "the top armored commander in the Army."[63] Rose had been validating that opinion daily on the drive to Cologne. The division commander's hard-charging task force commanders, and especially their great young officers, sergeants, and G.I.s, backed with their bravery, their brains, and their lives the battlefield checks that Maurice Rose wrote. In Namur, Belgium, months ago, Collins reprimanded Rose for endangering the men of Omaha Forward. By now, the VII Corps commander knew better. The Spearhead commander wasn't going to change. Collins left Rose to his work.

For the Cologne push, Rose didn't try anything overly clever. The Germans appeared pretty well wrung out. The opposition owned one more play: dumping the Hohenzollern Bridge. Getting there took priority. Rose considered all of his task forces and combat commands ready to lunge for the river span. But the current laydown made the pick for the major general. Brigadier General Doyle Hickey's Combat Command A received the mission. Colonel Tubby Doan's task force drew the zone that led straight to the Hohenzollern Bridge. Lieutenant Colonel Matt Kane's G.I.s would be right on TF Doan's north flank. Brigadier General Truman Boudinot's Combat Command B, with TF Hogan attached, planned to attack north of CCA. The 104th

Infantry Division prepared to take the southern half of Cologne.[64] But the Hohenzollern Bridge, the much-desired Rhine crossing—all eyes looked that way.

At 4:00 a.m. on March 5, the Americans attacked. Combat Command B advanced through the northwestern suburbs of Cologne. Task Force Lovelady took 160 prisoners and knocked out another Tiger tank; enemy action wrecked two Shermans, killed four G.I.s, and wounded twenty. Task Force Welborn methodically cleared streets, getting to the edge of the Cologne rail yard by dusk; that maze of derailed freight cars, full of German rear-guards, had to wait for March 6. To the north of CCB, tied in with the neighboring 99th Infantry Division on the near shore of the Rhine, 83rd Recon platoons engaged a series of German elements desperate to retreat north. The Germans killed three American scouts and wounded a dozen. Yeomans's recon men captured a damaged Panther, wrecked two more panzers, and gathered more than thirty German prisoners. Some Germans escaped to board overloaded river boats. Low clouds prevented American aircraft from intervening, although the all-weather U.S. artillery engaged.[65]

Combat Command A's Task Force Kane advanced steadily all morning until 11:09 a.m., when the point tanks ran into a Luftwaffe flak outfit at the city airfield. The first few crews threw their tanks into reverse and sought cover behind rubbled buildings. American TCs in the lead Shermans counted sixteen emplaced 88mm cannons, perhaps repurposed from the Cologne air defenses. The city's many factory complexes had often been bombed by both the Royal Air Force and the U.S. Army Air Forces. In any event, the German 88mm crews dominated the open runways. The Germans nailed TF Kane's lead vehicle, killing two Americans and wounding three. Matt Kane called for the 67th Armored Field Artillery to drop white phosphorus shells on top of the German 88mm gun locations. The brilliant white blossoms generated a thick smoke screen. As an added "benefit," the toxic hot chips of phosphorus burned holes in anything they struck, including German troops. Several German 88mm projectiles detonated due to these flaming shards. Once the smoke cloud grew thick enough, Kane's Shermans charged across the open airfield. Each tank carried riflemen of the 1st Battalion, 13th Infantry Regiment. Once they reached the enemy gun emplacements, they found a few dead Germans and no others. Surviving Luftwaffe crewman had apparently run off.[66]

Colonel Tubby Doan and his task force entered Cologne at 7:10 a.m., noting the city limits sign. As TF Doan moved along the highway from Stommeln, parallel to the nearby 104th Infantry Division, a few of the 3rd Armored Division troops took a few minutes to erect a large sign reading "Welcome to Köln [Cologne] Courtesy of the Spearhead Division." Maurice Rose in his trusty peep rolled right behind Doan.[67]

German antitank gun crews—either 75mm or 88mm, hard to be sure—opened fire at 9:08 a.m. The enemy had hauled junked vehicles and telephone poles into an underpass, compelling the Americans to fight through the blockage. To suppress the hostile antitank teams, Doan arranged a major artillery shoot, complicated by TF Kane's simultaneous clash at the Cologne airfield. Even the hardworking 67th Armored Field Artillery Battalion could only fire one major mission at the same time. At 11:40 a.m., the 67th delivered a thunderous series of howitzer volleys. Doan's rifle squads worked to the far side of the underpass. Engineers cleared the debris. The advance continued.[68]

One of the slow-moving Sherman crews detected an enemy rifleman shooting through a gap in a broken wall. Sergeant John Burleson saw the enemy soldier. The battlewise TC slewed the tank turret to frame the German in the gunner's sight. This kind of target usually merited a spray of .30 caliber coaxial machine gun fire. But gunner Corporal Hubert Foster went big. He belted out a 76mm main gun round.

The ear-splitting crack echoed in the street. Brick dust rose in a pall.

"Get him?" asked Burleson.

"Don't know," said Foster. "But he was standing behind that wall—now there ain't no wall."[69] So went the afternoon of March 5 in Cologne.

At 1:10 p.m., a disturbing report passed over the CCA command radio net. "Large explosion," the CCA command post duty NCO recorded. "Much smoke. Believed to be demolition of the main bridge."[70] After all of this . . .

Then again, explosions proliferated in Cologne. It would have been nice to put aloft a Piper Cub spotting plane and get a peek at the Hohenzollern's truss-work, but the murky weather precluded such flights. Maurice Rose, Doyle Hickey of CCA, and Tubby Doan agreed. Drive on. Believe it when you see it. But first, get there.

That wasn't going to happen on March 5. Combat Command B still had to clear the trashed rail yard and the factory quarter—visions of Stalingrad there. Task Force Doan moved block by block, slowly. "Infantry was to lead down the streets," Doan directed, "and the tanks would block side streets and support the infantry if needed." They were needed. By 6:55 p.m., the U.S. tankers demanded fuel and ammunition, the infantry wanted more bullets, too, and the engineers required a reissue of demolitions. Rose reluctantly let CCA stop for the night. The 104th Infantry Division also dealt with challenges in southern Cologne. German riflemen, machine gunners, and mortarmen kept the dark hours jumping. Americans heard clanking noises to the east. Panzers.[71] You just knew they'd be there. March 6 promised to be interesting.

——————

When to blow the Hohenzollern Bridge? For the Germans, it summarized what remained of their military options in Cologne. All of the boilerplate Hitler ranting and raving about defending "fortress city" Cologne to the last man and last bullet had not panned out. Some German soldiers fought. Most didn't. Maybe 120,000 of the city's unfortunate civilians cowered in basements, waiting for this final storm to pass. From 1940 to 1945, Cologne endured 167 Allied air raids and absorbed nearly 50,000 tons of air-delivered munitions. The great medieval cathedral, battered and pierced by far too much flying metal, still stood on the edge of the Rhine, right near the Hohenzollern Bridge. From all over the city, even in the late-winter haze of smoke and drizzle, you could just make out the cathedral's twin spires.[72] They beckoned the Americans forward to the medieval-era city center and the coveted three-arch river span.

The 3rd Armored Division stirred at its now-accustomed witching hour, 4:00 a.m. The 83rd Recon up north reported "all types of artillery and direct fire from east of the Rhine." Although voluminous, the enemy gunfire lacked accuracy. The Germans were simply flinging lead and explosives. Poor weather constrained the American response to artillery and some long-range 75mm gun engagements by the M24 Chaffee light tanks. Three hostile soldiers surrendered in a day the 83rd summed up as "static."[73]

Combat Command B cleared Cologne's factory quarter. Task Force Lovelady ended the day in and around a trashed-out rayon factory. The task force paced the advance with white phosphorus rounds. Reports of seven camouflaged panzers happily proved untrue. They might have been there the previous evening. Not anymore. The Germans had fled.[74]

Colonel Jack Welborn's task force spent the morning pushing through the city's vast rail yard. Bomb craters and artillery shell damage had torn up many of the steel train tracks. Some 800 intact freight cars were interspersed with derailed, burned-out carcasses of hundreds more. In one car, Welborn's G.I.s found a batch of new 75mm cannon tubes. Two others bulged with factory-packed mortar rounds. All kinds of other ammunition and supplies had been captured, to include a saltwater diving suit. Evidently no German would be using that anytime soon. After getting through the switching yard, Welborn's soldiers ended the day in the debris-filled parking lot of the Cologne Ford truck factory. Nobody in Detroit got a nickel from this one, of course; the Nazis commandeered the plant when the war began. The upper floor offered a fine vista of the Rhine River, although on March 6, light rain and smoke spoiled the view.[75]

Task Force Kane spent most of the day rooting out German *panzerfaust* men east of the airfield. The TF Kane tankers and riflemen worked through smashed-up shop fronts and what was left of two-story houses. Sergeant TCs up in the Sherman turrets sometimes glimpsed the cathedral spires in the distance.[76] A compelling view—but it wasn't their fight.

That belonged to Task Force Doan on March 6. Brigadier General Doyle Hickey of CCA and, of course, Major General Maurice Rose started early and spent their day right behind TF Doan's lead elements. The generals' presence generated urgency. Get to the bridge.[77]

Before the cloudy skies grayed, a passel of Allied war correspondents talked to Rose just as he was headed to link up with TF Doan in downtown Cologne. The general promised the journalists "quite a good fight." He also warned them to stay away from the cathedral. Naturally, that's exactly where every one of the reporters wanted to go.[78]

The general normally treated the eager press folks as part of the furniture. There were often a few correspondents coming or going from Omaha Forward. Rose treated them politely, but the division commander did not cultivate a media personality à la Monty or Patton. No, for the press people, Rose came across about as he was: well-uniformed, taciturn, resolute, and looking ever forward. The journalists went with that. They didn't dig deeper. That wasn't the nature of news work in that era.

In World War II, American reporters wore uniforms and handed over for censorship every word written and every photograph snapped. For the 3rd Armored Division, personable Major Haynes W. Dugan herded these cats. He graduated from the Columbia School of

Journalism before the war, so he spoke the language of the news business. In uniform though, Dugan worked for division G-2, the intelligence guys.[79] That showed how the U.S. Army of 1945 viewed the Fourth Estate. Let them do their jobs. Get some good human-interest stories. Be sure to include the hometowns of G.I.s. But if the journalists started to offer anything even remotely useful to the enemy, or at all controversial enough to upset the folks at home, men like Haynes Dugan knew the deal. Use the scissors.

The imminent fall of Cologne—and maybe a big Rhine bridge—brought out a lot of newsmen and two women, too: Ann Stringer of the United Press and Iris Carpenter of the *Boston Globe*. There were also soldier journalists, such as Staff Sergeant Andy Rooney of *Stars and Stripes* (the G.I. paper) and combat cameramen Tech-4 Jim Bates and Tech-3 Leon Rosenman.[80] Rooney would later become a celebrated figure at CBS television news. But on March 6, he was just another reporter hungry for a story. He'd get one. As the day wore on, Rooney and the rest of Dugan's charges gravitated to the action. And the action was in the lee of that soaring cathedral.

Spurred by Rose to move with energy, Colonel Tubby Doan counted on his tanks. The task force's 2nd Battalion, 32nd Armored Regiment led with the now-renowned T26E3 Pershing leading a company of medium tanks on one street and a company of Shermans a block over. Once the first few U.S. tanks gained control of the cathedral square, Doan intended to send up a company of speedy M5 Stuart light tanks with engineers aboard. They'd take the Hohenzollern Bridge in a single bound.[81]

At 2:10 p.m., 2nd Lieutenant Karl E. Kellner reported the cathedral in sight, maybe two blocks away. Slabs of collapsed buildings blocked the street. Kellner scanned the cathedral area and the nearby railway station. Grayish light limned holes in the station's upper floors. The ground level appeared very dark. Something down there looked wrong.

It was.

A 75mm armor-piercing slug ripped through Kellner's tank. A second followed. Kellner tumbled out of the turret, his left leg severed at the knee. Two more tankers scrambled out. Two never did.

Military journalist Andy Rooney, right there to see the big fight, helped a bold medic pull Kellner behind a brick pile. The medic did all he could. But the young officer didn't make it.[82] In his agony, the lieutenant sent back a final report.

Only a Panther could cause such pain.

That brought up the Pershing. One of Rose's TC fraternity, Staff Sergeant Bob Earley, told his driver to creep forward. That Panther was up there somewhere in front of the cathedral. Earley had become an old soldier by staying ahead of the enemy. That and luck. Both paid off.

As Earley's Pershing rolled, the German crewmen overplayed their hand. They'd been hiding in the shadows. Now the Panther clanked out into the gray square, crunching over glass fragments and cement pieces. Bob Earley noticed the movement. The Panther showed its side.

Three 90mm shots, wham, wham, wham, as fast as Earley's tankers could fire, then coax machine gun hosing all over the Panther. Tracer bullets skittered off at crazy, improbable angles. Be sure of it. Finish the job. In fact, the first American round did for the panzer, setting a raging gasoline fire. Five frightened Germans wriggled out of the various hatches. They ran.

From a good vantage point, Tech-4 Bates got it all on film. While there's a lot of generic war footage, this is one of the few episodes that shows friend and foe duking it out. The video lasts a few minutes, and the kill shots take a few spare seconds. It's in stark black and white.[83]

The faceless panzer men, though, accomplished something besides ending the lives of three Americans. They might have been crewing the last active fighting vehicle in the once-fearsome 9th

Panzer Division. By going down hard, they bought a handful of precious minutes.

At 2:55 p.m., the Germans blew the bridge. Two of the three iron arches tumbled into the waters of the Rhine.[84] Maurice Rose wanted it bad. That's the way he and his men got it. There was to be no easy crossing, and so no rapid breakthrough followed. The Rhine River stretched below the 3rd Armored Division soldiers like an evil moat, the kind without drawbridges. This war would drag on to the bitter end.

Still, the Americans held Cologne, or what was left of it. Editors at *Life* magazine deemed the metropolis a "desert" in their March 26, 1945, issue featuring photos taken in the wrecked city. One offered an aerial panorama of the devastated urban landscape, block upon block of roofless rectangles and spilled masonry. Another picture framed a vacant-eyed young German woman sitting on the dusty curb of a rubble-strewn street. A third image showed three solemn American generals—Rose, Hickey, and Boudinot—in their trench coats and steel helmets as they stood together on the shattered steps of the great cathedral. The scene called to mind Tacitus: "They make a desert and call it peace."[85] It didn't feel a lot like winning. Not yet.

CHAPTER 8

One Shot

Most of the killing you do in modern war is impersonal.
A thing few people realize is that you hardly ever see a
German. Very few men—even in the infantry—actually
have the experience of aiming a weapon at a German
and seeing the man fall.

Captain (Temporary Major) Fred Majdalanay[1]

At this time," said the corps commander, "we pause to remember those men who gave their lives so that we might be here." The loudspeaker echoed then died away.

Not a word came from the olive drab ranks, row on row of soldiers bracing at the position of attention. You didn't get a lot of ceremonies during the war. But Major General Joe Collins thought he owed it to the men who'd taken Cologne. So on the morning of Sunday, March 11, 1945, the VII Corps commander arranged a formation in the city sports stadium. The four divisions—the 99th, 3rd Armored, 104th, and 8th—and the corps troops—artillery, engineers, and the like—each arrayed an honor platoon behind their respective commanders. Unit battle flags swirled in the light breeze. United States Army outfits didn't carry their colors into action anymore. That kind of old-fashioned pomp went out with the Confederate surrender at Appomattox way back in 1865. But today, the old tradition was observed. There hadn't been an event like this since the G.I.s left England.

With Collins's short speech concluded, a select detachment of soldiers marched to a bare flagpole. All men saluted. A band crashed into "The Star-Spangled Banner," and the chosen men formally raised the U.S. flag over defeated Cologne. To close the proceedings, a squadron of American fighter-bombers passed overhead. "I believe," Collins wrote of the Americans present, "they will always remember that brief picture."[2]

A fitting gesture, simple and sincere, the gathering resonated. Yet it discomfited some, too, especially the long-time soldiers who attended. Maurice Rose said nothing about it one way or the other. Then again, he rarely did. You buried your dead and moved on. You didn't dwell on those lost. You dared not. The war wasn't over yet.

———

Much to his personal frustration, and despite his constant angling for the post, Field Marshal Bernard Law Montgomery was not the SHAEF land force commander, having overdone his prima donna act many times too many. By early March 1945, with all Allied field armies closed up near or at the Rhine, and no bridges at hand, it came down to Montgomery's old question: single thrust or broad front? Monty saw a chance to resurrect the single thrust idea—under his command, of course. General of the Army Ike Eisenhower had long championed the broad front. But the Rhine River barrier combined with Ike's innate urge to reinforce Anglo-American solidarity to allow one more waltz around that single thrust maypole.

Ike recognized that the Ruhr basin industries represented Nazi Germany's last extant arms production mills. The Russians seemed likely to go after Berlin, and good luck to them, as Hitler's last-ditch *Götterdämerung* in his ruined capital appeared all too likely to slaughter hundreds of thousands of Red Army soldiers. No, the Ruhr was the thing, and to take it, the tilt of the ground favored Monty's Twenty-First Army. Patton's Third Army aligned neatly with the secondary route toward Frankfurt. The Sixth Army Group down south would do what they could along the north fringes of the Alps. As for Hodges's First Army Group, well, taking Cologne impressed. But without an intact bridge, an assault crossing of the Rhine—a quarter mile wide in most spots—required a lot of firepower, engineers, and troops. So Ike ruled, much to Lieutenant General Omar Bradley's consternation. Priority went to Monty in the north.[3]

Montgomery made full use of Ike's largesse. The British commander prided himself on his mastery of the set-piece operation, the properly arranged and readied offensive, like El Alamein in 1942 or the Normandy landings in 1944. Therefore he concocted an elaborate orchestration, featuring 1.25 million soldiers arrayed in thirty-two divisions (eleven of them American, all of Ninth Army), a large airborne drop by Matt Ridgway's XVIII Airborne Corps (one U.S. and one British division), dozens of oceanic landing craft manned by the Royal Navy and the U.S. Navy, over a thousand assault boats and ferries, thousands of aircraft, thousands of artillery tubes, thousands of yards of treadway bridging, hundreds of tanks, miles-long smoke screens, and Prime Minister Winston L. S. Churchill in the spectators' gallery—there was one of those, too. As insurance, Monty demanded all ten divisions of the U.S. First Army remain on standby in case anything went haywire.[4] For those keeping count, and Omar Bradley certainly did, it all added up to Monty's old forty-division "full-blooded thrust" proposal. Again. You had to give it to the diminutive British field marshal for his consistency, if nothing else.

Such a large-scale offensive didn't coalesce overnight. Montgomery insisted on waiting until March 23, to get everything good and gripped up as only he could.[5] So for seventeen days, the rest of the entire Allied front, soldiers who'd just struggled like hell to get to the

Rhine, would sit on the west side of the wide river. For senior American commanders, this interlude suggested the term "anti-climax," and other, less printable things, too.

Then American tankers, armored infantrymen, and combat engineers grabbed a bridge, a good one. The successful task force wasn't from the 3rd Armored Division, frustrated at Cologne. They didn't come from the 1st Infantry Division, stymied at Bonn. Instead, on March 7, the opportunistic 9th Armored Division took the great Ludendorff Bridge at Remagen, 34 miles south of Cologne. The 9th Armored served in III Corps, part of First Army.[6] What would Ike do?

Here the map, that old bugbear, tripped up the American generals one more time. This time, even Bradley and Hodges were at first willing to be bold and cross in strength at Remagen, the former because he disdained waiting for another Monty extravaganza and the latter just because, in the same sense that even a stopped watch is right twice a day. When Bradley phoned in to SHAEF headquarters with the news, Ike said all the right things. But his chief G-3 officer, Major General Harold R. "Pink" Bull, doused the affair with a large bucket of cold water. "You've got a bridge," Bull agreed, "but it's in the wrong place. It just doesn't fit the plan." There you go. Ignore what the enemy's giving you. Stick to the script.

Bradley consulted the squiggles on his map. Sure enough, the road leading east of Remagen traced into forested high ground, the Westerwald, which exuded more than a whiff of the horrible Hürtgen. If, however, the problematic Westerwald could be surmounted—no guarantee with Hodges at the helm—six miles east ran a good Ruhr-Frankfurt autobahn. But then the Twelfth Army Group commander kept gazing at his map board, never a good thing for him. The more he thought about it, the more he agreed with SHAEF.

Bradley gradually talked himself out of the opportunity. Instead, with Bradley's concurrence, Eisenhower restricted the flow of forces into the bridgehead to five U.S. divisions and limited their advance to a thousand yards a day. "Ike and I were criticized then, and later, for moving too slowly and too cautiously," wrote Bradley. He went on: "I do not believe the criticism is warranted. There was no need to rush."[7] One wonders what Patton, Collins, or Rose might say, let alone the G.I.s anxious to end this accursed war and go home. For the staggering Germans, the delay served up an undeserved respite. Nevertheless, the orders went out. Build up slowly at Remagen. Wait for Monty.

It could be like waiting for Godot.

―――――

Hurry up and wait, say the old soldiers. March and march, roll fast, fight hard—and then you halt. And sit. And fret. The Rhine River had been there all along, and the top commanders and their expert staffers had been pondering this broad waterway for months. Yet the Allied plans for getting over the Rhine amounted to three: snag a bridge (like Remagen), make a deliberate assault (Monty's vast armada), and get lucky with small-scale, opportune crossings in odd places (roll the dice). Up north the Montgomery approach held sway. Down south, Patton's Third Army and the American-French Sixth Army Group chipped away, trying this and that. And in the middle, Hodges's First Army owned Remagen, the unwanted gift that came with all sorts of hand-wringing. While the Remagen situation percolated, most of First Army, including Maurice Rose's division, waited.

Waiting bred free time, and free time led to imagining, and for combat troops, that rarely turned out well. A nod to the far future, going home to see loved ones, could be OK, a pleasant vision, akin to looking forward to summer vacation in the bleak midwinter. As for thinking too much about lost comrades, let alone weighing one's chances of joining that unhappy assembly, well . . . don't go there. To avoid such disturbing ruminations, the Spearheaders tried to keep busy.

Task Force Lovelady's experiences typified this period. To the citizen soldiers who comprised the vast majority of the 3rd Armored Division, it seemed as if the grimy scrum of World War II took a break and the orderly Regular Army ways of 1941 Camp Polk were resurrected. Battalion surgeon A. Eaton Roberts observed that regardless of a few rumors of an immediate renewal of fighting

> nothing materialized, and we settled down to garrison life with its training programs, inspections, "B" rations [almost like real food], and recreational facilities. It was only natural for us to complain, as we had on similar occasions before, about the apparent incongruity of a training program directly after we had proved ourselves so admirably in combat. Most of us had been soldiers long enough to accept our fates resignedly, dismissing the proposal good-naturedly with an "Oh well, that's the army!" Actually, greater minds than ours had discovered through the years, that training is a progressive thing, which is just as necessary to the production and maintenance of elite troops, as it is to recruits. Retrospectively, we must agree that as these not-so-trying duty hours proceeded, we were quickly restored to neat, clean, good-looking human beings, proud of ourselves and of our unit. We felt better, slept better, and regained a healthy outlook on life.[8]

Men fixed overtaxed vehicles, practiced gunnery, rehearsed battle tactics, and even watched a few movies. As one of Roberts's "greater minds," Maurice Rose spent these days checking on the troops, looking at their gear, and catching up on his often-interrupted sleep. At forty-five, he was twice the age of most of his soldiers. And after two and a half years overseas at war and more than seven months in command of the 3rd Armored Division, even a fit man like Rose felt every one of his years. Had he been clinically evaluated—which of course he was not—it's likely that Rose hovered, as did most of the division's veterans, near the end of his tether. So every hour not under fire counted, helping to refill the general's leaking bucket of drive and courage, the same one shared by all soldiers. Some broke early. Some broke late. But sooner or later, if you kept going without letup, your spirit gave out.

In the vast campaigns of World War II not many American ground soldiers saw what we'd recognize as combat, but most G.I.s dealt with threats and anxieties luckily not often realized. Some—riflemen, scouts, tankers, medics, artillery forward observers, combat engineers, especially at the private, sergeant, and junior officer levels—lived, suffered, became wounded, and too often died squarely in the bull's-eye. The analogy of a circular target, ground zero (one's death) surrounded by a collection of concentric risk rings, is useful in parsing a soldier's potential emotional trauma. Most G.I.s had seen, heard, or smelled distant destruction by bombs or shells. Fewer experienced attacks by these distant, impersonal means, and these weapons were not to be discounted, as 60 percent of casualties in World War II came via artillery. The medical authorities didn't call breakdowns "shell shock" for nothing. Worse than random projectiles, like V-1 buzz bombs or harassing cannon shots, were concentrated artillery and mortar missions. That kind of pummeling could unnerve those in the beaten zone. A smaller minority of troops came under long-range—a thousand yards to a football field away—direct fire: panzer main guns, 88mm cannons, machine guns, and designated rifle fire, invariably called "sniping," although few Germans actually had the specialized training and the scoped shoulder arms that went with that method. Front soldiers discounted such fine distinctions. They mattered not at the receiving end. Most tank fights occurred at this thousand- to hundred-yard range. Inside a hundred yards, the participants were very few, and their tools—machine guns, rifles, hand grenades—quite lethal. Hand-to-hand combat rarely happened, Hollywood aside. But tossing a grenade into a bunker, or sweeping a BAR across a defended house's parlor, well, those things were nightmares known to but a few, thankfully.[9]

Each terrible target ring offered its own subset: sensing the threat, seeing a foe wounded or dead, seeing a friend fall, being wounded yourself, killing an enemy far away, and, finally, killing an enemy up close and personal. Combat veterans pulsed in and out through those horrible rings, day after day, night after night. In the U.S. Army of 1945, the limited number of divisions meant units stayed in the line and infused new individual replacements.[10] The veteran G.I.s stayed there as long as they could take it, or until their luck ran out. It's no wonder sane men faltered.

Maurice Rose had been inside those horrendous target circles in 1918 and now again since 1943. While the general had enough combat experience in both world wars to realize that all soldiers had their limits, Rose's understanding of combat exhaustion was inferred from day-to-day observation rather than any formal education in the subject. In 1945, officers didn't discuss such things. Rose and his generation did not know the term "post-traumatic stress disorder," nor its clinical details or proposed treatments. But Maurice Rose had been under fire a lot and knew what it did to people over time. Although demanding of himself and his subordinates, Rose didn't dismiss battle fatigue as some flighty excuse for cowardice. He didn't hold with generals like Georgie Patton slapping blubbering shell shock victims, although that probably said more about Patton's uneven mental state—perhaps that fierce competitor's own battle stress—than that of the soldiers he abused. Generals, too, could slide down into PTSD. Senior commanders who spent a lot of time getting shot at, and seeing their men wounded and killed, risked combat exhaustion right alongside the riflemen, tankers, forward observers, medics, and combat engineers. The bill will always come due.

In the aftermath of World War II, U.S. military psychiatrists described the path followed by Maurice Rose and his soldiers: becoming "battlewise," maximum efficiency, overconfidence/hyper-reactivity, emotional exhaustion, and then a "vegetative stage." The doctors debated how long it took to ascend then descend this awful parabola. Some thought sixty days of continuous combat was about the limit for most troops. Yet what constituted continuous combat? There had been time-outs even in the Normandy bocage or during the Bulge. Other researchers suggested that 200 to 240 "aggregate combat days" (these guys certainly had a way with words) would result in debilitating PTSD. In plain English, from six and a half to eight months of frontline action and a G.I. was fried. At that point, "practically all men in rifle battalions who are not otherwise disabled ultimately become psychiatric casualties."[11] The exact timing varied. The doleful trajectory did not.

The medical officers offered two exceptions. About 2 percent of humans did not succumb to combat fatigue. The bad news was that most of this group seemed to be psychopaths. The Waffen SS might see that as recruiting base, but not so the U.S. Army.[12] The other glimmer of hope involved breaks in combat. With rest, proper food, and meaningful activity—training and maintenance, for example— soldiers bounced back. Few seemed to come all the way back. Each bout of battle action stripped off another layer of emotional armor. Time off the line, however, slowed the degradation.[13] Unfortunately, the U.S. Army's policy of feeding individual backfills into units in contact—as in the Hürtgen Forest—made such quiet intervals infrequent. Divisions were supposed to keep fighting, not back off. In that sense, those three slow weeks in March came at the right time for Maurice Rose, the hard-charging task force commanders, and the old sweat TC brothers. Their personal aggregate days of combat had reached the danger zone, smack in the perilous 200 to 240 range.

To his considerable individual risks as a commanding general Rose added the fates of more than 14,000 of his fellow Americans. While 3rd Armored Division soldiers rightly celebrated their many

successes in battle in 1944–1945, the steady accumulation of G.I. casualties marked every panzer wrecked and every mile gained. Of the
sixteen U.S. Army armored divisions that served in World War II, the
Spearhead Division lost the most men (2,540 killed, 234 missing/cap-
tured, 7,331 wounded, and 6,017 nonbattle injuries) and the most
tanks (805).[14] All of that, too, went into Maurice Rose's emotional
rucksack. It was a load he could never put down, even if he wanted to
do so.

In 1945, a U.S. Army general flirting with combat exhaustion
would get zero sympathy from officialdom. Senior leaders excused
some recreational liquor, or the need for a few days' pass in Paris.
Dalliances outside of marriage happened. As long as your division
delivered results, minor lapses got overlooked. Most generals avoided
the circumstances of battle fatigue, so the top people didn't look for
signs. Maybe they should have, especially with a man wound as
tightly as Maurice Rose.

The military psychiatrists strongly urged those wrestling with
battle fatigue to discuss the matter, preferably with trained clini-
cians and fellow veteran soldiers. Yet Maurice Rose spoke only about
duty matters, nothing personal. Ever. His aide and driver barely
knew him. While Rose served and schooled with fellow cavalry officers Truman Boudinot and Bobby Howze during the 1930s, the major
general confided nothing to them. Rose didn't open up with Colonel
John Smith, the division chief of staff, nor Lieutenant Colonel Wesley
Sweat, the G-3 who accompanied his division commander day and
night on lengthy jaunts with forward task forces. As for Major General Joe Collins, who was friendly enough, the relationship remained
strictly professional. Collins assessed Rose as "not given to easy com-
radeship" due to being "somewhat stern." That "somewhat" was a
generous touch. Whatever boiled inside, Rose's armor held. "I never
knew a man," recalled reporter Hal Boyle, "who so ruthlessly and
cold bloodedly set about destroying an enemy."[15] Rose was what
he did.

One of Rose's peers, and only one, just plowed ahead and talked to Rose about the war, and command, and all the rest. But then again, Major General Terry de la Mesa Allen talked to everybody, from privates to five-star generals. Even after a long day at the front, Maurice Rose looked like he'd just marched in from a parade, tall and straight-backed. Terry Allen, by contrast, suggested an unmade bed—helmet askew, cigarette dangling from his lip, lanky and lean and loud. At a party, he'd be the one to end the night with a beer bottle in each hand and a lampshade on his head, leading a sing-along of off-color tunes. Allen told Rose (and all others) that he'd known the younger cavalry officer for twenty-five years. "We've been friends since he was a lieutenant," Allen asserted.[16] The two had never served a day together until 1943 in North Africa. Then and later, they were in different divisions. Yet Allen spoke of Rose as his pal. Allen didn't take no for an answer.

In March 1945, Terry Allen commanded the 104th Infantry Division. This wasn't his first rodeo. A free spirit, Allen bounced out of West Point, ex–Class of 1912, but immediately finished his degree at Catholic University. Commissioned into the cavalry by 1913, Allen led American horsemen in the Mexican "Punitive Expedition" of 1916–1917. He commanded an infantry battalion in World War I, earned the Silver Star for his bravery, and took a bullet through the jaw. It didn't curb his tongue.[17] Terry Allen loved to yak.

Between the wars, it appears Terry Allen and Maurice Rose might have passed each other at Fort Bliss, Texas, in 1932, although they served in two separate cavalry regiments. Allen was eleven years older and senior in rank to Rose. By 1942, Allen commanded the 1st Infantry Division. He led that famous outfit in North Africa and Sicily, and there he did meet Colonel, later Brigadier General, Rose. Brave, innovative, and dynamic, Terry Allen led from the front. Unlike Rose, though, Allen couldn't keep his mouth shut, and his 1st Infantry Division seemed overly rowdy. Allen ran afoul of his straight-laced corps commander in Sicily, Omar Bradley. Bradley fired Allen for his "cavalier attitude."[18]

Allen didn't stay fired. Army Chief of Staff General George C. Marshall thought Allen a great combat commander—which he was—and gave him a new division, the 104th. Allen took charge and never looked back. He taught his soldiers every bit of his own hard-earned tactical knowledge. His tough training regimen succeeded handily. Allen remained unkempt, but his division always fought with skill and will. The 104th Infantry Division "Timberwolves" became renowned for their night attacks, a particularly demanding task in the days before modern night vision sights.[19] Terry Allen was more than a decade older than many of his division-level colleagues, including Maurice Rose. And Allen never met a stranger, not even the laconic Rose.

Now this human cyclone whirled into VII Corps as one of Rose's fellow division commanders. At first Bradley had shunted the 104th off to Monty's Twenty-First Army Group, but eventually the fastidious Brad swallowed hard and accepted Allen's Timberwolves into the American fold, being careful to place the 104th under reliable Joe Collins and alongside steady Maurice Rose. When Bradley tried to make nice with Allen by saying that the 104th "ranked with the 1st and the 9th divisions as the finest combat divisions in the ETO [European Theater of Operations]," Allen smirked at his three-star superior. "Brad," retorted Allen, "the 1st and the 9th are in damn fast company." A group of G.I.s in earshot laughed, hooted, and hollered.[20] That was Terry Allen.

Allen chatted up Rose at every opportunity. The more the Spearhead commander clammed up, the more Allen stayed at it. Whenever their paths crossed, at commanders' meetings at VII Corps headquarters or out and about in the field, Allen teased Rose about old cavalry days—even though they'd not really shared any—about not drinking, about the younger general's consistently shined boots and clean-shaven, clean-scrubbed face. Allen didn't ask permission. He just rolled along. Now and then, curious 3rd Armored Division staff officers thought they detected a hint in Rose's unsmiling visage that possibly, a little bit, Rose enjoyed it.[21] Perhaps it reminded Rose that someone else knew the deal. It wasn't much. But it was something.

———

March 12, 1945, was a strange day for Rose. He traveled to First Army headquarters, by that point located in a damaged old barracks complex in dreary Duren, Germany. There, along with 136 other officers and enlisted men, Rose received a French Army award, in his case, the degree of *Officier de la Légion d'honneur*. Lieutenant General Marie-Louis Koeltz presented the medal with the usual double cheek kissing. If the effusive occasion made any impression on the stoic Rose, he didn't say. Rather, he left as soon as he could.[22] It was a long drive back to Omaha Forward in Cologne.

That night, Rose sat down with a typewriter and wrote a two-page letter to his family. He used official stationery. The division commander, not much of a typist, pecked out the division header: Headquarters, 3rd Armored "Spearhead" Division, Office of the Commanding General, A.P.O. [Army Post Office] #253, Postmaster NY [New York]. As he might with a formal report, the general inserted a subject line: Personal Correspondence with Maurice Roderick Rose.[23] His son, known as Reece, was a little more than four years old. Clearly Reece's mother, Rose's wife, Virginia, would be reading this one to the boy, and the general composed it with that in mind.

Rose wrote of the day's French award ceremony. He was sending the foreign medal and citation home, and he asked his son Reece to "accept them with my love." Rose also commented that unlike the other generals in theater, he did not wear his ribbons, even though Lieutenant General Hodges expressed his displeasure. Rose joked that the French bestowed the award because "they had some extra" and "needed to get rid of them." For Maurice Rose, this war wasn't about medals or promotions. It was about killing Germans. And he had his own very personal motivation there. It wasn't something he'd share with a four-year-old, or his wife, or anyone, really.

Then Rose mentioned his trust in the standard-issue M1911A1 .45 semiautomatic pistol. He explained that he'd picked up various German handguns, Lugers, Walthers, and the like. There's a reference to "Georgie," no doubt Patton with his famous ivory-handled revolvers. Rose, though, would stick with the good old .45.[24]

The general wrote a few lines concerning his aide Major Bob Bellinger. He also mentioned "that jar of Christmas caviar that my sweetie sent me," photos from Reece's fourth birthday celebration, and an Easter cable sent to the general's mother, his rabbi father, "Pops," and his brother "Arn" (Arnold).[25] It all hints at a private life and periodic correspondence that Rose did not open to his fellow soldiers. One wonders what Rose's Jewish family in Denver thought of receiving an Easter message. We do not know. Major General Maurice Rose wasn't the only member of the family who played his cards close to the vest.

His closing words speak of a side of Maurice Rose—"your devoted Pop"—he seldom revealed. Rose asked young Reece to cheer up his mother. "I know that she gets mighty lonesome at times," he wrote, "and that is a hard thing to overcome. But this thing can't last forever . . . I hope."[26] Him and several million G.I.s.

———

Whatever Rose thought of his family and home he bound tightly within. But another March letter demanded an official response. This March 18 missive came directly from General of the Army Dwight D. Eisenhower, the supreme commander. Ike didn't really know Rose. The SHAEF general had stopped by Omaha Forward at the Prym House in Stolberg back on November 8, 1944, and Rose shook Ike's hand at a commanders' conference at VII Corps headquarters on February 6, 1945.[27] In a pinch, Eisenhower might have been able to pick out Rose from a police lineup. Maybe.

So this document wasn't personal, but strictly duty-related. That bunch of correspondents in Cologne on March 6 filed some interesting stories, all right. It seems Ann Stringer, in particular, outsmarted Major Haynes Dugan, her minder at 3rd Armored Division headquarters, and actually broke real news. An editor plucked a contentious piece of hers off the wire and ran with it. Did they ever. The *Washington Post* went with "Nazi Tanks Excel Ours, Troops Say." Other headlines proved more dramatic. "American Tanks Not Worth a Drop of Water, Crews Say." "U.S. Tanks No Good in Battle, Say Crewmen After Losing Half of M-4 Machines." "American Tanks No Good, Assert Troops in Reich." Stringer quoted Staff Sergeant Bob Earley and his tankers by name. She got their hometowns right. And she made sure to tie them to the "Third Armored."[28]

Ike was not amused. His letter to Rose said as much:

> From time to time I find short stories where some reporter is purportedly quoting non-commissioned officers in our tank formations to the effect that our men, in general, consider our tanks very inferior in quality to those of the Germans. I realize that these sometimes spring from the human tendency to make startling statements in the hope that out of them will come a bit of publicity and self-notoriety. Possibly, also, certain reporters sometimes support their own views on such matters as these by quoting only those statements that support such views.[29]

At first blush, this looked like a five-star general worried about beating back some bad news. Ike stood taller than that. Although he lacked anywhere near Maurice Rose's front-line know-how, the SHAEF commander was no fool. In his second paragraph, Eisenhower admitted that "our men, in general, realize that the Sherman is not capable of standing up in a ding-dong, head-on fight with a

Panther." The Supreme Commander asked Rose for a no-kidding evaluation.[30] Where do we stand?

Rose didn't overreact. He seldom did. The major general immediately noticed that the message went to the 2nd Armored Division commander, too.[31] Rose's former outfit had been in theater even longer than the Spearheaders. Ike wanted feedback, not a scalp. One wondered if the SHAEF Commander might be the last American in Europe to realize the Sherman had serious shortcomings in firepower and protection. Rose ignored such unproductive speculation. He had to answer the mail.

The smooth answer, the politic reply, would be to regurgitate soothing bromides: Our Shermans have taken some licks, but they must be good enough. The production workers at home sure try hard and deliver swell tanks. The G.I.s are great guys and do their part with pride. Our tanks have many strengths. We're winning, after all.

The war's nearly over. Why rock the boat?

Anyone who knew Maurice Rose—and Ike didn't—expected a much more forthright reply. There'd be no spin, no happy talk, just the truth as Rose and his men saw it. That's exactly what Ike received.

Some generals would have churned their staff through a major data drill. Not Rose. He'd been out and about. The division commander ignored reams of statistics. Instead, Rose turned to his TC sergeants and frontline leaders. Their voices and their names went all the way to Ike.

The damning sentences burned like white phosphorus. Lieutenant Colonel Elwyn W. Blanchard, twice wounded as a tank battalion commander, said most Panthers had been struck by "our artillery or our air," and he'd only seen one of the big panzers wrecked by a 75mm Sherman cannon. Task force commander Lieutenant Colonel Matt Kane thought "our M4 is woefully lacking in armor and armament" against Panthers. Staff Sergeant Harry Wiggins observed that "I have seen very few Panthers knocked out by the M4. The air seems to have gotten most of them." His TC brother Staff Sergeant William

G. Wilson believed "the Mark V [Panther] is way out ahead of our M4 in thickness and design of armor and its gun." Two gunners—Corporal Albert E. Wilkinson and Private John A. Danforth, and driver Tech-4 Jerome O. Hararklu, agreed with the NCOs. Finally, Rose allowed Staff Sergeant Bob Earley, reporter Ann Stringer's primary source, to send his thoughts directly to General Ike. Earley shot straight: "I haven't any confidence in an M4."

Rose emphatically concurred with his soldiers, leading off in no uncertain terms: "It is my personal conviction that the present M4 and M4A3 tank is inferior to the German Mark V." Rose then explained how air, artillery, good crew gunnery, and smart maneuvering to get to the side and rear of Panthers combined to allow the 3rd Armored Division to fight effectively. But these tactics imposed an "excessive number of losses."[32]

It would be heartening to state that Eisenhower embraced these findings and took immediate remedial action. That didn't happen. Instead, the supreme commander sent a perfunctory thank-you note and promised to forward Rose's letter to the Department of War, where it would no doubt get answered circa 1948. Up at SHAEF, Ike had much bigger fish to fry, namely Montgomery's massive Rhine assault, strategic questions about Berlin and the Soviet Red Army, policy matters related to postwar occupation zones, and urgent correspondence with such impatient personages as Charles de Gaulle, I. V. Stalin, and Winston L. S. Churchill.[33] The SHAEF tank message had gone out. The answer came back. An acknowledgment was dispatched. The clerks checked the box. Done. All moved on.

One additional distressing matter caught Maurice Rose's attention. On March 8, TF Kane liberated *Staatsgefängnis* (state prison) Cologne. Amidst all the aerial bombardment and urban firefights, the forbidding gray Gestapo facility sustained only a few broken windows and a smattering of bullet and shell fragment chips and pits in the thick walls. As late as March 2, more than 800 captives had been crammed into the cells and surrounding spaces, but most of those unfortunates had been evacuated east of the Rhine by the Germans, no doubt to an appalling fate. Left behind were eighty-five "miserable human beings, some of them so weak they were unable to move," as the G.I.s reported. American battalion surgeons and medics treated the eighty-five survivors, all of them weakened by malnutrition and many ravaged by typhus. A good number of the victims were taken by field ambulance to rear-area military hospitals. Many of these "political enemies of the Third Reich" had been judged guilty of various contrived offenses that came down to being Jewish in Germany, the highest of high crimes in the twisted view of the Nazi Party. Rose, who understood both written and verbal German, thanks to his upbringing in a Yiddish-speaking home, made his own assessment, weighing this latest outrage among all the rest, real, rumored, and feared.[34] Here loomed another reason, a very serious one, for the Allied offensive to get rolling again immediately. How much more of this horror, and how much worse, waited on the far side of the Rhine?

The Ludendorff Bridge at Remagen collapsed on March 17, 1945, a most unlucky St. Patrick's Day. The hobbled German army couldn't retake it, so instead the enemy bombed it, shelled it, sent frogmen under it with explosives, and even tried two V-2 rockets. The various detonations further weakened the already damaged bridge. When it fell, ten American soldiers died in the wreckage, twenty-three went missing in the river, and sixty-three were wounded. By that time, though, First Army had dispatched 25,000 troops to the east side of the Rhine. Even better, ferries and two pontoon bridges also crossed the waterway, with more bridges to come.[35]

As with all First Army undertakings, the Remagen bridgehead reflected the influence, and lack thereof, of Courtney Hodges. The same day the Ludendorff span disintegrated into the river, the First Army commander removed the III Corps commander because "there has not been sufficient control" and there had been "a lack of accurate information." Never mind that this III Corps commander, Major General John Millikin, led Third Army's drive to Bastogne in December 1944, or that his corps units seized the only intact bridge on the Rhine.[36] He missed some reporting windows and so must go.

Millikin's real sin, of course, involved who he was not. "What a shame it was that VII Corps had not established the bridgehead," Hodges mused. "At the end of the first day he would have been out at the Autobahn [sic]." As Hodges's aides wrote, the First Army commander "personally took charge" at Remagen, and did so in his accustomed way. Hodges sent in Lightning Joe Collins and VII Corps headquarters to run the operation. And as night follows day, Maurice Rose's 3rd Armored Division followed.[37]

Collins, Rose, and most of their soldiers, eager to end this thing, chafed to get underway. All had to wait on Field Marshal Bernard Law Montgomery's elaborate Rhine River assault up north on March 23–24. Monty's huge attack went off splendidly, replete with a massive cannonade, a corps-scale parachute drop and glider incursion, darting landing craft, drifting smoke screens, and tanks on the move. By the time Monty's Twenty-First Army Group completed its ponderous crossing of the Rhine River, every other Allied field army—Hodges's First, Patton's Third, the American Seventh, and the French First already held enclaves east of the great German water barrier. But the wide advance, Ike's prescribed broad front, did not commence until Montgomery's forces joined the fray.[38] In that sense, at least, the peppery British field marshal surely made his influence felt.

For the 3rd Armored Division, the offensive east of the Rhine began at Maurice Rose's favorite hour, 4:00 a.m. on March 25. The division deployed Combat Command B, trailed by the 83rd Recon, to the north and Combat Command A to the south, with Combat Command Reserve trailing, ready to swing either way to reinforce success. Collins attached the 414th Infantry Regiment, 104th Infantry Division, Terry Allen's troops. Thus every Spearhead task force consisted of a battalion of tanks and another of infantry, either the half-tracked armored infantry of the 36th or the truck-carried riflemen of Terry Allen's well-trained 414th Timberwolves. The VII Corps order directed Rose's troops to go all the way to Altenkirchen, thirty miles away, and then beyond if possible. As Rose ordered, "advance would not be halted out of contact with the enemy." Bypass resistance centers and go hard.[39] For the first time since the West Wall back in September 1944, a real breakthrough, a war-winner, might be imminent.

Behind the Spearhead Division, outflanked German resistance would be handled by following elements of the 1st Infantry Division and Terry Allen's 104th Infantry Division (minus its 414th soldiers). Carried to the utmost, this attack would stretch a pincer along the south face of the entire German Army Group B defending the Ruhr manufacturing centers. The U.S. Ninth Army on the north face promised to do likewise. If the Ninth Army met the First Army, Falaise 2.0 and done right, the operation might well bag 300,000 German soldiers and excise the majority of the Third Reich's industrial base. [40]

Combat Command B paralleled the Sieg River, which the Germans held stoutly to protect their Ruhr factories. Brigadier General Truman Boudinot's G.I.s weren't interested in going north, but east. The enemy threw what they had in front of Boudinot's tanks. Afterward, G-2 analysts ticked off an impressive roll-call of hostile defenders: 5th Airborne Regiment, 62nd Volkgrenadier Division, 363rd Volksgrenadier Division, 3rd Panzergrenadier Division, and even 9th Panzer Division, 11th Panzer Division, and Panzer Lehr. These formations amounted to skeleton crews, a few platoons here, a couple panzers there, supplemented by game youngsters with *panzerfäusten* in hand. "The ordinary fighting man and the professional soldier have long seen the unnecessary continuance of fighting," one captured German general said. Yet he continued: "As long as the country is at war, they are honor-bound to fight."[41] Honor—it wasn't a word someone like Maurice Rose, nor most of his soldiers, associated with the German army of Adolf Hitler's Third Reich. Whatever the motivation, the opposition stayed at it.

Colonel Jack Welborn's task force ran into Germans before dawn. In a series of sharp village fights, the tankers and infantrymen banged into one roadblock after another. These Germans had plenty of *panzerfäusten* and used both mortars and artillery, too. Behind TF Welborn, Lieutenant Colonel Mike Yeomans's 83rd Recon moved up warily, posting teams to watch the Sieg River bridges for German leakers. At each spot of German opposition, the U.S. troops used a heavy dose of artillery. It all made for a long day, six hard-won miles, "a war of attrition," as one American put it, although most of the at-triting happened to the foe. At least the experienced officers and NCOs avoided friendly casualties.[42] Send a bullet, not a man. It worked, but it took time—no breakout here.

Lieutenant Colonel Bill Lovelady's task force found the Germans, too. Captain Roberts saw it as "heavy slugging," and it was. Right away, German mines blew treads off of two Sherman tanks. A Ger-man assault gun panzer nailed another Sherman. Lovelady's tankers and infantrymen destroyed five panzers, seventeen trucks, and three artillery pieces. The Americans took ninety-five prisoners. Like TF Welborn, Lovelady's men pushed out six difficult miles.[43]

In CCA, Task Force Kane found a lot of Germans, too. The war might be ending, but nobody told these hostiles. They kept fighting, little hard knots to be cut up. In the beat-up hamlets, Americans saw corpses hanging in the trees, with placards labeling the dead as de-serters and traitors. Clearly, the Gestapo had passed through ahead of Matt Kane's soldiers.[44] Some Germans evidently required more Nazi "inspiration" than others.

Kane's men battled determined crews of towed antitank guns and enemy machine gun nests covering hastily-laid minefields. Industri-ous German troops mixed nasty *glasmine-43* (glass mine model 1943) antipersonnel devices with bar-shaped Riegel tank track-busters. The *glasmine-43* looked like a Mason jar filled with trouble. It was triggered by foot pressure. Because its housing was glass, magnetic mine detectors missed it, and its needling glass splinters, difficult to detect by X-ray, often resulted in infections. As for the Riegel mine, simplicity itself, if a Sherman crunched the top plate into the bottom—wham! When American engineers tried to defuse them, Riegel mines tended to detonate immediately. A G.I. might survive a nearby *glasmine-43* explosion. But a Riegel mine? It could blow open the bottom plate of a 33-ton Sherman tank. What it did to a human was grisly. Task Force Kane made it a few miles despite the mines and the gunfire.[45] Good but not great—no one yet smelled open ground ahead.

To their immediate south, Tubby Doan's column surprised the first batch of German defenders. Those predawn starts sometimes paid off, and these Germans seemed worn out. One enemy crew handed over an intact Mark IV Panzer. Seventy opposition soldiers surrendered. Doan and his men wanted more. Urged by Maurice Rose, right there for the effort, Doan's G.I.s attacked throughout the day and into the night, thirty-six hours straight. "Our troops," reported Doan "although very tired, had completely disorganized the enemy." Task Force Doan found seventy-five serviceable enemy trucks abandoned, adding that prize to 329 German prisoners and the destruction or capture of three more panzers, seven antitank guns, ten 20mm antiaircraft guns, a half-track, and a howitzer. The task force had to stop for a few hours to refuel. They'd gone twelve miles to the east, the best advance in the 3rd Armored Division.[46]

So a bit over a day into the attack with twelve Americans killed and almost a hundred wounded, where did the division stand? The Germans slowed CCB more than CCA, and the northern task force of CCA (Kane) more than TF Doan on the most southerly route. Rose judged that the Germans were stretched. The division commander had seen it before in Normandy and Belgium. The foe didn't have much left. Push harder in the south—that would do it. Rose told Colonel Bobby Howze of CCR to be ready, and you didn't have to say that twice to the twin Texans, Sam Hogan and Rich Richardson. If Boudinot's CCB couldn't nudge aside their set of Germans, Rose intended to commit Howze's combat command to slip to the south to take Altenkirchen.[47] Maybe more.

Combat Command B started at 7:00 a.m. on March 26 and ran right into a buzz saw. German defenses slowed TF Welborn to a crawl. TF Lovelady faced a broad open field with Germans dug in on a low ridge concealed by trees. Overcast skies dribbled rain off and on. The American artillery, however, fired rain or shine. The gunners went to work. At midday, clearing skies allowed U.S. Army Air Forces forward controllers to bring in P-47 Thunderbolts. The pilots and ground troops combined to eliminate three panzers. Again, though, the day went by without appreciable movement. Bill Lovelady's outfit lost five tanks, four supply trucks, and a medical half-track. German 88mm gunners used the medic vehicle's red cross marker as a target indicator.[48] Honor indeed.

Things went better in the south. The Germans couldn't be strong everywhere, and CCB's constant pressure, combined with TF Doan's strong thirty-six-hour thrust, cracked something on the other side. Both TF Kane and TF Doan picked up the pace and pressed south of Altenkirchen. Rose sent in Colonel Howze's CCR to loop south of the stalled CCB and take Altenkirchen, and TF Richardson did so at about 5:00 p.m. on March 26. Now CCR would be to the north and CCA to the south, destination Marburg, sixty miles ahead. The slanting late afternoon sunlight, such as it was, lit the scene. As one soldier said later, "It was something like the breakthrough in Normandy, the same dust in the air—billowing clouds of it, pungent and stinging, laced with the stink of burning Nazi vehicles." At Rose's orders, the relatively fresh soldiers of CCR drove all night.[49] The old sweats grinned. Here we go.

Omaha Forward moved up to a dairy farm near the little town of Maulsbach just as things began to split open. At dusk on March 26, a few headquarters troops watched an impromptu fireworks show as two laden enemy ammunition trucks burned and exploded about a half mile away. Inside a commandeered house, Major Haynes Dugan entertained a trio of war correspondents, including the *Boston*

Globe's Iris Carpenter again, as well as Tom Henry of the *Washington Star* and Australian reporter Harold "Bunny" Austin. As Dugan explained the situation to the just-arrived journalists, a nearby German assault gun panzer pranged six quick rounds into the house and its gathered bunch of command post G.I.s, trucks, peeps, and half-tracks. As Dugan noted, "One man was slightly wounded and everyone 'played the walls' [took cover] while the projectiles screamed in." Brigadier General Truman E. Boudinot of CCB had been in the area and got roughed up by a blast, nothing bad, but enough to take notice.[50] If the traveling correspondents hoped for excitement, they didn't have to go far to find it. Omaha Way Forward lived up to its reputation.

Rose did, too. He spent March 27 up with the racing lead tanks of Combat Command Reserve and Combat Command A. From north to south ran task forces Hogan, Richardson, Kane, and Doan. Rose tucked up TF Welborn behind Richardson's column and TF Lovelady trailing Kane. The general was already thinking of sling-shotting Welborn and Lovelady through CCA to take Marburg. As CCR's log reflected, "Enemy resistance was light, but there was difficulty from terrain." A group of officers who studied the landscape found "the countryside was similar to the state of Oregon with wooded, rolling hills."[51] Not tank country, Lieutenant General Omar Bradley might declare. Yet as in the Ardennes, the tanks, half-tracks, and self-propelled howitzers, as well as the various trucks found a way. It helped that the Germans no longer possessed the wherewithal to form a coherent defensive line.

As the Americans overran isolated bands of German soldiers content to shoot once or twice then leg it, the roads teemed with refugees. Clearly the Gestapo had taken off. Americans saw shabbily dressed Russian, Polish, Romanian, Italian, French, Dutch, and Belgian slave laborers walking west, carrying what little they owned. Although tired, the former impressed workers flashed V-for-victory two-finger salutes. Some asked for cigarettes, and American soldiers tossed out packs of much-appreciated smokes. As the G.I.s rolled through the villages, sullen German civilians hovered in yawning doorways. A few children begged for candy. Enemy soldiers taken captive pleaded for food.[52] Clearly the Thousand Year Reich looked to be wrapping up about 988 years early. A good day's progress, this—enough to satisfy Maurice Rose. Tomorrow the 3rd Armored Division would surely be in Marburg.

It really felt like this drama had reached its final act.

———

Omaha Forward moved and set up twice on March 27, first to Altenkirchen, then to Atzelgift, and still the command post ended up thirty miles behind the fast-moving lead tanks. Only the need to refuel slowed aggressive commanders like Hogan and Richardson, and Maurice Rose gave orders for task forces CCB's Welborn and Lovelady to go through CCA at 7:00 a.m. on March 28 and take Marburg. Once that crossroads fell, the VII Corps commander wanted to link up with Rose and talk about a 90-degree turn, north toward Paderborn and a meeting with Ninth Army.[53] That move would be checkmate for the hundreds of thousands of German troops milling around in the Ruhr basin, soon to become the Ruhr Pocket.

Late on the afternoon on March 27, with the sun going down to close what had been a warm spring day, Maurice Rose's small command team sped west toward Omaha Forward in Atzelgift. Rose had spent the day with Combat Command A, watching the engineers, tankers, and rifle troops fight for bridging spots along the small but steep-banked Dill River. With that task completed, the general had some planning to do and orders to issue to get ready to meet Joe Collins on the morrow. The thirty-mile route back to Atzelgift was lousy with former slave workers shuffling west, platoons of G.I. supply trucks going both east and west, and small groups of confused German soldiers wandering here and there.[54] Most of that last bunch didn't want to play anymore. Some did.

Although Rose didn't know it—at that time, nobody in the 3rd Armored Division had gotten the word—a German patrol had already nabbed a peep with Lieutenant Colonel Jack Boulger aboard. The Spearhead Division G-1 certainly saw his share of action at Omaha Forward, an organization that in World War II lost nineteen men killed in action and earned a Distinguished Unit Citation (today's Presidential Unit Citation) for its series of firefights at Mons, Belgium, in September 1944.[55] Those kinds of distinctions normally go to tank or rifle companies, not division command posts. Boulger, like most of Rose's staff officers, figured on risks. He didn't figure on getting captured. Fortunately, he survived the war. But on the day he disappeared, all the soldiers at Omaha Forward could say was that Boulger had gone missing.

Although the neatly plotted maps in Maurice Rose's command post (and Adolf Hitler's Berlin Führerbunker, for that matter) showed front lines and unit markers, at this point in the war, those amounted to suggestions, not facts. The American armored columns rolled faster than the spots could be tagged by the mapping clerks, and the German divisions on both sides' charts really didn't exist in many cases. Central Germany in the last days of March 1945 had turned into the Wild West, with lots of pissed-off, desperate, exhausted men with loaded guns and bad attitudes. Rose's Americans certainly remained well-led and disciplined. The Germans? Who knew?

Now Rose and his little band passed through this dangerous wilderness.

The general moved with the usual team: two peeps (his with three personnel and Colonel Fred Brown's with two), two motorcycle messengers, and Lieutenant Colonel Wesley A. Sweat, his driver, and the three-man G-3 communications team on the M20 wheeled armored car. The M20 featured a .50 caliber heavy machine gun in a ring mount.[56] It couldn't stop a panzer, but it would do for whatever else the dozen-man group might encounter.

As the general's command group vehicles entered the east side of the little village of Rehe (prewar population 900 or so), Rose noticed movement on the roadway a quarter mile ahead. It was a line of gray-clad men crossing the road from north to south at the west end of the hamlet.[57] They carried weapons. Germans.

Some of the enemy troops must have heard the engines of the oncoming American trucks. Pale faces under coal-scuttle helmets and grimy fore-and-aft garrison caps turned toward Rose's quarter-ton peep, with Brown's behind it and the squat six-wheel angle-armored M20 behind that. It looked like way too much to face on an open road. Fight or flight? With or without a command—hard to tell—the German soldiers panicked, breaking what passed for their formation to get off the open road. They ran south in ones or twos. Some vaulted the chest-high brick wall of an enclosure. Others found an opening.[58]

The road was clear.

Fight or flight?

You didn't often see live Germans in the open like that. Rose sure hadn't. He'd served a day in the September 1918 St. Mihiel Offensive before being wounded by German shellfire; when he made it back to his outfit, he'd seen little action in the Meuse-Argonne.[59] In 1944–1945, Rose spent almost every day hearing every variety of German fire, sensing the dreaded zip-zip of the close ones, seeing the awful results, and yet, except for that one scrape at the West Wall, avoiding the worst. Rose had seen panzers rumbling and shooting a few hundred yards away. He'd dealt with tree bursts and Luftwaffe attacks and buzz bombs. Yet in two world wars the only individual German soldiers he'd seen had been dead or captured. And that accorded with the experience of the vast majority of soldiers, even those in the front lines. Hollywood heroics aside, modern firepower means most troops stayed behind cover. Being seen led to being hit, and being hit led to being killed.[60] Rose had long carried his .45 semiautomatic pistol but never fired it in anger. Now here were Germans right in front of him.

Fight or flight?

Never a doubt. "Look what's out there," Rose shouted to Major Bellinger and driver Tech-4 Shaunce. "Jerries!" Rose ordered Shaunce to pull over. He did.[61]

Fifty yards to the southwest, the enemy troops had all entered that walled enclosure. It looked like a cemetery. There were fifteen of them, maybe more: gray Germans, gray headstones, a gray wall, dark trees with spindly bare branches.[62] Already, with the long shadows, you could barely see them in there.

His quarter-ton vehicle had barely skidded to the road shoulder before Rose hopped out. The general pulled up the M1A1 .45 caliber Thompson submachine gun stored near the peep's right front seat. The 30-round stick magazine jutted out. Rose waved to Shaunce and Bellinger.[63] Follow me.

Colonel Fred Brown's peep slid to a halt and the artillery colonel jumped out, as did his driver, Private First Class A. C. Brazeal. The duo followed Rose and his guys. The M20 armored car was still two hundred yards behind.[64]

The Germans chose not to wait. A few began shooting with Mauser rifles and MP40 submachine guns. Rose and his quartet crouched at the cemetery wall. Most of the hostile bullets went high. A couple now and then nicked the brick wall.[65]

Rose didn't want to try the cemetery's front opening, a guaranteed fatal funnel. But the roadside wall showed a gap in the lee of a tree. The general read ground quickly and well, even little holes and hard points—that coup d'oeil thing. You either have it or you don't. Rose had it.

Rose sprang up, aimed his Tommy gun, and . . .

Nothing.

The general yanked the trigger; not a good idea, but he was desperate. Zippo.

Rose dropped the submachine gun and reached for his hip holster.[66]

The Germans kept right on shooting. High. Mercifully high.

Fred Brown's M1 Garand rifle barked. So did A. C. Brazeal's. Bellinger opened up as well. Shaunce, though, emulated his general. His Thompson gun didn't fire, either.[67]

Rose had his .45 pistol in his right hand. He shot once at what he thought might be a moving man. Hard to say.

Then a standing German raised a Mauser Kar98K. The black muzzle aimed right at Rose, a hole as deep and dark as a cavern. Twenty feet away. Rose squeezed his pistol trigger once.[68]

Crack!

The German collapsed like he'd been belted with a sandbag.

Rose turned to find his next target.

There wasn't one. Instead, twelve German soldiers stood with raised hands.

Rose waved his pistol, herding the Germans out of the graveyard. At the Rehe road, Lieutenant Colonel Wesley Sweat and the M20 crew waited with weapons trained on the cowed Germans. Motorcycle rider Private First Class James Omand watched Rose, the other Americans, and the line of silent prisoners and proclaimed it "a sight to behold."[69] It certainly was.

Killing people is not healthy. Over time, it's corrosive to one's character, morality, and stability. Shooting a person face-to-face stays with you unless you're one of the 2 percent of psychopaths. Maurice Rose definitely fell in the 98 percent of all the rest. Most G.I.s didn't have to handle the aftermath of slaying a man at close quarters. A hundred yards out, you could always tell yourself somebody else's bullet, or a machine gun burst, or the artillery, got him. But at pistol range? You owned that one and would the rest of your days.[70] Soldiers like Maurice Rose understood only one way to deal with it. Stay busy.

The Germans saw to that.

CHAPTER 9

"A Hell of a Fix"

So is death by the sword his atonement.

Aeschylus[1]

Omaha Forward got a little too much so a few hours after nightfall on March 28, 1945. In the timbered hills near Marburg, the German gunners spent the night lobbing rounds into the commandeered large house that hosted the division command post. The opposition made up in persistence what they happily lacked in accuracy and troop strength. The little bullets, for the most part, sounded like ricochets or spent rounds at the end of their range, cracking in tree tops and skipping off walls and roofs. The bigger items, though, packed a wallop. Explosive flashes lit the wood line, with booms and crashes right afterward. So far they hadn't struck anything important. But they did impact now and then. You couldn't see them in flight, but you could hear whizzing as hot fragments flew overhead. Now and then the misshapen razor-edged metal shards tinkled on the nearby pavement or smacked the house's northeastern exterior wall. Standing on the porch probably wasn't smart.

"Let's go indoors," Maurice Rose said. "I can't concentrate like this."[2]

Rose had a lot to think about. He'd just said goodbye to Major General Joe Collins. The VII Corps commander brought the orders Rose expected. Quit going east. Swing 90 degrees to the north. Aim for Paderborn, a hundred miles away. There, the 3rd Armored Division would link up with Ninth Army's 2nd Armored Division. Their firm connection promised to complete the encirclement of the 300,000 soldiers of German Army Group B as well as the remaining factory cities of the Ruhr basin, including Dortmund, Düsseldorf, Essen, Hagen, Hamm, Lippstadt, Remscheid, and Wuppertal.[3] Top Allied commanders had long sought a war-winning stroke. Here it was.

The shift in direction caught Rose running on two hours' sleep in the last twenty-four. You wonder how much the previous evening's shootout among the Rehe headstones affected the general, already plenty keyed up after a long day of combat. Still, Rose had long since found ways to press on, courtesy of G.I. coffee, Camel cigarettes, and his own implacable will.[4]

It was the eve of Passover (Erev Pesach) and the Wednesday before Easter, the stretch known as Holy Week to Christians. Holy—not the descriptor anyone might use for this cordite-stinking pursuit through the rubble of the Third Reich. Rose said nothing of these things. Yet his letter of March 12 suggests he certainly remembered. That all stayed private, as usual, to a man so often alone with his thoughts.

But Maurice Rose wasn't alone this evening. The division commander's subordinates had their own duties and had long learned to respect Rose's solitude. The dutiful Major Haynes Dugan, G-2 assistant and press escort, hovered nearby. He had some guests. Would the general be willing to spare a moment?

Normally Rose treated the press politely, said a few words, and moved on. He absolutely shunned the kind of personality profiles and "colorful" human interest stories that generals like Montgomery and Patton embraced. Rose wouldn't consider playing along with packaged puff pieces like the Ernie Pyle "G.I. general" shtick about Omar Bradley. The Spearhead division commander guarded his privacy. He gave standing orders to Haynes Dugan—no personal stuff. Ever. When Meyer Levin of the Overseas News Agency came by in the fall of 1944 to ask about Rose's Jewish background, Dugan gave him the stiff-arm. Rose would be happy to dish up some sentences concerning tanks and war. As for his upbringing, forget it.[5]

For whatever reason, this time things unfolded a little differently. Rose greeted his visitors, gestured to chairs, and took a seat himself. The five journalists sat down, notebooks open, pens and pencils ready. Rose recognized all of them: Bill Heinz of the *New York Sun*, Tom Henry of the *Washington Star*, Iris Carpenter of the *Boston Globe*, Staff Sergeant Andy Rooney of *Stars and Stripes,* and Jack Thompson of the *Chicago Tribune*.[6] Heinz was a very well-known sportswriter before the war. Henry followed the 3rd Armored Division's long push through France and Belgium in the summer of 1944 and had rejoined for the current attack. Carpenter and Rooney covered the battle for Cologne. Thompson's article from back in August 1944 gave the division its nickname "Spearhead." These reporters understood the ground rules. In whatever Rose told them, they'd avoid repeating operational details, and every word they composed had to be approved by military censors.

Rose spoke freely, uncharacteristically so. He summarized the previous day's fighting. The division's lead elements of Combat Command B took Marburg at noon. Some 2,700 hostile troops surrendered, and another 5,600 German Army patients and medical personnel in seven nearby military hospitals fell into American hands.[7] The wheels appeared to be coming off of the adversary's war machine.

Rose touched the map at Paderborn. That got attention. A journalist spoke up.

"When do you hope to reach your objective, general?"

"Tomorrow."

"You think you'll be there tomorrow," another asked, "better than a hundred miles?"

"You said hope," Rose responded. "I can hope, can't I?"

Then Rose asked a question of the press people. "Did you ever see anything like that before?"

The journalists stared at him. They didn't follow.

"Of course you have," Rose stated. "It's precisely Mons all over again—the same movement and the same object." The *Washington Star*'s Tom Henry nodded. He remembered.[8] The rest wrote it down, something to double-check later. Rose's mind leapt fast when talking tactics. Apparently coup d'oeil wasn't mentioned a lot in journalism school. To be fair, most of his own senior officers couldn't keep up when Rose started brainstorming.

Rose said way more than he typically did to reporters or anyone else, for that matter. "Yeomans [83rd Recon Battalion] will probably be the first man on the objective the way things look now," Rose mused. "He'll get there and then radio me some caustic note like 'The first team is here, when is the division coming?'"[9]

The correspondents scribbled furiously.

"I sent Yeomans a message today. It was sent in the clear so the Germans must have picked it up," continued Rose. "I told him I'd give him a case of scotch if he captured von Rundstedt, Kesselring, or Guderian and one bottle for Hitler dead or alive," offered the general, referring to famed German generals Gerd von Runstedt, Albert Kesselring, and Heinz Guderian. "The message was garbled," Rose went on "and someone put Göring in for Guderian. Suppose if he brings Göring in here I'll have to give him a case of scotch."[10] The case of liquor amounted to Rose's standard reward, although the despicable führer only rated a bottle.

Having laid out the plan and some chew-the-scenery "color," too, Rose ended with a challenge. "Coming along with us to try?"[11]

They were.

Then Rose did something very atypical. He showed the reporters a picture of his four-year-old-son, Reece. Because of the war, he barely knew the boy. The general talked about how much he looked forward to getting home.[12]

Of course, that depended on dozens of Sherman TC sergeants, hundreds of infantry NCOs, and thousands of weary G.I. privates. They, not the general, set the tempo now. Them and the Germans, of course. They were still out there.

———

The enemy didn't show a lot of spunk of March 29. As division staffers summarized, "Resistance was scattered and weak and unlocated." A warm, sunny day unleashed the P-38 Lightnings and P-47 Thunderbolts. The 3rd Armored Division's vehicle columns ran wild. By nightfall, the division moved 90-plus miles, not quite all the way to Paderborn, but pretty close.[13] It set the division record for the war.

As forecast, starting at 6:00 a.m., Mike Yeomans's 83rd Recon scouts led the way to the front door of Paderborn. "The day was one of the finest, if not the finest, in the history of this battalion in distance covered, prisoners captured."[14] They overran numerous halfhearted enemy defenses. An artillery NCO commented on the scouts' grim work:

> About 40 miles north of Marburg we were coming down winding roads around the edge of a hill. It was a sharp curve and when we got halfway around we could see a German peep stopped on the opposite side of the road. In the front seat were two German officers. The only trouble was that they didn't have any heads. Their heads were cut off very neatly, just even with their shoulders, and the blood was still gushing up out of the several arteries. Their heads, or parts of their heads, were nowhere to be seen. There wasn't a shrapnel hole in the peep so there was a lot of discussion as to just how it happened. The only logical

explanation is that they and a recon car of the 83rd came up on opposite sides of the blind curve and met head on, and the recon car fired a couple of rounds of 37 [mm] A.P. at them at point blank range, tearing off their heads. It wasn't a pleasant sight but war is war. Down the road were other Germans all shot up, but we soon passed this small pocket of what had been some resistance.[15]

Mike Yeomans's recon soldiers announced clear sailing all the way to the outskirts of Padenborn. From west to east, four task forces advanced, steel tentacles reaching toward Paderborn. By Rose's orders, the column commanders bypassed resistance when they could. Spearhead soldiers joked that they'd cleared the area "to the edge of the road." Behind them, riflemen of the 1st Infantry Division and 104th Infantry Division fought through German die-hards and collected prisoners. There were a lot.[16]

Colonel Bobby Howze's Combat Command Reserve led with Lieutenant Colonel Sam Hogan's troopers to the far west and Lieutenant Colonel Rich Richardson's soldiers toward the center of the division zone. Howze told both task force commanders, "Just go like hell!" That's what occurred. By noon Hogan's task force exceeded radio range and had to relay messages through following units from Combat Command A. Richardson's men pushed to within fifteen miles of Paderborn. The biggest delay all day came when happy American tankers found a warehouse filled with bottles of champagne. Aside from some hangovers, there were no casualties.[17]

To the east, Brigadier General Truman Boudinot had a much rougher time. Combat Command B pushed far north, but they paid for their mileage. Just east of TF Richardson, Task Force Welborn faced some scraps and took 150 prisoners. Lieutenant Colonel Bill Lovelady's tankers and infantrymen moved north on the easternmost division route. In a series of clashes, TF Lovelady captured 170 Germans and two large railcar-mounted cannons. They also destroyed five enemy trucks. The actions cost five Americans killed and nearly thirty wounded, plus two Shermans lost and three mired in the mud. Lovelady's force was down to sixteen functional M4 Shermans, about half strength.[18] Some of these damn Germans, too many, just never gave up.

Major General Rose spent time with Bill Lovelady's G.I.s, then shifted to Colonel Jack Welborn's task force as the day wore on. Corporal John Irwin, a Sherman tank gunner in TF Welborn, looked down from the turret at one point to see a peep sitting on the road, engine idling. Someone in the left front seat looked up at Irwin. The soldier had his helmet off. "He had a crew cut, stiff graying hair, a serious, handsome face, and a big frame," Irwin later said. The man touched his bare forehead. "My helmet's off to you men," the guy yelled. "Keep it up!" Then the peep sped away. Irwin had no idea who this older soldier might be. Buddies later goofed on him for not recognizing his division commander, Maurice Rose.[19] At the tank crew level, generals amount to passing curiosities. Some are more curious than others.

The long, long drive ended well after the sun set. The lead U.S. platoons halted to refuel, but it took most of the dark hours to tighten up extended vehicle columns and recover strays. Completely exhausted after the graveyard fracas, with hardly any sleep and multiple full days of movement and skirmishing, Maurice Rose found Omaha Forward about sixteen miles short of Paderborn. Home sweet home, it seemed, or what passed for it in the sour backwoods of the Third Reich.

But Rose wasn't there yet. In the narrow streets of the little German town, a 391st Armored Field Artillery Battalion half-track briefly blocked the road while its tired crew attempted a three-point turn. Frustrated, Colonel Fred Brown got out of his peep to "encourage" the driver. "General Rose himself was very nice about it," an artilleryman remembered, "and didn't seem worried at all but the underlings were evidently trying to make a few points." They did. The

half-track moved. And the command group reached Omaha Forward, not far away.

That did it for March 29 for the worn-down division commander.
He'd get some well-appreciated sleep, the slumber of the contented.
The division would be in Paderborn in the morning.[20] So Rose
believed.

The Germans thought differently. As the Americans gassed up,
ate, and caught some winks, the enemy assembled a formidable
force, SS *Ersatzbrigade Westfalen* (SS Replacement Brigade Westpha-
lia). The new brigade had received its local version of the universal
Third Reich directive of 1945: "Paderborn is to be held at all costs." Of
course. What else would SS troops do? Along with being a road and
rail junction, the city of 100,000 inhabitants served as a major panzer
training center for the Waffen SS and German Army Tiger battalions.
The Henschel & Son company owned a test site used to run trials for
prototypes of the original 63-ton Tiger I, the newer 77-ton Tiger II
(King or Royal Tiger), and the 72-ton Jagdtiger (Hunting Tiger) turretless tank destroyer bearing a wicked 128mm (5-inch) cannon in a
thick, blocky central casemate. Between the training center invento-
ries and the Henschel holdings, SS Ersatzbrigade Westfalen brought
together fifty-five panzers, mostly Tigers and some Panthers as well.
The German Army's *Schwere Panzer Abteilung* 507 (507th Heavy
Panzer Battalion), led by Russian front veterans, fleshed out their
ranks with Waffen SS panzer instructors, students, and school training vehicles. In addition to the armored punch, the SS Ersatzbrigade
brought in more than a thousand cadre and trainees organized in
five small infantry battalions. The 507th Heavy Panzer Battalion and
its supporting Waffen SS elements constituted the most dangerous
opponents the 3rd Armored Division faced since the Battle of the
Bulge. Panzers, Tigers no less, and Waffen SS—they were the stuff of
nightmares. Before sunup on March 30, these metal demons and
their pitiless masters waited in ambush a few miles south of
Paderborn.[21]

The division slept late, relatively speaking, on March 30. Rather than launch at 4:00 a.m., three of four task force columns cranked up at the leisurely hour of 7:00 a.m.[22] The extended motor march the day before took a lot out of men and equipment, so a few extra hours off-line was reckoned to be prudent. Given the way the day turned out, maybe the Spearheaders should have started earlier.

In the far west, Task Force Hogan hadn't even stopped moving until 3:45 a.m. In the dark, Sam Hogan's men tangled with gritty Germans willing to use *panzerfäusten*. Hogan's task force had to halt for a while to refuel and let the tank TCs and drivers, not to mention the long-suffering riflemen, clear their heads. They'd all get going again a few hours after sunrise.[23]

In front of TF Richardson and TF Welborn, Lieutenant Colonel Mike Yeomans's 83rd Recon kicked off at 6:00 a.m. They made it to the Borchen municipality on Richardson's route and to the west of Castle Hamborn on the Welborn path. Both areas were full of pugnacious dismounted German Waffen SS infantrymen. The enemy used *panzerfäusten* in volleys, and those in Borchen relied on the bazooka-like 88mm *panzerschreck*, too. The G.I.s found it tough to sort out the hamlet of Kirchborchen from the crossroads of Nordborchen. They simply called it all "Bazookatown." Yeomans's scouts didn't see any panzers. But they heard some in both places. Not good. With Rose's OK, Yeomans held up. Task Force Richardson and TF Welborn had to solve this.

Task forces Richardson and Welborn all went out on schedule at 7:00 a.m., as did Bill Lovelady's tankers and riflemen to their east. The weather people thought the day would start overcast and then clear by afternoon.[24] Maybe so. If there were panzers up ahead—and there were, a lot of them—the Spearheaders would need their aerial friends.

Rose went forward well before 7:00 a.m. He took his usual team: his own peep with aide and driver, Colonel Fred Brown's peep with his driver, the two motorcycle messengers, and Lieutenant Colonel Wesley Sweat with his driver and three radio men aboard the M20 armored car. Sweat brought an extra soldier, G-3 stenographer Technical Sergeant John T. "Africa" Jones, so nicknamed for his service in Tunisia. Jones had been included to document the upcoming linkup with the 2nd Armored Division. Wesley Sweat chose to leave behind the hulking .50 caliber heavy machine gun.[25] This made the scout car a bit roomier for what looked to be another long, boring day bouncing here and there in the dust trail of their energetic general.

As the peep motored north, Rose keyed his hand microphone: "OK, men, let's move out." Both Combat Command Reserve and Combat Command B acknowledged immediately, then Combat Command A in the rear did, too. For the final few miles to Paderborn, CCA would stay back. Rose planned to commit CCA only if things got gummed up.[26]

Back at Omaha Forward, Colonel John Smith and the staffers tracked the opening moves and informed VII Corps using the division's long-range radio set. Smith intended to push the command post up to Etteln, nine miles south of Paderborn. First TF Welborn had to clear the town, or at least most of it. Rose's headquarters men guessed they'd be in Etteln by dark.[27] If things really went well, they'd end up in Paderborn. It depended on the day's fighting.

On the way to find Colonel Jack Welborn's task force, Rose spotted a jeep coming from the other direction. The man in the front passenger seat looked familiar, a helmet with two white stars bobbing on his head. It was Major General Terry Allen of the 104th Infantry Division. Rose told Tech-4 Shaunce to pull over. Blowing by Terry Allen wasn't going to happen.

Allen's driver did likewise. Both generals got out. As usual, Allen started talking. Rose listened, his usual role in this odd-couple relationship. It's unclear what they discussed, or if Rose got a word in edgewise. At one point, Allen motioned to a nearby scout, Private Hugh Daly from the 104th. The officer who went by "Chief

Timberwolf" rather than "Commanding General" needed a light for his smoke. Allen always seemed to be bumming a light, a cigarette, or a snack, and his soldiers happily shared with him, as he did with them.

It's noteworthy that Daly and his two fellow privates weren't surprised to see either Allen or Rose so near the action. The Timberwolves' 414th Infantry Regiment had been working for the 3rd Armored Division since this operation began on March 25. All three young soldiers had seen plenty of both generals and heard even more. Some of it was probably true, too.

"Thank you, soldier," said Allen. "You men take care of yourselves."

Daly later commented: "What a thrill for us, such a distinguished person treating us lowly privates as peers, like his family." He had less to say of "the wonderful General Rose," nowhere near Terry Allen's caliber as an elbow-grabber and hand-shaker.[28] But Rose was out front. To privates, that mattered.

In his short discussion with Rose, the loquacious Allen may have mentioned a particular rifle platoon serving with the 2nd Battalion, 414th as part of TF Lovelady. This platoon was made up of African American infantrymen who'd just joined the division. Strapped for manpower, especially after the Battle of the Bulge, the senior U.S. Army generals finally noticed that a lot of their team remained on the bench. About an eighth of their country's potential soldiery could only serve in segregated outfits designated as "colored": black sergeants, corporals, and privates led by white officers and some white senior NCOs. A number of these units fulfilled combat roles. Most acted in logistics capacities. Black Americans were often truck drivers, ammunition haulers, fuel handlers, and "duty soldiers," Armyspeak for G.I. manual laborers. The autumn 1944 Red Ball Express convoys depended on the guts and diligence of segregated truck companies. Now, in response to the army's dire need for more riflemen, 4,562 African American service troops volunteered to join the infantry as individual replacements. Many black NCOs turned in their stripes to get this chance to fight as privates. The top American generals—Marshall the VMI graduate, Bradley of Missouri, Hodges of Georgia—wouldn't go all the way to man-by-man integration. The senior leadership compromised on black platoons as part of white rifle companies. It would take the Korean War to compel full-scale integration of the U.S. Army. Beating the Nazi Germans came first. In early 1945 ten of the sixty-one U.S. divisions in northern Europe received these unique African American infantry units.[29]

Terry Allen wanted some. His division had already worked with the 784th Tank Battalion (Colored) along the Roer River in January and February 1945; these tankers impressed Allen. When the new African American rifle platoons became available, Allen asked for and received his share, three of them. One went to each regiment. After the new platoons completed the standard 104th battle school for replacement soldiers, Terry Allen personally presented each new African American rifleman his division shoulder patch. "You are Black Timberwolves now," Allen said. "We expect great things from you." On March 30, the 414th Infantry Regiment's African American platoon worked for TF Lovelady.[30] They wanted to fight. They'd get their chance.

March 30 looked likely to provide plenty of combat for those seeking it. As Rose's peep linked in with the rumbling infantry half-tracks of TF Welborn, Major Bob Bellinger sought updates on the morning's attack. Task Force Hogan to the far west still hadn't gotten going yet. Task Force Richardson reported "no opposition." Task Force Welborn, as Rose could see, aimed at Etteln, where the 83rd Recon saw enemy troops in Waffen SS camouflage. Task Force Lovelady to the east said they were moving "rapidly." For the present, Rose stuck with Jack Welborn's infantrymen. Welborn had the most direct way to Paderborn. But maybe the general might shift to join Rich Richardson's axis if Etteln proved too tough a nut.[31]

By 11:30 a.m., all four task forces went beyond the 83rd Recon outposts and immediately smacked into the positions of the SS

Ersatzbrigade. Sam Hogan's soldiers to the west made it to Wewer, four miles outside Paderborn. There the Americans ran afoul of Waffen SS *panzerfaust* teams shooting from cellars, attics, and everywhere else, resistance judged "the strongest that had been met on the drive." The enemy took out three U.S. tanks and killed several infantrymen, too. Hogan's men would be busy all day.[32]

To the far east, Bill Lovelady's G.I.s hit a similar greeting at little Wrexen, ten miles short of Paderborn. There downed trees blocked the road. When Lovelady's first platoon held up, well-hidden *panzerschreck* teams knocked out three M5 Stuart light tanks, punching them out one after another. Three U.S. tankers died and a dozen fell wounded. When the next American armor company rolled up, hostile machine gunners forced the attached 414th Timberwolf infantrymen off the deck of the Sherman tanks; several of the American riflemen were killed outright, more wounded, and most disorganized. Two more tanks, both Shermans, were hit by *panzerfäusten*. Two American tank crewmen couldn't be found, perhaps dead in a burning vehicle, maybe captured. The Waffen SS men had a lot of ammunition.[33] They used it.

Lovelady's infantry included the African American platoon that nicknamed themselves the "Dusky Devastators." Among them was Sergeant Howard Williams, a former Golden Gloves boxer who'd been to Nazi Germany for the 1936 Olympics when the great sprinter Jesse Owens taught Adolf Hitler's people a thing or two about the Master Race. The African American platoon reinforced the lesson. They ran off, captured, or killed about forty Waffen SS defenders, wresting away two wooded knobs outside Wrexen.[34]

Anxious to see the Spearhead Division's efforts, Lightning Joe Collins flew in by Piper Cub in the afternoon. It was the only way the active VII Corps commander could keep up with the far-flung 3rd Armored Division. Collins's pilot bumped to a landing in a pasture, and Collins met Brigadier General Truman E. Boudinot. The CCB commander had a peep seat for Collins; Boudinot's aide had just been wounded. Collins's remaining entourage piled into other trucks. Off they went to find TF Lovelady. At one juncture, the two generals crouched on the friendly side of an embankment as an American medic struggled to save a stricken young SS *panzerfaust* man. The German had taken a bullet in his head. He didn't make it. Entangled in the fighting, the VII Corps commander ended up staying the night with Boudinot.[35]

It took until well past sundown to clean up the Wrexen mess. When the shooting ceased, Bill Lovelady's riflemen and tankers rounded up thirty-five sullen SS prisoners, finally out of tank-killing rounds.[36] The Germans ably held up TF Lovelady—no Paderborn run for them.

Task Force Richardson's progress stopped in the Borchen villages, "Bazookatown." Vicious, close-quarters fighting occurred in three separate hamlets. Villagers called the region the Jammertal, "The Vale of Sorrow."[37] It surely was on March 30, which just happened to be Good Friday. It was also the second day of Passover, as Jewish people would be aware. The only Jews in Bazookatown that afternoon wore G.I. olive drab.

Richardson's soldiers endured a brutal house-by-house contest. At one choke point near the Nordborchen crossroads, SS *panzerfaust* men punched holes through five Shermans in a few minutes. The Germans used the rocket launchers against tanks. They shot them at American riflemen. They even fired the things like mortars, using looping overhead trajectories to get at U.S. soldiers huddled behind cover. As the overcast lifted somewhat, Richardson's men brought in close air support against "very stubborn SS troops." The fighting went on well into the evening.[38] There'd be no thrust into Paderborn from Bazookatown.

If anyone made it into Paderborn to make good on Rose's promise, it had to be Colonel Jack Welborn's task force. Everybody else was grappling with gutsy Waffen SS foot troops—those guys again—determined to hold their ground. Task Force Richardson had reported two Panthers, and was dealing with them.[39] But nobody had seen the Tigers. They had yet to show up. Maybe the chronic German fuel shortages, courtesy of Allied heavy bombers, had finally drained the gas-thirsty Tiger fleet once and for all.

First, though, came Etteln, as full of Waffen SS *panzerfaust* men as all the rest of the towns south of Paderborn on March 30. Jack Welborn's tankers and infantrymen made good use of artillery and air strikes to clear the village. Rose and his artillery chief Brown helped in this effort, coordinating fires in support of TF Welborn. Tech Sergeant Africa Jones in the M20 armored car watched the proceedings. As stenographer, he maintained an informal log. The Etteln fracas started in earnest around 2:00 p.m. The aircraft kept on coming, bombing and strafing. When the planes took a break, American artillery shells chimed in.[40] It went on and on. Send a bullet, not a man. This was how it worked.

The general was fully absorbed in the ongoing battle. Artillery commander colonel Fred Brown, too, took an active role. Lieutenant Colonel George Garton, commander of the 391st Armored Field Artillery Battalion, pulled up his peep and joined the conclave. The G-3, Wesley Sweat, kept shuttling back and forth from Rose to the M20 vehicle's radio rack, sending news to Omaha Forward. German rounds, both small arms and heavier stuff, zipped and cracked, though nothing scary. It amounted to hearing fire and taking a bit, but not really receiving effective German attention. Not yet. And hopefully, as stenographer Tech Sergeant Jones opined, not ever on this day.[41]

The air strikes alternated with artillery concentrations. Lulls arose. During one of these brief gaps, Jones saw Colonel Brown and, he thought, Lieutenant Colonel Garton engaging distant Germans with M1 rifles. Jones could make out only so much from the open-topped armored car. He thought the German targets might be about 350 yards out. As near as Jones could tell, the American officers missed. Then they went back to working on artillery tasks.[42]

While this went on, Rose queried Colonel Bobby Howze of CCR about TF Richardson, then dropped down to talk directly to the task force lieutenant colonel himself. The division commander considered heading west to try that route. Richardson recommended not—too hot.[43] Rose elected to stick with Welborn.

At about 6:30 p.m., with dusk approaching, the few Waffen SS still alive in Etteln gave up. TF Welborn roared into the trashed town square. Rose's command group followed, with Garton's quarter-ton truck now along for the ride. Technical Sergeant Jones rated the place demolished. Still, the enemy was gone, although muffled sounds of TF Richardson's ongoing clashes came from the west. Jones glanced that way and turned to Wesley Sweat, also up in the turret ring.

"Look at that beautiful sunset," Jones marveled. "You would never imagine a war was going on."

"Yes," replied Sweat, "and it is appropriate because today is Good Friday."[44]

The crucifixion awaited.

———

Rose, Brown, Welborn, Sweat—they all trusted in the P-47 Thunderbolts, the beloved "Jugs," beefy aerial killing machines the beleaguered Germans called *verdammte jabos* (damned fighter-bombers). The Thunderbolt pilots sent exultant reports of blowing away panzer after panzer on the green, wooded hills around Castle Hamborn.[45] So the Tigers had been tamed. All hail the U.S. Army Air Forces.

Not this time.

American pilots took out many, many panzers in their day, but on March 30, 1945, they grossly overestimated the results of their efforts. The fighter-bombers used a new weapon, napalm, and the fire bombs looked awesome popping all around the parked Tigers. To the forward air controllers, it appeared the tanks had been burned out. In truth, only one had been singed, and it still worked just fine.[46] Worse, the Americans on the ground also thought the Tigers had been fried. Task Force Welborn's tankers and riflemen advanced with confidence, destination: Paderborn.

Colonel Jack Welborn led with a company of M4 Shermans, then a company of half-track infantry ready to dismount and clear roadblocks. The colonel's Willys peep rolled right behind the lead company. About five miles north of Etteln, Welborn took a hard left turn to head west, intending to move that way a mile before turning north up a sketchy farm track that passed the wooded hill of Castle Hamborn and then arrowed straight north six miles to Paderborn. That less obvious route might let the U.S. column wriggle through between these various Waffen SS *panzerfaust* nests. As Welborn's lead tanks made the hard left turn to the west, some of the American TCs looked to the north and saw the Germans hit by the air support, those nine knocked-out Tigers.[47]

They weren't knocked out, just silent, biding their time.

The westward route fronted farm fields on both sides. Shallow drainage ditches, two to three feet deep, paralleled the two-lane road, and on both sides a row of mature trees made for a lovely country lane. This quaint landscaping also meant the American vehicles passed one by one to the west. About a mile along, TF Welborn's lead vehicle, the powerful T26E3 Pershing, made the pivot to head north. It was a little after 7:00 p.m., last light.

Wham! Wham! Wham!

The German 88mm Tiger cannons belted the fifth Sherman tank in line, the one that hadn't turned north yet. They nailed the big Pershing, and then popped a lagging medical half-track at the east end, too, right near the intersection. The rest of the American vehicles halted, lined up, ducks in a row, a tank company and an infantry company, too, trapped between the two blasted ends of their column.

German panzer men later described the scene: "like shooting from a raised platform" at "food on a platter." The Tigers engaged from about 900 yards away. As usual, German gunners shot until they saw flames. They ventilated seven Shermans. Bright tongues of fire sprang up and oily smoke boiled as American gasoline ignited.[48] Task Force Welborn was in big trouble.

Colonel Jack Welborn in his peep and three Sherman tanks bumped north, swerving past the disabled Pershing. They made it to Castle Hamborn, pulled into shadowy spots under the trees, and tried to raise the rest of the task force on the radio. Two-thirds of TF Welborn was still coming up from Etteln. If the rest of the task force could get the word, and maneuver east or west, this still might work. It didn't pan out. No radio contact, and absolute confusion to the south ended any such hope. No joy.[49]

On the deadly road south of Castle Hamborn, surviving G.I. tankers and riflemen scrambled into the ditches, nuzzling up near tree trunks for cover. Some never made it out of the battered vehicles. Americans dragged wounded comrades below the road shoulders. The German panzers kept methodically working their way down the row of halted tanks and half-tracks. One after another, the American vehicles blazed up. Tracer bullets skipped off the pavement as German panzer machine gunners joined the fray, too. Soldiers burrowed deeper in the moist gullies.

Maurice Rose and his command group were right there in the ditches, too, their quarter-ton trucks and M20 armored car abandoned on the roadside. Radios could be heard, Omaha Five calling Omaha Six, Long John Smith asking for his general. All Rose could do was hang in the low ground, ducking the zip-zip-zip of near bullets, cradling his Tommy gun, pistol on his belt. At this point, Rose commanded nothing.

Brown and Garton, good artillerymen, crouched near their sidelined peeps, microphones in hand, still using the onboard radios. The two officers kept working to get artillery shells onto those damnable Tigers up the hill. It was getting dark, and firing deadly 105mm projectiles by guess and by God is not a good idea. So it took time to try different targeting solutions.[50] Meanwhile, the Germans kept right on going, banging away.

A few German tanks rolled through the open field to the north, brazenly stopping to play their machine guns up and down the stalled row of burning American vehicles. By now, every U.S. tank and half-track had been hit: seventeen Shermans, seventeen half-tracks, three two-and-a-half-ton trucks, two peeps (one of them Garton's) and an M36 Jackson tank destroyer to boot. An American soldier saw the German panzer crews and Waffen SS rifle troops atop their mighty armored beasts, whooping and hollering. The old heads among the enemy forces hadn't had a night like this since the glory days of the blitzkrieg.[51]

On the roadway, dozens of American soldiers lay dead and wounded; others were scattered or missing. The only blessing was that the onboard Tiger machine guns couldn't depress low enough to tear up the ranks of G.I.s nestled in the drainage ditches. Although plenty of bold Americans returned fire, no Tigers stopped.[52] They were like tyrannosaurs among sheep. Very weak sheep.

In the middle of this slaughter, prone Technical Sergeant Africa Jones felt hot metal whack his middle back. He didn't know what it was, some scorching fragment from enemy fire. "I'm hit," he shouted.

His G-3 officer crawled to Jones. Despite the gathering gloom, Lieutenant Colonel Sweat looked over and felt the impact site. The hot metal chip drew blood but had landed flat. Jones would be OK. The technical sergeant thought so. He comforted himself: "I'm with a major general who ought to be able to get us out of this."[53]

Ought to, but he had not done so yet. Thanks to Brown, Garton, and a lot of hardworking howitzer crewmen, the American artillery seemed to have done some good. The Tigers on the hill quit firing and moved off, perhaps going south to tangle with the rest of TF Welborn on the way north from Etteln. The other panzers that savaged the stalled vehicles had also left.[54]

Rose wasn't going out like this. No way. An old U.S. Army adage tells a leader under fire to do something, even if it's wrong. Rose began running through his options. They all started with one step. Get on the radio.

Heedless of the bullets, fragments, and flares zipping here and there, Rose scrambled to his peep. He grabbed the dangling hand microphone and called Omaha Five, Chief of Staff Long John Smith. Smith answered immediately.

Dispensing with radio call signs, Rose spoke firmly, no panic: "Smith, send somebody to close up this column. We have been cut. Two of our ambulances have been shot up." Colonel Smith acknowledged. Maybe Task Force Doan could get north to link up.[55] Maybe.

Rose tried to raise Welborn. Nothing. That colonel and his three tanks were half a mile away, holed up at Castle Hamborn. They might as well have been on Mars.

Wesley Sweat crouched nearby, visible in the intermittent light of the burning half-tracks. Rose remarked conversationally, as if commenting on the evening's weather, "We're in a hell of a fix now."

"We'll get out of it," Sweat said.[56] They all counted on their general.

Rose reviewed what he owned: the M20 armored car with six soldiers and those powerful radios, but no heavy machine gun. How that might have helped! But the weapon was back at Omaha Forward. Rose's team had two good peeps with seven men, counting himself; Garton's quarter-ton truck was trashed, useless. The motorcycles lay twisted on the roadway, tires shredded, their riders gone.[57] In the darkness, those two soldiers were on their own. Rose could deal with them later. If there was a later.

Colonel Fred Brown suggested dumping the vehicles and going cross-country south toward Etteln. That's how Sam Hogan and Olin Brewster and their troops shook loose when surrounded during the Battle of the Bulge. Rose disagreed. The general could count the blazing vehicles. Most of TF Welborn was still out there, probably gone around this fracas. The division commander couldn't say why, and he did not in this dire instance. But he wanted to mount up and keep going along the original route to find Welborn at Castle Hamborn. Then they'd all go back and sort out this carnage.[58]

It was now about 7:30 p.m., fully dark. Well, not fully—the burning American tanks, trucks, and half-tracks cast a lurid light and long shadows. Furtive creatures moved in the trees. Germans? Americans? Who knew?

Time to go. Rose's three vehicles started west. They threaded through the wreckage and then Brown spun north, nosing through a break in the trees, out into the open pasture north of the deadly road. Whatever was going through Rose's mind, his actions spoke. Press on.

———

The shooting and explosions seemed more distant now. Brown's peep led, with Garton and both of their drivers piled onto the seats atop large radio sets. The colonel drove.[59] The artillery officer wanted to be sure he made the correct turn toward Castle Hamborn. This wouldn't be a good night to screw up.

Rose's quarter-ton came next, the general staring intently as they approached the dirt trail. The M20 six-wheeler trailed, with Sweat up in the gunless turret ring. The vehicles slowly puttered over the meadow, hand-railing the trees along the road.

About three-quarters of a mile along, Brown spun the wheel. It was the muddy path to Castle Hamborn. Then Brown braked and halted. Behind the artillery colonel, Rose and Sweat stopped their vehicles. The hulking Pershing sat there, utterly inert.[60]

Brown and Garton got out, as did Private First Class A. C. Brazeal, Brown's driver. The Pershing's suspension system showed all kinds of damage, those lethal 88mm Tiger rounds at work. More of note, the artillerymen saw no tank tread marks on the earthen path running to the north of the dead Pershing. In truth, Colonel Jack Welborn's peep and his three Shermans had gone off the dirt trail to get around the stalled monster. In the darkness, that wasn't evident. Instead, Brown walked back to Rose's peep. The general had been trying in vain to contact Welborn on the SCR-506 radio.

Brown told Rose that it didn't look like Welborn had gone north. That settled it. The general told Brown to get back on the main road and head west. If they didn't find Welborn, they'd try to make their way to TF Richardson in the Borchen area. Brown nodded. It was about 7:45 p.m.[61]

In minutes the three American vehicles bounced back onto the hardtop. The peeps raced ahead, with the six-wheel M20 lagging as it worked from the dirt trail onto the pavement. Ahead, Brown saw the hazy, dark silhouettes of approaching tanks. The lead shape looked like a Pershing with a long 90mm cannon jutting forward. Fred Brown rejoiced: "That's one of Jack's new tanks."

As the artillery peep passed the first large tank, George Garton noticed two exhaust stacks.

A Pershing only had one.

"Holy shit!" Garton yelled. "It's a Tiger! Get off the road."[62]

There were three more Tigers as well, a dangerous quartet slowly clanking east. Brown muscled his peep's steering wheel and slid past number two, bounced off number three's side, and then whacked number four, too. A five-gallon gas can near Brown tore off. The colonel yanked the quarter-ton to his right, floored it, slithered into the drainage depression, and crossed the north tree line on the run, tires churning mud. The peep elevated briefly then landed on all four wheels in the open grassy field.

Behind Brown, Rose's driver Tech-4 Glenn Shaunce tried to follow suit. He swerved around Tiger one and glanced off the slab-like south side of the second one. Two more . . .

A hundred yards back, Tech Sergeant Africa Jones saw the four huge black shapes and the jittering, dodging U.S. peeps. "Why don't we head for the forest to our left [south]," Jones hollered at Sweat, "and try to join our own forces there?"

"No, no," the G-3 lieutenant colonel replied, "we must stay with the general."[63] They did.

Shaunce focused, hands gripping his Willys light truck's steering wheel. Tiger number three slewed a little, turning diagonally, trying to block Rose's onrushing peep. Shaunce drove for the gap ten yards ahead. The Tiger pivoted like a heavy bank vault door being pushed shut: slow, steady, and smooth.

And thus the bolt-hole closed.

A peep five feet wide crunched into a fat plum tree and a Tiger hull only four feet apart. Metal squealed. The peep motor gunned, then the light truck bounced backward, its front end crumpled. The peep's engine died.

Ten feet above the scarred pavement, the Tiger's turret hatch banged open. In the flickering half-light provided by flares and burning U.S. tanks, Shaunce glimpsed a person standing up, pointing a submachine gun at Rose's peep. The hostile form bellowed something, the words swallowed by the throaty roar of the panzer's huge Maybach engine. The German must be a TC, a man in a hurry. That MP-40 in the foe's hands meant business.

Maurice Rose and Bob Bellinger dismounted, hands up. Shaunce limped around the caved-in hood of his peep; his leg was fractured. He, too, raised his hands. The trio waited there near the right front of the massive Tiger, probably twelve feet from the enemy submachine gun's well-aimed barrel. Rose, the tallest, stood in the center. This was the end of the road, all right.

The German up top kept on yelling and gesturing. Rose tried to respond in German, but the enemy TC didn't hear him. One of the panzer man's words might have been *pistolen*.[64] Pistols, plural.

"I think he wants our guns," said the general.

Bellinger dropped his hands to unfasten his shoulder holster.

The German opened fire.

The burst rippled across the general, convulsing him with fourteen hammering impacts: right hand, chest, groin, head. Four in the head did the job. Rose's two-star helmet went spinning into the night air. Two 9mm rounds punctured it, too.[65]

Exit Maurice Rose.

EPILOGUE

Nordhausen D+309

The evil that men do lives after them.

William Shakespeare[1]

The 3rd Armored Division's light tanks did all the dirty work. With their 37mm main guns and thin armor, the 17-ton M5 Stuarts did not dare try to trade shots with any panzer, let alone a Panther or Tiger. Still, they were handy for going after enemy infantry, shooting up bunkers, dashing across bridges, guarding the fuel and maintenance trucks, and generic snooping around, "developing the situation," as the doctrinal euphemism went.[2] In plain English, U.S. Army Stuart crews found the enemy, often by banging right into them.

Every task force included at least one company of Stuarts. For his outfit's rotten little jobs, Lieutenant Colonel Bill Lovelady counted on the Stuart crews of Company B, 33rd Armored Regiment. And Company B relied on the "old man," 1st Platoon's Sergeant Aurio J. Pierro.

One of the charter members of the brotherhood of veteran Spearhead Division TCs, Pierro at age twenty-eight was one of the elders in his tank company. Of the twenty-man platoon of Stuart tankers that came ashore with him at Normandy way back in late June 1944, only Pierro remained on duty. All the rest had been killed, wounded, or gone missing. Pierro earned a Silver Star in the Battle of the Bulge. He'd had tanks shot out from under him and burned out. Pierro'd suffered wounds. He'd lost several crewmates. By April 1945, Pierro served as both the platoon sergeant and platoon leader, having lost yet another lieutenant near Marburg. Bill Lovelady recommended Pierro for a battlefield commission to 2nd lieutenant, but the paperwork wandered around somewhere among the ubiquitous "they" of higher headquarters.[3] So now Sergeant Aurio Pierro did lieutenant and staff sergeant work for buck sergeant pay.

This April 11, Pierro's platoon received orders. Check out a military compound in north Nordhausen. More dirty work, Pierro guessed. He didn't know the half of it. But Pierro didn't become an old soldier by being sloppy. He approached slowly, alert for trouble. "I came to a fence," he said. "I didn't know what it was, but there was a gate, and there was a barracks just on the other side of the fence." More SS diehards in there? Another bunch of *panzerfaust* teams? "And I didn't have any idea what it was," Pierro recalled, "No idea at all."[4]

Suddenly, a dozen men erupted from the shabby structure. A few pushed open the creaking gate. The scrawny inmates wore what looked to be filthy striped pajamas. These guys weren't German soldiers, nor were they Allied prisoners of war. Pierro remained up in his turret. He got on the radio—had to pass the word up the line. At the same time, he told his subordinate TCs to dismount a pair of men with Tommy guns. Check out those structures.

After a while, one of Pierro's privates came back. He stopped below Pierro's Stuart tank. "You gotta look in that building over there," the G.I. yelled. The soldier pointed to a dirty dull red-brick edifice.

Pierro climbed down and followed the soldier. When the sergeant walked into the unlit room, the smell almost bowled him over. He saw that "there was like an operating table, and there were dead prisoners, emaciated bodies there, tied hand and foot. On the floor, on the table—like an operating table, whatever it was."[5] Pierro had seen a lot of bad things in the war. But this . . .

An American artillery forward observer saw even worse in another building. "Thousands of poor wretches who had once been men," he wrote, "were starved until their shrunken skeletons looked as if they were going to punch holes through their parchment skin."[6] There were crematoriums full of ashes that had once been people.

Those V-1 buzz bombs and V-2 rockets? These were the slaves who built them, impressed Jews and other "undesirables" of the Thousand Year Reich. The warehoused dead numbered in thousands. This Nordhausen camp was part of a complex known as Dora-Mittelbau.[7] Ninety miles east of Paderborn, Pierro's platoon of Stuart tankers caught a blazing spark of the white-hot energy that had burned inside their dead general Maurice Rose. There's a reason Rose did what he did.

Pierro and his men had seen enough. The sergeant went back to his tank and reported what he'd seen in no uncertain terms to his company commander. This was one of those places murmured about in those terrible G.I. rumors. The blunt one-syllable words would be heard a lot in days to come: death camp.[8]

Sergeant Pierro's message rocketed right up, to Lieutenant Colonel Bill Lovelady, to Brigadier General Truman Boudinot, all the way to Brigadier General Doyle O. Hickey, the division commander. The doctors and medics came, as did the photographers and generals, to include Major General Joe Collins of VII Corps. Of a few hundred living prisoners liberated, only 254 men could be treated, and not all of them survived. Major Martin L. Sherman, a U.S. Army doctor, estimated that only half of those rescued lived to tell the sordid tale. The tidy German file boxes reflected some 60,000 inmates, of whom a third died by execution, exhaustion, and abuse. Those V1s and V2s had been built in a nearby tunnel complex in the Harz massif. The underground lair resembled Edvard Grieg's Hall of the Mountain King, although a particularly demented, diabolical version thereof. Spearhead soldiers heard that when Brigadier General Doyle Hickey walked through the fetid barracks, he almost chewed his brier pipe stem in half.[9]

———

The U.S. Army hews to its traditions, especially under dire conditions. No unit is ever without a commander. The second Major General Maurice Rose died, Brigadier General Doyle Hickey took command, even though it took until the morning of March 31, 1945, to confirm Rose's demise. There was a brief thought of shifting Major General Ernie Harmon, "Old Gravel Voice," from command of XXII Corps to backfill his late subordinate from Tunisia days. But in the end, the job stayed with Hickey.[10] He'd been with the 3rd Armored Division for three-plus years.

A patrol from TF Welborn went out after first light on March 31 to find the dead general. Staff Sergeant Arthur Hauschild, an experienced scout, led the squad. They found Rose right where he fell, the only body on the scene. Hauschild recognized the general immediately. Rose's signature tall brown cavalry boots still had some shine on them. "He lay on the ground near his [peep]," Hauschild reported later, "his helmet with bullet holes in it lay beside him, and his pistol still in its holster with the flap buttoned down." Rose's partially crushed quarter-ton peep was there, too, as well as the empty M20 armored car. The Germans hadn't taken a thing off Rose or the derelict U.S. vehicles. It appeared the enemy TC simply shot the tall guy in the middle and moved on. Nothing personal, just business—so it seemed. American radio code books and tactical map sheets remained on the peep and inside the M20. Hauschild's soldiers used their own Willys quarter-ton to ferry Rose, the marked maps, and the vital codes to Colonel Jack Welborn's little command post at Castle Hamborn.[11] Rose had nearly gotten there the night before, but in the final instance, the general zigged instead of zagged. A few minutes, a few yards, life and death—so it played out.

Although casualties among the ambushed companies of TF Welborn exceeded twenty-four killed and more than a hundred wounded, the only man slain in the division command group was Maurice Rose. Darkness swallowed many of the other Americans. The two artillery colonels and drivers eluded their pursuers. Both motorcycle riders got away cleanly and linked up with nearby elements of the 36th Armored Infantry Regiment. Tech-4 Glenn Shaunce crawled off on his broken leg, stopping to rest now and then. He finally found fellow soldiers just after sunup on April 1, Easter Sunday. Major Bob Bellinger didn't reach a friendly outfit until the next morning, but he, too, evaded capture.[12] How both men avoided all of those German submachine gun bullets remains an example of the fortunes of war. Somehow, they made it out.

Lieutenant Colonel Wesley Sweat, Tech Sergeant Africa Jones, and the four other men on the M20 armored car also survived, but did so the hard way. Taken captive by brusque Waffen SS ground troops, Sweat and his five fellow G.I.s endured more than two harrowing weeks shuttling between German prisoner of war compounds, finally reaching Stalag XIB near Hannover, Germany. The British 7th Armoured Division liberated them and about 17,000 other Allied prisoners on April 16, 1945.[13] Sweat, Jones, and their fellow soldiers, too, came home after the war.

The 3rd Armored Division didn't hesitate or stumble in the wake of Rose's death. Soldiers say that the best way to measure a commander's influence is to see what happens after he's gone. By that criteria, Rose and his Spearhead Division excelled. The G.I.s took Paderborn on April 1 and Lieutenant Colonel Matt Kane's task force met the 2nd Armored Division at nearby Lippstadt. The Ruhr Pocket, rechristened "Rose Pocket" to honor the late division commander, bagged more than 376,000 Germans, a greater number than anticipated. Humiliated and fearful of war crimes trials, Nazi hard case Field Marshal O. M. Walter Model shot himself. In the ruins of embattled Berlin, with Red Army soldiers at the doorstep of his bunker,

Adolf Hitler and many of his inner circle made the same choice. Thus in blood and pain, the vast European war ended on May 7, with the 3rd Armored Division in it to the very last. It's said that in and around Paderborn and during the several encounters that came after, not many Waffen SS troops surrendered, or at least not too many became Spearheader prisoners.[14] The men of 3d Armored Division were not in a magnanimous mood after Paderborn. Nordhausen only intensified such emotions.

The U.S. Army buried Major General Maurice Rose in a temporary grave at Ittenbach, Germany, on April 2, 1945, Easter Monday and the fifth day of Passover. The great men came to pay tribute: newly promoted General Omar N. Bradley, Lieutenant General Courtney H. Hodges, Lieutenant General George S. Patton, Jr., Major General J. Lawton Collins, Major General Ernest N. Harmon, and Major General Terry de la Mesa Allen. Soldiers said that Allen wept.[15]

America's Jewish community embraced Maurice Rose in death. The general's killing coincided with the spring 1945 wave of horrific film and stark photos documenting the multiple millions of brutal executions and tortures Nazi Germans had inflicted on European Jewry. Here in gallant Maurice Rose was the face of the U.S. Army's many soldiers who'd beaten Hitler's Germans and doing so ended what became widely known as the Holocaust. Few, if any, Americans asked what Rose said or thought about his heritage. He became the martyred Jewish general, slain by vicious Nazis. When the general's ninety-year-old father, Rabbi Sam Rose, died on July 10, 1945, most assumed it was due to a broken heart. Aware of the public interest, well-meaning military chaplains erected a Star of David over Rose's interim burial plot, replacing the original wooden cross. The wishes of Maurice Rose's wife, Virginia, or his adult son Mike (a Marine lieutenant serving in the Pacific theater) were solicited but not necessarily accepted.[16]

As to Rose's death, the details became confused and conflated, and it was none too clear exactly what happened at about 8:00 p.m.

on March 30, 1945, a quarter mile south of Castle Hamborn. Even Glenn Shaunce and Bob Bellinger couldn't quite agree, and the German shooter sure didn't raise his head, if he still existed, especially after the Nazi regime surrendered unconditionally. At the request of many, in and out of the U.S. Army, War Crimes Investigation No. 12-352A (Rose) began under the supervision of able military attorney (and future Watergate scandal special prosecutor) Colonel Leon Jaworski. After weighing the statements and subsequent interviews of the two eyewitnesses—Bellinger and Shaunce—and other peripheral figures like Fred Brown, Wesley Sweat, George Garton, John T. "Africa" Jones, and the other junior soldiers, none of whom saw the abrupt denouement, Jaworski agreed with his subordinate investigators that the killing was not intentional, but "made *in the heat of battle* [italics in original]."[17] It matched the verdict of frontline G.I.s. Rose spent a lot of time under fire and his luck ran out.

The U.S. Army saluted Rose. They named the Ruhr Pocket for him. They christened a troop transport ship, a barracks in postwar Vilseck, Germany, and a U.S. Army Reserve center in Middletown, Connecticut, with his name. The ship has been scrapped, but the facilities remain in use and continue to bear Maurice Rose's name. In Rose's hometown of Denver, a delegation led by his family's Jewish neighbors established a hospital named for the general. The medical center and a foundation derived from this effort still operate to this day.[18] All very proper, all very deserved, and yet, it's a bit less than might be expected for this bold frontline general. The suspicious might detect a whiff of anti-Semitism. Given the times, then and now, it cannot be ruled out.

There's a clue to what might have been going on or, rather, *not* going on, if you consider the immediate reactions to Rose's death among his superior officers in Europe. The lack of significant recognition wasn't due to anti-Semitism, as Major General Joe Collins, among many others, had no idea Rose was raised in a Jewish home until well after the Spearhead Division commander's death. Long before Jewish Americans began touting Rose's heritage, it fell to Collins, Hodges, Bradley, and Eisenhower to recognize the 3rd Armored Division commander's courage in his final hours. They simply took no action. The only military award Maurice Rose received for his last fight is one that isn't given, but earned—a Purple Heart to go with the one from World War I. When he died, Rose's bravery had been recognized with the Distinguished Service Cross for Belgium, two Silver Stars for Tunisia, another Silver Star for Sicily, and a Bronze Star with "V" (Valor) Device for the clash at Mons. Yet after September 1944—nothing. It's not as if Rose became any less daring before the West Wall, in the Bulge, at Cologne, or on that lonely road near Castle Hamborn. In many ways, though, he belonged to a bygone tradition, that of the frontline general. In the view of most of America's World War II senior commanders, men like Maurice Rose, Terry Allen, George Patton, Matt Ridgway, and Jim Gavin took far too many personal risks. Million-man armies and modern communications meant wars could (and, many thought, should) be run from a secure office, not from a quarter-ton truck, let alone on foot with a weapon in hand. The desk generals ruled—no need to encourage more of this immoderate old-school behavior. Joe Collins, who spent plenty of time up front, always sensed which way the wind blew. He let it ride.[19] The war ended. And Rose was gone.

Yet Maurice Rose was a lifelong soldier. In the end, the U.S. Army had its say, as it so often does for those who wear its uniform and sleep in its dust. On November 29, 1949, Mrs. Virginia Barringer Rose, the general's designated next of kin, received formal notification that her husband's grave would be marked with a Christian cross, as that was his recorded religious preference. Today he can be found in Plot C, Grave #1, Row #1 in the Netherlands American Cemetery and Memorial in Margraten.[20] He never served a day in that country. And he remains, now and always, a rabbi's son.

APPENDICES

3rd Armored Division Leadership

August 7, 1944, to March 30, 1945

Commanding General: Major General Maurice Rose[1]
Chief of Staff: Colonel John A. Smith, Jr.
G-1 (Personnel):
    Lieutenant Colonel Jack A. Boulger[2]
    Major George G. Otis (March 27, 1945)
G-2 (Intelligence): Lieutenant Colonel Andrew Barr
G-3 (Operations): Lieutenant Colonel Wesley A. Sweat
G-4 (Logistics): Lieutenant Colonel Eugene C. Orth
G-5 (Civil Affairs): Lieutenant Colonel William E. Dahl

Division Artillery: Colonel Frederic J. Brown[3]
54th Armored Field Artillery Battalion
    Lieutenant Colonel Robert G. Moore[4]
    Major John P. Sink (October 23, 1944)
    Lieutenant Colonel Mont Hubbard (December 4, 1944)
67th Armored Field Artillery Battalion: Lieutenant Colonel Edward S. Berry
391st Armored Field Artillery Battalion: Lieutenant Colonel George G. Garton

Division Trains: Colonel Carl J. Rohsenberger
3rd Ordnance (Maintenance) Battalion
    Lieutenant Colonel Joseph L. Cowhey
    Lieutenant Colonel Rager J. McCarthy (August 29, 1944)
Supply Battalion: Major Rodney J. Banta
45th Armored Medical Battalion: Lieutenant Colonel Charles L. Steyaart
Military Police Platoon

Division Troops (working directly for the division; subordinate units often
    assigned to combat commands)
Division Main Command Post (Omaha Forward) & Headquarters Company
Division Rear Command Post (Omaha Rear) & Service Company[5]
143rd Armored Signal Company: Captain John L. Wilson
83rd Armored Reconnaissance Battalion
    Lieutenant Colonel William L. Cabaniss
    Major John R. Tucker, Jr. (August 27, 1944)
    Lieutenant Colonel Prentice E. Yeomans (September 16, 1944)[6]
23rd Armored Engineer Battalion: Lieutenant Colonel Lawrence G. Foster
486th Anti-Aircraft Battalion: Lieutenant Colonel Raymond E. Dunnington[7]
703rd Tank Destroyer Battalion: Lieutenant Colonel Wilbur E. Showalter[8]

Combat Command A (CCA): Brigadier General Doyle O. Hickey
32nd Armored Regiment: Colonel Leander L. Doan[9]
1st Battalion, 32nd Armored Regiment
    Lieutenant Colonel Elwyn W. Blanchard[10]
    Captain Nicholas D. Carpenter (August 14, 1944)[11]
    Captain Foster F. Flegeal (August 17, 1944)[12]
    Major Frank S. Crawford (August 17, 1944)[13]
    Lieutenant Colonel John K. Boles (August 17, 1944)
    Major William G. Yarborough (August 19, 1944)
    Lieutenant Colonel Elwyn W. Blanchard (August 22, 1944)
    Lieutenant Colonel Matthew W. Kane (September 22, 1944)[14]
2nd Battalion, 32nd Armored Regiment
    Major Richard L. Bradley, Jr.[15]
    Major William K. Bailey (September 6, 1944)[16]
    Lieutenant Colonel Sydney T. Telford (September 10, 1944)[17]
    Lieutenant Colonel Clifford L. Miller (September 13, 1944)
3rd Battalion, 32nd Armored Regiment: Lieutenant Colonel Walter B.
    Richardson

Combat Command B (CCB): Brigadier General Truman E. Boudinot[18]
33rd Armored Regiment
    Colonel Dorrence S. Roysdon
    Lieutenant Colonel Littleton A. Roberts (August 31, 1944)
    Colonel John C. Welborn (September 4, 1944)
1st Battalion, 33rd Armored Regiment
    Lieutenant Colonel Rosewell H. King[19]
    Major Herbert M. Mills (August 29, 1944)
    Lieutenant Colonel Rosewell H. King (September 4, 1944)[20]
    Lieutenant Colonel Herbert M. Mills (September 14, 1944)[21]
    Major Kenneth T. McGeorge (November 18, 1944)[22]
    Major William S. Walker (January 8, 1945)
    Lieutenant Colonel Elwyn W. Blanchard (January 24, 1945)[23]
    Major Ralph M. Rogers (March 29, 1945)

2nd Battalion, 33rd Armored Regiment: Lieutenant Colonel William B. Lovelady
3rd Battalion, 33rd Armored Regiment: Lieutenant Colonel Samuel Hogan

Combat Command Reserve (CCR a.k.a. Division Reserve) and 36th Armored Infantry Regiment Colonel William W. Cornog, Jr.[24]
Lieutenant Colonel Jack R. Hutcheson (August 9, 1944)
Colonel Louis P. Leone (August 15, 1944)
Lieutenant Colonel Jack R. Hutcheson (September 2, 1944)
Colonel Carl J. Rohsenberger (acting, September 3, 1944)
Colonel Robert L. Howze, Jr. (September 24, 1944)

1st Battalion, 36th Armored Infantry Regiment
Major Paul W. Corrigan[25]
Major Theodore P. Mason (August 17, 1944)[26]
Captain Louis F. Plummer (September 9, 1944)[27]
Lieutenant Colonel William R. Orr (September 13, 1944)

2nd Battalion, 36th Armored Infantry Regiment
Lieutenant Colonel Vincent E. Cockefair[28]
Lieutenant Colonel Jack R. Hutcheson (August 9, 1944)[29]
Major Thomas G. Tousey, Jr. (August 20, 1944)[30]
Captain G. E. Smith (November 18, 1944)
Lieutenant Colonel Carlton P. Russell (November 19, 1944)
Major Robert E. Chaney (November 24, 1944)
Major R. T. Dunn (December 13, 1944)[31]
Major Thomas G. Tousey, Jr. (December 27, 1944)[32]
Captain G. E. Smith (January 4, 1945)[33]
Captain J. S. Metcalfe (January 5, 1945)
Lieutenant Colonel Thomas J. Moran (January 18, 1945)

3rd Battalion, 36th Armored Infantry Regiment
Major R. T. Dunn[34]
Captain (later Major) Thomas G. Tousey, Jr. (August 8, 1944)
Major R. T. Dunn (August 20, 1944)
Lieutenant Colonel Paul L. Fowler (September 27, 1944)[35]
Major Robert E. Chaney (January 6, 1945)[36]

Sources: Sergeant Frank Woolner, U.S. Army and Major Murray H. Fowler, U.S. Army et al., *Spearhead in the West 1941–1945: The Third Armored Division* (Frankfurt am Main, Germany: Kunst und Werbedruck, 1945), 9–95; U.S. Army Center of Military History, *Order of Battle of the U.S. Army—WWII—ETO—3d* [sic] *Armored Division* (Washington, DC: U.S. Army Center of Military History, March, 2001), at https://history.army.mil/documents/ETO-OB/3AD-ETO.htm, 435-439, accessed June 1, 2019.

3rd Armored Division Task Organization as of August 20, 1944

Command Group: Brigadier General Maurice Rose[1]

Division Main Command Post (Omaha Forward): Colonel John A. Smith, Jr.[2]

Division Trains: Colonel Carl J. Rohsenberger
Division Rear Command Post (Omaha Rear) & Service Company[3]
3rd Ordnance (Maintenance) Battalion (-): Lieutenant Colonel Joseph L.
      Cowhey
Supply Battalion: Major Rodney J. Banta
45th Armored Medical Battalion (-): Lieutenant Colonel Charles L. Steyaart
Military Police Platoon

Division Troops (working directly for the division)
143rd Armored Signal Company: Captain John L. Wilson
83rd Armored Reconnaissance Battalion: Lieutenant Colonel William L.
      Cabaniss

Combat Command A (CCA): Brigadier General Doyle O. Hickey[4]
32nd Armored Regiment: Lieutenant Colonel Leander L. Doan
   (Task Force Doan)
   1st Battalion, 32nd Armored Regiment: Lieutenant Colonel Elwyn W.
      Blanchard[5]
   1st Battalion (-), 36th Armored Infantry Regiment: Major Theodore P.
      Mason
   Company A, 23rd Armored Engineer Battalion (-)
   Company A, 703rd Tank Destroyer Battalion (-)
   Company A, 45th Armored Medical Battalion (-)
3rd Battalion, 32nd Armored Regiment: Lieutenant Colonel Walter B.
      Richardson[6]

(Task Force Richardson)
Company C, 1st Battalion, 36th Armored Infantry Regiment
Platoon, Company A, 23rd Armored Engineer Battalion
Platoon, Company A, 703rd Tank Destroyer Battalion
Platoon, Company A, 45th Armored Medical Battalion

54th Armored Field Artillery Battalion: Lieutenant Colonel Robert G. Moore[7]
67th Armored Field Artillery Battalion: Lieutenant Colonel Edward S. Berry
Battery A, 486th Anti-Aircraft Artillery Battalion
Detachment, 3rd Ordnance (Maintenance) Battalion

Combat Command B (CCB): Colonel Truman E. Boudinot[8]
33rd Armored Regiment: Colonel Dorrence S. Roysdon
    (Task Force Roysdon)
    1st Battalion, 33rd Armored Regiment: Lieutenant Colonel Rosewell H.
        King[9]
    2nd Battalion, 36th Armored Infantry Regiment (-): Major Thomas G.
        Tousey, Jr.
    Company D, 23rd Armored Engineer Battalion (-)
    Company B, 703rd Tank Destroyer Battalion (-)
    Company B, 45th Armored Medical Battalion (-)

2nd Battalion, 33rd Armored Regiment: Lieutenant Colonel William B.
    Lovelady[10]
    (Task Force Lovelady)
    Company D, 2nd Battalion, 36th Armored Infantry Regiment
    Platoon, Company D, 23rd Armored Engineer Battalion
    Platoon, Company B, 703rd Tank Destroyer Battalion
    Platoon, Company B, 45th Armored Medical Battalion

87th Armored Field Artillery Battalion: Lieutenant Colonel George F. Barber[11]
391st Armored Field Artillery Battalion: Lieutenant Colonel George G. Garton
Battery B, 486th Anti-Aircraft Artillery Battalion
Detachment, 3rd Ordnance (Maintenance) Battalion

Combat Command Reserve (CCR a.k.a. Division Reserve)
and 36th Armored Infantry Regiment: Colonel Louis P. Leone

2nd Battalion, 32nd Armored Regiment: Major Richard L. Bradley, Jr.[12]
3rd Battalion, 36th Armored Infantry Regiment: Major R. T. Dunn[13]
3rd Battalion, 33rd Armored Regiment: Lieutenant Colonel Samuel Hogan
23rd Armored Engineer Battalion (-): Lieutenant Colonel Lawrence G. Foster
703rd Tank Destroyer Battalion (-): Lieutenant Colonel Wilbur E. Showalter[14]
Company C, 45th Armored Medical Battalion (-)

183rd Field Artillery Battalion (155mm, towed): Lieutenant Colonel William C. George[15]

991st Armored Field Artillery Battalion (155mm, self-propelled): Lieutenant Colonel Edward S. Brannigan[16]

486th Anti-Aircraft Artillery Battalion (-): Lieutenant Colonel Raymond E. Dunnington[17]

Detachment, 3rd Ordnance (Maintenance) Battalion

Sources: Sergeant Frank Woolner, U.S. Army, and Major Murray H. Fowler, U.S. Army et al., *Spearhead in the West 1941–1945: The Third Armored Division* (Frankfurt am Main, Germany: Kunst und Werbedruck, 1945), 324–327; U.S. Army Center of Military History, *Order of Battle of the U.S. Army—WWII—ETO—3d* [sic] *Armored Division* (Washington, DC: U.S. Army Center of Military History, March 2001), at https://history.army.mil/documents/ETO-OB/3AD-ETO.htm, 435-439, accessed June 1, 2019; U.S. Department of War, Headquarters, 36th Armored Infantry Regiment, *History of the 36th Armored infantry Regiment* (Mühlheim, Germany: Headquarters, 36th Armored Infantry Regiment, July 31, 1945), 30. The war diary lays out the division task organization as of August 20, 1944.

Acknowledgments

Books don't spring out of thin air. This effort reflects the good ideas and patient wisdom of many. Special gratitude goes to my very talented agent, E. J. McCarthy. I must also salute the great publication team at Dutton/Caliber. The great editor Brent Howard, as well as Cassidy Sachs, LeeAnn Pemberton, John Parsley, and all the others deserve my full thanks. Their constructive input and smart suggestions greatly strengthened this work. My colleagues at North Carolina State University have been fully supportive, as always. Courtesy of these fine associates, I have learned a lot.

The primary sources for the 3rd Armored Division and Major General Maurice Rose reside in several archives. Of these, by far the most interesting and unusual is the Andrew Barr Collection of Third Armored Division Records at the University of Illinois at Urbana–Champaign. The 3rd Armored Division Association has lodged many of its holdings in this repository. Lieutenant Colonel Barr served as the G-2 (Intelligence Officer) for the 3rd Armored Division during World War II. His collection of combat logs, battle reports, personal accounts, and photographs is extensive, a real labor of love.

Other military archives are noteworthy. The U.S. Army Combined Arms Research Library at Fort Leavenworth, Kansas, is first-rate and includes many relevant documents from 1941–1945. Also useful is the similar collection held by the U.S. Army Heritage and Education

Center at the U.S. Army War College at Carlisle Barracks, Pennsylvania, which also highlights the recollections of key senior leaders. The U.S. Army Maneuver Center of Excellence Major General William J. Donovan Research Library at Fort Benning, Georgia, offers several unique tactical insights among its eclectic trove of documents. The U.S. National Archives and Records Administration remains an essential collection for any researcher studying the U.S. Army's campaigns in World War II. These fine institutions keep the U.S. Army's records and do so superbly.

Three extant works center on the life of Major General Maurice Rose. The 2003 biography by Steven L. Ossad and Don R. Marsh is a fine study of the man, his heritage, and his lifetime of service. Marsh served with Rose during part of World War II and historian Ossad dug deep in learning more about the general and his family. Also impressive is the 2015 biographical compilation by Marshal Fogel. This volume brings together numerous primary documents, an extensive selection of photographs and clippings, and a strong focus on Rose's background and legacy. Lastly, Dan Bauer's 2004 novel, written in the form of a wartime journal purportedly kept by Rose, draws on many interesting sources. Bauer's work is fiction, but because it's based on the wonderful Barr Collection, it offers interesting perspectives on key events and personalities. I am hopeful my book complements these worthy predecessors.

My ever patient wife, Joy, certainly has heard more about the 3rd Armored Division than most. Daughter Carolyn spent enough time around the army that she could probably tell even experienced military historians a thing or two. Son Philip fought in both Iraq and Afghanistan as an armor officer, so he knows the deal from the front end. Their support makes all things possible.

Wars are fought by real men and women. In chronicling the harrowing experiences of so many great Americans, to include division commander Maurice Rose, I've tried hard to get it right. They sure did. Any shortcomings in the current work are mine alone.

Notes

Prologue: Carentan D+7

1. Rick Atkinson, *The Liberation Trilogy*, 3 vols. (New York, NY: Henry Holt and Company, 2002–2013), vol. 3: *The Guns at Last Light: The War in Western Europe, 1944–1945* (2013), 632.

2. U.S. Department of the Army, Office of the Chief of Military History, *The United States Army in World War II, European Theater of Operations*, 10 vols. (Washington, DC: U.S. Government Printing Office, 1949–1990), vol. 2: Roland G. Ruppenthal, *Logistical Support of the Armies, Volume I: May 1941—September 1944* (1953), 418–421. For the British beaches (Gold, Juno, and Sword), including the Canadians (Juno Beach), Free French, and Poles, see Russell F. Weigley, *Eisenhower's Lieutenants: The Campaign of France and Germany, 1944–1945* (Bloomington: Indiana University Press, 1981), 107. The U.S. naval and air information also comes from Weigley, *Eisenhower's Lieutenants*, 69–70, 72, 105. The British assault forces included the Free French 1er Bataillon de Fusiliers Marins Commandos (1st Battalion, Marine Commando Fusiliers, a traditional name for infantry). By August 1, 1944, the 1st Polish Armoured Division also joined the British Twenty-First Army Group.

3. U.S. Department of War, Headquarters, European Theater of Operations, History Section, *Regimental Study Number 3: 506 Parachute Infantry Regiment in the Normandy Drop* (Versailles, France: Headquarters, European Theater of Operations, August 21, 1945), 35. The authors say of the German prisoners from the 6th Parachute Regiment, one of the better enemy outfits in Normandy: "Many were quite young; some were overage. They did not appear to be first-class troops physically. Though their ammunition supply was plentiful and their equipment was good. The majority were willing to talk." For the German point of view, see U.S. Department of Defense, Headquarters, U.S. Army Europe, Historical Division, *Foreign Military Studies B-839: A German Parachute Regiment in Normandy* (Heidelberg, Federal Republic of Germany, 1954), 8–10. This monograph was written by *Oberstleutnant* (Lieutenant Colonel) Friedrich, *Freiherr* (Baron) von der Heydte, the former regimental commander. He

noted that the new privates assigned averaged seventeen-and-a-half years of age, although he also observed that one-third of the officers and one-fifth of the noncommissioned officers were combat veterans who'd jumped in Crete, campaigned in North Africa, or fought in Russia.

4. The Cold War West German panzer force continued the tradition, naming their main battle tanks Leopards. The Leopard 2A7 is the current model.

5. Karl-Heinz Frieser with John T. Greenwood, *The Blitzkrieg Legend: The 1940 Campaign in the West,* trans. Gerald Lewis Geiger (Annapolis, MD: U.S. Naval Institute Press, 2005), 175–176. The incident involved the French 169th Artillery Regiment and supporting riflemen of the 55th Infantry Division at Bulson, France, on the evening of May 13, 1940. *Oberst* (Colonel) Karl-Heinz Frieser served as an infantry officer in the post-1955 Bundeswehr (Federal German Army). Collaborator John T. Greenwood is a noted U.S. military historian. Translator Gerald Lewis Geiger was a World War II veteran.

6. U.S. Department of War, *Field Manual 7-10: Rifle Company, Rifle Regiment* (Washington, DC: U.S. Government Printing Office, June 2, 1942), 79–80.

7. Gerald Astor, *The Bloody Forest: Battle for the Huertgen, September 1944– January 1945* (Novato, CA: Presidio Press, 2000), 138. Gerald Astor served in the European theater in World War II as an infantryman with the 97th Infantry Division.

8. The quotation is from Richard D. Winters with Cole C. Kingseed, *Beyond Band of Brothers: The World War II Memoirs of Major Dick Winters* (New York: Dutton Caliber, 2006), 108. Coauthor Kingseed is himself a former U.S. Army colonel of infantry and one of the premier historians of World War II. For the famous Company E, see Stephen E. Ambrose, *Band of Brothers: E Company, 506th Regiment, 101st Airborne From Normandy to Hitler's Eagle's Nest* (New York: Simon and Schuster, 1992), 98–101. The acclaimed miniseries is Dreamworks Television and HBO Films, *Band of Brothers* (Universal City, CA: Dreamworks Television, 2001), 10 episodes. Episode 3 is titled "Carentan." The name "Band of Brothers" evokes William Shakespeare's well-known speech in his play *Henry V.*

9. Clay Blair, *Ridgway's Paratroopers: The American Airborne in World War II* (New York: Dial Press, 1985), 327–328.

10. History Section, *Regimental Study Number 3: 506 Parachute Infantry Regiment in the Normandy Drop,* 56.

11. Ibid. 35, 68. Reporting was fragmentary during the Carentan battle, but the 506th Parachute Infantry Regiment estimated 1st Battalion at 225, 2nd Battalion at 300, 3rd Battalion at 175, and regimental and headquarters troops at 100. This put the regiment at well below half strength. Among these were some forty paratroopers from the 82nd Airborne Division who'd jumped off target. For the strength and disposition of all 101st Airborne Division regiments, see U.S. Department of War, Commanding General, 101st Airborne Division, "Operations of the 101st Airborne Division in the Invasion of France" (Newbury, UK: Headquarters, 101st Airborne Division, July 15, 1944), 2, 6–7.

12. Weigley, *Eisenhower's Lieutenants,* 11. For the limits of bazooka training see U.S. Department of the Army, Office of the Chief of Military History, *The United States Army in World War II: The Army Ground Forces,* 2 vols. (Washington, DC: U.S. Government Printing Office, 1947–1948), vol. 2: Robert R. Palmer, Bell I.

Wiley, and William R. Keast, *The Procurement and Training of Ground Combat Troops* (1948), 465, 571.

13. U.S. Department of the Army, Office of the Chief of Military History, *The United States Army in World War II: The Technical Services*, 23 vols. (Washington, DC: U.S. Government Printing Office, 1951–1997), vol. 20: George Raynor Thompson and Dixie R. Harris, *The Signal Corps: The Outcome (Mid-1943 through 1945)* (1966), 638.

14. Weigley, *Eisenhower's Lieutenants*, 28, 104, 106.

15. U.S. Department of War, *Field Manual 7-20: Infantry Battalion* (Washington, DC: U.S. Government Printing Office, October 1, 1944), 203–207.

16. Winters and Kingseed, *Beyond Band of Brothers*, 107.

17. U.S. Department of Defense, *generalmaior* [brigadier general equivalent, one star] Hermann Burkhart Mueller-Hillebrand, *Project #47: German Tank Losses*, trans. M Franks (Stuttgart, Germany: U.S. European Command Historical Division, November 10, 1950), 6. Mueller-Hillebrand served as chief of staff of Third Panzer Army during World War II. The German MG34 and MG 42 machine guns used by infantry and panzer forces fired the 7.92mm bullet, about one-third of an inch wide and an inch long.

18. Ralph Ingersoll, *The Battle is the Payoff* (New York: Harcourt Brace, 1943), 188.

19. George S. Patton, Jr., annotated by Paul D. Harkins, *War As I Knew It* (New York: Pyramid Books, 1970), 300. General George S. Patton, Jr., strongly advocated closing up with preparatory artillery fires in an attack. He'd learned that as a tank brigade commander in World War I. Paul D. Harkins served with Patton in World War II and went on to wear four stars and command the early U.S. effort in Vietnam in 1962–1964.

20. The 17th SS Panzergrenadier Division "Götz von Berlichingen" came from the Waffen SS (*Schutz Staffel*, Guard Force) Nazi Party troops. The SS divisions were named as well as numbered. Götz von Berlichingen (1480–1562) was a bold German mercenary knight known for his iron prosthetic hand, military prowess, and foul language. He supposedly once said of an opponent, "He can kiss my ass." Headquarters, U.S. Army Europe, Historical Division, *Foreign Military Studies B-839: A German Parachute Regiment in Normandy*, 30–31. For more on this attack, see Volker Greisser, *The Lions of Carentan: Fallschirmjäger Regiment 6, 1943–1945*, trans. Maria Taylor (Philadelphia, PA: Casemate Publishers, 2011), 118–119. Volker Greisser served as a Bundeswehr *fallschirmjäger*. His father, Eugen, served as an NCO in the regiment and was a source for the book. For the American assessment, see Commanding General, 101st Airborne Division, "Operations of the 101st Airborne Division in the Invasion of France," 7.

21. Greisser, *The Lions of Carentan*, 120.

22. Historical Division, *Foreign Military Studies B-839: A German Parachute Regiment in Normandy* (Heidelberg, Federal Republic of Germany, 1954), 20–25.

23. Ambrose, *Band of Brothers*, 100; Winters and Kingseed, *Beyond Band of Brothers*, 107.

24. Winters and Kingseed, *Beyond Band of Brothers*, 107; Commanding General, 101st Airborne Division, "Operations of the 101st Airborne Division in the Invasion of France" (July 15, 1944), 7.

25. Don Malarkey with Bob Welch, *Easy Company Soldier: The Legendary Battles of a Sergeant from World War II's "Band of Brothers"* (New York: St. Martin's Press, 2008), 107–108. See also Ambrose, *Band of Brothers*, 100.

26. Ambrose, *Band of Brothers*, 19. During the 506th Parachute Infantry Regiment's training at Camp Toccoa, Georgia, the paratroopers ran up Mount Currahee—Cherokee for "stands alone." The regiment's paratroopers adopted "Currahee" as their motto.

27. The tank-mounted M2HB .50 caliber machine gun fired a bullet a half-inch (12.7mm) wide and an inch and a half (39mm) long. Winters and Kingseed, *Beyond Band of Brothers*, 107–108. See also Larry Alexander, *Biggest Brother: The Life of Major Dick Winters, the Man Who Led the Band of Brothers* (New York: NAL Caliber, 2005), 75; and Malarkey and Welch, *Easy Company Soldier*, 108. For the official 101st Airborne Division view, see Commanding General, 101st Airborne Division, "Operations of the 101st Airborne Division in the Invasion of France" (July 15, 1944), 7. For the official 2nd Armored Division summary, see U.S. Department of War, Commanding General, Combat Command A, 2nd Armored Division, "Operations Report for Period 1–30 June 1944 Inclusive" (La Mine, France: Headquarters, Combat Command A, 2nd Armored Division, June 30, 1944), 3.

28. U.S. Department of the Army, Office of the Chief of Military History, *The United States Army in World War II, European Theater of Operations.* 10 vols. (Washington, DC: U.S. Government Printing Office, 1949–1990), vol. 4: Gordon A. Harrison, *Cross-Channel Attack* (1950), 365. For other times, see U.S. Department of War, Commanding General, Combat Command A, 2nd Armored Division, "Operations Report for Period 1–30 June 1944 Inclusive" (La Mine, France: Headquarters, Combat Command A, 2nd Armored Division, June 30, 1944), 3; as well as Malarkey and Welch, *Easy Company Soldier*, 108; Winters and Kingseed, *Beyond Band of Brothers*, 107; and Ambrose, *Band of Brothers*, 101.

29. Omar N. Bradley and Clay Blair, *A General's Life: An Autobiography* (New York: Simon and Schuster, 1983), 259–260; Ralph Francis Bennett, *Ultra in the West: The Normandy Campaign of 1944–45* (London: Hutchinson, 1979), 71–72. The author worked at Bletchley Park during World War II.

30. Bradley's by-name choice of Brigadier General Maurice Rose for the Carentan mission is found in the general's first autobiography, Omar. N Bradley, *A Soldier's Story* (New York: Henry Holt and Company, 1951), 293. For an eyewitness account of Rose at Carentan, see Steven L. Ossad and Don R. Marsh, *Major General Maurice Rose: World War II's Greatest Forgotten Commander* (Lanham, MD: Taylor Trade Publishing, 2003), 156. Sergeant Don R. Marsh served in the 142nd Armored Signal Company, 2nd Armored Division during World War II and had several personal interactions with General Rose, whom Marsh remembered well. See also Marshall Fogel, *Major General Maurice Rose: The Most Decorated Battletank Commander in U.S. Military History and the Naming of a Hospital in His Honor* (Aurora, CO: Frederic Publishing, 2017), 140–141. Fogel includes numerous primary source documents and photographs in his compilation honoring Rose's life and service.

31. U.S. Department of War, Headquarters 3rd Armored Division, *Spearheading with the 3rd Armored Division: In the Bulge, Duren-Cologne, the Ruhr Pocket,*

East to the Elbe (Halle an der Saale, Germany: Hallische Nachtrichten, 1945), insert "Order of Battle" immediately following page 28.

Chapter 1: Lightning Joe's Lament

1. Patton, *War As I Knew It*, 305.
2. For the phase line map, see Nigel Hamilton, *Monty*, 3 vols. (New York: McGraw-Hill, 1981–1987), vol. 2: *Master of the Battlefield: Monty's War Years, 1942–1944* (1983), 585. Nigel Hamilton's biography remains the standard work on the British field marshal. Hamilton knew Montgomery quite well for some twenty years.
3. Weigley, *Eisenhower's Lieutenants*, 100.
4. Michael D. Doubler, *Busting the Bocage: American Combined Arms Operations in France, 6 June—31 July 1944* (Fort Leavenworth, KS: Combat Studies Institute, November 1988), 32. Michael Doubler served as a U.S. Army armor officer during the Cold War. Doubler cited a study by Lieutenant Colonel Robert R. Ploger, commander of the 121st Engineer Combat Battalion, 29th Infantry Division. Ploger fought in Normandy.
5. For the estimate of 200 artillery shells to kill one German soldier during World War II, see Samuel Lipsman, Edward Doyle et al., *The Vietnam Experience*, 25 vols. (Boston, MA: Boston Publishing Company, 1981–1988), vol. 21, Edward C. Doleman, Jr., and the editors of Boston Publishing Company, *Tools of War* (1984), 48. For German troop strength opposing the U.S. First Army in Normandy by mid-July, 1944, see U.S. Department of the Army, Office of the Chief of Military History, *The United States Army in World War II, European Theater of Operations,* 10 vols. (Washington, DC: U.S. Government Printing Office, 1949–1990), vol. 5, Martin Blumenson, *Breakout and Pursuit* (1961), 30, 32–33. For a good statistical summary of U.S. Army artillery fires in the 1944 Normandy campaign, see Russell A. Hart, *Clash of Arms: How the Allies Won in Normandy* (Norman: University of Oklahoma Press, 2001), 280, 297n55.
6. Bradley's quote about his surprise can be found in Atkinson, *The Guns at Last Light*, 111. For the other comment, see Doubler, *Busting the Bocage*, 21.
7. James M. Gavin, *On to Berlin: Battles of an Airborne Commander, 1943–1946* (New York: Viking Press, 1978), 121.
8. Francis Ford Coppola and Edmund H. North, *Patton Shooting Script* (Century City, CA: Twentieth Century Fox, February 1, 1969), Scene 177 as found at https://thescriptsavant.com/pdf/Patton.pdf, accessed May 24, 2019. In the movie, the two generals were discussing the U.S. advance on Palermo, Sicily. General of the Army Omar N. Bradley, still alive at the time, served as a consultant on the film's production.
9. Martin Blumenson, editor, *The Patton Papers*, 2 vols. (Boston, MA: Houghton Mifflin Company, 1972–1974), vol. 2: *The Patton Papers, 1940–1945* (1974), 486. Patton stated that Bradley's pride in his knowledge of infantry tactics left him (Patton) "nauseated." Acclaimed as the premier scholar on the general, Martin Blumenson served as an officer in Patton's Third Army in 1944–1945.
10. Bradley and Blair, *A General's Life*, 45–46, 49, 54, 59, 60, 63, 74, 76, 94.
11. Carl von Clausewitz, *On War*, edited and translated by Michael Howard and Peter Paret (Princeton, NJ: Princeton University Press, 1976), 102.
12. Both Eisenhower and Bradley graduated in the West Point Class of 1915. Carlo D'Este, *Patton: A Genius for War* (New York: HarperCollins, 1995), 467–468, 479.

Former U.S. Army armor officer Carlo d'Este has established himself as a superb historian of the American and British efforts in the war on Germany.

13. Ibid., 467. D'Este quoted Brigadier General S. L. A. Marshall, who knew Bradley, Patton, Eisenhower, and the rest, and said this of Bradley: "The GIs were not impressed with him. They scarcely knew him. He's not a flamboyant figure and he didn't get out much to troops. And the idea that he was idolized by the average soldier is just rot. He didn't make that much of an imprint."

14. Bradley and Blair, *A General's Life*, 183, 258–259.

15. Patton, *War As I Knew It*, 91.

16. James H. Wellard, *The Man in a Helmet: the Life of General Patton* (London, UK: Eyre & Spottiswoode, 1947), 126. Wellard served as a combat correspondent with the U.S. Third Army in 1944–1945.

17. J. Lawton Collins, *Lightning Joe: An Autobiography* (Baton Rouge: Louisiana State University Press, 1979), 157. Collins's family produced four generals. Along with Joseph, his older brother James became a major general in the U.S. Army. Two of James's sons, James L. Collins, Jr., and Michael Collins, rose to the ranks of brigadier general, U.S. Army, and major general, U.S. Air Force Reserve, respectively. Michael Collins is better known as an astronaut who piloted the command module during the Apollo 11 moon landing in July 1969.

18. Ibid., 347.

19. Atkinson, *The Guns at Last Light*, 119. For Collins's progression to corps command in World War II, and that of his peers, see Robert H. Berlin, *U.S. Army World War II Corps Commanders: A Composite Biography* (Fort Leavenworth, KS: Combat Studies Institute, 1989), 6.

20. Earl F. Ziemke, *Department of the Army Pamphlet No. 20–271, The German Northern Theater of Operations 1940–1944* (Washington, DC: U.S. Government Printing Office, December 15, 1959), 183–184. For more on *Generaloberst* (colonel-general, equivalent to a U.S. four-star general) Eduard W. C. Dietl, see B. H. Liddell Hart, *The Other Side of the Hill: German Generals, Their Rise and Fall, with Their Own Accounts of Military Events 1939–1945* (London, UK: Cassell and Company, 1948), 52. Dietl died in a plane crash on June 23, 1944.

21. Blumenson, *The Patton Papers: 1940–1945*, 478.

22. The sentence, common even in today's U.S. Army, can be found as "It is better to send a bullet than a man" in Andrew F. Krepinevich, Jr., *The Army and Vietnam* (Baltimore, MD: Johns Hopkins University Press, 1986), 6. West Point graduate Krepinevich served as an officer during the Cold War. His study of the U.S. Army in Vietnam is a recognized classic and offers a reliable summary of the service's firepower tradition as proven in World War II and applied in Vietnam. Similar views have been expressed by General George S. Patton, Jr., General Matthew B. Ridgway, and many others. Russell F. Weigley, *The American Way of War: A History of United States Military Strategy and Policy* (Bloomington: Indiana University Press, 1973), 346–347 refers to the American air-land campaign in Europe in 1942–1945 as "The Strategic Tradition of U.S. Grant," pounding away against an outgunned foe with superior numbers of air squadrons and artillery.

23. Eric Bergerud, *Touched by Fire: the Land War in the South Pacific* (New York: Viking Press, 1996), 192–193. Bergerud described the massed, effective

firepower employed on January 10, 1943, in the opening attack of Collins's 25th Infantry Division on Guadalcanal. Six field artillery battalions fired six thousand rounds to complement effective bombing by Army Air Forces and Marine Corps aircraft. In three weeks of combat, the 25th Infantry Division took its terrain objectives, suffered 74 dead, and killed 1,100 dead of the defending Japanese.

24. Dr. Sidney T. Matthews, Dr. Howard M Smyth, Major Roy Lemson, and Major David Hamilton, Office of the Chief of Military History, "Interview with General of the Army George C. Marshall" (Washington, DC: The Pentagon, July 25, 1949). In the interview, Marshall said, "We had to go brutally fast in Europe. We could not indulge in a Seven Years' War. A king can perhaps do that, but you cannot have such a protracted struggle in a democracy in the face of mounting casualties."

25. Comparative Allied and German military numbers and a discussion of the overall U.S. policy come from Russell F. Weigley, *History of the United States Army: Enlarged Edition* (Bloomington: Indiana University Press, 1984), 438–439. For the U.S. Army's World War II manning concept, see Maurice Matloff, "The 90-Division Gamble," in Kent Roberts Greenfield, editor, *Command Decisions* (Washington, DC: U.S. Government Printing Office, 1960), 366–368. For the 40 percent tail supporting U.S. ground troops, see Victor Davis Hanson, *The Second World Wars: How the First Global Conflict Was Fought and Won* (New York: Basic Books, 2017), 215. The massive scale of the German-Soviet campaign of 1941–1945 is discussed in Hanson, *The Second World Wars*, 256–266.

26. Carlo D'Este, *Decision in Normandy* (New York: Harper Perennial, 1983), 252–259. D'Este offers a convincing explanation of how British manpower constraints limited options in Normandy in 1944.

27. Doubler, *Busting the Bocage*, 27. For Patton's comments, see Blumenson, editor, *The Patton Papers: 1940–1945*, 521.

28. Paul F. Gorman, *The Secret of Future Victories* (Fort Leavenworth, KS: Combat Studies Institute, 1992), II–78. General Paul F. Gorman fought in Vietnam and helped General William E. DePuy reform U.S. Army training in the 1970s. DePuy started in Normandy as a battalion S-3 (operations officer) and later commanded a battalion in the 90th Infantry Division. DePuy later commanded the 1st Infantry Division in Vietnam.

29. Weigley, *Eisenhower's Lieutenants*, 13. The quotation is from Lieutenant General Lesley J. McNair, the senior officer who organized and trained the army ground forces for World War II. For the unvarnished recollections of a U.S. Army infantry replacement in the 1944–1945 campaign in Europe, see Astor, *The Bloody Forest*, ix–x. Gerald Astor eventually ended up in the 97th Infantry Division.

30. Doubler, *Busting the Bocage*, 23.

31. Bradley is quoted in Weigley, *Eisenhower's Lieutenants*, 100.

32. Doubler, *Busting the Bocage*, 8.

33. Atkinson, *The Guns at Last Light*, 111–113.

34. Doubler, *Busting the Bocage*, 23–29. See also John Ellis, *The Sharp End: The Fighting Man in World War II* (New York: Charles Scribner's Sons, 1980), 60–65, 118–119.

35. Collins, *Lightning Joe*, 205–210.
36. Ibid., 206. See also Bradley and Blair, *A General's Life*, 262.
37. The quote from a First Army staff officer is found in Weigley, *Eisenhower's Lieutenants*, 98.
38. Collins, *Lightning Joe*, 210–225. For U.S. Army airborne forces casualties in Normandy, see Blair, *Ridgway's Paratroopers*, 348–349. The 82nd Airborne Division lost 5,245 men in thirty-three days of combat. For its part, the 101st Airborne Division lost 4,670 soldiers. Airborne operations came at a high price, especially when the lightly armed paratroopers and glider men remained in action as line infantry.
39. Weigley, *Eisenhower's Lieutenants*, 100.
40. Doubler, *Busting the Bocage*, 26–27, 48. The M1919 .30 caliber machine gun was the "little brother" of the M2HB .50 caliber heavy machine gun. The M1919 fired a .30 caliber bullet .30 inches wide and .85 inches long, or 7.8mm by 21.7mm. The M1918 Browning Automatic Rifle and Garand M1 rifle used this same cartridge.
41. Doubler, *Busting the Bocage*, 25, 37–38, and Weigley, *Eisenhower's Lieutenants*, 100.
42. Romie L. Brownlee and William J. Mullen, III, *Changing An Army: An Oral History of General William E. DePuy, USA, Retired* (Washington, DC: U.S. Government Printing Office, 1988), 82. Both interviewers were active duty U.S. Army infantry officers and Vietnam veterans.
43. Atkinson, *The Guns at Last Light*, 111–112, 128, offer several good descriptions of tanks in bocage fighting.
44. Doubler, *Busting the Bocage*, 31–32.
45. Ibid., 27–28, 36.
46. Collins, *Lightning Joe*, 229–230. See also Doubler, *Busting the Bocage*, 47–50 for a good description of the 83rd Infantry Division's preparatory training and problematic opening attack.
47. Bradley and Blair, *A General's Life*, 262. For an excellent discussion of the difficult command situation in the 90th Infantry Division in Normandy in the summer of 1944, see Thomas E. Ricks, *The Generals: American Military Command from World War II to Today* (New York: Penguin Press, 2012), 1–7.
48. Greisser, *The Lions of Carentan*, 120. The German 6th Airborne Regiment noted that after the battle of June 13, 1944, it took the Americans twenty-four days to move the twelve miles southwest of Carentan.
49. Hart, *The Clash of Arms*, 249–253.
50. Gorman, *The Secret of Future Victories*, II–43.
51. Quesada's account of the meeting is found in Samuel J. Lewis, "Interview With Lieutenant General Elwood R. 'Pete' Ouesada, USAF (ret.)" (Fort Leavenworth, KS: Combat Studies Institute, April 28, 1986).
52. Collins, *Lightning Joe*, 235–238. For the artillery numbers, see Blumenson, *Breakout and Pursuit*, 220. For the fire support plan, see James J. Carafano, *After D-Day: Operation Cobra and the Normandy Breakout* (Mechanicsburg, PA: Stackpole Books, 2008), 101, 107–108. A West Point graduate and Cold War field artillery officer, Carafano carefully explains the use of firepower in Operation Cobra.

53. Collins's thoughts on a reserve is found in Weigley, *Eisenhower's Lieutenants*, 150.

54. U.S. Department of War, Headquarters, VII Corps, "History of the VII Corps for the Period 1–31 July, 1944 Incl. Report After Action Against the Enemy [sic]" (St. Martin de Cennily, France: Headquarters, VII Corps, August 9, 1944), 22–25.

55. Collins, *Lightning Joe*, 233–237. For the American equivalent of German *panzergrenadier* divisions, see Hanson, *The Second World Wars*, 202, 221. See also Peter R. Mansoor, *The GI Offensive in Europe: The Triumph of American Infantry Divisions, 1941–1945* (Lawrence: University Press of Kansas,1999), 5, 37–39. West Point graduate Mansoor commanded an armor brigade combat team in Iraq in 2003–2004.

56. William C. Sylvan and Francis G. Smith, Jr., *Normandy to Victory: The War Diary of General Courtney H. Hodges and the First U.S. Army*, John T. Greenwood, ed. (Lexington: The University Press of Kentucky, 2008), 50–51.

57. Doubler, *Busting the Bocage*, 34–35, 56.

58. For more on Major General Watson's service in command, see Sergeant Frank Woolner, U.S. Army, *Division HQ: Third Armored Division Forward Echelon and Division Headquarters Company, April 15, 1941–May 8, 1945* (Frankfurt am Main, Germany: Kunst und Werbedruck, 1945), 2–6. Similar in format to a high school yearbook, this work chronicles the people and activities of the 3rd Armored Division headquarters.

59. Sergeant Frank Woolner, U.S. Army and Major Murray H. Fowler, U.S. Army et al., *Spearhead in the West 1941–1945: The Third Armored Division* (Frankfurt am Main, Germany: Kunst und Werbedruck, 1945), 327–330. This book includes extracts from division after-action reports on key engagements. See also Weigley, *Eisenhower's Lieutenants*, 130.

60. Woolner and Fowler, *Spearhead in the West 1941–1945*, 331–332. Major General Leland Hobbs of the 30th Infantry Division forced the relief.

61. Haynes W. Dugan, "The St. Lo [sic] Breakthrough" in *The Third Armored Division Saga in World War II* at http://www.3ad.com/history/wwll/dugan.pages/saga.pages/3france.htm#anchor498688 accessed May 23, 2019. Major Haynes W. Dugan served as assistant G-2 (Intelligence) and public relations officer for the 3rd Armored Division in 1944–1945. He completed his service as a lieutenant colonel. Dugan described Major General Leroy H. Watson as a "thoroughly nice man." For the comment on nice guys, see Leo Durocher with Ed Linn, *Nice Guys Finish Last* (New York: Simon & Schuster, 1975), 14.

62. Collins, *Lightning Joe*, 237.

63. Blumenson, *Breakout and Pursuit*, 178.

64. Collins, *Lightning Joe*, 238–239.

65. Headquarters, VII Corps, "History of the VII Corps for the Period 1–31 July, 1944," 27–28. For the German reaction and losses, see Blumenson, *Breakout and Pursuit*, 238.

66. Blumenson, *Breakout and Pursuit*, 234–235 describes the air attack. For Ernie Pyle's comment, see Atkinson, *The Guns at Last Light*, 143.

67. The summary of the casualties, to include the official assessment, can be found in Blumenson, *Breakout and Pursuit*, 236–237. For Bradley's reaction, see Bradley and Blair, *A General's Life*, 280.

68. Collins, *Lightning Joe*, 241; *Breakout and Pursuit*, 240.

69. Collins, *Lightning Joe*, 242; *Breakout and Pursuit*, 252.

70. Collins, *Lightning Joe*, 244. For the quote from a German prisoner of war taken in Normandy, see Doubler, *Busting the Bocage*, 26. See pages 55–58 for the training of the 22nd Infantry Regiment to mount and dismount M4 Sherman tanks.

71. Headquarters, VII Corps, "History of the VII Corps for the Period 1–31 July, 1944," 30–31. For his quote, see Collins, *Lightning Joe*, 242.

72. For Rose's advance, see Weigley, *Eisenhower's Lieutenants*, 156. The quotation comes from Ossad and Marsh, *Major General Maurice Rose: World War II's Greatest Forgotten Commander*, 181.

73. Blumenson, *The Patton Papers: 1940–1945*, 493. Patton wrote these words in a letter to his wife Beatrice dated July 31, 1944.

74. Headquarters, VII Corps, "History of the VII Corps for the Period 1–31 July, 1944," 34–39.

75. Collins, *Lightning Joe*, 245–246.

76. Ibid. See also Bradley and Blair, *A General's Life*, 281. To his credit, although reduced to colonel, Leroy H. Watson remained in theater. He became the deputy commander of the 29th Infantry Division at the end of August 1944, regained his general's rank in December, and served as a one-star through the rest of the war. He regained his major general rank before retiring from the U.S. Army in 1953.

77. Martin Blumenson, "Foreword" in Ossad and March, *Major General Maurice Rose: World War II's Greatest Forgotten Commander*, xi. After joining the armored force, Rose first commanded the 3rd Battalion, 13th Armored Regiment, 1st Armored Division. He was serving as executive officer (second in command) of the 1st Armored Brigade, 1st Armored Division at Fort Knox, Kentucky, when Patton chose him to be the chief of staff of the 2nd Armored Division at Fort Benning, Georgia.

78. Ernest N. Harmon with Milton MacKaye and William Ross MacKaye, *Combat Commander: Autobiography of a Soldier* (Englewood Cliffs, NJ: Prentice-Hall, 1970), 64, 122. For Bradley's comment, see Bradley, *A Soldier's Story*, 97.

79. Fogel, *Major General Maurice Rose: The Most Decorated Battletank Commander*, 71.

80. Mansoor, *The GI Offensive in Europe*, 63. Mansoor explains how this two-brigadier system worked in the 29th Infantry Division, a good example.

81. Yves J. Bellanger, *U.S. Army Armored Division 1943–1945: Organization, Doctrine, Equipment* (London, UK: Lightning Source, 2010), 1–4. Over the last century or so, the U.S. Army's two brigadiers per division have had different roles and titles. In the American phase of World War I (1917–1918), each brigadier commanded an infantry brigade of two regiments. The American part of World War II (1941–1945) saw airborne and infantry divisions employ the first one-star general as the assistant division commander (ADC) and the second as the artillery commander; armored divisions placed their brigadiers in command of CCA and CCB. This held true in the Korean War (1950–1953), too. By the Vietnam War (1965–1975), the brigadiers received the rather mundane

titles ADC-A and ADC-B. Post-Vietnam, these became the ADC-M (Maneuver), called the ADC-O (Operations) in light infantry formations, and the ADC-S (Support). In the Global War on Terrorism (2001–present), the positions were renamed deputy commanding general (DCG, Maneuver or Operations) and DCG (Support). The one consistent aspect has been two one-stars per division.

82. U.S. Department of War, Headquarters, 2nd Armored Division, "Historical Record—Operations of U.S. Second Armored Division (Kool Force)" (Palermo, Sicily: Headquarters, 2nd Armored Division, August 5, 1943), 6–8.

83. Harmon, MacKaye, and MacKaye, *Combat Commander*, 64.

84. For the definitive account of Marshall's selection of his key subordinates, Stephen R. Taaffe, *Marshall and His Generals: U.S. Army Commanders in World War II* (Lawrence: University Press of Kansas, 2011), especially 5–9. Taaffe includes Maurice Rose only for his wartime command of the 3rd Armored Division. Unlike so many others, Rose was not a prewar "Marshall man."

85. Woolner and Fowler, *Spearhead in the West*, 9. For Rose's high school transcript, see Fogel, *Major General Maurice Rose: The Most Decorated Battletank Commander*, 331–332. Maurice Rose only attended one high school. On his transcript, no marks are present past tenth grade. That could be as far as Rose went at Denver High School East Side, or it may reflect a more casual view of recordkeeping in 1912–1916. The transcript correctly lists Rose's birth state (Connecticut), home address, father's full name, and father's occupation, but records the student's first name as "Morris."

86. Fogel, *Major General Maurice Rose: The Most Decorated Battletank Commander*, 336–339. Future General of the Army Dwight D. Eisenhower also attended the Army Industrial College. Indicative of his identified potential for senior leadership, Ike had already graduated from the far more highly regarded U.S. Army War College a few years earlier. By 1946, the Army Industrial College became the Industrial College of the Armed Forces, and since 2012 the Dwight D. Eisenhower School for National Security and Resource Strategy.

87. Ibid., 337–338. Maurice and Venice Rose had one child, Maurice "Mike" Rose, who served thirty-one years in the U.S. Marine Corps, completing his service as a colonel.

88. "Rabbi S. Rose, 90, Father of Slain General, Is Dead," *Denver Post*, July 11, 1945, page 1. See also Ossad and Marsh, *Major General Maurice Rose: World War II's Greatest Forgotten Commander*, 38–40, 42, 46. In German, *rauss* means "out." At the time Samuel Rose emigrated from Poland in 1883, the region was the Duchy of Warsaw controlled by the Russian Empire.

89. Ibid., 74–75. Maurice and Virginia Rose's son Maurice Roderick "Reece" Rose became a senior law enforcement officer. The middle name Roderick honored Roderick R. Allen, one of then Lieutenant Colonel Maurice Rose's 1st Armored Division peers. Allen commanded the 12th Armored Division in 1944–1945 during the campaigns in France and Germany.

Chapter 2: Slaughter Pen

1. The transcript of Field Marshal G. A. F. von Kluge's telephone conversation with his chief of staff *general der infanterie* (equivalent to a U.S. lieutenant general, three stars) Günther Blumentritt on July 31, 1944, is quoted at length in Blumenson, *Breakout and Pursuit*, 323. In Blumenson's text, the cited transcript reads thusly: "It's a madhouse here . . . You can't imagine what it's like. Commanders are completely out of contact. [Colonel General Alfred J. F.] Jodl [chief of operations, German Armed Forces High Command] and [General of Artillery Walter] Warlimont [deputy chief of operations, German Armed Forces High Command] ought to come down and see what is taking place. [The whole mess had started] with [SS *Oberst-gruppenführer*, colonel group leader, equivalent to a U.S. lieutenant general, three stars] [Paul] Hausser's [commander, Seventh Army] fatal decision to break out to the southeast. So far, it appears that only the spearheads of various [American] mobile units are through to Avranches. But it is perfectly clear that everything else will follow. Unless I can get infantry and antitank weapons there, the [western] wing cannot hold. All you can do is laugh out loud. Don't they read our dispatches? Haven't they been oriented? They must be living on the moon."

2. The German reliance on immediate counterattack to restore the defense went back to World War I practice. See Timothy T. Lupfer, *Leavenworth Papers No 4, The Dynamics of Doctrine: The Changes in German Tactical Doctrine During the First World War* (Fort Leavenworth, KS: Combat Studies Institute, July 1981), 15–16, 19. West Point graduate Lupfer served in the U.S. Army as an armor officer during the Cold War.

3. For the deterioration over time of the Panzer Lehr Division, see Headquarters, VII Corps, "History of the VII Corps for the Period 1–31 July, 1944," 4, 18, 27.

4. D'Este, *Patton: A Genius for War*, 624, 640.

5. The Gestapo (*Geheime Staatspolizei*, Secret State Police) enforced Nazi Party directives. For a very readable assessment of Adolf Hitler's military service, see John Keegan, *The Mask of Command* (New York: Viking, 1987), 237–243. With regard to the military tensions between Hitler and his generals by the summer of 1944, see Matthew Cooper, *The German Army, 1933–1945: Its Political and Military Failure* (New York: Stein and Day, 1978), 507–510, 533–534. For the quoted examples of Adolf Hitler's anti-Semitic rhetoric, see Nigel Hamilton, *FDR at War*, 3 vols. (New York: Houghton Mifflin Harcourt, 2014–2019), vol. 3: *War and Peace: FDR's Final Odyssey, D-Day to Yalta, 1943–1945* (2019), 38.

6. Blumenson, *Breakout and Pursuit*, 457.

7. U.S. Department of War, Headquarters, 2nd Armored Division, "Extracts from Operational History, Second Armored Division, Phase I, Operation 'Cobra,' 26 July–31 July, 1944" (Hasselt, Belgium: Headquarters, 2nd Armored Division, September 12, 1944) II–4, III–3. Bradley's comments are from Bradley and Blair, *A General's Life*, 286–287.

8. U.S. Department of the Army, U.S. Army Center of Military History, *Order of Battle of the U.S. Army—WWII—ETO—3d* [sic] *Armored Division* (Washington, DC: U.S. Army Center of Military History, March 5, 2001), at https://history .army.mil/documents/ETO-OB/3AD-ETO.htm, 447, accessed May 28, 2019. This site lists the 3rd Armored Division's command post locations by day throughout 1944–1945.

9. Ossad and Marsh, *Major General Maurice Rose: World War II's Greatest Forgotten Military Commander*, 195–196.

10. Woolner and Fowler, *Spearhead in the West*, 333–336.

11. Collins, *Lightning Joe*, 247.

12. Ibid.

13. Harmon, MacKaye, and MacKaye, *Combat Commander*, 208.

14. U.S. Army Center of Military History, *Order of Battle of the U.S. Army—WWII—ETO—3d* [sic] *Armored Division* (Washington, DC: U.S. Army Center of Military History, March 5, 2001), at https://history.army.mil/documents/ETO-OB/3AD-ETO.htm, 447, accessed May 28, 2019. For the comments on the 3rd Armored Division commander's influence on command post personnel attitudes, see Woolner, *Division HQ: Third Armored Division Forward Echelon and Division Headquarters Company, April 15, 1941–May 8, 1945*, 1.

15. To find a good description of Rose's small command group, see Ossad and Marsh, *Major General Maurice Rose: World War II's Greatest Forgotten Military Commander*, 8, 24. The official organizational, manning, and equipping details can be found in Bellanger, *U.S. Army Armored Division 1943–1945: Organization, Doctrine, Equipment*, 12–13, 43–57, 473–481. With regard to Colonel Frederic J. Brown, Jr., see "Frederic Brown, Retired General," *New York Times*, March 17, 1971, 48.

16. The assigned organization, manning, and equipment, to include security forces, can be found in Bellanger, *U.S. Army Armored Division 1943–1945: Organization, Doctrine, Equipment*, 12–13, 43–50. Harmon's thinking on command group composition can be found in Harmon, MacKaye, and MacKaye, *Combat Commander*, 210–211.

17. Woolner and Fowler, *Spearhead in the West*, 16–17.

18. U.S. Department of the Army, Office of the Chief of Military History, *The United States Army in World War II, The Army Ground Forces*, 2 vols. (Washington, DC: U.S. Government Printing Office, 1947–1948), vol. 1: Kent Roberts Greenfield, Robert R. Palmer, and Bell I. Wiley, *The Organization of Ground Combat Troops* (1947), 318–335.

19. Ibid., 320–321. See also Steven J. Zaloga, *U.S. Army Armored Divisions: The European Theater of Operations, 1944–1945* (Oxford, UK: Osprey Publishing Company, 2004), 12–14.

20. Ibid., 327–328 quotes the August 1943 correspondence between Lieutenant General Lesley J. McNair of army ground forces in the United States and Lieutenant General George S. Patton, Jr., then commanding the Seventh Army in Sicily. For Harmon's thoughts, See Harmon, MacKaye, and MacKaye, *Combat Commander*, 202. Just after Harmon's departure from the theater in July, 1944, the 1st Armored Division in Italy converted to the new, lighter structure during a lull in operations. Harmon later arrived in France and resumed command of the 2nd Armored Division, his original assignment in 1942–1943.

21. Woolner and Fowler, *Spearhead in the West*, 11–12, 32–33. Combat Command A typically formed subordinate task forces (TFs) mixing tank and armored infantry units. Early in the war, CCA designated these X, Y, and, when used, Z. Later on, TFs routinely took the names of their commanders. While there was some attempt to speak of CC Hickey or CC Boudinot, that never really caught on. For an example of this rare usage, see Collins, *Lightning Joe*, 253.

22. Ibid., 13–14, 38–39. Early in the war, CCB designated its subordinate task forces 1, 2, and, when used, 3. As with CCA, as the war went on, TFs used the names of their commanders.

23. Ibid., 54–59.

24. Ibid., 90–95. See also Headquarters 3rd Armored Division, *Spearheading with the 3rd Armored Division*, insert "Order of Battle" immediately following page 28. For the death of Colonel Taylor, see Dugan, "Mortain Counterattack" in *The Third Armored Division Saga in World War II*, http://www.3ad.com/history/wwll /dugan.pages/saga.pages/3france.htm#anchor499008, accessed May 30, 2019.

25. Blumenson, *Breakout and Pursuit*, 461–462 offers an excellent description of the German scheme of maneuver.

26. Bennett, *Ultra in the West*, 119; Bradley and Blair, *A General's Life*, 291; Blumenson, *The Patton Papers: 1940–1945*, 503.

27. Blumenson, *Breakout and Pursuit*, 463. Generalleutenant (lieutenant general, equivalent to a two-star in the U.S. Army) Gerhard Graf von Schwerin commanded the 116th Panzer Division at Mortain. The Gestapo interrogated him and cleared him. He continued to serve throughout the war and died of natural causes in 1980.

28. D'Este, *Decision in Normandy*, 419. The quoted text comes from U.S. Department of War, Headquarters 3rd Armored Division, *Call Me Spearhead: Saga of the Third Armored "Spearhead" Division* (Versailles, France: European Theater of Operations Information and Education Division, 1945), 11. For the daily casualty names and numbers for 3rd Armored Division units, see 3rd Armored Division History Foundation, *3rd Armored Division Soldiers Who Gave Their Lives in World War II* at https://www.3ad.com/history/wwll/names.died.htm, accessed May 31, 2019.

29. Some sources refer to the key position as Hill 314. Weigley, *Eisenhower's Lieutenants*, 200; Blumenson, *Breakout and Pursuit*, 462, 474–475. The 120th Infantry regiment traced its heritage to the American Civil War 1st and 11th North Carolina regiments. Those regiments fought at Gettysburg in 1863 and most other major Civil War battles fought east of the Appalachian Mountains.

30. For CCA losses in the Mortain operation, see 3rd Armored Division History Foundation, *3rd Armored Division Soldiers Who Gave Their Lives in World War II* at https://www.3ad.com/history/wwll/names.died.htm, accessed May 31, 2019.

31. Woolner and Fowler, *Spearheading in the West*, 158.

32. William W. May, "The Death of a Colonel: An Eye-Witness Account," http:// www.3ad.com/history/wwll/memoirs.pages/may.htm, accessed May 31, 2019. May was a lieutenant in the 2nd Battalion, 36th Armored Infantry Regiment. See also U.S. Department of War, Headquarters, 36th Armored Infantry Regiment, *History of the 36th Armored Infantry Regiment* (Mühlheim, Germany: Headquarters, 36th Armored Infantry Regiment, July 31, 1945), 26. This document includes the entries for the regiment's daily war diary.

33. Blumenson, *Breakout and Pursuit*, 464. For estimated German losses, see Weigley, *Eisenhower's Lieutenants*, 200. In German, *kluge* means "clever."

34. Bradley and Blair, *A General's Life*, 296. Bradley spoke these words to visiting U.S. secretary of the treasury Henry Morgenthau.

35. For the destruction of Army Group Center in Belorussia in 1944, see Cooper, *The German Army, 1933–1945*, 474–475. German losses totaled 300,000 soldiers.

36. Hamilton, *Master of the Battlefield: Monty's War Years, 1942–1944*, 571–573, 785–786.

37. Weigley, *Eisenhower's Lieutenants*, 171.

38. Sylvan and Smith, *From Normandy to Victory*, 1–3 offers a fine short biographical sketch of Courtney H. Hodges. Sylvan and Smith's daily diary remains a wonderful source regarding the thoughts and actions of Hodges and his First Army Headquarters in 1944–1945.

39. Bradley, *A Soldier's Story*, 226; Blumenson, *The Patton Papers: 1940–1945*, 517.

40. Harmon, MacKaye, and MacKaye, *Combat Commander*, 208. Speaking of Hodges, Harmon stated, "I had the strong impression that he did little without the advice and support of Lieutenant General J. Lawton Collins."

41. Collins, *Lightning Joe*, 256.

42. Some might argue that the surrender of 238,243 Germans and Italians in Tunisia on May 13, 1943, constituted such an event. That one, though, reflected more on the achievement of Allied air and sea domination of the Mediterranean Sea rather than particularly shrewd maneuvering. The Germans and Italians were stuck in Tunisia and unable to withdraw as they couldn't cross the Allied-controlled Mediterranean. For more on this aspect, see Rick Atkinson, *The Liberation Trilogy*, 3 vols. (New York: Henry Holt and Company, 2002–2013), vol. 3: *An Army at Dawn: The War in North Africa, 1942–1943* (2002), 526–527; 537.

43. Captain Maurice Rose, U.S. Army, "Panama's Irregular Cavalry," *The Cavalry Journal* (July–August 1935): 26–27. This was the only professional article written by Rose before World War II.

44. For details of 3rd Armored Division Field Order No. 6, dated August 12, 1944, see Headquarters, 36th Armored Infantry Regiment, *History of the 36th Armored Infantry Regiment*, 27.

45. For this idea, see Major General Maurice Rose, U.S. Army, "An Operation of the Third Armored ('Spearhead') Division, *Military Review* (June 1945): 3. This article was likely cowritten, and perhaps ghost-written, by Lieutenant Colonel Wesley A. Sweat, the division G-3 (operations) officer. Then and now, *Military Review* is the official publication of the U.S. Army Command and General Staff College School (then the Command and General Staff School).

46. Woolner and Fowler, *Spearhead in the West*, 341–343.

47. For the guidance from Brigadier General Rose and the 6:00 a.m. start on August 13, 1944, see U.S. Department of War, Headquarters, 83rd Armored Reconnaissance Battalion, "Report of Action Against Enemy August 1944" (Namur, Belgium: Headquarters, 83rd Armored Reconnaissance Battalion, September 5, 1944), 2. For the specified 5:30 a.m. time of attack, see Woolner and Fowler, *Spearhead in the West*, 341–342.

48. The quoted phrase comes from Headquarters, 83rd Armored Reconnaissance Battalion, "Report of Action Against Enemy August 1944," 2.

49. Woolner and Fowler, *Spearhead in the West*, 155–163.

50. Ibid., 341–343. See also Headquarters, 36th Armored Infantry Regiment, *History of the 36th Armored Infantry Regiment*, 27. The German 728th Infantry Regiment was part of the 708th Infantry Division.

51. U.S. Department of War, Headquarters, 67th Armored Field Artillery Battalion, "Reports After Action Against Enemy, August 1944" (Charleroi, Belgium: Headquarters, 67th Armored Field Artillery Battalion, September 4, 1944), 10. The 67th Armored Field Artillery Battalion fired in support of both TF Richardson and TF Doan on August 13, 1944.

52. A. Eaton Roberts, *Five Stars to Victory: The Exploits of Task Force Lovelady, 2nd Bn. (Reinf.), 33rd Arm'd., 3rd Arm'd. Division U.S. Army in the War Against Germany 1944–1945* (Birmingham, AL: Atlas Printing and Engraving Co., 1949), 31–32. The author, Captain A. Eaton Roberts, served as the battalion surgeon in 1944–1945. For the official reports on each day's action, see U.S. Department of War, Headquarters, 2nd Battalion, 33rd Armored Regiment, "Log Book of Second Battalion" (Tilleda, Germany: Headquarters, 2nd Battalion, 33rd Armored Regiment, April 24, 1945), 6.

53. Woolner, *Division HQ: Third Armored Division Forward Echelon and Division Headquarters Company, April 15, 1941–May 8, 1945,* 6.

54. For a good sense of the ubiquity of modern U.S. Army communications, see Mary Blake French, editor, "Command Control, Communications, Computers and Intelligence (C4I) Systems and Capability Set 13" in *Army* (October 2012): 333–342. This article can be viewed at https://www.ausa.org/sites/default/files/weapons3_1012.pdf, accessed June 3, 2019.

55. Zaloga, *U.S. Army Armored Divisions: The European Theater of Operations, 1944–1945,* 46–48.

56. Patton, *War As I Knew It,* 303, 305, 307, 343, 352. While Patton relied on radios, as did all good World War II commanders, he well understood the limits of radio reports.

57. William Tecumseh Sherman, *Memoirs of General William T. Sherman* (Boston, MA: Da Capo Press, Inc., 1984), 408.

58. Roberts, *Five Stars to Victory,* 31–32.

59. Collins, *Lightning Joe,* 256; Sylvan and Smith, *Normandy to Victory,* 94–95; Headquarters, 36th Armored Infantry Regiment, *History of the 36th Armored Infantry Regiment,* 27.

60. Woolner and Fowler, *Spearhead in the West,* 341–344.

61. Headquarters, 36th Armored Infantry Regiment, *History of the 36th Armored Infantry Regiment,* 27–28; Headquarters, 2nd Battalion, 33rd Armored Regiment, "Log Book of Second Battalion," 7.

62. Weigley, *Eisenhower's Lieutenants,* 206–208. For the movements of Omaha Forward, see U.S. Army Center of Military History, *Order of Battle of the U.S. Army—WWII—ETO—3d* [sic] *Armored Division* (Washington, DC: U.S. Army Center of Military History, March 5, 2001), at https://history.army.mil/documents/ETO-OB/3AD-ETO.htm, 447.

63. Woolner and Fowler, *Spearhead in the West,* 341–344.

64. Headquarters, 36th Armored Infantry Regiment, *History of the 36th Armored Infantry Regiment,* 28.

65. Headquarters 3rd Armored Division, *Call Me Spearhead: Saga of the Third Armored "Spearhead" Division,* 16; Woolner and Fowler, *Spearhead in the West,* 78–80. For a good short discussion of American versus German tank reliability, see Zaloga, *U.S. Army Armored Divisions: The European Theater of Operations, 1944–1945,* 33.

66. Headquarters, 36th Armored Infantry Regiment, *History of the 36th Armored Infantry Regiment*, 28; Woolner and Fowler, *Spearhead in the West*, 343–344.

67. Headquarters, 2nd Battalion, 33rd Armored Regiment, "Log Book of Second Battalion," 7.

68. 3rd Armored Division History Foundation, *3rd Armored Division Soldiers Who Gave Their Lives in World War II* at https://www.3ad.com/history/wwll/names .died.htm, accessed June 3, 2019.

69. Sylvan and Smith, *Normandy to Victory*, 97.

70. For the quote on the French and the actions of TF Hogan, see Woolner and Fowler, *Spearhead in the West*, 155, 344–346. See also Headquarters, 83rd Armored Reconnaissance Battalion, "Report of Action Against Enemy August 1944," 2, and Dugan, "Closing the Falaise Gap," *The Third Armored Division Saga in World War II*, http://www.3ad.com/history/wwll/dugan.pages/saga .pages/3france.htm#anchor499895, accessed June 5, 2019.

71. For the actions of the 1st Battalion, 32nd Armored, see Woolner and Fowler, *Spearhead in the West*, 44–48. See also Headquarters, 36th Armored Infantry Regiment, *History of the 36th Armored Infantry Regiment*, 28.

72. Headquarters, 2nd Battalion, 33rd Armored Regiment, "Log Book of Second Battalion," 7.

73. Roberts, *Five Stars to Victory*, 32. For the view from First Army, see Sylvan and Smith, *Normandy to Victory*, 100. Major General Pete Quesada, U.S. Army Air Forces, offered the "good hunting" quote.

74. For Sergeant Donald Ekdahl's quote, see Woolner and Fowler, *Spearhead in the West*, 96–97. For the day's operations by TF Lovelady, see Headquarters, 2nd Battalion, 33rd Armored Regiment, "Log Book of Second Battalion," 7, and Roberts, *Five Stars to Victory*, 36.

75. 3rd Armored Division History Foundation, *3rd Armored Division Soldiers Who Gave Their Lives in World War II* at https://www.3ad.com/history/wwll/names .died.htm, accessed June 4, 2019.

76. Collins, *Lightning Joe*, 256. Collins spent most of the week with the 1st Infantry Division and 9th Infantry Division.

77. For the quotation, see Bradley and Blair, *A General's Life*, 298. For a good overview of the debate of command responsibility for failure to close the Falaise Pocket, see D'Este, *Decision in Normandy*, 445–447. Montgomery's frustration with Crerar is discussed in Hamilton, *Master of the Battlefield: Monty's War Years 1942–1944*, 780–781.

78. Blumenson, *Breakout and Pursuit*, 555–558. Some estimates suggest as few as 20,000 Germans escaped the Falaise Pocket.

79. Dwight D. Eisenhower, *Crusade in Europe: A Personal Account of World War II* (New York: Doubleday and Company, 1948), 279.

Chapter 3: War on the Michelin Map

1. "Audacity, audacity, always audacity!" Ladislas Farago, *Patton: Ordeal and Triumph* (New York: Ivan Obolensky, 1963), 447. In the 1970 film *Patton*, the general says he is quoting Frederick the Great. The sentence is more closely associated with Georges Jacques Danton, a leader of the French Revolution. In any event, it was a favorite Patton expression. The chapter title is suggested by Hubert Essame, *Patton: A Study in Command* (New York: Charles Scribner's

Sons, 1974), 146. Essame was a World War I and World War II veteran. He commanded an infantry brigade in northwest Europe in 1944–1945 and completed his British army service as a major general. For Patton's own use of the Michelin map, see Patton, *War As I Knew It*, 91.

2. Woolner and Fowler, *Spearhead in the West*, 53, 157.

3. Bradley and Blair, *A General's Life*, 309.

4. Larry Collins and Dominique Lapiere, *Is Paris Burning?* (New York: Penguin Books, 1965), 230, 231, 295–296, 348–349.

5. Sylvan and Smith, *Normandy to Victory*, 114.

6. Hamilton, *Master of the Battlefield: Monty's War Years, 1944–1945*, 772.

7. Eisenhower, *Crusade in Europe*, 286; Bradley and Blair, *A General's Life*, 369–370; Blumenson, *The Patton Papers: 1940–1945*, 608.

8. For an excellent short summary of Montgomery's background, see Carlo D'Este, *Bitter Victory: The Battle for Sicily, 1943* (New York: E. P. Dutton, 1988), 93–97. Montgomery's comment is in Hamilton, *Master of the Battlefield*, 772.

9. Hamilton, *Master of the Battlefield*, 773.

10. U.S. Department of War, *Field Manual (FM) 100-5 Field Service Regulations: Operations* (Washington, DC: U.S. Government Printing Office, May 22, 1941), 131.

11. Patton, *War As I Knew It*, 91. Patton borrowed from Alexander Pope's *An Essay on Man* (1733).

12. Roberts, *Five Stars to Victory*, 39. For the reference to ordinary maps, see Woolner and Fowler, *Spearhead in the West*, 163. The value of the Michelin map is noted in Essame, *Patton: A Study in Command*, 146.

13. Headquarters, 83rd Armored Reconnaissance Battalion, "Report of Action Against Enemy August 1944," 3.

14. Dugan, "90-Degree Shift Toward Mons, Belgium" in *The Third Armored Division Saga in World War II*, http://www.3ad.com/history/wwll/dugan.pages/saga.pages/3france.htm#anchor1115164, accessed June 7, 2019; Roberts, *Five Stars to Victory*, 36, 38, 39.

15. Headquarters, 36th Armored Infantry Regiment, *History of the 36th Armored Infantry Regiment*, 30. For the order banning acceptance of drinks from happy French villagers, see Roberts, *Five Stars to Victory*, 36.

16. Headquarters, 36th Armored Infantry Regiment, *History of the 36th Armored Infantry Regiment*, 31; Headquarters, 2nd Battalion, 33rd Armored Regiment, "Log Book of Second Battalion," 8. For the 23rd Engineer bridging effort, see Headquarters, 3rd Armored Division, *Call Me Spearhead*, 20.

17. Roberts, *Five Stars to Victory*, 38.

18. Daniel O. Magnussen, "The General Cried at Dawn," at http://www.3ad.com/history/wwll/memoirs.pages/magnussen.htm, accessed June 7, 2019. Magnussen was a captain assigned to the Division G-3 (Operations) Section. He knew Rose well and interacted with him regularly. The general in the title was not Maurice Rose, but Major General Terry de la Mesa Allen, one of Rose's peers. Allen commanded the 1st Infantry Division (1942–1943) and then the 104th Infantry Division (1944–1945) during World War II. Magnussen offered a contrasting view between the popular, gregarious Terry Allen and the much more forbidding, close-mouthed Maurice Rose.

19. The story of Haldeman's company defense is covered well in Woolner and Fowler, *Spearhead in the West*, 167–169. For the effects of this German

counterattack on timing, see Headquarters, 2nd Battalion, 33rd Armored Regiment, "Log Book of Second Battalion," 8.

20. Headquarters, 2nd Battalion, 33rd Armored Regiment, "Log Book of Second Battalion," 8; Woolner and Fowler, *Spearhead in the West*, 169.

21. Headquarters, 36th Armored Infantry Regiment, *History of the 36th Armored Infantry Regiment*, 31.

22. Haynes W. Dugan, "George Patton and I," [sic] at http://www.3ad .com/history/wwll/dugan.pages/articles.pages/patton.htm, accessed June 7, 2019.

23. Headquarters, 83rd Armored Reconnaissance Battalion, "Report of Action Against Enemy August 1944," 3.

24. Headquarters, 36th Armored Infantry Regiment, *History of the 36th Armored Infantry Regiment*, 31.

25. Roberts, *Five Stars to Victory*, 38; Headquarters, 2nd Battalion, 33rd Armored Regiment, "Log Book of Second Battalion," 8.

26. Roberts, *Five Stars to Victory*, 38.

27. Headquarters, 2nd Battalion, 33rd Armored Regiment, "Log Book of Second Battalion," 8.

28. George Bailey, "Excerpts from The Biography of an Obsession: Germans," http:// www.3ad.com/history/wwll/memoirs.pages/bailey.htm accessed June 7, 2019. Bailey served as a 1st lieutenant in the Division G-2 (Intelligence) Section. For more on Château de Ferrières, see "Château de Ferrières" at The Rothschild Archive at https://family.rothschildarchive.org/estates/9-chateau-de-ferrieres, accessed June 7, 2019.

29. Headquarters, 83rd Armored Reconnaissance Battalion, "Report of Action Against Enemy August 1944," 3.

30. Headquarters, 36th Armored Infantry Regiment, *History of the 36th Armored Infantry Regiment*, 32.

31. Headquarters, 2nd Battalion, 33rd Armored Regiment, "Log Book of Second Battalion," 8.

32. Roysdon's courageous foot charge is covered in Roberts, *Five Stars to Victory*, 18. The lieutenant's comment was from Belton Y. Cooper, *Death Traps: The Survival of an American Armored Division in World War II* (Novato, CA: Presidio Press, 1998), 40. Then Lieutenant Cooper served in the 3rd Ordnance (Maintenance) Battalion in 1944–1945.

33. Roysdon's "favorite 'pep' talk" is quoted in Roberts, *Five Stars to Victory*, 22.

34. There are two accounts of this incident by World War II veterans. The first is found in Haynes W. Dugan, "An Interesting Excerpt," *3rd Armored Division Association News* (June 1963), 23. The second is in Cooper, *Death Traps*, 94. An excellent description of the action at the railroad bridge is included in Ossad and Marsh, *Major General Maurice Rose: World War II's Greatest Forgotten Commander*, 201.

35. Collins, *Lightning Joe*, 261; Headquarters, 36th Armored Infantry Regiment, *History of the 36th Armored Infantry Regiment*, 32.

36. Headquarters, 36th Armored Infantry Regiment, *History of the 36th Armored Infantry Regiment*, 32; Headquarters, 83rd Armored Reconnaissance Battalion, "Report of Action Against Enemy August 1944," 3.

37. Headquarters, 3rd Armored Division, *Call Me Spearhead*, 22.

38. Dugan, "90-Degree Shift Toward Mons, Belgium," *The Third Armored Division Saga in World War II*, http://www.3ad.com/history/wwll/dugan.pages/saga.pages/3france.htm#anchor1115164, accessed June 8, 2019. The general's account is at Rose, "An Operation of the 3rd Armored ('Spearhead') Division," 4. For a fine discussion of the distinction between German Waffen SS and panzer crew uniforms, see Adam Makos, *Spearhead: An American Tank Gunner, His Enemy, and a Collision of Lives in World War II* (New York: Ballantine Books, 2019), 149.

39. Woolner and Fowler, *Spearhead in the West*, 170–172, 350–354.

40. Woolner, *Division HQ: Third Armored Division Forward Echelon and Division Headquarters Company, April 15, 1941–May 8, 1945*, 6.

41. Ibid., 6–7.

42. Headquarters, 3rd Armored Division, *Call Me Spearhead*, 23.

43. Woolner and Fowler, *Spearhead in the West*, 78–80. For more on this change of command, see Cooper, *Death Traps*, 81–83. Cooper served under both commanders of the 3rd Ordnance (Maintenance) Battalion.

44. Headquarters, 36th Armored Infantry Regiment, *History of the 36th Armored Infantry Regiment*, 32.

45. Roberts, *Five Stars to Victory*, 40.

46. Headquarters, 2nd Battalion, 33rd Armored Regiment, "Log Book of Second Battalion," 8; 3rd Armored Division History Foundation, *3rd Armored Division Soldiers Who Gave Their Lives in World War II* at https://www.3ad.com/history/wwll/names.died.htm, accessed June 8, 2019.

47. Collins, *Lightning Joe*, 360–361.

48. Headquarters, 36th Armored Infantry Regiment, *History of the 36th Armored Infantry Regiment*, 32; Headquarters, 83rd Armored Reconnaissance Battalion, "Report of Action Against Enemy August 1944," 4; Woolner and Fowler, *Spearhead in the West*, 350–353.

49. Headquarters, 36th Armored Infantry Regiment, *History of the 36th Armored infantry Regiment*, 32.

50. Rose, "An Operation of the 3rd Armored ('Spearhead') Division," 6. In this article, Rose carefully describes what CCA, CCB, and CCR did on August 31, 1944.

51. Ibid., 3.

52. Woolner and Fowler, *Spearhead in the West*, 352–353.

53. Headquarters, 3rd Armored Division, *Call Me Spearhead*, 23.

54. Collins, *Lightning Joe*, 261; Rose, "An Operation of the 3rd Armored ('Spearhead') Division," 6.

55. Weigley, *Eisenhower's Lieutenants*, 275. See also Bradley, *A Soldier's Story*, 407–408; Sylvan and Smith, *Normandy to Victory*, 115; Collins, *Lightning Joe*, 261. The air reconnaissance effort is described in Blumenson, *Breakout and Pursuit*, 679. Blumenson's official history was published before the Ultra decrypts could be discussed in public forums. Both the Bradley/Blair and Collins books came out after the Ultra code-breaking secrets were publicly disclosed in 1974; both works acknowledge the importance of Ultra. As VII Corps commander, Collins did not qualify for Ultra access in 1944–1945. Ultra intelligence was restricted to field army commanders and above. John Greenfield's thorough editor's notes for Sylvan and Smith's First Army war diary also refer to Ultra on 505–506.

56. Rose, "An Operation of the 3rd Armored ('Spearhead') Division," 5, features an excellent sketch map derived from the one used on the real mission. See also Headquarters, 83rd Armored Reconnaissance Battalion, "Report of Action Against Enemy August 1944," 4.

57. Woolner and Fowler, *Spearhead in the West*, 351–353.

58. Headquarters, 36th Armored Infantry Regiment, *History of the 36th Armored Infantry Regiment*, 32; Rose, "An Operation of the 3rd Armored ('Spearhead') Division," 7; Headquarters, 2nd Battalion, 33rd Armored Regiment, "Log Book of Second Battalion," 8; 3rd Armored Division History Foundation, *3rd Armored Division Soldiers Who Gave Their Lives in World War II* at https://www.3ad.com/history/wwll/names.died.htm, accessed June 9, 2019.

59. Woolner and Fowler, *Spearhead in the West*, 51–52 covers the basics. For the quotation, see Ossad and Marsh, *Major General Maurice Rose: World War II's Greatest Forgotten Commander*, 198.

60. Haynes W. Dugan, "Closing the Falaise Gap," *The Third Armored Division Saga in World War II*, http://www.3ad.com/history/wwll/dugan.pages/saga.pages/3france.htm#anchor499895, accessed June 9, 2019.

61. U.S. Department of War, Headquarters, 83rd Armored Reconnaissance Battalion, "After Action Report September 1944" (Büsbach, Germany: Headquarters, 83rd Armored Reconnaissance Battalion, October 5, 1944), 1; Headquarters, 36th Armored Infantry Regiment, *History of the 36th Armored Infantry Regiment*, 32–33; Sylvan and Smith, *Normandy to Victory*, 117.

62. Roberts, *Five Stars to Victory*, 40–41. For the unit roll-up, see Headquarters, 2nd Battalion, 33rd Armored Regiment, "Log Book of Second Battalion," 9.

63. Headquarters, 36th Armored Infantry Regiment, *History of the 36th Armored Infantry Regiment*, 32–33; Woolner and Fowler, *Spearhead in the West*, 352–353.

64. Headquarters, 36th Armored Infantry Regiment, *History of the 36th Armored Infantry Regiment*, 32–33.

65. Ibid., 33; 3rd Armored Division History Foundation, *3rd Armored Division Soldiers Who Gave Their Lives in World War II* at https://www.3ad.com/history/wwll/names.died.htm, accessed June 10, 2019.

66. Roberts, *Five Stars to Victory*, 42; Headquarters, 36th Armored Infantry Regiment, *History of the 36th Armored Infantry Regiment*, 33.

67. Woolner and Fowler, *Spearhead in the West*, 352–354; Headquarters, 83rd Armored Reconnaissance Battalion, "After Action Report September 1944," 1.

68. Woolner, *Division HQ: Third Armored Division Forward Echelon and Division Headquarters Company, April 15, 1941—May 8, 1945*, 8. See also George Bailey, "Excerpts from The Biography of an Obsession: Germans" at http://www.3ad.com/history/wwll/memoirs.pages/bailey.htm accessed June 10, 2019.

69. Woolner and Fowler, *Spearhead in the West*, 353–354; Collins, *Lightning Joe*, 263.

70. Collins, *Lightning Joe*, 261.

71. U.S. Department of War, *Field Manual 101-5: Staff Officers' Field Manual: The Staff and Combat Orders* (Washington, DC: U.S. Government Printing Office, August 19, 1940), 43–44.

72. Roberts, *Five Stars to Victory*, 42.

73. Headquarters, 36th Armored Infantry Regiment, *History of the 36th Armored Infantry Regiment*, 34; Headquarters, 3rd Armored Division, *Call Me*

Spearhead, The German generals captured were *Generalleutenant* (equivalent to a U.S. major general, a two-star) Rudiger von Heyking (commander, 6th Parachute Division), *Generalmaior* (equivalent to a U.S. Army brigadier general, one star) Hubertus von Aulock (commander of a defense unit from the former Paris garrison), and *Generalmaior* Karl Wahle (another former garrison commander).

74. Headquarters, 36th Armored Infantry Regiment, *History of the 36th Armored Infantry Regiment*, 34–35.

75. Richard W. Van Horne, "History of the 991st Field Artillery Battalion," at http://www.3ad.com/history/wwll/feature.pages/991st.pages/991st.history.htm, accessed June 13, 2019. These 155mm cannons were similar to those in the main battery (6-inch guns) of U.S. Navy light cruisers in World War II.

76. Woolner, *Division HQ: Third Armored Division Forward Echelon and Division Headquarters Company, April 15, 1941—May 8, 1945*, 8. The Germans in the armored half-track are identified as *panzergrenadiers* earlier on that same page. *Panzergrenadiers* were the German equivalent of U.S. Army armored infantry. Both militaries assigned half-tracks to these rifle troops, but shortages in German production consigned many *panzergrenadiers* to wheeled cargo trucks. *Panzergrenadiers* preferred to use the Sd.Kfz. (*Sonderkraftfahrzeug*, "special motor vehicle") 251 half-track, which carried ten troops in addition to the two-man crew. The vehicles could carry as many as twenty soldiers packed in tightly. It mounted an MG34 or MG42 7.92mm machine gun.

77. Woolner and Fowler, *Spearhead in the West*, 354–355.

78. Headquarters, 2nd Battalion, 33rd Armored Regiment, "Log Book of Second Battalion," 9.

79. Blumenson, *Breakout and Pursuit*, 684.

80. Woolner and Fowler, *Spearhead in the West*, 355; Collins, *Lightning Joe*, 263–264.

81. Atkinson, *The Guns at Last Light*, 231; 3rd Armored Division History Foundation, *3rd Armored Division Soldiers Who Gave Their Lives in World War II* at https://www.3ad.com/history/wwll/names.died.htm, accessed June 10, 2019

82. Woolner and Fowler, *Spearhead in the West*, 355–356.

Chapter 4: Dragon's Teeth

1. Sylvan and Smith, *Normandy to Victory*, 121. First Army war diarists Sylvan and Smith paraphrased the words of Lieutenant General Courtney H. Hodges spoken on September 6, 1944.

2. Headquarters, 2nd Battalion, 33rd Armored Regiment, "Log Book of Second Battalion," 9.

3. Cooper, *Death Traps*, 154; Blumenson, *Breakout and Pursuit*, 696.

4. Blumentritt is quoted in Nigel Hamilton, *Monty*, 3 vols. (New York: McGraw-Hill Book Company, 1981–1987), vol. 3: *Final Years of the Field Marshal, 1944–1976* (1987), 3–4.

5. Woolner and Fowler, *Spearhead in the West*, 9.

6. The Sambre River ran east through Charleroi to Namur, where it joined the Meuse River. U.S. Department of War, Headquarters, 3rd Armored Division, "Fragmentary Order to Field Order No. 13" (Namur, Belgium: Headquarters, 3rd Armored Division, September 5, 1944), 1; Headquarters, 36th Armored

Infantry Regiment, *History of the 36th Armored Infantry Regiment*, 34–35. For the military service of Major Alton Glenn Miller and "A String of Pearls," see Dennis M. Spragg, *Glenn Miller Declassified* (Lincoln: University of Nebraska Press, 2017), 23. Miller died in a December 15, 1944, air crash in the English Channel. Miller, Flight Officer John Robert Stuart Morgan, and Lieutenant Colonel Norman Francis Baessell remain missing in action.

7. U.S. Army Center of Military History, *Order of Battle of the U.S. Army—WWII—ETO—3d* [sic] *Armored Division* (Washington, DC: U.S. Army Center of Military History, March 5, 2001), at https://history.army.mil/documents/ETO-OB/3AD-ETO.htm, 436, accessed June 17, 2019.

8. U.S. Department of War, Headquarters, 33rd Armored Regiment, "After Action Report for the Month of September 1944" (Stolberg, Germany: Headquarters, 33rd Armored Regiment, October 7, 1944), 3; Headquarters, 2nd Battalion, 33rd Armored Regiment, "Log Book of Second Battalion," 9.

9. Roberts, *Five Stars to Victory*, 43.

10. For more on Colonel John C. "Jack" Welborn, see Woolner and Fowler, *Spearhead in the West*, 49–52. For more on the 70th Tank Battalion (originally drawn from the 1st Battalion, 67th Armored Regiment, 2nd Armored Division), see Shelby L. Stanton, *Order of Battle: U.S. Army World War II* (Novato, CA: Presidio Press, 1984), 291, 299.

11. Headquarters, 33rd Armored Regiment, "After Action Report for the Month of September 1944," 3.

12. Headquarters, 36th Armored Infantry Regiment, *History of the 36th Armored Infantry Regiment*, 35; Woolner and Fowler, *Spearhead in the West*, 180–181.

13. Headquarters, 36th Armored Infantry Regiment, *History of the 36th Armored Infantry Regiment*, 35.

14. Headquarters, 83rd Armored Reconnaissance Battalion, "After Action Report September 1944," 1.

15. Collins, *Lightning Joe*, 264.

16. Haynes W. Dugan, "Mons to Eupen—In Another Light" in *The Third Armored Division Saga in World War II*, http://www.3ad.com/history/wwll/dugan.pages/saga.pages/4belgium.htm#anchor1265271, accessed June 12, 2019.

17. Ibid., 264–265; Blumenson, *Breakout and Pursuit*, 694.

18. Collins, *Lightning Joe*, 265. For examples of other such Collins-directed diversions of forces from 3rd Armored Division, see Collins, *Lightning Joe*, 247, 253, 272–273, 278, and 285. Collins pointedly noted Rose's objections on 247 and 278, the only negative comments about Rose in Collins's memoirs.

19. Ossad and Marsh, *Maurice Rose: World War II's Greatest Forgotten Commander*, 237.

20. Headquarters, 83rd Armored Reconnaissance Battalion, "After Action Report September 1944," 1.

21. Roberts, *Five Stars to Victory*, 44; Headquarters, 2nd Battalion, 33rd Armored Regiment, "Log Book of Second Battalion," 9.

22. Headquarters, 33rd Armored Regiment, "After Action Report for the Month of September 1944," 4.

23. Ibid.; Woolner and Fowler, *Spearhead in the West*, 178. This act formed part of the basis for Rose's Distinguished Service Cross. See U.S. Department of War, Headquarters, First Army, "General Orders No. 86," (Spa, Belgium:

Headquarters, First Army, November 25, 1944), 1. See also U.S. Department of the Army, Headquarters, U.S. Army Europe, "General Orders Number 13: Designation of Rose Barracks" (Heidelberg, Germany: Headquarters, U.S. Army Europe, September 15, 1952), 1. The dedication order includes details from the documentation for Rose's Distinguished Service Cross.

24. Headquarters, 33rd Armored Regiment, "After Action Report for the Month of September 1944," 4. See also Blumenson, *Breakout and Pursuit*, 694; Collins, *Lightning Joe*, 265.

25. Headquarters, 33rd Armored Regiment, "After Action Report for the Month of September 1944," 4.

26. Headquarters, 36th Armored Infantry Regiment, *History of the 36th Armored Infantry Regiment*, 35.

27. For a good summary of the Liege fortifications by an officer involved in the operation, see Cooper, *Death Traps*, 117–118.

28. Headquarters, 3rd Armored Division, *Call Me Spearhead*, 27.

29. Headquarters, 83rd Armored Reconnaissance Battalion, "After Action Report September 1944," 2.

30. Woolner and Fowler, *Spearhead in the West*, 179–181.

31. U.S. Department of War, Headquarters, 67th Armored Field Artillery Battalion, "Reports After Action Against Enemy, September 1944," (Stolberg, Germany: Headquarters, 67th Armored Field Artillery Battalion, October 5, 1944), 5–6.

32. The description of the staff car comes from Headquarters, 3rd Armored Division, *Call Me Spearhead*, 27; Roberts, *Five Stars to Victory*, 44–45; Headquarters, 33rd Armored Regiment, "After Action Report for the Month of September 1944," 4–5; Headquarters, 2nd Battalion, 33rd Armored Regiment, "Log Book of Second Battalion," 9. Captive Generalmaior Bock von Wolfingen was involved in German military government in Belgium.

33. Headquarters, 36th Armored Infantry Regiment, *History of the 36th Armored Infantry Regiment*, 36.

34. Ibid. See also Headquarters, 3rd Armored Division, *Call Me Spearhead*, 28.

35. Headquarters, 83rd Armored Reconnaissance Battalion, "After Action Report September 1944," 2; Collins, *Lightning Joe*, 265. Collins spent time with Rose on September 8, 1944, in Liege.

36. Headquarters, 83rd Armored Reconnaissance Battalion, "After Action Report September 1944," 2.

37. Woolner and Fowler, *Spearhead in the West*, 358. For a description of the coil defensive technique, see Cooper, *Death Traps*, 315.

38. Lucian Heichler, *Chapter III: The Germans Opposite VII Corps in September 1944* (Washington, DC: Office of the Chief of Military History, December 1952), 5.

39. Cooper, *The German Army 1933–1945*, 517.

40. Headquarters, 33rd Armored Regiment, "After Action Report for the Month of September 1944," 5.

41. Captain Paul H. Bowdle, U.S. Army, Technician Fifth Grade Edward R. Broadwell, U.S. Army, and Corporal Bertram Bendit, U.S. Army, *Combat History of the 391st Armored Field Artillery Battalion* (Neu Isenberg, Germany: Derndruck Publishers, 1945), 81. See also Technician 5th Grade H. Glenn Jenkins, U.S. Army, *Combat History of "A" Battery, 391st Armored Field Artillery*

Battalion, 24 June 1944 to 24 April 1944 (Neu Isenberg, Germany: Derndruck Publishers, 1945), 52.

42. 3rd Armored Division History Foundation, *3rd Armored Division Soldiers Who Gave Their Lives in World War II* at https://www.3ad.com/history/wwll/names .died.htm, accessed June 16, 2019; Roberts, *Five Stars to Victory*, 45. This incident was included in determining the award of the Distinguished Service Cross to Rose. See Headquarters, First Army, "General Orders No. 86," 1, and Headquarters, U.S. Army Europe, "General Orders Number 13: Designation of Rose Barracks," 1.

43. Ibid.; Roberts, *Five Stars to Victory*, 45; Headquarters, 2nd Battalion, 33rd Armored Regiment, "Log Book of Second Battalion," 10.

44. Headquarters, 33rd Armored Regiment, "After Action Report for the Month of September 1944," 5.

45. Ibid., 6; Headquarters, 2nd Battalion, 33rd Armored Regiment, "Log Book of Second Battalion," 10.

46. Headquarters, 3rd Armored Division, *Call Me Spearhead*, 28–29; Woolner and Fowler, *Spearhead in the West*, 183, 358.

47. Headquarters, 83rd Armored Reconnaissance Battalion, "After Action Report September 1944," 2; 3rd Armored Division History Foundation, *3rd Armored Division Soldiers Who Gave Their Lives in World War II* at https://www.3ad .com/history/wwll/names.died.htm, accessed June 13, 2019.

48. Headquarters, 36th Armored Infantry Regiment, *History of the 36th Armored Infantry Regiment*, 36.

49. Headquarters, 2nd Battalion, 33rd Armored Regiment, "Log Book of Second Battalion," 10. The quotations comes from Roberts, *Five Stars to Victory*, 45.

50. Roberts, *Five Stars to Victory*, 45.

51. Blumenson, *The Patton Papers: 1940–1945*, 410, 419, 470–471.

52. Hamilton, *Master of the Battlefield: Monty's War Years 1942–1944*, 807. For Montgomery's earlier arguments along the same line, see Hamilton, pages 498–499 (January 7, 1944), 511–512 (January 21, 1944), 563–564 (April 7, 1944), and 588–589 (May 15, 1944).

53. For Monty's reference to a "full-blooded thrust," refer to Hamilton, *Final Years of the Field Marshal, 1944–1976*, 24. For his numbers, see Hamilton, *Master of the Battlefield: Monty's War Years 1942–1944*, 809, 815. The American numbers can be found in Bradley and Bair, *A General's Life*, 283.

54. Hamilton, *Master of the Battlefield: Monty's War Years 1942–1944*, 804, 809, 818. For the German view, see Note 4 above as well as Cooper, *The German Army 1933–1945*, 514–518. The German 1914 offensive through neutral Belgium took its name from Field Marshal Alfred Graf von Schlieffen (1833–1913), who devised the scheme but did not live to carry it out. Of note, Major General J. Lawton Collins, whose VII Corps inherited the former Schlieffen Plan routes, saw the parallel between 1914 and 1944. See Collins, *Lightning Joe*, 264.

55. Bradley and Blair, *A General's Life*, 321.

56. For a very succinct summary of these two routes into Germany, see Weigley, *Eisenhower's Lieutenants*, 254.

57. Bradley and Blair, *A General's Life*, 314–315. Bradley's recollections of this issue are among the most passionate passages in his book.

58. Weigley, *Eisenhower's Lieutenants*, 261.

59. For a particularly good summary of the logistics situation, see Carlo D'Este, *Patton: A Genius for War* (New York: HarperCollins, 1995), 645–649.

60. Ibid., 268–271, 281–282. Weigley's analysis is very clear and very sobering.

61. Hamilton, *Final Years of the Field Marshal, 1944–1976*, 51.

62. Weigley, *Eisenhower's Lieutenants*, 281–282. The "bridge too far" quote originated with Lieutenant General Frederick A. M. "Boy" Browning, commander of the British I Airborne Corps. See Cornelius Ryan, *A Bridge Too Far* (New York: Popular Library, 1974), 9.

63. Atkinson, *The Guns at Last Light*, 250.

64. U.S. Department of the Army, Office of the Chief of Military History, *The United States Army in World War II, European Theater of Operations*, 10 vols. (Washington, DC: U.S. Government Printing Office, 1949–1990), vol. 7, Charles B. MacDonald, *The Siegfried Line Campaign* (1963), 30. MacDonald served as a rifle company commander in the U.S. Army's 2nd Infantry Division during the 1944–1945 campaign in northwestern Europe. The World War I German defensive line was called the *Siegfriedstellung* (Siegfried Position) although the British, French, and Americans referred to it as the Hindenburg Line, using the name of German Army Chief of the General Staff Field Marshal Paul von Hindenburg. In U.S. Army reports and official histories of World War II, the term Siegfried Line predominates.

65. For Dickson's report, see Weigley, *Eisenhower's Lieutenants*, 300–301. For Hodges's words, see Sylvan and Smith, *Normandy to Victory*, 125.

66. Sylvan and Smith, *Normandy to Victory*, 124. On September 10, 1944, Hodges referred to "the VII Corps which will be the main spearhead in the [First] Army's drive into Fortress Germany."

67. Collins, *Lightning Joe*, 266.

68. U.S. Department of the Army, Committee 23, Armored Officers Advanced Course, *Armor in the Attack of Fortified Positions* (Fort Knox, KY: U.S. Army Armored School, May 1950), 25. The six majors and two captains who wrote this study included veterans of the 3rd Armored Division's September 1944 assault on the West Wall. For the construction of the West Wall, see MacDonald, *The Siegfried Line Campaign*, 30–31.

69. U.S. Department of War, 1st Lieutenant Fred L. Hadsel and Private First Class Ridgeley C. Dorsey, "Rough Draft of Interview with Colonel Leander L. Doan and Lieutenant Colonel William R. Orr, 'Cracking the Siegfried Line: Task Force Doan, Combat Command A, 13–19 September 1944'" (Spa, Belgium: 2nd Information and Historical Section, First Army, November, 1944), 1.

70. Headquarters, 83rd Armored Reconnaissance Battalion, "After Action Report September 1944," 2.

71. Roberts, *Five Stars to Victory*, 48.

72. Headquarters, 33rd Armored Regiment, "After Action Report for the Month of September 1944," 6; Headquarters, 2nd Battalion, 33rd Armored Regiment, "Log Book of Second Battalion," 10.

73. Hadsel and Dorsey, "Rough Draft of Interview with Colonel Leander L. Doan and Lieutenant Colonel William R. Orr," 1.

74. Ibid., 1–2.

75. Woolner and Fowler, *Spearhead in the West*, 359–360.

76. Committee 23, Armored Officers Advanced Course, *Armor in the Attack of Fortified Positions*, 28. For Patton's description of the tactic, see Patton, *War As I Knew It*, 300.

77. Committee 23, Armored Officers Advanced Course, *Armor in the Attack of Fortified Positions*, 14–21. This monograph includes excellent diagrams and photographs. The Germans referred to the first West Wall belt as the Scharnhorst Line, named after Lieutenant General Gerhard J. D. von Scharnhorst and the second band as the Schill Line, after Major Ferdinand B. Schill, both Prussian heroes of the Napoleonic Wars.

78. Hadsel and Dorsey, "Rough Draft of Interview with Colonel Leander L. Doan and Lieutenant Colonel William R. Orr," 2.

79. Ibid. See also Woolner and Fowler, *Spearhead in the West*, 359–361.

80. Hadsel and Dorsey, "Rough Draft of Interview with Colonel Leander L. Doan and Lieutenant Colonel William R. Orr," 2.

81. Committee 23, Armored Officers Advanced Course, *Armor in the Attack of Fortified Positions*, 47. For efforts to reduce the dragon's teeth by demolitions, see Colonel Julian Drayton, U.S. Army, Lieutenant Colonel H. A. Miller, U.S. Army, and Lieutenant Colonel Shaffer F. Jarrell, U.S. Army, "Immediate Report No. 61: Breaching of Siegfried Line" (Luxembourg City, Luxembourg: Headquarters, Twelfth Army Group, September 22, 1944), 1–2. This survey offers comments from both Colonel Truman E. Boudinot, commander of Combat Command B, 3rd Armored Division and Lieutenant Colonel Wesley A. Sweat, G-3 (operations officer) of the 3rd Armored Division. Both explained that explosives did not work well against the dragon's teeth.

82. Hadsel and Dorsey, "Rough Draft of Interview with Colonel Leander L. Doan and Lieutenant Colonel William R. Orr," 3.

83. Woolner and Fowler, *Spearhead in the West*, 361.

84. Heichler, *Chapter III: The Germans Opposite VII Corps in September 1944*, 12, 23–26.

85. Committee 23, Armored Officers Advanced Course, *Armor in the Attack of Fortified Positions*, 47–49; Collins, *Lightning Joe*, 270. In his memoirs, Collins misidentified the reinforcing unit as being from the 16th Infantry Regiment.

86. Hadsel and Dorsey, "Rough Draft of Interview with Colonel Leander L. Doan and Lieutenant Colonel William R. Orr," 4.

87. 3rd Armored Division History Foundation, *3rd Armored Division Soldiers Who Gave Their Lives in World War II* at https://www.3ad.com/history/wwll/names .died.htm, accessed June 16, 2019.

88. Headquarters, 33rd Armored Regiment, "After Action Report for the Month of September 1944," 7.

89. Headquarters, 2nd Battalion, 33rd Armored Regiment, "Log Book of Second Battalion," 10; Jenkins, *Combat History of "A" Battery*, 54; Headquarters, 36th Armored Infantry Regiment, *History of the 36th Armored Infantry Regiment*, 37. German civil engineer and ardent Nazi Fritz Todt (1891–1942) ran his namesake labor organization starting in 1938, and later incorporated its work into his duties as Reich Minister for Armaments and Ammunition. Todt died in an airplane crash in 1942. His successor was Albert Speer.

90. Committee 23, Armored Officers Advanced Course, *Armor in the Attack of Fortified Positions*, 31–33; Headquarters, 33rd Armored Regiment, "After Action Report for the Month of September 1944," 7.

91. Headquarters, 2nd Battalion, 33rd Armored Regiment, "Log Book of Second Battalion," 10; Headquarters, 83rd Armored Reconnaissance Battalion, "After Action Report September 1944," 2–3; Heichler, *Chapter III: The Germans Opposite VII Corps in September 1944*, 25–27.

92. Headquarters, 33rd Armored Regiment, "After Action Report for the Month of September 1944," 7. Woolner and Fowler, *Spearhead in the West*, 365–367.

93. Headquarters, 2nd Battalion, 33rd Armored Regiment, "Log Book of Second Battalion," 11.

94. Ibid.; Roberts, *Five Stars to Victory*, 54–56; Woolner and Fowler, *Spearhead in the West*, 367. For tank losses, see Cooper, *Death Traps*, 127–129.

Chapter 5: The Dark Wood of Error

1. Ernest Hemingway, *Across the River and into the Trees*, (Scotts Valley, CA: CreateSpace Independent Publishing Platform, 2014), 138. Originally published in 1950, Hemingway's novel incorporates his own experiences as a war correspondent serving with the 4th Infantry Division during combat operations in the Hürtgen Forest. Passchendaele was a notorious bloody British Army trench offensive in 1917. The novel's title comes from the last words of Lieutenant General Thomas J. "Stonewall" Jackson, Confederate States Army. The chapter title refers to the imagery found in the first verses of the first canto of Dante Alighieri's *Divine Comedy*.

2. Ryan, *A Bridge Too Far*, 599. Montgomery's characterization is quoted on page 591. The British 1st Airborne Division assaulted with 10,005 men. Only 2,163 British paratroopers and glider men successfully withdrew from the Arnhem area on September 26, 1944. For Montgomery's own misgivings in the wake of the failed operation, see Hamilton, *Final Years of the Field Marshal, 1944–1976*, 88–90. Public bravado and some ungracious blame-casting aside, Montgomery immediately took responsibility for the defeat in private correspondence.

3. For the quotation from Patton's letter of September 21, 1944, see Blumenson, *The Patton Papers*, 552. The comments about the Metz region are at page 589. Third Army losses for September 1944 are found in Patton, *War As I Knew It*, 119, 135.

4. Collins, *Lightning Joe*, 269–271. MacDonald, *The Siegfried Line Campaign*, 617.

5. Charles B. MacDonald, *The Operations of VII Corps in September 1944* (Washington, DC: Office of the Chief of Military History, March 1953), 31.

6. Collins, *Lightning Joe*, 271; Headquarters, 2nd Battalion, 33rd Armored Regiment, "Log Book of Second Battalion," 12; Headquarters, 36th Armored Infantry Regiment, *History of the 36th Armored Infantry Regiment*, 41–42.

7. Hamilton, *War and Peace: FDR's Final Odyssey, D-Day to Yalta, 1943–1945*, 369, 401–402, 543–544n.

8. Sylvan and Smith, *Normandy to Victory*, 138.

9. See the Appendix 1 for details.

10. Woolner and Fowler, *Spearhead in the West*, 11–14.

11. Brigadier General Theodore Roosevelt, Jr., earned the Medal of Honor for his leadership under fire on Utah Beach on D-Day. His father, President Theodore

Roosevelt, earned the Medal of Honor for his leadership in the charge up San Juan/Kettle Hill in the 1898 Spanish-American War. For more on the younger Roosevelt's death and those of the other U.S. generals in the northwestern Europe campaign in 1944, see Robert S. Rush, "Generals and Flag Officers Killed in War," originally posted August 7, 2014, at *War on the Rocks* at https://warontherocks.com/2014/08/general-and-flag-officers-killed-in-war/ accessed June 18, 2019. Command Sergeant Major Rush served in the infantry and earned his doctorate in history. His 2001 book *Hell in Hürtgen Forest: The Ordeal and Triumph of An American Infantry Regiment* is a classic account of that bloody battle.

12. Woolner, *Division HQ: Third Armored Division Forward Echelon and Division Headquarters Company, April 15, 1941—May 8, 1945,* 10.

13. Woolner and Fowler, *Spearhead in the West,* 66–67, 72–74; Headquarters, 83rd Armored Reconnaissance Battalion, "After Action Report September 1944," 3. For the Tank Destroyer Corps motto, see Christopher R. Gabel, *The U.S. Army GHQ Maneuvers of 1941* (Washington, DC: U.S. Government Printing Office, 1991), 176.

14. 3rd Armored Division History Foundation, *3rd Armored Division Soldiers Who Gave Their Lives in World War II* at https://www.3ad.com/history/wwll/names.died.htm, accessed June 19, 2019.

15. Woolner and Fowler, *Spearhead in the West,* 44–45; Ossad and Marsh, *Maurice Rose: World War II's Greatest Forgotten Commander,* 98; Harmon, MacKaye, and MacKaye, *Combat Commander,* 134–136, 195.

16. Jack Thompson, "Tank Men from Chicago Help Beat Nazi Best, Third Division Feat Wins Name 'Spearhead,'" *Chicago Tribune,* August 22, 1944, 1–2.

17. Woolner and Fowler, *Spearhead in the West,* 96–99, 110; Roberts, *Five Stars to Victory,* 19. Roberts referred to the "staid, Victorian motto 'Always Dependable.'" For other armored division mottos, see Zaloga, *U.S. Armored Divisions: The European Theater of Operations, 1944–1945,* 76–92. There was a post-1945 attempt to nickname the 4th Armored division "Breakthrough," but it never caught on.

18. Woolner and Fowler, *Spearhead in the West,* 367. At full strength, the division comprised 830 officers and 13,850 enlisted soldiers.

19. For 3rd Armored Division authorized strengths by type, see Greenfield, Palmer, and Wiley, *The Organization of Ground Combat Troops,* 320–321. For the Third Army commander's views, see Patton, *War As I Knew It,* 314.

20. Palmer, Wiley, and Keast, *The Procurement and Training of Ground Combat Troops,* 382, 421–422; Cooper, *Death Traps,* ix–x. The quote from the inspector's report is from Atkinson, *The Guns at Last Light,* 409.

21. Weigley, *Eisenhower's Lieutenants,* 374. For the 3rd Armored Division integration of replacements in autumn 1944, see Woolner and Fowler, *Spearhead in the West,* 368–369.

22. David W. Hogan, Jr., *A Command Post at War: First Army Headquarters in Europe, 1943–1945* (Washington, DC: U.S. Government Printing Office, 2000), 188. See also Weigley, *Eisenhower's Lieutenants,* 371.

23. 3rd Armored Division History Foundation, *3rd Armored Division Soldiers Who Gave Their Lives in World War II* at https://www.3ad.com/history/wwll/names.died.htm, accessed June 19, 2019.

24. Committee 23, Armored Officers Advanced Course, *Armor in the Attack of Fortified Positions*, 61.

25. U.S. Department of War, *Technical Manual 9-759 Medium Tank M4A3* (Washington, DC: U.S. Government Printing Office, August 4, 1942), 23–33.

26. Woolner and Fowler, *Spearhead in the West*, 367; Cooper, *Death Traps*, 129–130.

27. Woolner and Fowler, *Spearhead in the West*, 367; Committee 23, Armored Officers Advanced Course, *Armor in the Attack of Fortified Positions*, 61.

28. Cooper, *Death Traps*, 117.

29. Ibid., 113. As a U.S. Army ordnance officer, Cooper studied the relative performance of the 75mm and 76mm guns. For the distribution of 76mm gun Sherman tanks, see Zaloga, *U.S. Armored Divisions: The European Theater of Operations, 1944–1945*, 30.

30. Samuel W. Mitcham, Jr., *Retreat to the Reich: German Defeat in France, 1944* (Mechanicsburg, PA: Stackpole Books, 2006), 217–223.

31. Charles B. MacDonald, *A Time for Trumpets: The Untold Story of the Battle of the Bulge* (New York: Bantam Books, 1985), 18.

32. Ibid. See also Peter Caddick-Adams, *Snow and Steel: The Battle of the Bulge, 1944–45* (Oxford, UK: Oxford University Press, 2015), 64, and Weigley, *Eisenhower's Lieutenants*, 256. For more on German panzer production numbers, see Mueller-Hillebrand, *Project #47: German Tank Losses*, 41–42.

33. For Churchill's quote, see Winston L. S. Churchill, "Speech in the House of Commons on June 18, 1940" at https://winstonchurchill.org/resources/speeches/1940-the-finest-hour/their-finest-hour, accessed June 20, 1940. This is often referred to as the "Finest Hour" speech. For the effects of V-1 and V-2 attacks, see Weigley, *Eisenhower's Lieutenants*, 258–259. For V-1 buzz bombs passing over the 3rd Armored Division, see Headquarters, 3rd Armored Division, *Call Me Spearhead*, 24. Lieutenant Belton Y. Cooper saw the German V-1s fly and the V-2s launch as recorded in Cooper, *Death Traps*, 127–128, 182, 269.

34. G. E. Patrick Murray, *Eisenhower Versus Montgomery: The Continuing Debate* (Westport, CT: Praeger Publishers, 1996), 56–60.

35. Weigley, *Eisenhower's Lieutenants*, 350–353, 402–403, 410.

36. Bradley and Blair, *A General's Life*, 340.

37. Ibid., 340, 352–353.

38. Hogan, *A Command Post at War*, 122. For Hodges's six trips forward to see the 3rd Armored Division commander, see Sylvan and Smith, *Normandy to Victory*, 97 (August 16, 1944), 165 (November 5, 1944), 303 (February 22, 1945), 313 (February 28, 1945), 323 (March 7, 1945), and 345 (March 24, 1945).

39. MacDonald, *The Siegfried Line Campaign*, 22. Brigadier General John G. Hill wrote that statement in 1954. During the war, he'd served as G-3 of V Corps.

40. Sylvan and Smith, *Normandy to Victory*, 76. Hodges offered these thoughts to XIX Corps commander Major General Charles H. Corlett on July 30, 1944, during the Operation Cobra breakout.

41. Hogan, *A Command Post at War*, 160–162. An additional armored division (the 7th) in XIX Corps was involved with helping their British neighbors in the Peel Marshes to the immediate north.

42. MacDonald, *The Siegfried Line Campaign*, 252.

43. Collins, *Lightning Joe*, 271; Hogan, *A Command Post at War*, 170.

44. MacDonald, *The Siegfried Line Campaign*, 252, 281. The Second Reich was the 1871–1918 German regime that fought World War I.

45. Collins, *Lightning Joe*, 272, 277. Collins judiciously referred to "difficulties arranging corps boundaries and supporting fires" with XIX Corps.

46. Ibid., 272–273.

47. U.S. Department of War, Headquarters, 33rd Armored Regiment, "After Action Report for the Month of October 1944" (Stolberg, Germany: Headquarters, 33rd Armored Regiment, November 2, 1944), 5.

48. Ibid.; Woolner and Fowler, *Spearhead in the West*, 368–369.

49. Woolner and Fowler, *Spearhead in the West*, 368–369; Headquarters, 33rd Armored Regiment, "After Action Report for the Month of October 1944," 6.

50. MacDonald, *The Siegfried Line Campaign*, 317–319.

51. For Hodges's movements from October 2, 1944, to October 21, 1944, see Sylvan and Smith, *Normandy to Victory*, 141–153. Hodges went to XIX Corps (October 2), VII Corps (October 3), 30th Infantry Division and V Corps (October 7), VII Corps and 1st Infantry Division (October 9), and then VII Corps and 1st Infantry Division again (October 19).

52. MacDonald, *The Siegfried Line Campaign*, 303, 319. The famous quote from Voltaire ("to encourage the others") referred to the execution of British admiral John Byng in the wake of a bungled sea battle off Minorca in 1756.

53. 3rd Armored Division History Foundation, *3rd Armored Division Soldiers Who Gave Their Lives in World War II* at https://www.3ad.com/history/wwll/names .died.htm, accessed June 20, 2019.

54. MacDonald, *The Siegfried Line Campaign*, 493.

55. Collins, *Lightning Joe*, 279. For the geography of the Hürtgen, see Astor, *The Bloody Forest*, 37–38.

56. Astor, *The Bloody Forest*, 57, 61, 72.

57. Ibid., 60, 199, 268.

58. The 47th Infantry Regiment lost 201 killed and 1,264 wounded in September and October 1944 in the Hürtgen Forest. See U.S. Department of War, Headquarters, 9th Infantry Division, Office of the Surgeon, "Report of Medical Activities for the Month of September 1944," (Rötgen, Germany: Headquarters, 9th Infantry Division, October 2, 1944), 1–2; U.S. Department of War, Headquarters, 9th Infantry Division, Office of the Surgeon, "Report of Medical Activities for the Month of October 1944," (Elsenborn, Belgium: Headquarters, 9th Infantry Division, November 1, 1944), 1–2; U.S. Department of War, Headquarters, 9th Infantry Division, Office of the Surgeon, "Report of Medical Activities for the Month of November 1944," (Elsenborn, Belgium: Headquarters, 9th Infantry Division, December 2, 1944), 1–2; U.S. Department of War, Headquarters, 9th Infantry Division, Office of the Surgeon, "Report of Medical Activities for the Month of December 1944," (Eupen, Belgium: Headquarters, 9th Infantry Division, January 3, 1945), 1–2. For unit strength of an infantry regiment, see Stanton, *Order of Battle U.S. Army World War II*, 15. For 3rd Armored Division losses, see 3rd Armored Division History Foundation, *3rd Armored Division Soldiers Who Gave Their Lives in World War II* at https://www.3ad.com/history/wwll/names.died .htm, accessed June 21, 2019.

59. Cooper, *Death Traps*, 139–141.

60. Hogan, *A Command Post at War*, 171–172.

61. Collins, *Lightning Joe*, 273–274. Major Jack A. Houston of the 9th Infantry Division G-2 section prepared the report quoted by Collins.

62. MacDonald, *The Siegfried Line Campaign*, 406.

63. Ibid., 399–400; Hogan, *A Command Post at War*, 182–184.

64. Sylvan and Smith, *Normandy to Victory*, 165.

65. Ossad and Marsh, *Maurice Rose: World War II's Greatest Forgotten Combat Commander*, 225.

66. Ibid., 246.

67. Bailey, "Excerpts from The Biography of an Obsession: Germans," at http://www.3ad.com/history/wwll/memoirs.pages/bailey.htm accessed June 22, 2019. See also Woolner, *Division HQ: Third Armored Division Forward Echelon and Division Headquarters Company, April 15, 1941–May 8, 1945*, 10.

68. James A. Sawicki, *Infantry Regiments of the U.S. Army* (Dumfries, VA: Wyvern Publications, 1981), 120–121.

69. Collins, *Lightning Joe*, 137, 151, 204; See also Patton, *War As I Knew It*, 307–308. Patton wrote that issuing a plan constitutes 5 percent of a commander's duty. Supervision is the other 95 percent. He also stated, "Never tell people *how* to do things. Tell them *what* to do and they will surprise you with their ingenuity." (Italics in original.)

70. Collins, *Lightning Joe*, 247.

71. Ibid., 275.

72. Woolner and Fowler, *Spearhead in the West*, 370–371. Haynes W. Dugan, "3AD's Role in the Winter Offensive" in *The Third Armored Division Saga in World War II* at http://www.3ad.com/history/wwll/dugan.pages/saga.pages/5germanyl.htm#anchor1561120, accessed June 22, 2019.

73. Sylvan and Smith, *Normandy to Victory*, 175; Bradley and Blair, *A General's Life*, 343; MacDonald, *The Siegfried Line Campaign*, 412. For a unit-level view, see Roberts, *Five Stars to Victory*, 65.

74. MacDonald, *The Siegfried Line Campaign*, 411–413.

75. Ibid., 414; Sylvan and Smith, *Normandy to Victory*, 176.

76. Roberts, *Five Stars to Victory*, 67; U.S. Department of War, Headquarters, 33rd Armored Regiment, "After Action Report of the 33rd Armd Regt [sic] for the Month of November 1944" (Stolberg, Germany: Headquarters, 33rd Armored Regiment, December 2, 1944), 6.

77. Headquarters, 33rd Armored Regiment, "After Action Report of the 33rd Armd Regt [sic] for the Month of November 1944," 6–7; 3rd Armored Division History Foundation, *3rd Armored Division Soldiers Who Gave Their Lives in World War II* at https://www.3ad.com/history/wwll/names.died.htm, accessed June 21, 2019.

78. Roberts, *Five Stars to Victory*, 67; Headquarters, 2nd Battalion, 33rd Armored Regiment, "Log Book of Second Battalion," 15.

79. U.S. Department of War, Headquarters, 36th Armored Infantry Regiment, "Action Against Enemy, Reports After/After Action Reports November 1944" (Stolberg, Germany: Headquarters, 36th Armored Infantry Regiment, November 30, 1944), 5–6.

80. Headquarters, 33rd Armored Regiment, "After Action Report of the 33rd Armd Regt [sic] for the Month of November 1944," 8.

81. MacDonald, *The Siegfried Line Campaign*, 423–424.

82. Haynes W. Dugan, "General Rose and the Railway Workers" at https://www
.3ad.com/history/wwll/dugan.pages/articles.pages/railway.workers.htm, accessed June 22, 1944.

83. Headquarters, 33rd Armored Regiment, "After Action Report of the 33rd Armd
Regt [sic] for the Month of November 1944," 8.

84. Ibid., 9, 11–14.

85. Bradley and Blair, *A General's Life*, 343.

86. Collins, *Lightning Joe*, 278.

87. Ibid., 276; MacDonald, *The Siegfried Line Campaign*, 492; Woolner and Fowler,
Spearhead in the West, 375–376.

88. U.S. Department of War, Headquarters, 36th Armored Infantry Regiment, "Action Against Enemy, Reports After/After Action Reports December 1944"
(Havelange, Belgium: Headquarters, 36th Armored Infantry Regiment, December 31, 1944), 4–6, 13–21.

89. Haynes W. Dugan, "The Bulge—Miscellaneous Reports" at http://www.3ad
.com/history/wwll/dugan.pages/saga.pages/6bulge.htm#anchor1838093, accessed June 22, 2019. Dugan served in the 3rd Armored Division G-2 section
and recounts the indicators before the German Ardennes counteroffensive.

Chapter 6: Panthers in the Snow

1. Lanrezac is quoted in MacDonald, *A Time for Trumpets*, 23. *Général de division*
(major general, two stars) Charles Lanrezac commanded the French Fifth
Army in August 1914 at the outset of World War I. Lanrezac was relieved of
command on September 3, 1914.

2. Bradley and Blair, *A General's Life*, 356.

3. MacDonald, *A Time for Trumpets*, 24, 43–45, 81–84.

4. Bradley and Blair, *A General's Life*, 357. For what he called "the doctrinal response," see Weigley, *Eisenhower's Lieutenants*, 465, 469–470.

5. Stanton, *Order of Battle U.S. Army World War II*, 15. See also Blair, *Ridgway's
Paratroopers*, 48–49, 426–430. For artillery, the airborne units used 75mm
pack howitzers (range 9,475 yards) and 105mm "snub-nose" howitzers (range
8,000 yards).

6. Bradley and Blair, *A General's Life*, 357–358; Blumenson, *The Patton Papers:
1944–1945*, 595–598. Hogan, *A Command Post at War*, 213.

7. Sylvan and Smith, *Normandy to Victory*, 214–215.

8. Ibid.; Hogan, *A Command Post at War*, 209.

9. Sylvan and Smith, *Normandy to Victory*, 214. The First Army commander had
the choice of two armored divisions, the 3rd and the 5th. Stanton, *Order of
Battle U.S. Army World War II*, 51, 54. For the actual alert orders (six hours for
CCA, one hour for CCB), see Headquarters, 36th Armored Infantry Regiment,
"Action Against Enemy, Reports After/After Action Reports December 1944," 7.

10. U.S. Department of War, Headquarters, First Army, "General Orders No. 86," 1.
For the brief ceremony at First Army Headquarters on December 12, 1944, see
Sylvan and Smith, *Normandy to Victory*, 205. Hodges's high opinion of Rose is
found in the same source, 274.

11. U.S. Department of War, Headquarters, European Theater of Operations,
"General Orders No. 165" (Paris, France: Headquarters, European Theater of
Operations, 1945), 1. This was Bradley's only valor award.

12. Hogan, *A Command Post at War*, 212, 215. See also Peter Caddick-Adams, *Snow and Steel*, 406–408.

13. U.S. Department of War, Headquarters, 3rd Armored Division, *Spearheading with the 3rd Armored Division* (Halle an der Saale, Germany: Hallisch Nachrichten, 1945), 10.

14. Griesser, *The Lions of Carentan*, 219–226. The German airborne task force commander was *Oberst* (colonel) Friedrich August von der Heydte, who also commanded the 6th Airborne Regiment at Carentan.

15. U.S. Department of the Army, Committee 3, Armored Officers Advanced Course, *Armor under Adverse Conditions: 2nd and 3rd Armored Divisions in the Ardennes Campaign, 16 December 1944 to 16 January 1945* (Fort Knox, KY: U.S. Army Armored School, June 1949), 11–12. The three majors and four captains included veterans of both divisions.

16. U.S. Department of War, Headquarters, 33rd Armored Regiment, "After Action Report for the Month of December 1944" (La Fourche, Belgium: Headquarters, 33rd Armored Regiment, January 5, 1945), 4. For the contents of the fuel depot, see MacDonald, *A Time for Trumpets*, 238. Some sources estimate as much as three million gallons on site.

17. Headquarters, 36th Armored Infantry Regiment, "Action Against Enemy, Reports After/After Action Reports December 1944," 7.

18. Cooper, *Death Traps*, 162–165. Cooper was part of this difficult road movement.

19. Hogan, *A Command Post at War*, 215; Sylvan and Smith, *Normandy to Victory*, 220–221.

20. Woolner and Fowler, *Spearhead in the West*, 205–208. See also "General Rose of Denver Has Close Brush with Buzz Bomb," *Denver Post*, December 28, 1944, 1.

21. U.S. Department of the Army, Office of the Chief of Military History, *The United States Army in World War II, European Theater of Operations*, 10 vols. (Washington, DC: U.S. Government Printing Office, 1949–1990), vol. 8, Hugh M. Cole, *The Ardennes: Battle of the Bulge* (1965), 345.

22. Blair, *Ridgway's Paratroopers*, 411.

23. Matthew B. Ridgway, as told to Harold R. Martin, *Soldier: The Memoirs of Matthew B. Ridgway* (New York: Harper and Brothers, 1956), 115.

24. Ibid. See also Blair, *Ridgway's Paratroopers*, 441–442 and U.S. Department of War, Headquarters, 83rd Armored Reconnaissance Battalion, "After Action Report December 1944" (Lierneux, Belgium: Headquarters, 83rd Armored Reconnaissance Battalion, January 14, 1945), 2.

25. Ridgway and Martin, *Soldier*, 115.

26. George C. Mitchell, *Matthew B. Ridgway: Soldier, Statesman, Scholar, Citizen* (Mechanicsburg, PA: Stackpole Books, 2002), 25, 29–30, 37–38, 45–47; Blair, *Ridgway's Paratroopers*, 438, 442.

27. Weigley, *Eisenhower's Lieutenants*, 507–508.

28. Headquarters, 3rd Armored Division, *Spearheading with the 3rd Armored Division*, 10–11.

29. Steven J. Zaloga, *Panther vs. Sherman Battle of the Bulge 1944* (Northants, UK: Osprey Publishing, 2011), 28. For the December 1944 number of 3rd Armored Division M4 Shermans with 76mm cannons, see Zaloga, *U.S. Armored*

Divisions: The European Theater of Operations, 1944–1945, 30. For comparisons between German and American tanks, see Cooper, *Death Traps*, 306–309. As a U.S. Army ordnance officer, Cooper studied both American and German tanks during his military coursework, then examined these vehicles in the field in 1944–1945 while carrying out his duties as a maintenance officer.

30. Mueller-Hillebrand, *Project #47: German Tank Losses*, 41–42; Zaloga, *Panther vs. Sherman*, 38–40.

31. Zaloga, *Panther vs. Sherman*, 28, 29–31.

32. Cooper, *Death Traps*, 308. This is the primary thesis of the author's book. Along with a personal account of the 3rd Armored Division's campaigns in 1944–1945, Cooper indicts the U.S. Army for the qualitative shortcomings of the M4 Sherman vs. its German adversaries, notably the Panther. The title speaks for itself. For the views of American and German tank crewmen, see Makos, *Spearhead: An American Tank Gunner, His Enemy, and a Collision of Lives in World War II*, 20, 203.

33. Major General Maurice Rose, U.S. Army, "Personal Correspondence with General of the Army Dwight D. Eisenhower" (Hermelheim, Germany: Headquarters, 3rd Armored Division, March 21, 1945), 1.

34. Zaloga, *Panther vs. Sherman*, 31; Mueller-Hillebrand, *Project #47: German Tank Losses*, 18–20, 27.

35. Stephen B. Patrick, "Tank!: A Weapons System Survey," *Strategy & Tactics Magazine* no 44 (May/June 1974): 9–11.

36. Cooper, *Death Traps*, 148. As an ordnance officer, Cooper worked to install these modifications. For the ground pressure comparison, see Zaloga, *Panther vs. Sherman*, 29–31.

37. Rose, "Personal Correspondence with General of the Army Dwight D. Eisenhower" (March 21, 1945), 1–2.

38. U.S. Department of the Army, Ballistics Research Laboratory, *Report No. 758: Data on World War II Tank Engagements Involving the U.S. 3rd and 4th Armored Divisions* (Aberdeen Proving Ground, MD: Ballistic Research Laboratory, 1954), 27–28, 45–46.

39. Department of War, *Technical Manual 9-759 Medium Tank M4A3*, 3–6, 28–30. Even on today's M1A2 Abrams main battle tanks, the U.S. Army uses a human loader rather than the autoloader favored by many foreign designers. Not only is a well-trained loader more efficient, but the position remains a good entry-level way to learn tank turret tasks.

40. Haynes W. Dugan, "3rd Armored Division World War II Tank Aces," https://www.3ad.com/history/wwll/pool.pages/dugan.article.htm, accessed June 30, 2019; Zaloga, *Panther vs. Sherman*, 42, 46. See also Sergeant Frank Woolner, U.S. Army, "Texas Tanker," *Yank: The Army Weekly* (September 22, 1944), 10–12. Determining how many panzers a particular U.S. tank crew destroyed was difficult. There were no established counting rules and most ground fights included multiple armored vehicles, artillery, infantry bazooka fire, and air support. Even in Pool's case, some contemporary accounts list twelve "confirmed" German panzer kills. For Pool's connection to movies, see Fogel, *Major General Maurice Rose: The Most Decorated Battletank Commander in U.S. Military History*, 119, and David Nye, "World War II Tank Crew that Inspired the Movie *Fury*," *Real Clear Defense* (September 9, 2015) at https://www

.realcleardefense.com/articles/2015/09/10/wwii_tank_crew_that_inspired _the_movie_fury_108455.html, accessed July 1, 2019.

41. 3rd Armored Division History Foundation, *3rd Armored Division Soldiers Who Gave Their Lives in World War II* at https://www.3ad.com/history/wwll/names .died.htm, accessed June 30, 2019.

42. Bellanger, *U.S. Army Armored Division 1943–1945: Organization, Doctrine, Equipment*, 44–45, 49, 61–63.

43. Committee 3, Armored Officers Advanced Course, *Armor under Adverse Conditions*, 23. For map locations, see U.S. Department of War, U.S. Army Map Service, *France and Belgium 1:50,000, Sheet 92 Durbuy* (Washington, DC: U.S. Army Map Service, 1944), 1.

44. 1st Lieutenant Fred I. Hadsel, U.S. Army, "Combat Interview with Major General Maurice Rose, CG [Commanding General], 3rd AD [Armored Division]," (Spa, Belgium: 2nd Information and Historical Section, First Army, January 26, 1945), 1–3.

45. Headquarters, 36th Armored Infantry Regiment, "Action Against Enemy, Reports After/After Action Reports December 1944," 7–8. For an excellent overview of the situation, see Gregory Fontenot, *Loss and Redemption at St. Vith: The 7th Armored Division in the Battle of the Bulge* (Columbia, MO: University of Missouri Press, 2019), 178. Colonel Greg Fontenot is an accomplished historian and tank commander who commanded an armor battalion task force in the 1990–91 Iraq War and the first American brigade combat team in Bosnia in 1995.

46. Ossad and Marsh, *Major General Maurice Rose: World War II's Greatest Forgotten Commander*, 261.

47. William Castille, "The Story of Task Force Hogan, Part One" at http://www.3ad .com/history/wwll/memoirs.pages/castille.htm, accessed June 27, 2019. During World War II, Castille served as the S-2 (intelligence officer) for Combat Command B, 3rd Armored Division. See also Committee 3, Armored Officers Advanced Course, *Armor under Adverse Conditions*, 25.

48. Committee 3, Armored Officers Advanced Course, *Armor under Adverse Conditions*, 25. See also MacDonald, *A Time for Trumpets*, 537–538; and Fontenot, *Loss and Redemption at St. Vith*, 178.

49. Committee 3, Armored Officers Advanced Course, *Armor under Adverse Conditions*, 25–27.

50. Headquarters, 36th Armored Infantry Regiment, "Action Against Enemy, Reports After/After Action Reports December 1944," 8–9.

51. Woolner, *Division HQ: Third Armored Division Forward Echelon and Division Headquarters Company, April 15, 1941–May 8, 1945*, 10; MacDonald, *A Time for Trumpets*, 538–539. For the role of the combat engineers, see 1st Lieutenant Fred I. Hadsel, U.S. Army, "Combat Interview with Major Jack Fickessen, Executive Officer, 23rd Armored Engineer Battalion," (Bra, Belgium: 2nd Information and Historical Section, First Army, January 7, 1945), 1.

52. Headquarters, 36th Armored Infantry Regiment, "Action Against Enemy, Reports After/After Action Reports December 1944," 8–9.

53. Committee 3, Armored Officers Advanced Course, *Armor under Adverse Conditions*, 27.

54. Headquarters, 36th Armored Infantry Regiment, *History of the 36th Armored Infantry Regiment*, 70–71.

55. Gavin, *On to Berlin*, 230.

56. Bradley and Blair, *A General's Life*, 358–359; Hogan, *A Command Post at War*, 216.

57. Weigley, *Eisenhower's Lieutenants*, 499–501; Cole, *The Ardennes: Battle of the Bulge*, 19, 22, 69. For the Ultra aspect, see Caddick-Adams, *Snow and Steel*, 625 and MacDonald, *A Time for Trumpets*, 61.

58. Atkinson, *The Guns at Last Light*, 420, 430, 445–447.

59. Weigley, *Eisenhower's Lieutenants*, 507, 509–10, 532, 547–548. For the "Russian High," see Cole, *The Ardennes: Battle of the Bulge*, 649. For division arrival dates, see Stanton, *Order of Battle U.S. Army World War II*, 63 (11th Armored Division was in France on December 17, 1944), 141 (75th Infantry Division arrived in France on December 13, 1944), and 159 (87th Infantry Division landed in France on December 5, 1944).

60. D'Este, *Patton: A Genius for War*, 700–702. The headline came from a December 30, 1944, *Washington Post* editorial.

61. Cole, *The Ardennes: Battle of the Bulge*, 423–427; Bradley and Blair, *A General's Life*, 363–366; Hamilton, *Final Years of the Field Marshal, 1944–1976*, 210–211.

62. Hamilton, *Final Years of the Field Marshal, 1944–1976*, 213, 222. For the comment on Hodges by Brigadier General Robert W. Hasbrouck, commander of the 7th Armored Division in the Battle of the Bulge, see Caddick-Adams, *Snow and Steel*, 407. On Montgomery's request to remove Hodges, see Hogan, *A Command Post at War*, 220.

63. Hamilton, *Final Years of the Field Marshal, 1944–1976*, 214; Collins, *Lightning Joe*, 282.

64. Headquarters, 36th Armored Infantry Regiment, *History of the 36th Armored Infantry Regiment*, 72–73.

65. Castille, "The Story of Task Force Hogan, Part One" at http://www.3ad.com/history/wwll/memoirs.pages/castille.htm, accessed June 27, 2019.

66. Headquarters, 36th Armored Infantry Regiment, "Action Against Enemy, Reports After/After Action Reports December 1944," 10; Committee 3, Armored Officers Advanced Course, *Armor under Adverse Conditions*, 28.

67. Headquarters, 36th Armored Infantry Regiment, *History of the 36th Armored Infantry Regiment*, 73.

68. MacDonald, *A Time for Trumpets*, 544.

69. Ibid., 540–541.

70. Woolner and Fowler, *Spearhead in the West*, 388–390.

71. Castille, "The Story of Task Force Hogan, Part One" at http://www.3ad.com/history/wwll/memoirs.pages/castille.htm, accessed June 27, 2019.

72. Headquarters, 36th Armored Infantry Regiment, "Action Against Enemy, Reports After/After Action Reports December 1944," 11.

73. Committee 3, Armored Officers Advanced Course, *Armor under Adverse Conditions*, 13.

74. Ibid., 13–14.

75. MacDonald, *A Time for Trumpets*, 544–546.

76. Ibid., 198, 222; Headquarters, 33rd Armored Regiment, "After Action Report for the Month of December 1944," 5–6.

77. U.S. Department of the Army, Committee 1, Armored Officers Advanced Course, *The Armored Division in the Defense* (Fort Knox, KY: U.S. Army Armored School, May 1950), 59–60.

78. Blair, *Ridgway's Paratroopers*, 448–449; Hamilton, *Final Years of the Field Marshal, 1944–1976*, 224–228. The reference to straightening the ways refers to Isaiah 40:3-4 in the Old Testament of the Bible.

79. Rose's orders are summarized in Headquarters, 36th Armored Infantry Regiment, *History of the 36th Armored Infantry Regiment*, 73–75. For weather and air operations, see Sylvan and Smith, *Normandy to Victory*, 230, 232, 236–237. For available artillery battalions, see MacDonald, *A Time for Trumpets*, 559.

80. Committee 1, Armored Officers Advanced Course, *The Armored Division in the Defense*, 60–61.

81. Ibid., 61–63.

82. This firefight is covered in detail in Zaloga, *Panther vs. Sherman*, 50–67. See also Committee 3, Armored Officers Advanced Course, *Armor under Adverse Conditions*, 29–30.

83. Woolner and Fowler, *Spearhead in the West*, 389–392.

84. Castille, "The Story of Task Force Hogan, Part One" at http://www.3ad.com /history/wwll/memoirs.pages/castille.htm, accessed June 28, 2019.

85. Headquarters, 33rd Armored Regiment, "After Action Report for the Month of December 1944," 7.

86. Cole, *The Ardennes: Battle of the Bulge*, 588–590; and Fontenot, *Loss and Redemption at St. Vith*, 245–249.

87. MacDonald, *A Time for Trumpets*, 559.

88. Ibid., 554–555; Woolner and Fowler, *Spearhead in the West*, 203–224.

89. Olin Brewster, "What Really Happened, Belle Haie, Belgium, December 1944, Task Force Y [TF Richardson]," *3rd Armored Division Association Newsletter*, (September 1990), 14–28.

90. MacDonald, *A Time for Trumpets*, 553–554; Ossad and Marsh, *Major General Maurice Rose: World War II's Greatest Forgotten Commander*, 274–277.

91. Hadsel, "Combat Interview with Major General Maurice Rose, CG [Commanding General], 3rd AD [Armored Division]," 1–2.

92. Woolner and Fowler, *Spearhead in the West*, 407–409; 3rd Armored Division History Foundation, *3rd Armored Division Soldiers Who Gave Their Lives in World War II* at https://www.3ad.com/history/wwll/names.died.htm, accessed June 28, 2019.

93. Woolner and Fowler, *Spearhead in the West*, 407–409.

Chapter 7: To the Rhine

1. James Jones, *WWII* (New York: Ballantine Books, 1975), 208. Author of the novels *From Here to Eternity* and *The Thin Red Line*, James Jones served as a rifleman in the 25th Infantry Division in World War II. He earned the Purple Heart when wounded during combat on Guadalcanal in January 1943.

2. For the damage to the dams, see U.S. Department of the Army, Office of the Chief of Military History, *The United States Army in World War II, European Theater of Operations*, 10 vols. (Washington, DC: U.S. Government Printing Office, 1949–1990), vol. 9, Charles B. MacDonald, *The Last Offensive* (1972), 80–83. For First Army casualties, see MacDonald, *The Siegfried Line Campaign*, 617.

3. MacDonald, *A Time for Trumpets*, 187.

4. MacDonald, *The Last Offensive*, 82–83, 143.

5. Cole, *The Ardennes: Battle of the Bulge*, 674–676, goes with 67,000 German casualties. MacDonald, *A Time for Trumpets*, 618, suggests 100,000. Caddick-Adams, *Snow and Steel*, 635, offers two possible figures based on incomplete German records: 67,261 or 84,834. Given the degraded state of German military record-keeping by January 1945, it's difficult to know with any certainty.

6. Hamilton, *Final Years of the Field Marshal 1944–1976*, 266–270; Collins, *Lightning Joe*, 295.

7. For a brilliant description and partial transcript of Monty's press conference, see Atkinson, *The Guns at Last Light*, 483. For Monty's perspective, see Hamilton, *Final Years of the Field Marshal 1944–1976*, 274–279, 300–306.

8. 3rd Armored Division History Foundation, *3rd Armored Division Soldiers Who Gave Their Lives in World War II* at https://www.3ad.com/history/wwll/names .died.htm, accessed June 29, 2019. The quotation is from Atkinson, *The Guns at Last Light*, 485. For German practice, see Joseph Balkoski, "Operation Grenade: The Battle for the Rhineland, 23 Feb.–5 Mar. '45," *Strategy & Tactics Magazine* (January/February 1981), 14.

9. U.S. Department of War, Headquarters, 32nd Armored Regiment, "Actions Against Enemy, Reports After/After Action Reports, Month of February 1945" (Cologne, Germany: Headquarters, 32nd Armored Regiment, March 8, 1945), 1.

10. Cooper, *Death Traps*, 181, 230; Zaloga, *Panther vs. Sherman*, 19.

11. Woolner and Fowler, *Spearhead in the West*, 78–80.

12. Zaloga, *U.S. Armored Divisions: The European Theater of Operations, 1944–1945*, 34.

13. Cooper, *Death Traps*, 21–22, 138. For the Ronson nickname, see Ellis, *The Sharp Edge*, 150.

14. Cooper, *Death Traps*, 35–36.

15. Makos, *Spearhead*, 149; Headquarters, 3rd Armored Division, *Spearheading with the 3rd Armored Division*, 26–27; Sylvan and Smith, *Normandy to Victory*, 303. The T26E3 eventually became standardized as the M26 Pershing. Its name honored General John J. Pershing, a former cavalry officer and the commander of the American Expeditionary Force in France in World War I.

16. Zaloga, *U.S. Armored Divisions: The European Theater of Operations, 1944–1945*, 30; U.S. Department of War, Headquarters, 83rd Armored Reconnaissance Battalion, "After Action Report February 1945" (Cologne, Germany: Headquarters, 83rd Armored Reconnaissance Battalion, March 10, 1945), 2. The M24 was named to recognize Major General Adna R. Chaffee, Jr., a key organizer of America's World War II armored force.

17. Cooper, *Death Traps*, 225–228.

18. Atkinson, *The Guns at Last Light*, 183–184, 371. The Soviet Red Army liberated the death camp at Majdanek, Poland, on July 23, 1944. The French First Army liberated the Natzweiler-Struthof death camp on November 23, 1944.

19. Sylvan and Smith, *Normandy to Victory*, 302; Collins, *Lightning Joe*, 298.

20. Sylvan and Smith, *Normandy to Victory*, 305.

21. MacDonald, *The Last Offensive*, 157–161; Collins, *Lightning Joe*, 299.

22. Weigley, *Eisenhower's Lieutenants*, 610–611; MacDonald, *The Last Offensive*, 160.

23. MacDonald, *The Last Offensive*, 159; Sylvan and Smith, *Normandy to Victory*, 305–308.

24. Headquarters, 83rd Armored Reconnaissance Battalion, "After Action Report February 1945," 2–3.

25. Woolner and Fowler, *Spearhead in the West*, 410–414.

26. Roberts, *Five Stars to Victory*, 71.

27. U.S. Department of War, Headquarters, 33rd Armored Regiment, "After Action Report for the Month of February 1945" (Neideraussem, Germany: Headquarters, 33rd Armored Regiment, March 3, 1945), 2–3.

28. Woolner and Fowler, *Spearhead in the West*, 228–230.

29. Ibid., 228–229.

30. Headquarters, 2nd Battalion, 33rd Armored Regiment, "Log Book of Second Battalion," 23.

31. Headquarters, 83rd Armored Reconnaissance Battalion, "After Action Report February 1945," 3.

32. Headquarters, 32nd Armored Regiment, "Actions Against Enemy, Reports After/After Action Reports, Month of February 1945," 3–4.

33. Woolner and Fowler, *Spearhead in the West*, 410–414.

34. Ibid., 230–231.

35. Headquarters, 83rd Armored Reconnaissance Battalion, "After Action Report February 1945," 3.

36. Headquarters, 33rd Armored Regiment, "After Action Report for the Month of February 1945," 3.

37. Roberts, *Five Stars to Victory*, 72.

38. Headquarters, 2nd Battalion, 33rd Armored Regiment, "Log Book of Second Battalion," 24.

39. Headquarters, 32nd Armored Regiment, "Actions Against Enemy, Reports After/After Action Reports, Month of February 1945," 4–5; 3rd Armored Division History Foundation, *3rd Armored Division Soldiers Who Gave Their Lives in World War II* at https://www.3ad.com/history/wwll/names.died.htm, accessed July 2, 2019.

40. Dugan, "Heavy Fighting As Push to Rhine Continues," *The Third Armored Division Saga in World War II*, https://www.3ad.com/history/wwll/dugan.pages/saga.pages/7germany2.htm#anchor321456, accessed July 2, 2019.

41. Headquarters, 36th Armored Infantry Regiment, *History of the 36th Armored Infantry Regiment*, 99–101; Ossad and Marsh, *Major General Maurice Rose: World War II's Greatest Forgotten Commander*, 287–288.

42. Sylvan and Smith, *Normandy to Victory*, 310–11, 313.

43. Woolner and Fowler, *Spearhead in the West*, 70–71, 415–418; 3rd Armored Division History Foundation, *3rd Armored Division Soldiers Who Gave Their Lives in World War II* at https://www.3ad.com/history/wwll/names.died.htm, accessed July 3, 2019.

44. Sylvan and Smith, *Normandy to Victory*, 312–313

45. Van Horne, "History of the 991st Armored Field Artillery Battalion," http://www.3ad.com/history/wwll/feature.pages/991st.pages/991st.history.htm, accessed July 3, 2019.

46. Harmon, MacKaye, and MacKaye, *Combat Commander*, 208.

47. Sylvan and Smith, *Normandy to Victory*, 313.

48. Headquarters, 3rd Armored Division, *Spearheading with the 3rd Armored Division*, 23.

49. Collins, *Lightning Joe*, 301–302. The Hohenzollern Bridge was named for the Prussian royal dynasty that included Frederick the Great (ruled 1740–1786) and Kaiser Wilhelm II (ruled 1888–1918).

50. U.S. Department of War, Headquarters, 83rd Armored Reconnaissance Battalion, "After Action Report March 1945" (Nordborchen, Germany: Headquarters, 83rd Armored Reconnaissance Battalion, April 5, 1945), 2; Headquarters, 36th Armored Infantry Regiment, *History of the 36th Armored Infantry Regiment*, 104–105.

51. Roberts, *Five Stars to Victory*, 73.

52. U.S. Department of War, Headquarters, 32nd Armored Regiment, "Actions Against Enemy, Reports After/After Action Reports, Month of March 1945" (Sanhgerhausen, Germany: Headquarters, 32nd Armored Regiment, April 30, 1945), 3–4.

53. U.S. Department of War, Headquarters, 36th Armored Infantry Regiment, "Action Against Enemy, Reports After/After Action Reports March 1945" (Etteln, Germany: Headquarters, 36th Armored Infantry Regiment, March 31, 1945), 4.

54. U.S. Department of War, Headquarters, 33rd Armored Regiment, "After Action Report for the Month of March 1945" (Nordborchen, Germany: Headquarters, 33rd Armored Regiment, April 4, 1945), 3.

55. Headquarters, 2nd Battalion, 33rd Armored Regiment, "Log Book of Second Battalion," 25.

56. Headquarters, 33rd Armored Regiment, "After Action Report for the Month of March 1945," 3. Woolner and Fowler, *Spearhead in the West*, 419.

57. Headquarters, 36th Armored Infantry Regiment, "Action Against Enemy, Reports After/After Action Reports March 1945," 5; Headquarters, 36th Armored Infantry Regiment, *History of the 36th Armored Infantry Regiment*, 106.

58. Headquarters, 83rd Armored Reconnaissance Battalion, "After Action Report March 1945," 2.

59. Ibid.; Headquarters, 2nd Battalion, 33rd Armored Regiment, "Log Book of Second Battalion," 25.

60. Ibid. The M36 Jackson tank destroyer took its name from Confederate Lieutenant General Thomas J. "Stonewall" Jackson.

61. Roberts, *Five Stars to Victory*, 74–75. Headquarters, 32nd Armored Regiment, "Actions Against Enemy, Reports After/After Action Reports, Month of March 1945," 3.

62. Collins, *Lightning Joe*, 314.

63. Ibid.

64. Woolner and Fowler, *Spearhead in the West*, 235–238, 419–423.

65. Headquarters, 2nd Battalion, 33rd Armored Regiment, "Log Book of Second Battalion," 25; Headquarters, 33rd Armored Regiment, "After Action Report for the Month of March 1945," 3; Headquarters, 83rd Armored Reconnaissance Battalion, "After Action Report March 1945," 2–3.

66. Headquarters, 32nd Armored Regiment, "Actions Against Enemy, Reports After/After Action Reports, Month of March 1945," 5, 25–26; U.S. Department of War, Headquarters, 67th Armored Field Artillery Battalion, "Reports After

Action Against Enemy, March 1945" (Brakel, Germany: Headquarters, 67th Armored Field Artillery Battalion, April 7, 1945), 5.

67. Iris Carpenter, *No Woman's World: From D-Day to Berlin, a Woman Correspondent Covers World War II* (Boston, MA: Houghton Mifflin Company, 1946), 262. For a photograph of the sign, see Fogel, *Major General Maurice Rose: The Most Decorated Battletank Commander in U.S. Military History*, 211.

68. Headquarters, 33rd Armored Regiment, "After Action Report for the Month of March 1945," 3.

69. Woolner and Fowler, *Spearhead in the West*, 235–237.

70. Headquarters, 32nd Armored Regiment, "Actions Against Enemy, Reports After/After Action Reports, Month of March 1945," 26.

71. Ibid., 5; Headquarters, 36th Armored Infantry Regiment, *History of the 36th Armored Infantry Regiment*, 107.

72. "The Desert of Cologne: Germany's Fourth Largest City is War's Biggest Ruin," *Life*, March 26, 1945, 36–38.

73. Headquarters, 83rd Armored Reconnaissance Battalion, "After Action Report March 1945," 2.

74. Roberts, *Five Stars to Victory*, 75; Headquarters, 2nd Battalion, 33rd Armored Regiment, "Log Book of Second Battalion," 26.

75. Headquarters, 33rd Armored Regiment, "After Action Report for the Month of March 1945," 3. Woolner and Fowler, *Spearhead in the West*, 235–236. For a description of the Ford factory, see Cooper, *Death Traps*, 237.

76. Headquarters, 32nd Armored Regiment, "Actions Against Enemy, Reports After/After Action Reports, Month of March 1945," 5, 27.

77. Headquarters, 3rd Armored Division, *Spearheading with the 3rd Armored Division*, 26–27.

78. Carpenter, *No Woman's World*, 262.

79. Haynes W. Dugan, "Those Damn Dams on the Roer River," The 3rd Armored Division Saga in World War II at http://www.3ad.com/history/wwll/dugan.pages/saga.pages/7germany2.htm#anchor320094, accessed July 5, 2019.

80. Makos, *Spearhead*, 232, 274, 278. See also Ossad and Marsh, *Major General Maurice Rose: World War II's Greatest Forgotten Commander*, 290–292.

81. Headquarters, 32nd Armored Regiment, "Actions Against Enemy, Reports After/After Action Reports, Month of March 1945," 5, 28.

82. Andy Rooney, *My War* (New York: Public Affairs Books, 1995), 249–250.

83. This well-known footage is available in many formats. For a good example, see https://www.youtube.com/watch?v=NBI9d0-IfEM, accessed July 5, 2019. For the best account of the tank battle, see Makos, *Spearhead*, 201–217. It's the centerpiece of this superb book. Along with Staff Sergeant Robert Earley, the rest of the Pershing crew were Corporal Clarence Smoyer (gunner), Corporal John "Johnny Boy" DeRiggi (loader), Tech-5 William "Woody" McVey (driver), and Private Homer "Smokey" Davis (assistant driver).

84. Headquarters, 32nd Armored Regiment, "Actions Against Enemy, Reports After/After Action Reports, Month of March 1945," 5, 28–29.

85. "The Desert of Cologne," 36–39. For the quotation, see K. B. Townsend, editor and translator, *Tacitus: Agricola and Germania* (London, UK: Methuen and Co., 1894), 34. The famous line comes from the last sentence of *Agricola* Part XXX.

Chapter 8: One Shot

1. Fred Majdalanay, *The Monastery* (Boston, MA; Houghton Mifflin Co., 1946), 67. Captain (temporary Major) Majdalany served in the Lancashire Fusiliers Regiment of the British Army in World War II. He fought in North Africa, Sicily, and Italy. He was wounded in action and earned the Military Cross. His novel *The Monastery* concerns the difficult battle for Monte Cassino in Italy.
2. Woolner and Fowler, *Spearhead in the West*, 355; Collins, *Lightning Joe*, 104.
3. MacDonald, *The Last Offensive*, 294.
4. Ibid., 296–297, 305; Bradley and Blair, *A General's Life*, 402–403; Hamilton, *Final Years of the Field Marshal, 1944–1976*, 421–423; Weigley, *Eisenhower's Lieutenants*, 639–641, 644–646. Montgomery's planned Rhine crossing included 49,000 engineers (22,000 Americans) and 5,481 artillery pieces (2,070 American).
5. Hamilton, *Final Years of the Field Marshal, 1944–1976*, 420.
6. Atkinson, *The Guns at Last Light*, 548–551. The Remagen railroad bridge took its name from *General der Infanterie* (equivalent to a U.S. lieutenant general, three stars) Erich F. W. Ludendorff, the 1916–1918 *generalquartiermeister* (quartermaster-general, operations chief, equivalent to the U.S. Army G-3 in Washington, DC) of the German High Command during World War I.
7. Bradley and Blair, *A General's Life*, 410. For a predictably contrasting view, see Collins, *Lightning Joe*, 305.
8. Roberts, *Five Stars to Victory*, 76.
9. Samuel A. Stouffer et al., *Studies in Social Psychology During World War II: The American Soldier*, 4 vols. (Princeton, NJ: Princeton University Press, 1949), vol. II: *The American Soldier: Combat and Its Aftermath* (1949), 59–104. For the effectiveness of artillery in World War II, see James F. Dunnigan, *How to Make War: A Comprehensive Guide to Modern Warfare* (New York: William Morrow and Company, 1988), 97.
10. Weigley, *Eisenhower's Lieutenants*, 12–14.
11. For the phases of breakdown, see Roy L. Swank and Walter E. Marchand, "Combat Neuroses: Development of Combat Exhaustion," *American Medical Association: Archives of Neurology and Psychology* (March 1946): 236–43. Swank and Marchand studied American soldiers in the Normandy campaign of 1944. For the official military findings, see Palmer, Wiley, and Keast, *The Procurement and Training of Ground Combat Troops*, 228.
12. Dave Grossman, *On Killing: The Psychological Cost of Learning to Kill in War and Society* (New York: Back Bay Books, 1996), 43–44. Grossman served as a U.S. Army infantry officer, to include duty in Ranger and airborne units. He taught psychology to cadets at the U.S. Military Academy at West Point, New York.
13. Ibid., 48–50.
14. U.S. Army Center of Military History, *Order of Battle of the U.S. Army—WWII— ETO—3d* [sic] *Armored Division* (Washington, DC: U.S. Army Center of Military History, March 5, 2001), at https://history.army.mil/documents/ETO-OB /3AD-ETO.htm, 436-437, accessed July 6, 2019; Zaloga, *U.S. Armored Divisions: The European Theater of Operations, 1944–1945*, 92.
15. Collins, *Lightning Joe*, 314; Hal Boyle, "Views of the War: General Rose" (April 1, 1945) in Fogel, *Major General Maurice Rose: The Most Decorated Battletank Commander in U.S. Military History*, 275. Boyle wrote for the Associated Press

and served as a correspondent with both the 2nd and 3rd Armored Divisions in 1943–1945.

16. Magnussen, "The General Cried at Dawn," at http://www.3ad.com/history/wwll/memoirs.pages/magnussen.htm, accessed July 10, 2019.

17. Gerald Astor, *Terrible Terry Allen: Combat General of World War II: The Life of an American Soldier* (New York: Presidio Press, 2003), 14, 20, 41–42.

18. Ibid. 78, 115, 131; Ossad and Marsh, *Maurice Rose: World War II's Greatest Forgotten Commander*, 99; Bradley and Blair, *A General's Life*, 195.

19. Atkinson, *The Guns at Last Light*, 334; Weigley, *Eisenhower's Lieutenants*, 354, 660. See also Astor, *Terrible Terry Allen*, 239–241.

20. Astor, *Terrible Terry Allen*, 309; Collins, *Lightning Joe*, 274–275.

21. Ossad and Marsh, *Maurice Rose: World War II's Greatest Forgotten Commander*, 245.

22. Sylvan and Smith, *Normandy to Victory*, 330–331. Napoleon Bonaparte established the French Légion d'honneur in 1802.

23. Ossad and Marsh, *Maurice Rose: World War II's Greatest Forgotten Commander*, 294–295, 409n23. This single typed letter is the only surviving correspondence between Maurice Rose and his family. Mrs. Virginia Rose stated that all letters had been lost in a postwar flood. Fellow soldiers, including the general's personal secretary Tech 4 Nathaniel Peavy, said later they'd never seen Rose type anything, let alone letters to his family. Peavy didn't even know Rose could type. Rose was indeed a very private man.

24. Ibid., 296. For Patton's pistols, see Martin Blumenson, *Patton: The Man Behind the Legend, 1885–1945* (New York: William Morrow and Company, 1985), 169–170, 210, 235 (photo).

25. Ossad and Marsh, *Maurice Rose: World War II's Greatest Forgotten Commander*, 296–297.

26. Ibid., 297.

27. Sylvan and Smith, *Normandy to Victory*, 168, 291.

28. Makos, *Spearhead*, 314–315.

29. General of the Army Dwight D. Eisenhower, U.S. Army, "Personal Correspondence with Commanding Generals, 2nd Armored Division and 3rd Armored Division" (Versailles, France: Headquarters, Supreme Headquarters Allied Expeditionary Force, March 18, 1945), 1.

30. Ibid., 1–2. See also Makos, *Spearhead*, 315.

31. Ibid., 1.

32. Major General Maurice Rose, U.S. Army, "Personal Correspondence with General of the Army Dwight D. Eisenhower" (Hermulheim, Germany: Headquarters, 3rd Armored Division, March 21, 1945), 1–3.

33. General of the Army Dwight D. Eisenhower, U.S. Army, "Personal Correspondence with Commanding Generals, 3rd Armored Division" (Versailles, France: Headquarters, Supreme Headquarters Allied Expeditionary Force, March 27, 1945), 1; MacDonald, *The Last Offensive*, 305, 319–320, 321, 328–334, 339–343.

34. Woolner and Fowler, *Spearhead in the West*, 237–238; Ossad and Marsh, *Maurice Rose: World War II's Greatest Forgotten Commander*, 46. For the prison and the Gestapo's depredations in Cologne, see National Socialist Documentation Center of the City of Cologne, https://museenkoeln.de/ns-dokumentationszentrum/default.aspx?s=715, accessed July 7, 2019.

35. MacDonald, *The Last Offensive*, 227–230.

36. Sylvan and Smith, *Normandy to Victory*, 326, 336–337. After his relief from command of III Corps, Millikin took over the 13th Armored Division on April 17, 1945, when its prior commander was wounded in action.

37. Ibid., 331, 334; Collins, *Lightning Joe*, 306, 309.

38. Weigley, *Eisenhower's Lieutenants*, 640–646.

39. Headquarters, 36th Armored Infantry Regiment, *History of the 36th Armored Infantry Regiment*, 112.

40. Collins, *Lightning Joe*, 309–311, 316.

41. Balkoski, "Operation Grenade: The Battle for the Rhineland, 23 Feb.–5 Mar. '45," 14.

42. Headquarters, 33rd Armored Regiment, "After Action Report for the Month of March 1945," 4; Headquarters, 83rd Armored Reconnaissance Battalion, "After Action Report March 1945," 3. For the quote, see Headquarters, 3rd Armored Division, *Spearheading with the 3rd Armored Division*, 33.

43. Roberts, *Five Stars to Victory*, 94; Headquarters, 2nd Battalion, 33rd Armored Regiment, "Log Book of Second Battalion," 27.

44. Woolner and Fowler, *Spearhead in the West*, 239–242.

45. Ibid.; Headquarters, 3rd Armored Division, *Spearheading with the 32rd Armored Division*, 32; Headquarters, 32nd Armored Regiment, "Actions Against Enemy, Reports After/After Action Reports, Month of March 1945," 6–7, 38.

46. Headquarters, 32nd Armored Regiment, "Actions Against Enemy, Reports After/After Action Reports, Month of March 1945," 6–7.

47. 3rd Armored Division History Foundation, *3rd Armored Division Soldiers Who Gave Their Lives in World War II* at https://www.3ad.com/history/wwll/names .died.htm, accessed July 8, 2019. Woolner and Fowler, *Spearhead in the West*, 425–429.

48. Headquarters, 33rd Armored Regiment, "After Action Report for the Month of March 1945," 4; Headquarters, 2nd Battalion, 33rd Armored Regiment, "Log Book of Second Battalion," 28; Roberts, *Five Stars to Victory*, 96.

49. Woolner and Fowler, *Spearhead in the West*, 243–248.

50. Ibid., 249; Woolner, *Division HQ: Third Armored Division Forward Echelon and Division Headquarters Company, April 15, 1941–May 8, 1945*, 12. Harold "Bunny" Austin reported for the *Sydney Morning Herald* during World War II. Because Thomas Austin (1815–1871) is widely reputed to have introduced rabbits into the Land Down Under, "Bunny" has become a common nickname for those Australians who share the surname.

51. Headquarters, 36th Armored Infantry Regiment, "Action Against Enemy, Reports After/After Action Reports March 1945," 12. For an excellent terrain analysis, see U.S. Department of the Army, Committee 12, Armored Officers Advanced Course, *Armored Encirclement of the Ruhr* (Fort Knox, KY: U.S. Army Armored School, May 1949), 61–62.

52. Ibid., 65–66. For a more detailed description of the released impressed workers, see William B. Ruth, Sr., "Across the Rhine: Buschbell to Paderborn," 3rd Armored Division History Foundation at http://www.3ad.com/history/wwll /memoirs.pages/ruth.pages/across.rhine.htm, accessed July 9, 2019. Ruth was a junior NCO in Service Company, 33rd Armored Regiment during combat operations in 1944–1945.

53. Headquarters, 2nd Battalion, 33rd Armored Regiment, "Log Book of Second Battalion," 28; Headquarters, 36th Armored Infantry Regiment, *History of the 36th Armored Infantry Regiment*, 113–114; U.S. Army Center of Military History, *Order of Battle of the U.S. Army—WWII—ETO—3d* [sic] *Armored Division* (Washington, DC: U.S. Army Center of Military History, March 5, 2001), at https://history.army.mil/documents/ETO-OB/3AD-ETO.htm, 446-447, accessed July 9, 2019.

54. Woolner and Fowler, *Spearhead in the West*, 247–250.

55. Woolner, *Division HQ: Third Armored Division Forward Echelon and Division Headquarters Company, April 15, 1941–May 8, 1945*, 12; 3rd Armored Division History Foundation, *3rd Armored Division Soldiers Who Gave Their Lives in World War II* at https://www.3ad.com/history/wwll/names.died.htm, accessed July 8, 2019; Headquarters, 3rd Armored Division, *Spearheading with the 3rd Armored Division*, 30.

56. Zaloga, *U.S. Armored Divisions: The European Theater of Operations, 1944–1945*, 22–25.

57. Woolner and Fowler, *Spearhead in the West*, 250–252.

58. John Thompson, "General's Pistol Helps Rout 30 and Capture 12 Nazis," *Chicago Tribune*, April 1, 1945, 1. Various accounts list the number of Germans as twelve to thirty. Fifteen is the number used by Lieutenant Colonel Wesley A. Sweat and Colonel Frederic Brown.

59. Ossad and Marsh, *Maurice Rose: World War II's Greatest Forgotten Commander*, 69–72.

60. Richard Holmes, *Acts of War* (New York: The Free Press, 1985), 149. Holmes served in the British army during the Cold War and taught at the Royal Military Academy at Sandhurst.

61. Thompson, "General's Pistol Helps Rout 30 and Capture 12 Nazis," 1.

62. Headquarters, 3rd Armored Division, *Spearheading with the 3rd Armored Division*, 35.

63. Thomas R. Henry, "Gen. Rose's Death Army's Greatest Loss," *Chicago Sentinel*, April 12, 1945, 1.

64. Woolner and Fowler, *Spearhead in the West*, 250–252.

65. Thomas R. Henry, "Masters of Slash and Surprise: 3rd Armored Division," *Saturday Evening Post*, October 19, 1946, 7. American soldiers usually called the MP40 the "Schmeisser," a reference to Hugo Schmeisser, designer of the MP18 submachine gun used during World War I. Schmeisser did not develop the World War II version.

66. Thompson, "General's Pistol Helps Rout 30 and Capture 12 Nazis," 1. Although he never said one way or the other, it appears Rose did not switch the submachine gun from safe to fire.

67. Headquarters, 3rd Armored Division, *Spearheading with the 3rd Armored Division*, 35. Shaunce apparently also did not switch his Thompson gun from safe to fire.

68. Thompson, "General's Pistol Helps Rout 30 and Capture 12 Nazis," 1. The Karabiner 98 Kurz (carbine 1898 model short) was the standard German Army bolt-action rifle.

69. "General Rose Shoots It Out with Group of 30 Nazis," *Denver Post*, March 31, 1945, 1; Headquarters, 3rd Armored Division, *Spearheading with the 3rd Armored Division*, 35.

70. Grossman, *On Killing*, 114–119.

Chapter 9: "A Hell of a Fix"

1. R. S. Trevelyan, editor and translator, *The Oresteia of Aeschylus*: *Agamemnon, Choephohori, Eumenides* (Cambridge, UK: Bowes and Bowes, 1920), 62.
2. Carpenter, *No Woman's World*, 283.
3. Collins, *Lightning Joe*, 311.
4. Henry, "Masters of Slash and Surprise: 3rd Armored Division," 7.
5. Gabriel Cohen, "Meyer Levin Examines his Way of Life," *Chicago Tribune*, June 11, 1950, sec. 4, p. 4. Cohen reviewed Levin's book *In Search: An Autobiography*, which included comments about his attempt to interview Major General Maurice Rose.
6. Staff Sergeant Andy Rooney, U.S. Army, "Killing of Rose Cost U.S. Army One of Top 3 Tankers: Leader Down Where They Fight," *Stars and Stripes*, April 6, 1945, 10. See also Carpenter, *No Woman's World*, 283; Henry, "General Rose's Death Army's Greatest Loss," 1. Carpenter appears to have arrived during Rose's impromptu discussion.
7. MacDonald, *The Last Offensive*, 351; Headquarters, 33rd Armored Regiment, "After Action Report for the Month of March 1945," 4; Roberts, *Five Stars to Victory*, 97.
8. Henry, "Masters of Slash and Surprise: 3rd Armored Division," 7.
9. Rooney, "Killing of Rose," 10.
10. Ibid. Rose named Field Marshal Gerd von Rundstedt, Luftwaffe Field Marshal Albert Kesselring, Colonel-General (four stars) Heinz Guderian, and Luftwaffe Reichsmarschall (supreme marshal) Hermann Göring.
11. Carpenter, *No Woman's World*, 283.
12. Henry, "General Rose's Death Army's Greatest Loss," 1.
13. Woolner and Fowler, *Spearhead in the West*, 433–434.
14. Headquarters, 83rd Armored Reconnaissance Battalion, "After Action Report March 1945," 4.
15. Jenkins, *Combat History of "A" Battery*, 96–97.
16. MacDonald, *The Last Offensive*, 351–352.
17. Howze's quote is in John Toland, *The Last 100 Days* (New York: Random House, 1966), 309. Headquarters, 36th Armored Infantry Regiment, "Action Against Enemy, Reports After/After Action Reports March 1945," 12.
18. Roberts, *Five Stars to Victory*, 98; Headquarters, 33rd Armored Regiment, "After Action Report for the Month of March 1945," 4; Headquarters, 2nd Battalion, 33rd Armored Regiment, "Log Book of Second Battalion," 30; 3rd Armored Division History Foundation, *3rd Armored Division Soldiers Who Gave Their Lives in World War II* at https://www.3ad.com/history/wwll/names.died.htm, accessed July 11, 2019.
19. Makos, *Spearhead*, 342.
20. Jenkins, *Combat History of 'A' Battery*, 97.
21. MacDonald, *The Last Offensive*, 352. For a superb laydown of the Paderborn fighting, see J. R. W. Graves, A. P. L. Halford MacLeod, G. C. Middleton, and D. R. Summers, *The Battle of Paderborn: 29 March–3 April 1945* (Paderborn Garrison, Germany: Headquarters, British Army of the Rhine, September 1985), 2–4. The British army study of the battle was composed by serving officers. They drew on local witnesses, former German Army soldiers who fought at Paderborn, and 1945 German military records.

22. Headquarters, 36th Armored Infantry Regiment, *History of the 36th Armored Infantry Regiment*, 115; Headquarters, 33rd Armored Regiment, "After Action Report for the Month of March 1945," 4.

23. Headquarters, 36th Armored Infantry Regiment, "Action Against Enemy, Reports After/After Action Reports March 1945," 13.

24. Headquarters, 2nd Battalion, 33rd Armored Regiment, "Log Book of Second Battalion," 29.

25. Technical Sergeant John T. Jones, U.S. Army, "Personal Experience, March 30, 1945" (Etteln, Germany: Headquarters, 3rd Armored Division, 1945), 1. This rank was superior to technician 3rd grade (tech-3). In today's U.S. Army, this rank is sergeant first class (E-7).

26. Charles Whiting, *Ike's Last Battle: The Battle of the Ruhr Pocket, April 1945* (London, UK: Leo Cooper, 2002), 75. Whiting served as a sergeant in the British army in France, Holland, Belgium, and Germany in 1944–1945. See also Headquarters, 36th Armored Infantry Regiment, *History of the 36th Armored Infantry Regiment*, 115.

27. Robert S. Gamzey, "Epic Saga of Gen. Rose told here by Col. Smith," *Denver Jewish News*, September 13, 1945, 1. See also Woolner, *Division HQ: Third Armored Division Forward Echelon and Division Headquarters Company, April 15, 1941–May 8, 1945*, 12; U.S. Army Center of Military History, *Order of Battle of the U.S. Army—WWII—ETO—3d* [sic] *Armored Division* (Washington, DC: U.S. Army Center of Military History, March 5, 2001), at https://history.army.mil /documents/ETO-OB/3AD-ETO.htm, 446-447, accessed July 12, 2019.

28. Astor, *Terrible Terry Allen*, 314.

29. Ibid., 313. For the official history of African American soldiers in World War II, see U.S. Department of the Army, Office of the Chief of Military History, *The United States Army in World War II, Special Studies*. 10 vols. (Washington, DC: U.S. Government Printing Office, 1952–1992), vol. 4: Ulysses Lee, *The Employment of Negro Troops* (1965), 688, 693, 695. The African American rifle platoons went to the 1st, 8th, 9th, 69th, 78th, and 104th infantry divisions in First Army, the 99th and 106th in Third Army, and the 12th and 14th armored divisions in Seventh Army, part of Sixth Army Group in southern France and southern Germany. African American combat units included field artillery, tank, and tank destroyer battalions and the separate 24th Infantry Regiment. The African American 92nd Infantry Division fought in Italy in 1944–1945. The African American 93rd Infantry Division (incorporating the initially separate 25th Infantry Regimental Combat team) served in the Pacific Theater in 1944–1945.

30. Headquarters, 36th Armored Infantry Regiment, *History of the 36th Armored Infantry Regiment*, 112; Headquarters, 36th Armored Infantry Regiment, "Action Against Enemy, Reports After/After Action Reports March 1945," 10; Astor, *Terrible Terry Allen*, 313; Lee, *The Employment of Negro Troops*, 675. Allen stated that the 784th Tank Battalion (Colored) "ably supported the division in defense."

31. Headquarters, 36th Armored Infantry Regiment, "Action Against Enemy, Reports After/After Action Reports March 1945," 13; Headquarters, 2nd Battalion, 33rd Armored Regiment, "Log Book of Second Battalion," 29.

32. Headquarters, 36th Armored Infantry Regiment, *History of the 36th Armored Infantry Regiment*, 115.

33. Headquarters, 2nd Battalion, 33rd Armored Regiment, "Log Book of Second Battalion," 29; Roberts, *Five Stars to Victory*, 100.

34. Ann Stringer, "Dusky Devastators" *The Times* (Shreveport, Louisiana), April 3, 1945, 1. Stringer previously covered the 3rd Armored Division's attack into Cologne.

35. Collins, *Lightning Joe*, 313.

36. Headquarters, 2nd Battalion, 33rd Armored Regiment, "Log Book of Second Battalion," 29; Roberts, *Five Stars to Victory*, 100.

37. Graves, MacLeod, Middleton, and Summers, *The Battle of Paderborn: 29 March–3 April 1945*, 9.

38. Headquarters, 36th Armored Infantry Regiment, "Action Against Enemy, Reports After/After Action Reports March 1945," 13; Committee 12, Armored Officers Advanced Course, *Armored Encirclement of the Ruhr*, 72.

39. Graves, MacLeod, Middleton, and Summers, *The Battle of Paderborn*, 9; Woolner and Fowler, *Spearhead in the West*, 433–434.

40. Jones, U.S. Army, "Personal Experience, March 30, 1945," 2.

41. Ibid. For the American effort to take Etteln, see Headquarters, 33rd Armored Regiment, "After Action Report for the Month of March 1945," 4.

42. Jones, U.S. Army, "Personal Experience, March 30, 1945," 2–3.

43. Graves, MacLeod, Middleton, and Summers, *The Battle of Paderborn*, 10.

44. Jones, U.S. Army, "Personal Experience, March 30, 1945," 3.

45. Graves, MacLeod, Middleton, and Summers, *The Battle of Paderborn*, 14.

46. Ibid. For the use of napalm from the P-47 aircraft, see Atkinson, *The Guns at Last Light*, 581.

47. Graves, MacLeod, Middleton, and Summers, *The Battle of Paderborn*, 15.

48. The quotes come from Makos, *Spearhead*, 351, and Ossad and Marsh, *Major General Maurice Rose: World War II's Greatest Forgotten Commander*, 23.

49. Headquarters, 33rd Armored Regiment, "After Action Report for the Month of March 1945," 4.

50. Graves, MacLeod, Middleton, and Summers, *The Battle of Paderborn*, 16.

51. For the German crew celebration, see Jenkins, *Combat History of "A" Battery*, 99. For the U.S. losses, see Cooper, *Death Traps*, 256. The author participated in the postbattle maintenance recovery effort.

52. Woolner and Fowler, *Spearhead in the West*, 265–268, 433–434. For U.S. casualties, see 3rd Armored Division History Foundation, *3rd Armored Division Soldiers Who Gave Their Lives in World War II* at https://www.3ad.com/history/wwll/names.died.htm, accessed July 13, 2019.

53. Jones, U.S. Army, "Personal Experience, March 30, 1945," 3–4.

54. Graves, MacLeod, Middleton, and Summers, *The Battle of Paderborn*, 16.

55. Makos, *Spearhead*, 352; Ossad and Marsh, *Major General Maurice Rose: World War II's Greatest Forgotten Commander*, 33.

56. Ossad and Marsh, *Major General Maurice Rose: World War II's Greatest Forgotten Commander*, 35.

57. Jones, U.S. Army, "Personal Experience, March 30, 1945," 1, 4.

58. Graves, MacLeod, Middleton, and Summers, *The Battle of Paderborn*, 16.

59. Jones, U.S. Army, "Personal Experience, March 30, 1945," 4.

60. Fogel, *Major General Maurice Rose: The Most Decorated Battletank Commander in U.S. Military History*, 224, 270–272. Fogel includes aerial and ground-level photographs of the incident area. See also Woolner and Fowler, *Spearhead in the West*, 265–268, 433–434.

61. Jones, U.S. Army, "Personal Experience, March 30, 1945," 4–5; Committee 12, Armored Officers Advanced Course, *Armored Encirclement of the Ruhr*, 73.

62. Graves, MacLeod, Middleton, and Summers, *The Battle of Paderborn*, 16.

63. Jones, U.S. Army, "Personal Experience, March 30, 1945," 5.

64. Collins, *Lightning Joe*, 314. Collins personally interviewed Major Robert M. Bellinger, Rose's aide, a few days after the firefight. Tech-4 Glenn Shaunce later said he'd heard Rose say "*no versteh*," German for "no understand." Rose both spoke and read German.

65. For Rose's autopsy diagram and description of wounds incurred, see Ossad and Marsh, *Major General Maurice Rose: World War II's Greatest Forgotten Commander*, 341–343.

Epilogue: Nordhausen D+309

1. William Shakespeare, *Folger Shakespeare Library: Julius Caesar*, ed. Barbara A. Mowat and Paul Werstine (New York: Simon and Schuster, 2011), 250. The famous line spoken by the character Marc Antony in his funeral oration for Julius Caesar. It can be found in act 3, scene 2, line 84. The next line is also well known: "The good is oft interred with their bones."

2. Steven J. Zaloga, *U.S. Armored Units in the North African and Italian Campaigns, 1942–1945* (Oxford, UK: Osprey Publishing Company, 2006), 40–41.

3. Aurio J. Pierro, "Profile of a Tanker: Platoon Sgt. [sic] Aurio J. Pierro," 3rd Armored Division History Foundation at http://www.3ad.com/history/wwll /memoirs.pages/pierro.htm, accessed July 14, 2019.

4. Michael Hirsh, "Aurio J. Pierro Oral History Interview," June 30, 2008, at Scholar Commons, University of South Florida at https://scholarcommons.usf .edu/cgi/viewcontent.cgi?referer=&httpsredir=1&article=1118&context=hgstud _oh, accessed July 14, 2019. This interview was part of the research for Michael Hirsh's superb book *The Liberators: America's Witness to the Holocaust* (New York: Random House, 2010).

5. Ibid., 12–13.

6. Jenkins, *Combat History of "A" Battery*, 107.

7. Roberts, *Five Stars to Victory*, 102; Woolner and Fowler, *Spearhead in the West*, 272–274.

8. U.S. Department of War, Headquarters, 33rd Armored Regiment, "After Action Report for the Month of April 1945" (Sangerhausen, Germany: Headquarters, 33rd Armored Regiment, May 2, 1945), 3.

9. Headquarters, 3rd Armored Division, *Spearheading with the 3rd Armored Division*, 47–48; Collins, *Lightning Joe*, 323–324. The V-2 guided missile reflected the design and engineering of a team led by SS *Sturmbannführer* (major) Werner von Braun. After the war, he and his rocket team worked for the United States. Von Braun's engineers played a big role in designing early U.S. missiles, to include the Saturn series that took Americans to the moon.

10. Sylvan and Smith, *Normandy to Victory*, 355–356; Collins, *Lightning Joe*, 316–317; Harmon, MacKaye, and MacKaye, *Combat Commander*, 252. Had Harmon taken over after Rose, "Old Gravel Voice" would have had the distinction of commanding the 1st, 2nd, and 3rd armored divisions. Harmon supported leaving Hickey in command.

11. Haynes W. Dugan, "Aftermath of General Rose's Death," 3rd Armored Division History Foundation, http://www.3ad.com/history/wwll/dugan.pages /articles.pages/rose.death.htm, accessed July 14, 2019.

12. Ibid. The two motorcycle riders were Private Fort Class James Omand and Private First Class Aaron Nichols. For American casualties on March 30, 1945, near Hamborn, see 3rd Armored Division History Foundation, *3rd Armored Division Soldiers Who Gave Their Lives in World War II* at https://www.3ad .com/history/wwll/names.died.htm, accessed July 14, 2019. See also Fogel, *Major General Maurice Rose: The Most Decorated Battletank Commander in U.S. Military History*, 266.

13. David J. Fleischer, "Searching for My Dad," 3rd Armored Division History Foundation at http://www.3ad.com/history/wwll/association.pages/guest .speaker.2005.htm, accessed July 14, 2019. Those captured were Lieutenant Colonel Wesley A. Sweat (Division G-3 officer) and Technical Sergeant John T. "Africa" Jones (G-3 stenographer), and Private James Stevenson (G-3 driver), as well as Tech-4 Neil Fleischer, Tech-4 Wesley Ellison, and Private First Class William Hatry, all from the 143rd Armored Signal Company. For the Germans, *Stalag* was an abbreviation for *Kriegsgefangenen-Mannschafts-Stammlager* (Prisoner of War Group Camp).

14. Graves, MacLeod, Middleton, and Summers, *The Battle of Paderborn*, 18, 21–22. The British authors allege that German villagers near Paderborn reported, "At around this time 80–100 captured SS men were shot out of hand." The Germans surrendered at SHAEF headquarters at 2:41 a.m. on May 7, 1945, and in Berlin to the Soviet Red Army at 12:16 a.m. on May 9, 1945.

15. Sylvan and Smith, *Normandy to Victory*, 356. For U.S. Army Signal Corps film of the ceremony, see https://www.youtube.com/watch?v=k19eiwCTZME, accessed July 14, 2019. The general officers who attended are visible just over the right shoulder of the chaplain, who is wearing a black stole that blows in the wind. For Allen's emotional reaction, see Magnussen, "The General Cried at Dawn," at http://www.3ad.com/history/wwll/memoirs.pages/magnussen .htm, accessed July 14, 2019.

16. "Rabbi S. Rose, 90, Father of Slain General, Is Dead," *Denver Post*, July 11, 1945, page 1; Ossad and Marsh, *Major General Maurice Rose: World War II's Greatest Forgotten Commander*, 360–361; For more on the wartime service of Jewish Americans, see Lisa Ades, director, *GI Jews: Jewish Americans in World War II* (New York: Turquoise Films, 2017). This superb documentary aired on PBS stations. It draws on an equally impressive book: Deborah Dash Moore, *GI Jews: How World War II Changed a Generation* (Cambridge, MA: Belknap Press, 2006).

17. Leonidas (Leon) Jaworski, U.S. Army, "Memorandum to Colonel Hall, Subject: File No. 12-352A (Rose) (Washington, DC: U.S. Army War Crimes Office, Judge Advocate General Division, June 11, 1945), 1–2. See also Leon Jaworski, *After*

Fifteen Years (Houston, TX: Gulf Publishing Company, 1961), 59–60, 65. In 1973–1974 Leon Jaworski served as the second and final special prosecutor empowered to investigate the Watergate scandal.

18. Fogel, *Major General Maurice Rose: The Most Decorated Battletank Commander in U.S. Military History*, 457–459, 506, 519; Headquarters, U.S. Army Europe, "General Orders Number 13: Designation of Rose Barracks," 1.

19. Collins, *Lightning Joe*, 314; Bradley and Blair, *A General's Life*, 420; Gavin, *On to Berlin*, 252–253; Ridgway, *Soldier*, 13, 115–116; Harmon, MacKaye, and Mac-Kaye, *Combat Commander*, 251–252. Harmon, no shrinking violet in combat, summarized thusly: "I have always thought that the commander and staff of a rapidly advancing division should never move toward the front at night because of just this type of danger. During a rapid armored advance, there are almost always enemy stragglers in hiding or maneuvering to return to their own lines before they are captured or killed. Unhappily Rose decided to take a chance; it cost him his life and left the Third Armored Division without a commander at a critical moment of the campaign." Harmon called Rose's death "tragically unnecessary."

20. For the burial plot of Major General Maurice Rose, see U.S. American Battle Monuments Commission, Netherlands American Cemetery and Memorial at https://www.abmc.gov/node/388455, accessed July 15, 2019.

Appendices: 3rd Armored Division Leadership

1. Initially assumed command as a brigadier general; promoted to major general on September 5, 1944.
2. He was captured by German forces on March 27, 1945, and released as the war ended.
3. Division artillery battalions habitually aligned with 54th (CCR), 67th (CCA), and 391st (CCB). In addition, two to three nondivisional artillery battalions were often added to increase division firepower backing the combat commands.
4. Wounded in action October 23, 1944.
5. The Division Rear Command Post habitually moved with the division trains. Omaha Rear included the division special staff: the adjutant general, chaplain, finance, inspector general, judge advocate general, ordnance, postal services, quartermaster (supply), and special services (morale programs).
6. Killed in action on April 18, 1945.
7. Attached throughout the command tenure of Major General Maurice Rose.
8. Attached throughout the command tenure of Major General Maurice Rose, with the exception of December 17, 1944, to January 2, 1945.
9. Initially assumed command as a lieutenant colonel, later promoted to colonel.
10. Wounded in action August 14, 1944.
11. Wounded in action and captured on August 14, 1944. He did not survive captivity.
12. Wounded in action August 17, 1944.
13. Wounded in action 1944.
14. Wounded in action on April 21, 1945.
15. Wounded in action on September 6, 1944.

16. Wounded in action September 10, 1944.
17. Killed in action on September 13, 1944.
18. Initially assumed command as a colonel; promoted to brigadier general on September 24, 1944.
19. Wounded in action on August 29, 1944.
20. Returned to command, then wounded in action September 14, 1944.
21. Initially assumed command as a major; promoted to lieutenant colonel. Killed in action on November 18, 1945.
22. Wounded in action on January 8, 1945.
23. This officer returned from wounds twice, first to resume command of the 1st Battalion, 32nd Armored and then to take command of the 1st Battalion, 33rd Armored. He suffered a nonbattle injury on March 29, 1945.
24. Killed in action on August 9, 1945.
25. Wounded in action August 17, 1944.
26. Killed in action September 9, 1944.
27. Wounded in action on September 13, 1944.
28. Killed in action on August 9, 1944.
29. Normally the executive officer (second in command) of the 36th Armored Infantry Regiment, Hutcheson succeeded to command of both 2nd Battalion (fully engaged in repelling the Mortain counterattack) and the 36th Armored Infantry Regiment.
30. Wounded in action on November 18, 1944. He also briefly commanded the 3rd Battalion, 36th Armored Infantry Regiment in August–September, 1944.
31. Wounded in action on December 27, 1944. He also briefly commanded the 3rd Battalion, 36th Armored Infantry Regiment in August, 1944.
32. Wounded in action on January 4, 1945. This was his second stint in command of the 2nd Battalion, 36th Armored infantry Regiment.
33. Wounded in action on January 5, 1945. He twice commanded the battalion for brief periods.
34. Wounded in action on August 8, 1944.
35. Wounded in action on January 6, 1945.
36. Killed in action on April 15, 1945. Earlier, he briefly commanded the 2nd Battalion, 36th Armored Infantry Regiment.

Appendices: 3rd Armored Division Task Organization as of August 20, 1944

1. The Command Group also included Colonel Frederic J. Brown, the Division artillery commander and Lieutenant Colonel Wesley A. Sweat, the Division G-3 (operations) officer.
2. The Division's general staff officers worked in Omaha Forward.
3. The Division Rear Command Post moved with the division trains.
4. At the start of operations in Normandy, CCA designated its task forces as X, Y, and (when used), Z. Over time, task forces were designated by their commanders' last names. In some records, CCA is known as CC Hickey, but this was not typical.
5. The battalion consisted of three tank companies, A (M5 Stuart), D (M4 Sherman), and G (M4 Sherman). The official table of organization and equipment of the 32nd Armored Regiment included the 1st Battalion (M5 Stuart light

tanks), 2nd Battalion (M4 Sherman medium tanks), and 3rd Battalion (M4 medium tanks). In Normandy, the division permanently reorganized both armored regiments to create six identical tank battalions with three companies: one light (M5 Stuarts) and two medium (M4 Shermans).

6. The battalion consisted of three tank companies, C (M5 Stuart), H (M4 Sherman), and I (M4 Sherman).

7. The 54th Armored Field Artillery Battalion habitually supported CCR, but artillery was not usually left in reserve.

8. At the start of operations in Normandy, CCB designated its task forces as 1, 2, and (when used) 3. As with CCA, CCB later designated task forces by their commanders' last names. In certain records, CCB is identified as CC Boudinot, but this was not common.

9. The battalion consisted of three tank companies, A (M5 Stuart), F (M4 Sherman), and I (M4 Sherman).

10. The battalion consisted of three tank companies, B (M5 Stuart), D (M4 Sherman), and E (M4 Sherman).

11. This non-divisional unit supported the 3rd Armored Division during operations in France from July 9, 1944, to August 28, 1944.

12. The battalion consisted of three tank companies, B (M5 Stuart), E (M4 Sherman), and F (M4 Sherman).

13. The battalion consisted of three tank companies, C (M5 Stuart), G (M4 Sherman), and H (M4 Sherman).

14. Attached throughout the command tenure of Major General Maurice Rose, with the exception of December 17, 1944, to January 2, 1945.

15. This nondivisional unit supported the 3rd Armored Division during operations in France from August 12, 1944, to September 20, 1944.

16. This nondivisional unit supported the 3rd Armored Division during operations in France from August 12, 1944, to September 20, 1944.

17. Attached throughout the command tenure of Major General Maurice Rose.

Index

About the Author

Daniel P. Bolger served thirty-five years in the U.S. Army, retiring as a lieutenant general in 2013. He commanded troops in Iraq and Afghanistan. His military awards include five Bronze Stars (one for valor) and the Combat Action Badge.